Shades of Decolonial Voices in Linguistics

GLOBAL FORUM ON SOUTHERN EPISTEMOLOGIES

Series Editors: Sinfree Makoni *(Pennsylvania State University, USA)*, **Rafael Lomeu Gomes** *(University of Oslo, Norway)*, **Magda Madany-Saá** *(Pennsylvania State University, USA)*, **Bassey E. Antia** *(University of the Western Cape, South Africa)* and **Chanel Van Der Merwe** *(Nelson Mandela University, South Africa)*

This book series publishes independent volumes concerned primarily with exploring peripheralized ways of framing and conducting language studies in both the Global South and Global North. We are particularly interested in the 'geopolitics of knowledge' as it pertains to language studies and aim to illustrate how language scholarship in the Global North is partially indebted to diverse traditions of scholarship in the Global South. We are also keen to explore interfaces between language and other areas of human and non-human scholarship. Ultimately, our concern is not only epistemological; it is also political, educational and social. The books are part of the Global Forum, which is open and politically engaged. The Global Forum fosters collegiality and dialogue, using the technologies essential to productivity during the pandemic that have served our collective benefit. In the book series, we experiment with the format of the book, challenging the colonial concept of a single monologic authorial voice by integrating multiple voices, consistent with decoloniality and the democratic and politically engaged nature of our scholarship.

Full details of all the books in this series and of all our other publications can be found on http://www.multilingual-matters.com, or by writing to Multilingual Matters, St Nicholas House, 31–34 High Street, Bristol, BS1 2AW, UK.

GLOBAL FORUM ON SOUTHERN EPISTEMOLOGIES: 2

Shades of Decolonial Voices in Linguistics

Edited by
Sinfree Makoni, Cristine Severo, Ashraf Abdelhay, Anna Kaiper-Marquez and Višnja Milojičić

MULTILINGUAL MATTERS
Bristol • Jackson

DOI https://doi.org/10.21832/MAKONI8530
Library of Congress Cataloging in Publication Data
A catalog record for this book is available from the Library of Congress.
Names: Makoni, Sinfree, editor. | Severo, Cristine Gorski, editor. | Abdelhay, Ashraf, editor. | Kaiper-Marquez, Anna, editor. | Milojičić, Višnja, editor.
Title: Shades of Decolonial Voices in Linguistics/Edited by Sinfree Makoni, Cristine Severo, Ashraf Abdelhay, Anna Kaiper-Marquez and Višnja Milojičić.
Description: Bristol; Jackson: Multilingual Matters, [2023] | Series: Global Forum on Southern Epistemologies: 2 | Includes bibliographical references and index. | Summary: "This book argues that Linguistics has been shaped by colonization. It outlines how linguistic practices may be decolonized and the challenges which this poses to linguists, before concluding that decolonization in Linguistics is a process with no definite end point, which cannot be completely successful until ocieties are decolonized too"— Provided by publisher. Identifiers: LCCN 2023011045 (print) | LCCN 2023011046 (ebook) | ISBN 9781800418523 (paperback) | ISBN 9781800418530 (hardback) | ISBN 9781800418554 (epub) | ISBN 9781800418547 (pdf)
Subjects: LCSH: Linguistics. | Decolonization. | Imperialism and philology. | LCGFT: Essays.
Classification: LCC P41 .S44 2023 (print) | LCC P41 (ebook) | DDC 410.1—dc23/eng/20230530 LC record available at https://lccn.loc.gov/2023011045
LC ebook record available at https://lccn.loc.gov/2023011046

British Library Cataloguing in Publication Data
A catalogue entry for this book is available from the British Library.

ISBN-13: 978-1-80041-853-0 (hbk)
ISBN-13: 978-1-80041-852-3 (pbk)

Multilingual Matters
UK: St Nicholas House, 31-34 High Street, Bristol, BS1 2AW, UK.
USA: Ingram, Jackson, TN, USA.

Website: www.multilingual-matters.com
Twitter: Multi_Ling_Mat
Facebook: https://www.facebook.com/multilingualmatters
Blog: www.channelviewpublications.wordpress.com

Copyright © 2023 Sinfree Makoni, Cristine Severo, Ashraf Abdelhay, Anna Kaiper-Marquez, Višnja Milojičić and the authors of individual chapters.

All rights reserved. No part of this work may be reproduced in any form or by any means without permission in writing from the publisher.

The policy of Multilingual Matters/Channel View Publications is to use papers that are natural, renewable and recyclable products, made from wood grown in sustainable forests. In the manufacturing process of our books, and to further support our policy, preference is given to printers that have FSC and PEFC Chain of Custody certification. The FSC and/or PEFC logos will appear on those books where full certification has been granted to the printer concerned.

Typeset by Nova Techset Private Limited, Bengaluru and Chennai, India.
Printed and bound in the UK by the CPI Books Group Ltd.

Contents

	Dedication	vi
	Interlude: In Memory of Átila Calvente *Magda Madany-Saá*	ix
	Gratitudes	xiii
	Foreword *Peter E. Jones*	xv
	Why 'Shades of Decolonial Linguistics'? *Sinfree Makoni, Cristine Severo, Ashraf Abdelhay, Anna Kaiper-Marquez and Višnja Milojičić*	1
1	Living Theory and Theory that Kills: Language, Communication and Control *David Bade*	13
2	An Iconoclast's Approach to Decolonial Linguistics *Salikoko S. Mufwene*	44
3	Giving Jack His Jacket: Linguistic Contact in the Danish West Indies *Robin Sabino*	68
4	Challenging the Dominance of Mind over Body in the History of Language Analysis *John Joseph*	88
5	Keywords for India: A Conceptual Lexicon for the 21st Century *Peter de Souza and Rukmini Bhaya Nair*	120
6	Queer Anger: A Conversation on Alliances and Affective Politics *Tommaso Milani*	142
7	Identity and the African Storybook Initiative: A Decolonial Project? *Bonny Norton*	163
8	Domination and Underlying Form in Linguistics *Nick Riemer*	190
9	Decolonizing Multilingualism: A Practice-Led Approach *Alison Phipps and Piki Diamond*	210
	Epilogue *Višnja Milojičić and Rafael Lomeu Gomes*	237
	Index	241

Dedication

Atila,

How and where are you now, dearest friend? What do the newer horizons drawing your core to action look like this time? We miss you here, in this plane of reality that is currently under fire.

You were a force of mad lucidity driven by the very pulse of the Earth. When we met at that gathering, it was as if we instantly recognized a mutual hunger in one another: the urgency to translate fateful dreams of change into action. You introduced yourself as a seventy-something-year-old academic farmer from Brazil. Your energy was volcanic. The aura of your stories reflected an ineffable depth that bore the stain of the times you faced violence while defending the forest against man-made predators.

You were incarcerated, you told me, between lettuce bites, and you mentioned something to do with 'imposed dictatorship problems;' which has become a common code between people from Latin America. I suggested that we talk more, so we walked over to the edge of campus on College Ave, CC, you and I, and, as we spoke we became swallowed by a torrential conversation involving everything that we cared about and the issues we desperately wanted to change for the benefit of all. What we shared resonated in each other's hearts and we let ourselves become inebriated by its effects.

The three of us sitting at that table might as well have been from different planets. We all shared differences in age, race, ability, gender, nationality, height and class, among other things, but we were all moved by the same prospective dream: liberation from capitalism as a system of global domination. We longed for a life free of the fear for the unknown that we all have within and that we are taught to project as hate for others.

It was then that you told us of your work in the Amazon in the 1970s when you witnessed the interventions made by the World Bank on small farms, affecting the territories of the Indigenous Paiter Suruí people due to the presence of the military government. You went through graduate school and used the resources you found there to develop a working model that you called the 'Cacaio Project,' and that worked as a 'backpack of survival tools for populations at risk.' Your PhD thesis, in reflection of your life's mission, was dedicated to raising awareness about the violence that young people in vulnerable conditions are subjected to in the context of favelas around Río de Janeiro and in your beloved Petrópolis.

You gave those of us who were lucky to have met you the most precious of gifts: the heartfelt knowledge of how to grow your own food in reciprocal collaboration with the Earth. In a world ruled by money, where agonism, greed and inequality are ever-increasing, it is pressing that people teach each other to become self-sufficient in ways that re-connect them with the sources of life that all of us are meant to care for. In that we agreed.

I told you about my work as a community artist in Chiapas and Zambia and how I created dialogic drawing exercises as a means for people to open themselves to the wonders that anti-colonial forms of sensibility grant to those who dare to feel deeply in connection to everything. Empowerment for us involves dealing with the inferiorization that is particular to Latinxs. It is a hellish limbo of constant uncertainty that we are forced to navigate.

We also spoke about our transnational collective, Bruxas Bruxas and the mycorrhizal ecologies of care that we conjured within the prison system of Pennsylvania while teaching art. As community artists we sought to connect experiences of subaltern alterities with hegemonic discursive formats through which we could repurpose the fine art gallery setting to work as a platform from which to raise awareness against the structural causes behind police brutality and labor-based exploitation.

After we said goodnight, the vibrant residue of that encounter compelled us to stay in touch. You traveled back to Brazil and carried on with your workshops for building vegetable gardens with children from local schools. We emailed often and started an action group with your students Andressa and Roberto and my colleague Megan from rural sociology. We began meeting regularly online to conspire in the crafting of a replicable model for our idea of developing rooted, and connective forms of awareness of nature. Our aim was to perform sustenance horizontally and collectively. We intended to give our initiative the capacity to spread around the world like fungal spores carried by the wind.

But then the pandemic hit.

The anxiety was shared by us all. You were adamant when we called and you said: 'We need to do something now! We need to convince other people to help us plant 7 billion trees!'

My reaction was the only one I could have possibly had: 'But of course! Yes! Let's do this!' I could not even fathom such a quantity in my head, if I am honest. But you spoke with such power, Atila, and I knew we would never be stopped. You let me know of your frustration with what you saw as a lack of involvement on behalf of universities in organizing actions against the greater corporate forces actively destroying our livable landscapes.

So, in response, we dreamed up a holistic, transdisciplinary and non-formal educational project that merged the community-building practices of artmaking and food growing via the playful conceptualization culture-as-cultivation. However, after some consideration, we decided to begin smaller, planning to plant one billion trees first. You responded: 'Yes, but then we also need to build 700 vegetable gardens!' to which I responded: 'naturally!' My next email led us to the title: 'I know! Bruno Munari has a drawing exercise in which he challenges people to perceive a tree as a slow explosion of a seed and to draw one as such. If our aim is to plant 1 billion trees, then let's call this project 'One Billion Slow Exploding Seeds!'" It sounded funnily appealing, this way to use playfulness in signaling an absurdly factual need. So, we drafted an abstract that read like a manifesto, we poured our souls into the writing and hoped for the best when applying for conferences. Soon after we had three opportunities lined up and a paper on the way. You and I presented 1BSES in South Africa, the UK and Brazil. I became absorbed by my dissertation while waiting to present at MLA in Glasgow and we lost touch for a moment when I got the news of your passing. Your last message read as if you barely had any energy left. I had called a couple of days prior, but it was too late.

If I were to explain love in its most powerfully connective phase, it would be by channeling your fierce tenderness in caring for the living and the dying as part of a dynamic, ever-unfolding whole that is our home. Your very being is proof of the value intrinsic to the core teachings of Latina/x writers who are building affective and conceptual bridges to heal colonial divides among the oppressed. There is a hard and complex truth in the lessons of anti-colonial scholars who are presently trying to demonstrate to the rest of the world that it is possible to work together across differences toward a common dream in spite of the hardships that we face. It becomes easier to face them together. That is a kind of math that I can grapple with. Driven by the memory of your being, we are daring to dream into reality the material possibility for all people who are suffering from domination to be able to lead a dignified life with the proper metabolic conditions and in reciprocity with the Earth's processes, which is what ecosocialism and marxist ecological feminisms fight for.

We have so much work to do. We are shedding the human to be recognized as compostable humus. As fungi. You left when the party had just begun. I couldn't believe that you were gone, it was as if the entire world skipped a heartbeat. Days became heavier. But, as I am telling Andressa and Roberto in the group chat that we still interact on: our project is actively being embraced by incredible people from around the world. I wish you could be here for it. There are so many kind and willing beings trying to make a difference and we are getting together to make your dream come true. We will plant 1 billion trees and 700 vegetables gardens by forming mycorrhizal coalitions between universities and cultural institutions to get academics (professors and students) to join in the fun. I wish you had been there for the conversation that happened in Glasgow after I presented 1BSES for the first time without you. I screened a video of you speaking about the project and it got through to people because of how genuinely and fiercely you spoke.

I am now summoning a river of images to express the gratitude that I feel for the moments where we were able to join forces and weave a common envisioning for a future grounded in non-egotistical comradely love. For that is the type of love that we must cultivate against all rifting forces of ego. Love like that will heal the agonistic divide.

Oh, Atila. We will someday share a glass of cachaça de banana, as we promised, while traversing the mycorrhizal afterworlds, and in celebration of the life that you dedicated to caring after our home.

Desde el corazón,
Xalli

~ ~~ ~ ~~ ~ ~~ ~ ~~ ~ ~~ ~ ~~ ~ ~~ ~ ~~ ~ ~~ ~ ~~ ~ ~~ ~ ~~ ~ ~~ ~ ~~~

Dedication originally presented in:

A Maelstrom of Peace: Atila Calvente's Billion Slow Exploding Seeds
Re-membering Anti-colonial Life-forms Through the Cultivation of Love
A Project by Atila Calvente† and Xalli Zúñiga.

Interlude: In Memory of Átila Calvente

Magda Madany-Saá

Átila worked for over 20 years in Petrópolis with neighborhood schools in the favelas and the rural countryside, bringing farmers and disadvantaged children together to plant school vegetable gardens and learn about the origin of the foods they eat, and how it relates to their own lifestyles as they grow. In addition, he had experience among settlers in the Amazon, ranchers and indegenous on the Ilha do Bananal in Tocantins, as well as his own experience as an organic coffee and dairy farmer in the Atlantic Forest in the Serrana area of Rio.

Átila initiated The Cacaio Project: Education for Environmental, Aesthetic and Moral Development on which he extensively talked about during our GVF sessions. He was above all a great humanist and an insatiable seeker of knowledge to try to make sense out of global and local problems that afflict youth and their families everywhere. After contributing to planting hundreds of school and community gardens in his beloved Petrópolis, his last (perhaps quixotic) quest to plant 1 billion native trees was emblematic of his energy and willingness to give so much of himself to the poor and to Nature. His trees survive and honor him...

In a personal email to Magda Madany-Saá in May 2021, he wrote:

I have learned so much in the Penn State Virtual Group. Today my work seeks to take advantage of the aspect that encourages the decolonization of science and research methods (Smith, 2008), looking for new onto-epistemological bases on a relationship with nature, silence and ecopoetry. Language and communication do not come exclusively from the brain–mind–body, but also from some energy/spirit. As a farmer in Brazil I can bring to vulnerable children concrete experiences for them to get involved in abstract thinking. The rain teaches softness and lightness. Soils teach humility. Domestic animals teach rationality. Silence allows the expansion of attention and concentration. The lakes cultivate serenity. The sun, an awakening of life. The forest is like a synonym for diversity. The streams, the movement of life itself. To learn from the peasant woman, the vital force. Children abandoned by governments and societies, characterize challenges for an unthinkable future. Cecília Meireles said, 'Words fly, and sometimes they land'. We work to create a fertile environment so that children can seize opportunities to be protagonists of their own stories.

In one of the last emails to his colleague Magda Madany-Saá in September 2021, he wrote: 'Iniciei o projeto no Morro do Alemão e falei para os traficantes se afastarem do meu/nosso projeto. I shall plan to go back there October 10th.'

And he added: 'At the Posse community we are going on October 2th to amplify the vegetable garden, plant trees alongside the local river and play with the children different Cacaio educational practices.'

I would like to ask the wind, the moon, the wild tender flowers of the Cerrado, and the souls of my Suruí children from the Amazon, a word to build the most beautiful, aesthetic, true and silent friendship. (Á. Calvente, personal communication, September 2021)

~ ~~ ~ ~~ ~ ~~ ~ ~~ ~ ~~ ~ ~~ ~ ~~ ~ ~~ ~ ~~ ~ ~~ ~ ~~ ~ ~~ ~ ~~ ~ ~~ ~ ~~

The above narrative about Átila Calvente was shared by Magda Madany-Saá at the opening of Bonny Norton's Global Virtual Forum (GVF) talk in October of 2021. Below, you can view some of the Zoom chat comments which our GVF participants posted in response to Magda's announcement of Átila's passing:

Clarissa Jordao: This sounds like a prayer.... beautiful
Busi Makoni: It's as if he could foresee the end of his life and left us with some words of wisdom.
Anna Kaiper-Marquez: Thank you Magda for this.
Ashraf Abdelhay: Thank you very much for this presentation. It is very sad to lose a friend. Our hearts are with his family. May his soul rest in peace.
Magdalena Madany-Saá: RIP dear Atila. Thank you everyone for honoring his memory today.
Anisa Caine: Thank you Magda for this moving tribute. Atila's poetic spirituality has made a lasting impact on us all, we celebrate his life with deep sadness and gratitude.

If you share Átila's passion for rural education and place-based education, we encourage you to read his articles:

Calvente, A.T. (2015) The Cacaio project: Education for environmental, aesthetic and moral development. *Contemporary Aesthetics (Journal Archive)* 13 (1), 7.
Calvente, A.T. (2022) Abstract critical thinking, language and school vegetable gardens: Improving the Cacaio garden of education and praxis. In S. Makoni, A. Kaiper-Marquez and L. Mokwena (eds) *The Routledge Handbook of Language and the Global South/s* (pp. 430–446). New York: Routledge.

Gratitudes

This volume, *Shades of Decolonial Voices in Linguistics*, is our second volume in our series of the Global Forum on Southern Epistemologies. The First Volume was *Decolonial Voices, Language and Race*, and the third is provisionally *Foundations of Decolonial and Southern Epistemologies*. In this volume, we argue, as many people have argued before us, that linguistics has been shaped by colonialism and outline strategies which may be deployed to decolonize linguistics. We conclude, however, that the decolonization of linguistics is an open-ended process and will not be successfully concluded until society has been decolonized as well.

Like our other projects, we managed to get the volumes to a successful conclusion not because of any single individual capability, but because of the commitments of many people. This includes the organizing and editorial team of the Global Virtual Forum, the guests who have generously contributed to each session of the Global Forum, our global audience, and many other people who have advertised and promoted the Forum in their social and educational circles.

One of the many defining features of the series of the Global Forum on Southern Epistemologies is that the expertise we rely on is largely, though not exclusively, from among those who take part in the Global Forum. For example, we are grateful to a colleague who designed the cover for the book series. We are also grateful to the colleagues who produced the videos which accompany the volume, thus making the volumes multimodal in both theory and practice and increasing accessibility. Further, we are grateful to our global audience including those who weekly attend our forums, at times twice a week, and those who download and make various uses of our videos from across the globe.

The development of the Global Forum has been an ongoing journey for us. It has been more successful than we would have envisioned at the beginning. Its success has depended largely on the contributions and commitments of fellow colleagues, friends, associates, and acquaintances at different stages in their careers and life trajectories, making the project an experiment in intergenerational communication as well.

It is not feasible to individually cite the names of all the people who have actively contributed to this developing project and have shaped our scholarship on this life changing writing and living journey. Thus, following Catherine Walsh (2023), perhaps these acknowledgements ought to be more properly accurately construed as 'gratitudes' rather than acknowledgements.

Foreword

It is my singular honour to invite readers to feast on *Shades of Decolonial Voices in Linguistics*, the second instalment of the ground-breaking *Global Forum on Southern Epistemologies* series. Like its predecessor, this new volume infuses incisive argument and personal testimony from its keynote presenters with the cut and thrust of real conversation and debate. It is in such interaction, in such a novel forum as this, where the sheer scale of the challenge of a decolonial linguistics is being grasped and, perhaps, some of its initial pathways staked out.

As our authors jointly attest, the decolonization of linguistic and communicational disciplines is both necessary and urgent. To create a new vision of our communicational powers worthy of all humanity, free of the despotic mental and institutional shackles of Eurocentric and Northern tradition, giving pride of place, and voice, to those who have been silenced and to those suffering and resisting discrimination, domination and worse – is there a more inspiring, a more noble, aim in the history of any intellectual endeavour? But it's no walk in the park. Indeed, it's a task unprecedented in our time and will demand an effort that is out-and-out *Hanumanian* (de Souza & Nair, Chapter 5).

Furthermore, as the discussions here show, it is a collective and inclusive project to which we all have something to offer if we are willing. The means and ideologies of cultural and symbolic violence, accompanying and enabling colonial seizure, displacement and domination of the Global South, both shape and are shaped by the linguistic and communicational weapons used against the oppressed and exploited within the Northern colonizing states themselves and clothed in the same threadbare epistemologies (Pennycook, 1998). The colonizers' perspective on the linguistic poverty of 'primitive peoples', with their exclusively 'concrete' (rather than 'abstract') cognitive capacities, became entrenched in Northern linguistic theory and educational systems for which the unsponsored written trumps the embodied oral, where rumination on the decontextualized products of linguistic activity represents the height of rationality. The masses, at the other end, bristle with 'language deficits' or plunge into the notorious 'word gap'.

Accordingly, a crucial point of departure for the decolonial project, as our co-editors, Sinfree Makoni, Cristine Severo, Ashraf Abdelhay, Anna Kaiper-Marquez and Višnja Milojičić, argue is to settle accounts with the positivism and scientism of Eurocentric linguistic tradition – to stop trying to pin languaging down with structures, postulates or frameworks or, most importantly, to shoehorn linguistic experience and know-how into boxes with language names on them. If philosophers are out of their 'skulls' and psychologists have lost their 'minds' (John Joseph, Chapter 4), then we linguists must prepare to lose our tongues.

What we gain is the chance to share our communicational philosophies and experiences across the globe, the possibility of creating together, where we can, common goals for this liberating venture along with programmes of enquiry and teaching fitted to and informed by practical interventions to address linguistic and communicational problems, injustices and wrongs. The extent to which the methods and achievements of Eurocentric scholarship will survive the critical fire brought by this insurgent intellectual movement remains an open question, but, as our contributors show, careful and self-critical re-examination of such scholarship together with productive engagement with internal Eurocentric/Northern nonconformist traditions (e.g. with Bourdieu, see Joseph, Chapter 4, or with Harris's integrationism, see Bade, Chapter 1; Makoni *et al.*, 2021; Pablé *et al.*, 2022) is both necessary and fruitful.

The contribution that linguists can make to advance the pursuit of what Boaventura de Sousa Santos (2018) calls 'cognitive justice' is of course inseparable from the broader life-and-death struggle for global social justice. As William Jamal Richardson (2018: 242) puts it so simply and straightforwardly: 'Decolonisation means prioritising the survival of colonised peoples above other interests'. 'The core mechanism by which we can begin to disrupt these processes of structural Eurocentrism', he goes on, 'is by ensuring that colonised and marginalised people don't die'. This blunt truth puts all our efforts into perspective. In effect, for those of us steeped in Eurocentric methods, within privileged Northern institutions, our entire professional training and disciplinary commitments are at stake. This is not just a question of adding to our reading lists but a profound and arduous journey of intellectual discovery, of self-criticism, self-doubt. And this is not just about the content of university curricula but about the universities themselves as institutions and their deep and continuing complicity in live colonial and oppressive economic and political systems. It is in this overall context of decolonizing practice, then, that this volume makes its singular and timely contribution.

In their congenial opening, 'Why "Shades of Decolonial Linguistics"?', Sinfree Makoni, Cristine Severo, Ashraf Abdelhay, Anna Kaiper-Marquez and Višnja Milojičić deftly set the scene for the verbal fireworks to come, suitably laying out a set of four questions which encourage the contributors to adopt the 'what if approach': what would be 'the implications for their professional practices, if linguistics were to be decolonized'? In response, the invited contributors provide starting points, thinking points, talking points, from their own life experiences and very different areas of research, opening out into an expanded dialogic free-for-all with plenty of time for questions, challenges and reflections articulated in a spirit of cooperation and mutual respect. The topics addressed are diverse, demonstrating something of the scope of the decolonial challenge in intellectual matters generally, as well as in linguistics in particular.

David Bade (Chapter 1: 'Living Theory and Theory that Kills: Language, Communication and Control') talks about 'how I integrated my life as a librarian, a linguist and a shepherd'. Bade notes how, in Chomsky's English there is 'no hint of ethnicity, race, religion, poverty, joy, old age, sickness or death, much less Buddhism, nor is there any hint of communication, of winter, summer, of children or animals' and addresses the baleful impact of mechanistic linguistic models, largely constructed on (and in) English. Salikoko Mufwene explores turning points in his own ongoing critical journey away from linguistic orthodoxy in Chapter 2: 'An Iconoclast's approach to Decolonial Linguistics'. Mufwene shows how European imperialists and colonizers devised and applied self-serving 'hierarchies of grammatical structure' in their self-proclaimed civilising mission. He calls out to 'all of us trained in the Western paradigm' to 'step back and put things in context and re-examine our analyses'.

In Chapter 3, Robin Sabino's 'Giving Jack His Jacket: Linguistic Contact in the Danish West Indies' aims to bring the forgotten people, and in particular, 'subaltern agency and identity', back into our understanding of linguistic creativity and development, noting that racist assumptions and an understanding of linguistic change as decay motivated the view that Caribbean creoles were corrupt reductions of European targets. John Joseph's Chapter 4: 'Challenging the Dominance of Mind over Body in the History of Language Analysis' takes on the pervasive biological reductionism of neurolinguistic research with the help of a '4E' perspective, exposing the legacy of racist assumptions, as well as the commercial and institutional interests, at work in 'locating language' in the brain.

'Keywords for India: A Conceptual Lexicon for the 21st Century' (Chapter 5) is Peter Ronald de Souza and Rukmini Bhaya Nair's account of their own attempt to 'use language to breach the fortress of hegemony of the Global North'. Through selecting and focusing on 200 keywords 'from the Indian linguistic space' (e.g. *jootha, time pass, swaraj*), the authors target the comfort zones of the hegemonic Eurocentric conceptual universe and provide 'a tactic, if not a high-level strategy, for democratizing the linguistically colonized, dominated by English, hierarchy of languages that we still have in India'. In his 'Queer Anger: A Conversation on Alliances and Affective Politics' (Chapter 6), Tommaso Milani stirs up a powerful discussion with his audience about the value and place of rage and disobedience in scholarly commitment and practice, focusing on the need to take account of complexities and ambivalences in identities and political allegiance. For instance, Israel, he argues, uses LGBTQ rights in creating 'new forms of discriminations' against the Palestinian people, the victims of Israeli erasure and dispossession. Bonny Norton (Chapter 7: 'Identity and the African Storybook Initiative: A Decolonial Project?') also raises a chat storm in exploring the significance and implications of the African Storybook Initiative and subsequent language projects (e.g. Global Storybooks) in enabling and promoting a linguistic citizenship through the expansion of identity options for decolonial subjects.

In his 'Domination and Underlying Form in Linguistics' (Chapter 8) Nick Riemer argues that mainstream linguistics education, and notably undergraduate linguistics teaching, 'plays a role in normalizing the unjustifiable and unaccountable exercise of power' both inside and outside the academy. The university linguistic classroom, in Riemer's view, is a key site for 'habituat[ing] students to a certain exercise of arbitrary symbolic authority', a situation crying out for critical challenge and transformation. In Chapter 9, 'Decolonizing Multilingualism: A Practice-Led Approach', part convivial dialogue, part artistic performance, Alison Phipps and Piki Diamond address fundamental issues of decolonial practice in relation to multilingualism and the epistemicidal tendencies of the Western academy. In contrast to research methodologies which 'extract' the surface *what* of cultural being, they propose 'additive' journeys of collaborative creation, communal forms of calling forth 'coming from a place of the *why*'.

There we have it: a heady brew indeed. And so, without further ado, let the show begin!

Peter E. Jones
Department of Humanities
Sheffield Hallam University

References

Makoni, S., Verity, D. And Kaiper-Marquez, A. (eds) (2021) *Integrational Linguistics and Philosophy of Language in the Global South*. Abingdon: Routledge.

Pablé, A., Severo, C., Makoni, S. and Jones, P.E. (2022) Integrationism and Language Ideologies. *Fórum Linguístico* 19, special issue.

Pennycook, A. (1988) *English and the Discourses of Colonialism*. London: Routledge.

Richardson, W.J. (2018) Understanding Eurocentrism as a structural problem of undone science. In G.K. Bhambra, D. Gebrial and K. Nişancıoğlu (eds) *Decolonising the University*. London: Pluto Press.

Santos, B. de Sousa (2018) *The End of the Cognitive Empire: The Coming of Age of Epistemologies of the South*. Durham: Duke.

Why 'Shades of Decolonial Linguistics'?

Sinfree Makoni, Cristine Severo, Ashraf Abdelhay, Anna Kaiper-Marquez and Višnja Milojičić

Decolonial Voices, Language and Race, our inaugural volume in the Global Forum on Southern Epistemologies (GFSE) series, was published by Multilingual Matters in 2022. The current volume develops the theme of decolonization via a focus on linguistics, addressing the following four questions:

(1) What does decolonization mean?
(2) What does it mean to decolonize linguistics?
(3) Why should we decolonize linguistics?
(4) How is decolonial linguistics practised?

This volume is based on sessions by scholars including David Bade, Salikoko Mufwene, Robin Sabino, John Joseph, Peter de Souza, Rukmini Bhaya Nair, Tommaso Milani, Bonny Norton, Nick Riemer, Alison Phipps and Piki Diamond.

What Does Decolonization Mean?

The title of the volume, *Shades of Decolonial Voices in Linguistics*, highlights the different iterations of commitment to decolonization among the scholars assembled in this volume. Scholarly commitment ranges from the explicit articulation of and commitment to decolonial linguistics to a broader critical orientation within the teaching of linguistics to undergraduate students. We opted for the term 'shades' because, although everyone is affected by colonization, the impact and nature of decolonization vary depending on whether it is a settler or an extractive colonization that the project aims to undo or contain.

We have also used this title because the meaning of decolonization varies according to the geopolitical location and analytical tradition within which the analysis is situated. For example, in the United States, decolonization is associated with settler colonialism on the one hand, and the quest for social justice and demand for reparations on the other. Meanwhile, in postcolonial Africa, decolonization emphasizes addressing the legacy of colonialism, such as via the redistribution of land in post-apartheid South Africa.

It is necessary to study decolonial linguistics even if we do not refer to ourselves as decolonial linguists. We cannot move beyond an approach of 'coloniality' if we are using the 'segregationist' orientations towards languages (Harris, 1998) that treat them as discrete, nameable entities. That approach created the analytical problems of 'colonial linguistics' that we find embedded across the entire colonial legacy (Heller & McElhinny, 1997; Rajagopolan, 2020). Decolonizing linguistics also means challenging the tendency to view language as an object, which renders languages as ensembles of positive facts that are the consequence of freezing dynamic interpersonal social processes and converting them into monological texts (Riemer, forthcoming).

In this context, 'coloniality' refers to the residue of and legacy of colonialism beyond the formal end of colonialism (Mignolo, 2021). Coloniality is a much more amorphous concept than colonialism, which describes the actual domination of one country by another. Kramsch (2022) elaborates on the concept:

> Coloniality is the permanent process of material and symbolic exploitation, both domestic and abroad, very much linked to racial policies, racism, ethnic discrimination, and all kinds of other discriminations or dominations of the gender related kind. Mary Louise Pratt makes the distinction between *descolonisación* and decolonization. The concept of decolonization comes from Latin America, under the name of *descolonisación*. It is understood, however, in Latin America as a political process of historical change against capitalism and neoliberalism in all its forms. So, whenever we look at research in decolonization that comes from Latin America, it will always have an anti-capitalist, anti-neoliberal flavor that you do not [necessarily find] in the term decolonization as it is being applied more widely in applied linguistics. Decolonization in English is an unspecified movement against inequities of race and gender and for greater social justice.

For Kramsch, the issue concerns the language used to frame decolonization, which is not necessarily the language in which the concept originates. Therefore, the issue concerns the politics of translation. The word may carry different meanings as it is used in Spanish compared to how it is used in English, Swahili or Arabic. The decolonial challenge requires considering how decolonization might be framed in the numerous languages that are rarely used to discuss decolonization. This involves recognizing that our understanding of decolonization is not as broad as it should be. For example, Wright (2022) indicates that the Muslim community of Niasse – which comprises 'tens of millions of adherents' – has been engaged in discourses of decolonization, but that engagement is largely unfamiliar to language scholars in the Global North and Global South outside Islamic studies.

For Norton (this volume), a decolonial project is one that seeks to expand the range of 'identity options' available for decolonial subjects. Norton's argument for decolonization is partially founded on Stroud's (2001) notion of linguistic citizenship. Like Stroud, Norton believes it is a decolonial concept. There is a potential contradiction here: although the idea of citizenship might be liberatory in some contexts, it is potentially discriminating in other contexts, because the criteria for citizenship enable not only inclusion but also exclusion.

What Does it Mean to Decolonize Linguistics?

The decolonization of linguistics requires reworking the analytical frameworks of linguistics to create alternative analytical heuristics that also consider the political implications of revising the orthodox linguistic paradigms. These heuristics enable us to engage with the other cultures and ways of being, thinking and communicating that might have been overlooked or suppressed by the status quo.

Another characteristic of the decolonization of linguistics is that it is an open-ended and never-ending process, much like the decolonization process itself (Mayo, 2022). The decolonization of linguistics can be practised by questioning the pluralization, enumerability and nameability of languages as fruitful ways of capturing linguistic diversity (Makoni & Pennycook, 2024) because some areas of human and social experiences (e.g. water) are not easily amenable to counting.

Furthermore, the decolonization of linguistics is predicated on an awareness that the very notion of language is a recent ideological idea of questionable relevance to non-Western societies. From that perspective, language is not universal (Makoni & Pennycook, 2007; Masters & Makoni, 2019; Pennycook & Makoni, 2020) or, as integrationists following Roy Harris emphatically argue, it is a 'myth' (Harris, 1998). When we argue that language is a 'myth' or an 'invention' (Makoni & Pennycook, 2007), we do not mean that language does not exist, but that languages – similar to other phenomena, including race – are socially constructed and should be understood within very specific discourses and particular institutional ideologies that have created notions about languageness reinforced by literacy. Consider, for example, the postcolonial context of Africa. African languages do not exist; instead, what exists is 'human speak' (*ukulumisinthu*) (isiNdebele or isiZulu), sometimes rendered as *unotaura chivanhu* (you speak human speak) (chiShona).

Decolonial linguistics is not necessarily an anti-Global North linguistics project, as evidenced by its strategic alliances with the Integrational Linguistics associated with the work of Harris (1998), late professor of Linguistics at Oxford University in the UK. That is, decolonial linguistics and Integrational Linguistics can collaborate in the critical project of decolonizing language studies (see Makoni *et al.*, 2021, 2022b; Pable *et al.*, 2022). However, tensions and contradictions between the two exist. For example, Harris suggests that the language user 'has the only concept of a language worth having and everyone is a linguist' (Harris, 1998: 20). This has strong decolonial and liberating potential because some contexts (e.g. African grammars) have seen linguistic descriptions informed by missionaries and outsiders with limited knowledge of the languages and communicative contexts within which they were functioning.

Therefore, decolonial linguistics seeks to analyze the nature of language not from a linguistics perspective but from the perspective of the speaker, the language user. In some cases, the language user may be a disenfranchised 'native speaker' (Pable *et al.*, 2022), a term we are adamant about retaining in the context of African decolonial scholarship because it enables us to identify who has been disenfranchised.

This means that not all native speakers are privileged because that depends on the language. For example, native speakers of African languages, especially minority African languages, were disenfranchised by the European missionaries and linguists that described their languages from a European perspective or using a European analytical grid (Makoni, 2011). In such cases, decolonization involves a process of disinventing African languages by viewing them through different lenses (Makoni

& Pennycook, 2007), which entails cultivating the importance of native speakers of African languages. Arguing for the importance of native speakers in such contexts is not a reiteration of the colonial perspective. Instead, it is a liberatory strategy distinct from its employment in Western European scholarship, which is rife with colonial connotations (Joseph, this volume; Davies, 2003).

In the practice of the decolonization of linguistics, 'instability', conflict and inconsistency are the norm. Consequently, decolonial linguistics is anti-linguistics: 'a systematic questioning and inverting of the basic premises and arguments of traditional linguistic theory' (Stewart, 1983: 266).

Characteristic Features of Decolonized Linguistics

For Nick Riemer (this volume), it is necessary to cast a critical lens on linguistics because of the potential impact its teaching has on the thousands of students who are exposed to it at the undergraduate level. Riemer argues that teaching linguistics encourages ethnocentricity, homeogeneism and Eurocentricism, producing habituated mindsets because students are rarely provided with any rationale for why a specific analytical model should be adopted for the purposes of pedagogy. Additionally, he contends that linguistics is frequently taught in a manner that suggests that there is a single solution to the problem sets that students are given to address, an approach that might be carried out of the classroom.

It is Eurocentrism and coloniality's characteristic discursive and epistemological certainty that decolonization seeks to challenge by focusing on adopting epistemological 'uncertainties' towards social, educational, political and linguistic problems. However, although we seek to shift away from Eurocentricism – one of the defining features of coloniality – we are cognizant of the complications associated with a complete breakaway or 'delinking' from a Eurocentric approach to linguistics.

The call to decolonize linguistics has been accompanied by calls to decolonize other disciplines, including anthropology (Comaroff & Comaroff, 2015), political science (Shilliam, 2019), and sociology (Connell, 2018). Meanwhile, there is increasing fervour around notions of decolonizing international relations, physics, medicine and African studies, alongside university structures and formal education models. Central to this shift is the struggle over whose knowledge matters and should therefore be regarded as legitimate (Makoni *et al.*, 2022b). In this context, the need to be sensitive to issues about sexuality in decoloniality has been recognized as a vital project. Addressing this, Milani (this volume) argues in favour of a queered multilingualism by debunking the bias against LGBTQ in the research on multilingualism, which addresses ethnicity, race and social class (among other factors) but is silent on the issue of sexuality.

One of the objectives of decolonial linguistics is to go beyond the 'world of English', to borrow Bade's phrase. That objective can be interpreted in at least two ways. First, it might mean analyzing languages other than English or Indo-European languages. Of course, only analyzing languages other than English does not necessarily qualify the analysis as sufficiently decolonial, although it at least expands linguistic analysis 'beyond English', thereby making linguistic analysis less Eurocentric and creating opportunities for a decolonial linguistics to emerge.

Second, it describes the emergence of a more critical orientation towards linguistic analyses of English. Mufwene (this volume) argues that there is an unfortunate tendency to analyze other languages based on analytical categories that pertain to English, calling for a reworking of analytical frameworks and resistance against understanding the rest of the universe in terms of the linguistic status quo.

The 'world beyond English' is multilingual, but the meaning of multilingualism will differ substantially across diverse contexts. Clearly, multilingualism should mean different things in the Global North than in the Global South/s (Makoni *et al.*, 2022a), the plurality of which reflects the concept's heterogeneity and multiplicity. However, even in the 'Global South/s' (Makoni *et al.*, 2022a), the meaning of multilingualism will inevitably vary, hence the preference for the term 'southern multilingualisms'.

One type of knowledge evoked by practices of decolonization is indigenous knowledges, including the use of indigenous languages. We consider it imperative to resist romanticizing in the process of adopting indigenous and traditional knowledges and believe that advocacy for indigenous languages cannot successfully lead to decolonization if the underlying assumptions about language remain Eurocentric. Inspirations from indigenous cosmological visions (without uncritically romanticizing indigeneity) include notions of *nite* (Diagne, 2020), *ubuntu and nepantla* (Pennycook & Makoni, 2020) and *Allin Kghaway, buen vivir, sumak kawsay* or *Suma Qamaña* (Cusicanqui, 2010; Quijano, 2014). These ideas and theories argue that engagement with decolonial voices demands a commitment not only to local people but also to challenging white, heterosexual, middle-class and Euro-American males. Our commitment to indigenous perspectives as a project that contributes to decolonizing linguistics should also consider the evolving nature of indigenous knowledge and eschew a crystalized and essentialized notion of indigeneity. This means problematizing the use of generic and hierarchical identity categories, such as the terms 'indigenous', 'native peoples', 'forest peoples', 'native peoples', 'Aborigines' and 'peoples of the fourth world'. Furthermore, the notion of indigeneity itself must be always subject to review (Mignolo, 2007).

However, Riemer (forthcoming) cautions us that the decolonization of linguistics as theory should not 'be substituted either for the decolonizing of the discipline as institutional practice, or for the decolonizing of society more broadly'.

This volume belongs to the genre of 'conversational books' (see the Preface to Volume 1). As such, it aims to expand the genre of scholarly books. Most academic books, even those arguing for decolonization, are typically predicated on the conception of a monoglossic book, which reinforces coloniality via the linearity of their introductions and conclusions, among other monoglossic features. For Piki Diamond and Alison Phipps (this volume), decolonization involves 'messing around with academic monographs'.

Furthermore, decolonization involves retaining a transmodal form of publishing that tries to capture the multiple voices and polyglossia of the interactions upon which the books are based. Because this particular book 'originates' in the Global Virtual Forum's recorded audiovisual conversations, which have been converted into supplementary materials, it (and all of our conversational books) seeks to reflect and enhance polyglossic characteristics by creating texts in which the audience is a partner in the decolonial investigation of established knowledge, ultimately challenging the notion of a unitary author.

Pennycook and Makoni (2020) contribute to decolonial linguistics by questioning some of the underlying assumptions that form the basis of linguistics. The authors expose some of the biases inherited from the colonial period that permeate contemporary practices of linguistics as a profession, which, notably, originated in the 19th century, coinciding with European expansion and colonization.

The analysis of decolonial linguistics should be based on various very specific processes, and these should go beyond arguments that analysis should be conducted in indigenous languages. Following de Souza and Nair (this volume), we propose that the metalanguage used in decolonial linguistics be grounded in four principled actions: (i) infiltration, (ii) population, (iii) elevation and (iv) appropriation. The terms will be drawn from local plurilingual contexts, raising theoretical and ideological issues about the politics of metalanguage, an under-researched topic in sociolinguistics, as Hutton (2022) has argued:

> The relationship between specialist and lay vocabulary in the social sciences is an under-studied topic, and it arguably cuts to the heart of many of the key questions that these disciplines confront. Technical terms may eventually circulate in mainstream usage and lay terms are sometimes selected for 'disembedding' as technical terms. It is argued that stipulated definition is a fundamental form of conceptual engineering and it follows that disciplinary metalanguages are in unstable and dynamic interaction with lay discourse. There are strong arguments for a detached or 'alienated' metalanguage, since social analysis requires distance from social mainstream, yet this very alienation threatens to delegitimate disciplinary metalanguages since they are at cross purposes with the conceptual world under study.

Authorship and Decolonizing Multilingualism

According to Alison Phipps (this volume), decolonizing multilingualism has implications for issues of authorship:

> What it means to author in the Global North within the academy is very different to what I've experienced authorship as being through Piki. And in many ways, even though Piki has not necessarily written the words of the *Decolonising Multilingualism* book that I have written, she was very much one of the key authors of the experiences that form a third of that book and have formed much more of the work that we've done together. I'm using the word 'work' there in the sense of *mahi*, in the sense of the 'wider work' in the world. The word mahi, meaning a broader understanding of what we're here to do rather than what we're necessarily paid to do, transactionally.

The issue concerns not only decolonizing multilingualism but also researching multilingually across different disciplines. However, decolonizing multilingualism appears counterintuitive to the 'multilingual turn'. In this context, it is worth considering Phipps' suggestion that much of her research constitutes 'a struggle to decreate'. Simone Weil has spoken about de-creation as a struggle at the roots of the mind that individuals undertake when they realize that the ways in which they have been inadvertently created (Weil, 1997). As a component of de-creating, decolonizing multilingualism means de-centring particular types of multilingualism, the types of multilingualism associated with hierarchical views of language. Decolonizing language, de-centring and de-creating also demand developing an awareness that so many of the ways in which we used to know the world and used to know language have been lost to the academy's particularly narrow view of knowledge.

Decolonizing Linguistics and Extractivist Ideologies of Research Methodologies

One of the primary objectives of decolonizing linguistics is to break with the violent extractivist ideologies of research methodologies which reflect 'a fossil fuel of rhetoric[:] We mine data. We codify it. We analyze it' (Cronin, as cited by Phipps, this volume). Overall, the ways that we – in applied linguistics, in sociolinguistics, in linguistic disciplines, in disciplines of modern languages, and even in literary studies – have looked at languaging, at the ways we use and deploy language within the Anthropocene, have been largely extractivist.

Non-extractivist approaches mean starting with practice and with art and with improvising and devising rather than starting with a plan, a linear chart, a project scheme, a book outline or a set of questions about what data to be obtained from where and when. This puts researchers in a less identifiable place. Non-extractivist methodologies are cooperative and involve multiple exegeses. For example, the dance project in Ghana demonstrates a non-extractivist approach to research that corresponds to the decolonization of research methods: it was conducted in 20 languages, it was spontaneous, and it was additive.

Sociolinguistics has never taken a clear position on this, oscillating between a universal commitment to social engineering with its evocation of romantic authenticity and embrace of postmodern fluidity. Decolonizing linguistics radically challenges sociolinguistics by bringing a decolonizing perspective to an already fraught relationship between academic metalanguage and the social realities under study (Hutton, forthcoming). For Hutton, sociolinguistics has no way of answering the critique from Southern Theory because Southern Theory and decolonial linguistics are agents of 'disambiguation'. Central to sociolinguistics is the notion that language is 'socially constituted' (Hymes, 1974: 195) but also needs to develop a metalanguage apparatus that is consistent with the requirements and expectations of Western social sciences.

Decolonization and Black Female Scholarship

According to Busi Makoni (2021, 2022), black female scholars are subjected to conditions of invisibility, exclusion and silencing, facing structural and systemic barriers that range from greater difficulties accessing graduate education to an absence of administrative and academic support. This process is evidenced by statistics concerning the number of citations of work by black female scholars, reflecting the patriarchal and white domination of scholarship.

Decolonization in An Unequal Digital World

Given our decision to hire a commercial transcription company in India whose ideologies (we later discovered) were rooted in a colonial mindset towards language use, we have had the unfortunate experience of witnessing the *racing* of, and *linguistic discrimination* towards, our chapter authors' bodies and speech. Particular to this volume, we have experienced our chapter authors' language being judged against the yardstick of standard language ideology (SLI) on numerous occasions.

One case in point is the work of Phipps and Diamond (this volume), wherein the chapter authors' translanguaging was labelled with the note 'speaking a foreign language' by our transcribers, and whose chapter was rife with transcription errors when we first received it. For instance, Phipps and Diamond's frequent references to linguistic and cultural phenomena outside the Global North resulted in confusion on the transcribers' part, such that terms like 'Ga speaker' would be transcribed as 'guest speaker' on numerous occasions. Crucially, the reality of this situation pushed us, as co-editors, to reflect on the impetus to align our future transcription hires with the values of our forum series.

Since our forum's first transcription company exhibited values and behaviors aligned with racial and linguistic discrimination, even as our forum organizers worked to align our forum series with the values of equality and inclusivity, we have done our best to remedy this disalignment in values by cutting ties with our old transcription company last year. As of today, our forum has newly hired a non-commercial transcriber based in Ghana.[1]

Organization of The Volume

Building on this overview of approaches to decolonial linguistics and de-creating multilingualism, this section provides short summaries of this publication's conversational chapters:

In Chapter 1, 'Living Theory and Theory that Kills: Language, Communication and Control', David Bade introduces his own interest in linguistics as a child and how this interest led him to abandon his plan to become a missionary and instead become a student of linguistics in the 1970s. During this time, he was alarmed by the degree to which theories had been developed based on English alone and not tested in real-world contexts or in the context of other languages. He was also unsettled by the widespread strict observation of an approach to linguistics based entirely on Chomsky. Bade's introduction to alternative philosophies of language and communication, particularly in Library Sciences, was sparked by his initial readings of Roy Harris. These readings, in combination with Sinfree Makoni's arguments on the links between African languages and colonial missionary history, led Bade to explore new forms of communication, including how humans communicate with animals. Thus, this first chapter explores how the decolonization of linguistics can happen at a personal level and can transcend human communication. At the same time, a controversial issue which emerged during the discussion about Harris was the allegation that he was sexist towards women. Comparable allegations have been made against other linguistic scholars, including Dell Hymes. Addressing such allegations remains a considerable challenge for decolonial scholarship, which must continue to grapple with such issues.

In Chapter 2, 'An Iconoclast's Approach to Decolonial Linguistics', Salikoko Mufwene draws on his own experiences as an 'iconoclast' (as one reviewer referred to him) to explore the history of colonization and the necessity of decolonial linguistics. However, decolonial linguistics is complicated because 'not everybody that claims to do decolonial linguistics really does decolonial linguistics'. In this chapter, Mufwene expands on several key arguments connected to decolonial linguistics, including the need for careful analysis of languages not familiar to us, the substantial contributions of non-native speakers to the development of linguistics, and the complex history of European colonization in Africa, Asia and South America. This chapter provides a basis for rethinking colonial-embedded linguistic practices and expanding notions of decolonization to recognize the 'delicate work that we are engaging in, in which we have to resist the danger of throwing the baby out with the bath water' (Mufwene, this volume).

In Chapter 3, 'Giving Jack His Jacket: Linguistic Contact in the Danish West Indies', Robin Sabino depicts a complex and dense history of the colony, paying specific attention to 'the agency and rich cultural resources of the West African persons forced to make the small, island of St. Thomas their home'. Philosophically, this monograph begins from the documentation of Virgin Islands Dutch Creole as categorized into three distinct varieties: Negerhollands, developed by Africans and their descendants; Hoch Kreol, developed by the Euro-Caribbean settler population; and the Liturgical Lect, created by missionaries. The linguistic development of the colony is then framed in terms of the 'inter and intra speaker variation' that originally developed as Africans incorporated local linguistic resources and the semiotic practices of their oppressors as strategies for communication and self-identification. Sabino also discusses the notion of conventionalization and argues that it occurs as entrenchment progresses, with speakers not only conventionalizing but also re-conventionalizing over time, producing linguistic change.

In Chapter 4, 'Challenging the Dominance of Mind over Body in the History of Language Analysis', John Joseph understands language in terms of how it is embodied, embedded, enacted and extended, which he calls 4E cognition. Using the 4E prism as a basis for analysis, Joseph explores the role of Chomskyan linguistics in notions of the 'native speaker'. He uses Davies' ideas of the native speaker being a 'myth' to argue that extended/distributed cognition liberates us from conceptions of language that are restricted to representations stored in the brain and from research programmes that assume that a brain born with a particular structure for storing such representations develops in an automatic way with minimal exposure to input data. Finally, Joseph explores concepts of translanguaging and posthumanism to expand conversations on disrupting concepts of the 'native speaker'.

In Chapter 5, 'Keywords for India: A Conceptual Lexicon for the 21st Century', Peter de Souza and Rukmini Bhaya Nair centre on the 'enslavement of minds', the continuation of intellectual enslavement even after the end of colonialism that is enabled and enhanced by the domination of specific analytical frameworks. They argue for challenging these 'formidable forces of domination' not by using indigenous languages instead of 'colonial languages' but by drawing on local plurilingual contexts as resources for analytical inputs. This chapter represents a conversation between de Souza and Nair, with de Souza analyzing the specific processes involved in decoloniality and Nair posing the question of whether decoloniality is (i) a state of mind, (ii) a social process or (iii) a hybrid production, using the history of British colonialism in India to interrogate these ideas. The authors conclude by establishing four approaches to enacting scholarship that can enable the conduct of decolonial discussions with humility.

In Chapter 6, 'Queer Anger: A Conversation on Alliances and Affective Politics', Tommaso Milani argues for the importance of 'queering multilingualism'. Drawing on the history of LGBTQ rights in Israel and Palestine, he explores the many contradictions regarding these rights and suggests that the paradoxes involved in the discourse surrounding LGBTQ rights convert the Israeli support for LGBTQ rights into a tool of self-identity that works to justify its violations of the human rights of Palestinians. Using these examples, Milani contends that research on multilingualism is biased against the LGBTQ: despite addressing, for example, ethnicity, race and social class, it is silent on the issue of sexuality.

In Chapter 7, 'Identity and the African Storybook Initiative: A Decolonial Project?', Bonny Norton explores three interconnected issues: (i) the relationship between linguistic citizenship and the African Storybook initiative; (ii) the decolonial nature of the African Storybook; and (iii) the expansion of the range of identity options for decolonial subjects. She proposes a decolonial approach to language that engages with recent debate concerning 'linguistic citizenship' (Stroud, 2001, 2018) and reflects on the role of digital technology in the identity of African peoples in relation to themselves and their communities. For Norton, the use of technology for improving multilingual literacy practices and empowering local people exemplifies a set of actions that can contribute to addressing the global disparity in literacy skills.

In Chapter 8, 'Domination and Underlying Form in Linguistics', Nick Riemer explores political epistemologies of linguistics to identify the nature of linguistics in relation to climate catastrophe in contexts of political authoritarianism. He explores the political and ideological consequences of beliefs that language in general, or particular languages, have a single underlying form, linking this to the teaching and learning of linguistics in undergraduate education. For Riemer, undergraduate students are subjected to notions that model society as orderly, rule-governed, hierarchical and amenable to dispassionate decision-making, prerequisites to the contemporary bureaucratic administration that facilitates modern governmentality. In this context, perspectives from the Global South may contribute to decolonizing universities and teacher training by expanding our understanding of what it means to teach and learn languages, ultimately contributing to shifting the geography of reason that represents the foundation of the Western university system (Gordon, 2021).

In Chapter 9, 'Decolonizing Multilingualism: A Practice-Led Approach', Alison Phipps and Piki Diamond expand on decolonial approaches to multilingualism by problematizing the Eurocentric geography of reason that has shaped what is considered knowledge and the languages used to produce and disseminate that knowledge.

Reflecting on the challenges they confronted conducting a £2.5 million multilingual project involving 11 countries and 22 researchers, they exemplify how financial support can enhance collaboration instead of reinforcing power relations based on economic advantage and disadvantage. By exposing the ethical, political, cognitive and economic challenges they faced, Phipps and Diamond emphasize the value of experience for decolonial projects, for scholars from the Global North, the Global South, and the spaces in-between. Their personal narratives demonstrate how meanings are never static. Instead, they are produced by continuous processes of negotiation, change, and adjustment, processes that always take time.

We are grateful to Alastair Pennycook and John Joseph for providing critical feedback on two drafts of this introduction.

Note

(1) Our current transcriber is Emmanuel Paddy of Emmanuel Paddy Transcription Services.

References

Abdelhay, A., Makoni, S. and Severo, C. (forthcoming) Colonial heteronormative ideologies and the racializing discourse of language families. In E.H. Lutz, K. Nancy and Z. Jochen (eds) *The Oxford Guide to Bantu Linguistics*. Oxford: Oxford University Press.

Comaroff, J. and Comaroff, J.L. (2015) *Theory from the South: Or, How EuroAmerica is Evolving Toward Africa*. New York: Routledge.

Connell, R. (2018) Decolonizing sociology. *Contemporary Sociology* 47 (4), 399–407.

Cusicanqui, S. (2010) *Ch'ixinakax utxiwa*: una reflexión sobre prácticas y discursos descolonizadores. Buenos Aires: Tinta Limón, 2010.

Davies, A. (2003) *The Native Speaker: Myth and Reality*. Clevedon: Multilingual Matters.

Diagne, B.S (2020) On cultural and linguistic specificities. In B. Diagne and J.L. Amselle (eds) *In Search of Africa(s)* (pp. 50–60). Cambridge: Polity Press.

Gordon, L. (2021) *Freedom, Justice, and Decolonization*. New York: Routledge.

Harris, R. (1998) *Integrational Linguistics: A First Reader*. Oxford: Pergamon Press.

Heller, M. and McElhinny, B. (2017) *Language, Capitalism, Colonialism: Toward a Critical History*. Toronto: University of Toronto Press.

Hutton, C. (2022) Can there be a politics of language? Reflections on language and metalanguage. In B. Antia and S. Makoni (eds) *Southernizing Sociolinguistics* (pp. 17–32). New York: Routledge.

Hymes, D. (1974) *Foundations in Sociolinguistics: An Ethnographic Approach*. Philadelphia: University of Pennsylvania Press.

Kramsch, C. (2022) Decolonizing foreign language education. *African Studies Global Virtual Forum Series*. The Pennsylvania State University. https://www.youtube.com/watch?v=VXuNzQbuUnE

Makoni, S.B. (2011) Sociolinguistics, colonial and postcolonial: an integrationist perspective. *Language Sciences* 33 (4), 680–688.

Makoni, B. (2021) Black female scholarship matters. *Journal of Language and Sexuality* 10 (1), 48–58. https://doi.org/10.1075/jls.00013.mak.

Makoni, B. (2022) Black female scholarship matters: Erasure of black African women's sociolinguistic scholarship. In B. Antia and S. Makoni (eds) *Southernizing Sociolinguistics: Colonialism, Racism, and Patriarchy in Language in the Global South* (pp. 131–146). New York: Routledge.

Makoni, S. (2011) Sociolinguistics, colonial and postcolonial: An integrationist perspective. *Language Sciences* 3 (4), 680–688.

Makoni, S. and Pennycook, A. (eds) (2007) *Disinventing and Reconstituting Languages*. Clevedon: Multilingual Matters.

Makoni, S. and Pennycook, A. (2024) Looking at multilingualisms from the Global South. In C. McKinney, P. Makoe and V. Zavala (eds) *The Routledge Handbook of Multilingualism* (2nd edn). Abingdon: Routledge.

Makoni, S., Severo, C. and Abdelhay, A. (2020) Colonial linguistics and the invention of language. In A. Abdelhay, S. Makoni and C. Severo (eds) *Language Planning and Policy Ideologies, Ethnicities, and Semiotic Spaces of Power* (pp. 211–228). Newcastle upon Tyne: Cambridge Scholars Publishing.

Makoni, S., Kaiper-Marquez, A. and Mokwena, L. (eds) (2022a) *The Routledge Handbook of Language in the Global South*. Abingdon: Routledge.

Makoni, S., Severo, C., Abdelhay, A. and Kaiper-Marquez, A. (2022b) *The Languaging of Higher Education in the Global South: De-Colonizing the Language of Scholarship and Pedagogy*. New York: Routledge.

Makoni, S., Verity, D. and Kaiper-Marquez, A. (eds) (2021) *Integrational Linguistics and Philosophy of Language in the Global South*. New York: Routledge.

Masters, K.A. and Makoni, S. (2019) Gazing at language crossing in the global north but doing crossing in the global south. *Journal of Multicultural Discourses* 14, 295–300.

Mayo, P. (2022) 20 years of engagement in postcolonial education: A retrospective. *African Studies Global Virtual Forum Series*. The Pennsylvania State University.

Mignolo, W. (2007) Delinking: The rhetoric of modernity, the logic of coloniality and the grammar of decoloniality. *Cultural Studies* 21, 449–514.

Mignolo, W. (2021) *The Politics of Decolonial Investigations*. Durham: Duke University Press.

Pablé, A., Severo, C., Makoni, S. and Jones, P. (2022) Integrationism and Language Ideologies. *Fórum Linguístico* 19, special issue.

Pennycook, A. and Makoni, S. (2020) *Innovations and Challenges in Applied Linguistics from the Global South*. New York: Routledge.

Quijano, A. (2014) 'Bien vivir': entre el 'desarrollo' y la des/colonialidad del poder. In A. Quijano (ed.) *Cuestiones y horizontes: de la dependencia histórico-estructural a la colonialidad/descolonialidad del poder* (pp. 847–859). Buenos Aires: CLACSO.

Rajagopalan, K. (2020) Linguistics, colonialism, and the urgent need to enact appropriate language policies to counteract the latter's baleful fallout on former colonies. In A. Abdalhay, S. Makoni and C. Severo (eds) *Language Planning and Policy: Ideologies, Ethnicities, and Semiotic Spaces of Power* (pp. x–xiii). Newcastle upon Tyne: Cambridge Scholars Publishing.

Riemer, N. (forthcoming) Racism and ideology in linguistics. In S. Makoni, S. Rudwick and B. Antia (eds) *Language and Race*. Abingdon: Routledge.

Shilliam, R. (2019) Behind the Rhodes statue: Black competency and the imperial academy. *History of the Human Sciences* 32 (5), 3–27.

Stewart, S. (1983) Shouts on the street: Bakhtin's anti-linguistics. *Critical Inquiry* 10 (2), 265–281.

Stroud, C. (2001) African mother tongue programs and the politics of language: Linguistic citizenship versus linguistic human rights. *Journal of Multilingual and Multicultural Development* 22 (4), 339–355.

Stroud, C. (2018) Linguistic citizenship. In L. Lim, C. Stroud and L. Wee (eds) *The Multilingual Citizen: Towards a Politics of Language for Agency and Change* (pp. 17–39). Bristol: Multilingual Matters.

Weil, S. (1997) *Gravity and Grace* (A. Wills, Trans.). Lincoln: University of Nebraska Press.

Wright, Z. (2022) Islam, Blackness, and African cultural distinction: The Islamic Negritude of Shaykh Ibrahim Niasse. *Journal of African Religions* 10 (2). https:doi.org/10.5325.

witnessed the mass conversion of linguists in response to the latest pastoral epistle of Mr Chomsky.[2] I had been told rather condescendingly that religious people were incapable of intellectual curiosity and unwilling to acknowledge the force of intellectual argument. Yet here were linguists flocking to the altar like Pentecostal converts. It was clear to me then – I think I was 20 years old in 1979 – that the structures of authority and belief were even more pronounced in the university than I have ever met in churches – we argued a lot in churches; I assume that many of you have the same experience. But in the university, all I saw was herd following leaders. I really was astounded as a young man at what I saw in universities. It wasn't at all what I'd been told.

In those days I was especially struck by Chomsky's attitude that all one needs to study language is to look closely at the English language. I was studying Palestinian Arabic, Chinese, Croatian, Biblical Hebrew, Japanese, Kimeru, Russian and Spanish – all as an undergraduate – while dreaming of studying Burmese, Mongolian and Tibetan, languages they didn't teach there, and all the other languages of Africa, Asia and America, past and present, as well as speaking in tongues in my church. A linguistics based on English only, I considered a criminal enterprise. Indeed, a monstrous crime against humanity. But I could not argue with one point: if there were a universal grammar that underlay all languages, then theoretically one should be able to discover it and describe it no matter what language and no matter how many or how few languages one investigated.

On this matter of a linguistics based on English only, Talbot J. Taylor made a marvellous critique in a book review published in 1995.[3] In his review he praised *The Encyclopedia of Language and Linguistics* for including authors from 75 countries. In his final paragraph he writes this:

> We, I am myself an American linguist, need to be told at this particular time that American linguistics is not simply another expression for linguistics, just as at an earlier time European grammarians needed to be told that Latin grammar is not a synonym for grammar. It was the first descriptive grammars of the Native American languages, grammars which struggled to be independent of the Latinizing paradigm, that were finally able to affect this therapeutic transformation of the grammarian's picture of language structure.

So, here we see the core issue clearly: it is only by paying attention to those other languages, listening to the voices of those others, that the American linguist and the English-only theorist will confront the non-universality of English, and the differences with which speakers around the globe exuberantly or carefully express themselves.

So, now let me jump ahead 30 years to that moment when I realized what was wrong with Chomskyan linguistics. This was under the influence of my discovery of Roy Harris. Chomsky never even looked at English, much less any other language. All it takes to realize that, and it took me 30 years to see what was plain as day, is to look at Chomsky's own examples in his published writings. So let me read a few of Chomsky's English, upon which universal grammar is based:

Colorless green ideas sleep furiously.

The man hit the ball.

What do you think that Mary fixed?

How did John wonder what Mary fixed?

John believes sincerely that Mary is clever.

John wants to go.

John wants Bill to go.

John tries Bill to win.

Now that last example Chomsky's language organ apparently produced in order to support his argument that it is a syntactic string that no one's language organ produces. Presumably, the argument does not apply to linguists, whose language organs generate this kind of nonsense all the time. In fact, Chomsky writes the first example sentence quoted above in *The Logical Structure of Linguistic Theory* in 1955,[4] again in the 1956 paper 'Three models for the description of language' (Chomsky, 1956) and for a third time in *Syntactic Structures* in 1957 (Chomsky, 1957) Moreover, searching that phrase today using Google indicates that Chomsky's grammatical though nonsensical 'Colorless green ideas sleep furiously' appears 47,300 times in documents on the internet.

Although disguised as John, Bill and Mary, Chomsky never goes beyond Dick, Jane and Sally. For those of you who didn't grow up in 1930s-to-1960s United States, I can explain later. Language and life are hitting, wanting, winning, and balls all the way. In Chomsky's English there is no hint of ethnicity, race, religion, poverty, joy, old age, sickness or death, much less Buddhism, nor is there any hint of communication, of winter, summer, of children or animals. The only time Chomsky ever comes close to admitting the real world is in that famous phrase repeated 47,303 times now. Colorless: Chomsky's English is colorless. Yet it is green, tinged with envy. And it sleeps furiously, the envious middle-class white man's troubled unconscious. In Chomsky's linguistics, we find the real world abolished through envious repression, replaced by the ideological world of Dick, Jane and Sally. In contrast to his linguistics, Chomsky's political writings are the furious repudiation of that colorless green intellectual sleep that is required for the promotion of the ideal English speaker/listener and the homogenous speech community upon which his linguistics is based. His political writings vehemently criticize the United States precisely because his linguistics is the pure expression of the American ideology of the melting pot, the perfectly homogenous community in rigid conformity with its inherited biological rules for the production of social order.

Anyone who looks at real English will have to consider the world shaking and world making significance of English in the real world. Here I offer a few instances of the language that made me and those who made it. Probably too many instances, but it's really hard sometimes to stop.

'And God saw everything that he had made and behold it was very good.' That's
from the King James Bible.
'Therefore, get up with determination and fight.' That's from the Bhagavad Gita.

'Tat tvam asi.' That's from the Chandogya Upanishad.
'For a boy who is supposed to be so smart you sure are stupid.' That's what my dad said.
'Knowledge is power.' Thomas Hobbes.
'It is easier to build strong children than to repair broken men.' Frederick Douglas.
'Love needs reality.' Simone Weil.
Here's one of my favorites, my dearly beloved Yoko Ono: 'The odds of not meeting in this life are so great that every meeting is like a miracle. It's a wonder that we don't make love to every single person we meet.' That was one of the great, great words directed to me when I was 18. I read that on the liner notes to one of her records. It really turned my whole life around.
Another significant moment was when the head of the department in my library said to me in his office, 'Get out of here.' It was sort of the end of my career.
Then another one: my wife and I said to each other 'I do.'

These are all examples of real language, the language that has made me who I am, how I think and how I live. Voices that speak across millennia. 'Tat tvam asi' may appear to some of you to be a Sanskrit phrase (if I didn't butcher it), which it is. But it is also in the *Encyclopedia Britannica*, and I repeat it often, even though I don't know Sanskrit, so I have to consider it good English as well, just like Schatzi, amigo, Jihad, Kung Fu. To these linguistic life changers that have great significance for me, we might add the following for many others:

'In the country well-governed, poverty is something to be ashamed of.' Confucius.
'There is no God but Allah and Muhammad is his prophet.' That's every anglophone Muslim I assume.
'Here I stand, I can do no other.' Martin Luther.
'I think, therefore I am.' Descartes.
'Let them eat cake.' Marie Antoinette.
'Give me liberty or give me death.' Patrick Henry.
'Workers of the world unite!' The *Communist Manifesto*.
'Change the world, it needs it.' Somebody, maybe everybody, says that.
Then 'Make America great again.'

The significance of each of these sentences is determined by who says, hears, writes or reads it, when, where and why. Notice also that a lot of that comes from some other language. Although once again I cannot provide a reference, when I asked Roy Harris, he suggested that Michael Toolan was the one who made the remark, 'What linguists often forget is that people sometimes fall in love.' Yet before Michael Toolan or Roy Harris, Eugen Rosenstock-Huessy had blown me away, throwing me forever outside the theoretical confines of the standard theory with his discussion of how language establishes relationships, using as his primary example those two little words 'I do.' Rosenstock-Huessy was not simply making a comment on speech act theory, an example of a performative verb. He was saying that language brings you and another person into a relationship that, in the case of 'I do,' alters not just one's own life but that of another; it establishes not just one relationship, but multiple relationships: backwards through the past, as well as forward into the future with kinship ties; and that by establishing such relationships, it reveals its political origin. 'I do' has the power to bring together people of different, and perhaps antagonistic, genders, families, classes, castes, nations, races and religions.

If you have followed this far, you should be able to see how a Chomskyan examination of 'I do' – noun plus verb – does not get anywhere near language as a socially responsible act of political commitment and relationship. To even think of language in terms of the rules of grammar, or of '*a* language', or of 'the English language', is to completely miss everything that is vital and necessary about language. One can easily pursue this line of thinking to the conclusion: the idea that universal grammar underlies language is a theoretical idea that prohibits any relationship between language and (1) communication, (2) social relationships and (3) political realities.

So, having extricated myself from the theoretical fictions and restrictions of the standard theory, I could turn my attention south and east to studying all those real languages, rather than universal grammar. Then one day Sinfree Makoni informed me that all those real languages of Africa were the creation of Protestant and Catholic missionaries and colonial administrators.

Sinfree's studies of the politics of colonial linguistics in Africa brings me back to Chomsky's remarks in *Language and Responsibility* about science, and linguistics as a science in relation to the political realm, namely that scientific theory has no political dimension, linguistic theory has no connection whatsoever with political matters, however much scientists and linguists themselves may devote their energies to political issues.[5] Language is a product of the language organ, and science the product of the science organ: no political origin, no political implications for language or science, both of these being bodily excretions like saliva and urine.

It is this conception of language and science as being the products of some internal organs, and moreover organs whose operations are described as the rule-governed generation of particular kinds of objects in the biological world, which all my experience in the library revealed to be unacceptable, precisely because of its denial of the political dimensions of language. For me the library is the place where all the voices of the world are gathered together so that they can all participate in our conversations about who we are and what we should do. The library is an institutional effort to bring about encounters across time, space, language and culture. My task as a librarian has always been to ensure that each of those authors writing in their various languages would be integrated into the collection in such a manner as to promote their discovery and study by students and scholars. I had to assume that they each had something to say, that there were people like myself who did want to learn what they had to say. Yet the orientation and attitudes I found among library managers and professors of library science was that we are simply managing information, neither authors nor readers are relevant to our work, which is understood to be a technical operation of cataloguing and classification, warehousing, archiving, storage and retrieval, managing publishers' contracts, etc. Instead of Rosenstock-Huessy's insistence that people speak because they have something to say, library science and library management offer us information considered as something independent of its makers and readers in a process in which both are irrelevant.

Into that situation, the once-upon-a-time linguistics student struggled to make sense of his responsibilities to the authors of the books, and to the library's readers. I was thrilled to be given the responsibility to ensure that those books in African and Asian languages would be made available for anyone who wanted to read them. I very quickly realized my own limitations and it did not take me long to see that the problems that I had were the same as those that probably every other research library in the United States and the world had. Most of us librarians did and continue to do what is perhaps the most responsible action that we can take: we wait for someone else to catalogue those books, someone who can actually read them well enough to have something to say about them. We keep searching for those books in our shared library databases and when someone else provides a record, we copy it and feel relieved that the work has been accomplished. Yet I knew that many of those records were being deliberately input by persons who did not know what they were doing, who couldn't read what they were cataloguing but who were being ordered to do it anyway by library administrators. The idea had occurred to some library manager who considered him or herself technologically savvy that his or her staff could enter an incomplete and erroneous record and wait for someone else to fix it, to fill it out and correct its errors and omissions. Then they could just download that corrected record for the library to use. We call that cooperative cataloguing. It's a splendid idea, isn't it? Except that everyone was doing the same thing, every library was waiting for someone else to complete the work and give it back to us perfect. Noun phrase added to verb phrase, we have produced language. Fill in the blanks of an empty computer template, complete it with default settings and we have access to information. Unfortunately, in that world colorless green ideas sleep furiously and they are not the only ones to do so. Like medieval alchemists, we stick fool's gold into our computers and expect the system to turn it back to us as pure gold. There is no communication involved at all.

In 2002 as I struggled with this ideological, technical and linguistic situation in the library, I sat down and read Roy Harris for the first time. I immediately grasped what he was arguing in *The Language Machine* because I was living in the innermost circle of that hell. Instead of a theoretical linguistics that denied the political and ethical dimensions of speaking and writing before anything could even be said or written, here was a theory of language that made everything in my library world come alive. What I was up against in the library was the institutional incarnation of the language machine, the bureaucratic and technological production and circulation of language that was absolutely meaningless and useless. Harris' discussion of Saussure's blank bald talking heads, speech machines with no gender, no age, no class, no religion, no desires, no hopes, no fears, no education, no political goals, no personality at all, *and nothing to say* seemed to me to be a profound critique not only of Chomsky, but of scholarly communication as understood by information scientists and librarians.[6]

With my first paper drawing on Harris' ideas, the library administration at the University of Chicago sought to terminate my employment because of that paper. I had been ordered not to let anyone read it, but someone did read it and wrote to the Library of Congress about it and someone there wrote to my employer, and the

Associate Provost at the university eventually ruled in my favor on the grounds that the University of Chicago actually does encourage research and publication. I was very glad to hear that! But in the meantime, before that judgement came down, I moved back to the farm, totally expecting to be disemployed at any moment. Exercising one's academic freedom, that is to say, one's freedom of speech, can be costly. That is how at 46 years old I suddenly became a cowherd like Krishna and chose to remain one. Life with cattle, sheep and goats is far more rewarding than life in a university bureaucracy. Like Krishna, I dance with a peacock, play with calves and wade in the river. Like Simone Weil, I need that reality because I love it.

If speaking in the library can be absurd on the one hand, or end your career on the other, living both of those realities concurrently made it impossible for me to think of linguistics as though I were in an ivory tower, to elaborate theory as though it had absolutely nothing to do with the social and political realities within which we live. Speaking to cattle, sheep and foxes in the barn, however, took me in entirely unexpected directions: language doesn't make communication possible, rather, the desire for communication makes language possible. Cattle, horses, pigs and foxes do not speak English, nor the universal grammar of the standard theory, much less read about it, yet to the attentive cowherd they speak volumes. The peacock, for instance, has to lead the dance.

Information science was more or less born with Norbert Wiener's book *Cybernetics: Control and Communication in the Animal and the Machine* (Wiener, 1948) and it should be no surprise that in information science, communication and control are coupled not only in the animal and the machine, but in theory as well. In the library world, a demonstrated control over the materials in the library is uncritically assumed to foster scholarly communication, just as in orthodox linguistics, communication is seen to be made possible by the proper functioning of the language organ, or even is nothing but the proper functioning of the language organ. There are no relationships of freedom nor responsibility, only relationships of obedience and necessity, the inevitable predictability of mechanical operations. But the world isn't like that at all. Not in the library, not in the pasture, not in the barn.

I have on occasion heard professors remark that English is the language of science, and it alone suffices, even that the whole world looks to the United States for scientific leadership, so we need not concern ourselves with those un-American voices, et cetera. Yet the science of Harvard and MIT gives us a language organ. In my work as a librarian, I have come to understand that no one can rely on the authority of science, of English scholarship and American theory. What the folks in Ulaanbaatar, Nouakchott or Mumbai have to say cannot be any worse than what comes out of MIT. Just as linguists of an earlier day needed to pay attention to Native American languages in order to see their own theoretical blindness, so today linguists need to look for those voices not rendered sterile by adherence to American ideologies of language. Hence this forum.

The connections that are often made between communication and control present us with that issue which is at the very core of Roy Harris' critique of linguistic theory and philosophy of language as we generally hear it (MIT, Chomsky, the standard theory, etc.): the freedom and responsibility of the language maker, both as speaker and writer and as hearer and reader. Here I would like to draw back to a remark by Edward Said that I really love: 'There is after all a profound difference between the will to understand for purposes of co-existence and humanistic enlargement of horizons, and the will to dominate for the purposes of control and external enlargement of horizons, and the will to dominate for the purposes of control and external domination.' That's from the introduction to the 25th Anniversary edition of *Orientalism*. (Said, 2003). When communication is understood as a practice following a will to dominate for the purposes of control, we are led to cybernetics, information theory, library science, the Standard Theory in linguistics, atomic physics and some all-too-common approaches to prayer. But that is not all: we are led directly to violence.

At this point, I would like to close with two short comments, and then open the forum up for a more conversational approach than the 'I talk, you listen' style that you've had to suffer these last few minutes. The first closing remark concerns Byung-Chul Han's book, *What is Power?* (2018). Here and now, I wish only to point out that in his conclusion to that book, Han suggested it is naming that gives us power, that by giving ourselves no name, we may be able to give ourselves to the world in acts that will not involve the exercise of power and violence. I don't know what all follows from that, but I was really profoundly moved by that conclusion to his book. My final remark concerns the horse trainer Monty Roberts and his understanding of establishing relations of communication among horses. Communication among horses, Roberts claims, always involves establishing relations of trust, and violence always destroys trust.[7] Roberts has developed a way of working with horses, communicating with them in body language, movements and gestures that seeks to talk them into cooperating with the trainer, in doing things that both the horse and the trainer will enjoy. Unlike traditional horse training methods, he does not try to dominate or control the horse, he seeks to communicate to the horse that he, the trainer, can be trusted, that they can do things together for their mutual enjoyment. In that world, violence is anathema: the horses won't stand for it, and neither will Monty Roberts. In other words, with love and devotion and all the right moves, Roberts gets his horses to say, 'I do.' That's it. Sinfree?

Sinfree Makoni

Thank you very much. I think everyone can now understand why I thought inviting you would be very helpful. [*Claps*] Let's clap for David. [*Warm laughter and clapping*]

David Bade

Thank you.

Sinfree Makoni

I have a couple of issues that I want to discuss with you, David. The first one is just more informative before we get into a discussion. Some of the members of the forum may know something about Chomsky but have hardly read any material about Roy Harris because of the skewed nature of linguistic theories and practices. And if you are ostracized from the discipline of linguistics, whatever you say doesn't really matter. Roy Harris may not be very widely known, so can you just give us a bit of a background about who Roy Harris was and what his main ideas were, for example? I only got to know more about Roy Harris when I'd left University of Cape Town. Even though at the University of Cape Town there was Nigel Love, who was working on Roy Harris and integrationism, I just thought he was doing things on language and philosophy that had little relevance to what I was talking about. It was only after I had left Cape Town that I discovered that, no, this guy called Nigel Love seems to be talking about things of interest. So, why don't you give us some more information about who this guy called Roy Harris was, and what you think his impact is on your way of thinking about linguistics?

David Bade

Well, I'll back up just a minute. When I studied linguistics in the 1970s, it was with Robert Lees, one of Chomsky's first students. Lees founded the department at the U of I [University of Illinois at Urbana-Champaign], and so he hired people there who knew Chomskyan linguistics, but they knew nothing else.[8] When I studied linguistics, every other approach to language prior to Chomsky was dismissed as irrelevant. The debate was to argue that we had a scientific revolution in linguistics, and everything before Chomsky was now pre-scientific, so we didn't need to know anything about the history of linguistics. Now, Braj Kachru taught me the history of linguistics in a class, so he would probably object to that statement, but pretty much the linguists in the 1970s at the University of Illinois where I studied, they didn't know the history of linguistics. They didn't know anything that wasn't Chomsky. We were all just taught Chomsky, well, at that time of course it was generative grammar – Chomsky's students, who were doing something that Chomsky later squashed. But, there was no awareness of any other approach in linguistics. So, when I looked at Rosenstock-Huessy's books and Roy Harris' books, when I saw them in bookstores or the library, I paid no attention to them because they were speaking a language that had nothing to do with generative transformational grammar; I didn't realize there could be anything valuable there.

It was when I first sat down to read Eugen Rosenstock-Huessy, when I first came to the University of Chicago in '95, that I realized he's really hard to understand because of my own limited background in linguistics, but his basic idea was that people speak because they have something to say and therefore language has a political origin. Well, that is just totally unlike Chomskyan linguistics, as far from that as you can get. But when I read Roy Harris then in 2002, I realized Harris and Rosenstock-Huessy were starting at the same place: language is a political act. It has political origins. It matters. And it is not just abstract structures that the mind generates for no reason whatsoever. Now, that means that Harris' books address none of the questions that Chomsky addresses. There is nothing in any of Harris' books that responds to anything like these separate domains of linguistic theory that we have in our classes: syntax, phonology, semantics. I mean, Harris *does* speak about meaning and semantics, but he does not speak about it in terms of generative semantics or the semantic component, or any of this kind of theoretical ideas. Harris is a philosopher. He is a thinker with a profound sense of our political responsibility. So, you can't read Harris, looking for an analysis of linguistic artefacts. You read Harris to understand why people speak, why there is language, what it means that we speak to each other. It is a completely different approach to language that has a completely different set of orienting questions. I find it wonderful.

Sinfree Makoni

My first encounter with Chomsky was when I was an undergraduate student in the University of Ghana. What I couldn't understand, but now I partially do, was that in the halls of residence, there were lots of mosquitoes, and we didn't have electricity. But we would spend nights trying to draw these tree diagrams, and I remember asking a friend of mine, what do tree diagrams have to do with these mosquitoes? I couldn't see the connection between the notions of language that they were teaching us in linguistics and the struggles that we were faced with. That's why sociolinguistics became very interesting to me – because I could at least relate to it. I couldn't understand what they were talking about. And let me move on to the other point that you make, which I've always found very interesting because of your experience. You make the point that – from your perspective, and I see where you are coming from – that language is the product of communication. So, if that is the case – if language is the product of communication, and it's not the language that produces communication – when you are talking to your horses, the language of communication with horses will be different from the way you communicate, let's say, with your pigs and your goats, for example. So, are there different varieties of language, depending on the species of animals that you are interacting with on your farm?

David Bade

Well, to be honest my animals don't really pay much attention to me... [*Laughter*] Unless I'm carrying hay. Monty Roberts has actually written a book where he does... it's like a book of sign language, and he shows what movements mean what among horses (Roberts, 2014). So, if they move their head this way, that way, if they walk a certain way; things like, at a certain point, they will poop. And it actually signifies something in the particular kinds of relationships, when (for example) a horse has been banished from the herd for bad behavior, young boy horses, often, when they want to get back in – because obviously banished from the herd means death – they want back in, and they will show signs of submission and willingness to follow the rules of the herd, and a certain manner of walking. But he sets out the steps of how this communication among horses takes place; and it's like reading a manual of sign language: the drawings of this move means that, and this gait means that; I think he says there are about 150 motions that he has identified, that they communicate – and, of course, they only communicate in specific situations. You can't just make that move and have it mean something, all by itself, out of nothing. But in their life together, in certain situations, they need to indicate certain things. And he, as a trainer, does the same thing.

And if you watch any of his videos, it is absolutely astounding how he works with horses. So, there is a sense in which he has written a grammar, it's a pedagogical grammar, to show people what moves mean what in what situations. But he stresses the fact that, first of all, it's learned behavior, and that it goes for almost all horses, I mean all horses that he knows in all breeds all over the world, have the same motions. So that these motions, they have some connection to how horses move in the real world, and they make it mean something. I mean, they're not arbitrary, they're learned, so he says that it can't be some program. It's definitely learned behavior. But it is pretty much the same in all horses. And he's also studied deer, wild deer – he believes that the same is there with deer, and that one may have... Now, I don't know, he hasn't written it up – he doesn't write theoretical treatises, so it's kind of hard to know how all to go. That's what I'm working on, anyway, to understand that.

But they don't have the kind of flexibility that our mouth and tongue afford us. I mean, the human ability to speak and to make distinctions *is* really dependent on our physiology, the way our anatomy works. Talbot Taylor has worked with apes. It's absolutely astounding, too. They can't do sign language, like American Sign Language. They tried to teach them that but then their hands, their bodies aren't coordinated in the way to do it. But they were trying to teach a young ape sign language, and they were talking all the while among themselves. That ape had a baby. Well, that baby grew up in this whole environment, almost as a human child. And they had no idea that it was paying attention or learning anything. It never showed any interest in anything. Then they took the mother away one day, and the baby was left there with the researcher, Sue Savage-Rumbaugh.[9] And it understood English. When they were talking, it would do something to show that, you know... it would go grab a banana and give it to them, if they said they needed a banana, or something like that. And they realized that it couldn't talk a word, it knew no sign language, but it could understand what they were saying and follow directions. Absolutely astounding. Talbot Taylor has written quite a bit on this, and it's absolutely fascinating that this young monkey could understand English but could not speak. Just like children: they learn to understand before they can actually speak. Now, the ape couldn't ever learn to speak because of its own mouth and facial, you know, the anatomical problem. But the apes, that baby ape: two things that it could do that absolutely astounded me was it enjoyed make-believe games, to play make-believe games with these trainers, Sue Savage-Rumbaugh and her colleagues. The fact that an ape can engage in make-believe games just... I was stunned: what that may mean for our understanding of animals. Do horses play make-believe games? I've watched foxes playing in the barn, and I am sure they have that kind of imaginative life, too.

But the other thing was Savage-Rumbaugh and her crew played a trick on another one of the apes. And this little ape that understood English ran right to their symbol board where he can point to things to show what he means. And he said, 'You're bad.' Now, an ape can judge human behavior in terms of good and bad. Well, I'll leave it for you to think about. I mean, the day after I read that, I walked out in the barn and I was thinking to myself, 'Would you guys say, 'You're bad!' if you could?' It really changed the way I interact with my animals, just the thought that perhaps they're judging me the way I judge Chomsky and Donald Trump and all these other – are my cats and my sheep and my cattle looking at me and saying, 'You're bad.'? So, this recent exploration of mine in the world of animal communication has *profoundly* affected my own behavior and the way I act around my animals.

Sinfree Makoni

Let me ask you a question that I should be directing to myself, but I will pose it to you anyway. If you were to advise me on what a decolonial approach to animal communication with horses would look like, what would you say?

Comments from the chat box

Salikoko Mufwene: May jump in here to answer this question?

David Bade

Well, I think Monty Roberts has pretty much done that. First, he learned to communicate with horses. When he was a 13-year-old boy, he went out to trap horses to sell to the rodeos. He went out in the Nevada desert by himself and just watched the horses. And this is where he learned, where he realized that they were communicating. He realized that their motions, that their body language, their gestures, their movements were significant for *them*. He learned how to respond in the same fashion so that they would respond to him as one of the herd. Now the thing was, *all* horse training that he's aware of – and he's looked through the history to try to find out how people trained horses throughout the history of the domestication of horses – that it's all been in order to dominate and control the horse. And – it's violent. Horse training has always been violent. And, for Monty Roberts, the whole point was: work *with* the horses. Let's do things together, let's have fun. And that's why, when I closed my talk… he's not trying to dominate horses. He's not trying to bring them under his control. He's establishing a relationship very much like a marriage, where you choose to do things together. Not separately, not against each other, not controlling each other, but to say, 'Yes! Let's live a life together and do things because we enjoy each other's company.' Now, if north and south, Englishman and Zimbabwean could live together with this agreement of, 'Yes, let's work together! Let's live together. Let's manage a life that we *both* can enjoy.' Well, that I think, is the whole point of a decolonial linguistics – is to get to that kind of conversation, that kind of linguistic interaction. Rather than the 'I'm the authority, you listen.' 'Science says you have to believe.' But to have a whole different kind of relationship. So, I think that Roberts, by taking horse training out, away from control and domination, and making it a joint activity – that's language at its best.

> **Comments from the chat box**
>
> **Cristine Severo:** Thanks a lot David for your inspiring talk. Our concept of rationality has contributed to reinforce the anthropocentric concept of language (and vice-versa). That is so violent because it contributes to reinforce the idea of animals and nature as things and objects.

Sinfree Makoni

That's interesting. Sali, you wanted to jump in.

Saliko Mufwene

Yes, thank you. The question is a very good one. And thank you, David, you answered very well, so I have very little to add to it now. What I was going to say is that we have been colonial to animals.

David Bade

Exactly.

Salikoko Mufwene

And imposing ourselves as superior to them. And, as David just said by the end of his answer, we have to en*gage* with them and realize that, just like it is hard for them to speak, to sign, it's hard for us to learn *their* means of communication. You know? How successful are we to figure out how horses communicate among themselves, how chimps communicate among themselves? Are we anatomically and mentally capable of doing what they do, and why do we expect them to do what we do?

David Bade

Exactly. We cannot expect horses and apes to learn Shona *or* English, but that doesn't mean they won't communicate with us if we will just pay attention. But that is very, I mean, I am just blown away at what Monty Roberts was able to learn from horses. But he did it as a little boy who loved horses. That was the whole thing. He went out to capture horses, but he spent a month learning first. And that was the most important month of his life. And, *he* says that. In fact, he sends out a flyer when you order his books or videos, or whatever, and he has a picture of him with the two horses behind him. And the caption on the flyers is, 'Meet the professors.' He regards the horses as his professors. And he promotes the horses as the teachers. That is wonderful. [*Laughs*] That's absolutely wonderful.

> **Comments from the chat box**
>
> **Mari Haneda:** I would like to ask quick question.

Magdalena Madany-Saá

We have a question from Mari, and Rafael also is paying attention to the chat.

Rafael Gomes

Yeah, and Sangeeta – sorry, Mari – Sangeeta had written to me before, saying that she wanted to make an intervention.

Sangeeta Bagga-Gupta

I was probably going on a different direction, but I could come in. Thank you very much. First comment relates to this ongoing discussion on decoloniality of how we approach animals. I mean, in a number of world philosophies... David, you actually talk about them initially in your presentation – there isn't this hierarchy of humans at the pinnacle, there is much more horizontal relationships. So, everything from Ubuntu, how the Saami relate to nature, and a number of so-called indigenous communities, ways of being, connects very much to what you're saying. And I'm wondering whether those – you would also include those in this decoloniality towards animals. So, you could comment on that. Furthermore, I was floored when you took up *tat tvam asi*, particularly because I used that in the introduction to a double special issue that comes out in a week or so (Bagga-Gupta, 2022) and to which some colleagues on the screen have contributed (Bandung, 2022). And I'd like you to comment on that. I can read Devanagari – but my Sanskrit is very rusty – for a number of different reasons, I use it together with *tattva mimamsa*. And these two phrases, which are not completely unknown, but may be in the Anglo-Saxon world, there is not much attention paid to these concepts or to Ubuntu. In European spaces, some of these concepts are kind of modern, fashionable concepts, but they are not attended to in depth.

So, what I do with *tat tvam asi*, I think of it as a gloss that points to ontological, epistemological bases of who I am, who you are, who we are, who living things are. So, I mean I am thinking also in connection with Thich Nhat Hanh, the Zen master who passed away last weekend, the way in which he elaborates on life: being, becoming, and continuing. So, these kinds of thinkings kind of brings home our naiveté of understanding language in the way that you have explored, something that I became aware of after leaving my doctoral studies in communication sciences. And then kind of tipping into what gets glossed as linguistics. So, I don't have this linguistics background, but I've had to learn that in order to be able to teach, for instance. So, *tat tvam asi* for me would be, unlearning to learn in the way you are also trying to say

– what you have had to *un*learn in order to *re*learn, because what you were offered was not fitting into what you were seeing. And that is what I heard – Sinfree, you also point out that, the mosquitoes kind of helped you see that what you are learning is not connecting to the reality that you are in. So, could you comment on *tat tvam asi*?

> **Comments from the chat box**
> **Sangeeta Bagga-Gupta:** तत् त्वम् असि (Tat Tvam Asi)

David Bade

My encounter with that phrase goes back a long way, but I don't remember the origin. I remember I was reading the *Bhagavad Gita* in the early 80s. At that time, I was particularly interested in Buddhism and studying Buddhism. But I read an essay about the *Bhagavad Gita* and this phrase that I used that the, the one about 'therefore fight.' It was, 'What does Krishna mean? Is he arguing that war is okay?' I mean, it's a *huge* issue. And that was why I was reading it; because I couldn't understand it, and I was trying to understand it. And all I can say is, I've spent the next 40 years thinking about it, without ever coming to some definitive answer – I keep thinking about it. And the *tat tvam asi* was roughly at the same time – to realize that I cannot set myself above others in judgment. That – well, I don't know what to say more about it. I can just say that that phrase has resounded with me throughout the years since, for 40 years, I've lived with it. And I don't know that I can offer any more explanation, except that that phrase comes to mind a lot of times. Partly in the sense of acknowledging my kinship with the world, but partly also to stop myself from that arrogant assumption that my judgments over against the world, should not be turned around as self-judgments. In fact, when I read Nietzsche, my first thought after reading several of his works, was that all of the nasty, cruel things he says about this, this and the other, probably are an admission of self-knowledge. He is blasting away all these people because he sees that as himself, and he cannot admit it. So, the *Tat tvam asi* for me is very much to keep me from ranting and raving like a Nietzsche and putting everybody else down; to acknowledge that we're in this together; we're a lot more alike than unlike. Our differences are real, but I guess – this again is a lifelong question for me – is the nature of, can we communicate, can we actually meet each other? Is there a possibility? I mean, there are so many intellectual currents that say, well you can't, it's a prison house of language; you can't get out of it. Or the constructionist epistemology, where everything is actually your own mental activity; you don't ever actually encounter the world. I mean, there are all sorts of things like this. And my own experience, quite simply, was that meeting a young Romanian woman in college changed me *forever*. [*Laughter*] I mean, it's simple; it's just simple. I cannot say she was a product of my imagination, that she was just a linguistic fiction. She was real. The fact that she wasn't interested made it a real dilemma for me. But that is basically it. I have stumbled upon foxes, kits, baby foxes playing in the barn and will never forget the experience. It was – they didn't know I was there, and I walked in, and they're playing. It was an out-of-this-world experience for me. I will remember it on my deathbed. It was just incredible. Well, that's a real encounter. I lived in the real world. So, any theory that says that I *don't* live in the real world, I just reject. And the *tat tvam asi* is, was, very much an important thing for me to recognize, that we are together, we do share this world, we do experience things together. Which doesn't mean that I understand everything that goes on in your mind, or that I understand everything you say, or that my knowledge is absolute and certain. I mean, philosophers argue about certainty and all that. And I think it's just a silly argument. We live in a real world, and we love it or we reject it. But the more we love it, the more we know it. Sorry, that's not a very good answer to *tat tvam asi*! [*Laughs*]

Sangeeta Bagga-Gupta

Thank you for sharing. I think you make a point, when you say it is about the relationships. And, what you said earlier on about world shaking, and world making of language in the real world. And I think that is also the essence of it. Who I, or who you, or who we are, rather than that there is this essentialistic way of understanding. So, thank you.

Sinfree Makoni

Thank you.

Rafael Gomes

Thank you, Sangeeta. Thank you, David. We have now a question from Mari Haneda. Mari?

Mari Haneda

Yes, thank you. Thank you for a fascinating talk. I really appreciate it. I was nodding along. So, I have two questions. I just wondered if you have encountered Hallidayan linguistics, and if you felt any affinity toward it, because it sort of shares fundamental premises with integrational of linguistics. The second is a more personal one. I attended Theory of Mind Conference at the University of Toronto. That was organized by a psychologist David Olson. So, Harris' lecture was really excellent. But then, there are just sort of numerous complaints by female keynote speakers and graduate students that Harris was an absolute pig, like he was real sexist. And David was really plagued with complaints that people wanted Harris to leave, a huge number of women. So, this sort of like begs a question of – you know, the anti-racist and feminist people who are saying right now – for example, at the University of Pennsylvania, they removed the name of, not Gumperz, but who is the other one? Dell…

Sinfree Makoni

Dell Hymes.

Mari Haneda

Okay – from the name of the center, because of his mistreatment of graduate students, female graduate students, and so forth. So, my anti-racist or feminist colleague would say that I shouldn't be using either Dell Hymes or John Gumperz because of their personal behavior. So, Harris really displayed really incredibly condescending behavior toward women, belittling us. And I just wondered if you consider, like, separating the printed word from the individual and appreciate the work, or are they integrated? I don't know. So, if you could sort of, like, explore the two questions, I would be really grateful. Thank you.

> **Comments from the chat box**
>
> **Sangeeta Bagga-Gupta:** I'd like to follow up later on Mari's important second question

David Bade

Well, the first one is easy to answer. I've never read Halliday. When I left linguistics in 1979, I pretty much left it for good until I stumbled on Roy Harris in 2002. I didn't read linguistics, and I wasn't following linguistics at all. And, since Harris I've just – I've had too little time to explore things that I would... I have, I believe, five or six of Halliday's books on my shelf, but they remain unread, like many other of my books. So, I can't really say anything about Halliday. I don't have any opinions because I have absolutely no knowledge. As far as Harris, Harris was... I only met Harris once. I visited him at his home in 2009 at a seminar he had for a number of younger – well, I shouldn't say younger. I certainly wasn't young. But, people who had discovered his works since he'd retired, was basically the people he had there. My own relationship with Harris was always positive. He was very... a wonderful support to me. Since I'm not a woman, I cannot really comment about his attitude towards women. I do know Harris, from all accounts, was very difficult to get along with, even among those of his admirers. As far as rejecting a thinker because of their attitudes or beliefs, it's a really hard one, because I think we would all be rejected. I don't know of any academics who could set themselves up as a model. We listen to each other, we try to learn from each other and we criticize each other. So, I dislike... I will give one example.

In my youth, I was very much interested in Paul Goodman, the anarchist theorist. Well, Goodman was kicked out of every job he had for sexually harassing his students, male and female. Goodman was absolutely appalling in personal attitudes and behaviors, but I found a lot of what he wrote to be very, very interesting. Now, it was a dilemma for me for years, because I was inspired by his writing; I was absolutely appalled at his behavior. Now, I find Harris' writing, his ideas, his questions, the orientation of his research, to be absolutely marvellous – nothing like it. I *really* appreciate Harris. That he was hard to get along with, that he had some pathological issues in dealing with people... For instance, he *never* wrote about other people's writings with praise unless they were his students. Well, that's a problem. That is a real problem. Now, in private communication he admitted to me that he had been influenced by Hume and that he really thought that R.G. Collingwood was greatly underrated. Now, that correspondence followed my own acknowledgement that I was profoundly influenced by Collingwood and by Hume. So, he was responding to something *I* had written. But Harris had some serious problems as a human being. I don't think anyone who knew him would deny that. I find his attitude towards language and our political responsibilities toward each other to be very amenable to a feminist approach. Now, that feminists would reject Harris and his ideas and attitudes, I'm in no position to make judgments on that.

If I can go apart from Harris a minute: one of my other big major influences is Eugen Rosenstock-Huessy. He is a totally marginal character. If anyone read that paper I wrote, you'll get some idea. Now, what is not in that paper is one of the most extraordinary things that made me *keep* at trying to understand Rosenstock-Huessy. Rosenstock-Huessy once wrote somewhere, that the most important issue for human beings, all of us, always, is that men and women should somehow find a way to live a life together that they can both say yes to. He says, this is more important than religion, than science, than politics. It is *the* fundamental issue that we face, and we should be prepared to jettison *everything else* to meet that need of ours. Because there is no human future, without our learning to make a world in which both of us, men and women, can live together and embrace the world we make together. Now, that to me is the most profound feminist orientation that I have ever read. Because it is not just for boys or just for girls. It is an orientation and a *foundational* assumption about life. But no one would ever call Rosenstock-Huessy a feminist. Rosenstock-Huessy wrote a lot of things that would offend a lot of people. And if you're a feminist, you probably *shouldn't* read Rosenstock-Huessy. If you're a Marxist, you probably shouldn't read Rosenstock-Huessy. He was heretical in everything that he wrote, but he began on that assumption. And that's all I can say. That was his primary objective: in trying to fashion a world with language and communication that men and women can both say yes to. Now, one can reject Rosenstock-Huessy for many things that he said and wrote. And one can reject him for his attitudes towards horses or women – I don't know; he was dead before I ever went to college, so I never met him; I have no experience. I know from his writings that he's incredibly difficult for people to handle. But I find those kind of things in his writing, and I am grateful. I don't find that anywhere else. Now, Harris, I think, is in probably the same boat as Rosenstock-Huessy. Rosenstock-Huessy criticized everybody, so did Roy Harris. But they, each of them, had something to offer us; and I would hate to throw out the baby with the bath water.

Mari Haneda

Thank you. That's sort of the position I've been taking, despite criticism from my staunch feminist friends, because otherwise you erase people, you erase the intellectual history of a particular discipline. And that's like erasing the history of linguistics before Chomsky, right? So, we would be making a mistake. So, thank you for that response. And, I think Sangeeta has a follow-up question online, right? Thank you.

Sangeeta Bagga-Gupta

Could I just jump in? I just wanted to comment, and this is a question I ask myself. When I started working with language studies – what I prefer to call linguistics – of course, you can't then – and this was during my post doc career – you can't then avoid John Gumperz. Having known and done fieldwork during my doctoral studies in Mumbai, Pune and Delhi, I was a bit puzzled to see John Gumperz's work never giving any recognition to scholars, or interpreters, or whoever, in the Indian landscape. It slowly dawned on me that, I don't know, I couldn't make sense of what he was saying in terms of, I couldn't relate to the theorizing he was doing, and unconsciously I refused to reference him. And this is where my question comes – this is long before what has now happened with Dell Hymes, and what is happening with Rhodes Must Fall now, and all those movements. This is much, much – two decades ago. So, my question is that if we have scholars who are saying the same things as scholars we happen to have met, and who don't meet up to a model yard stick, call it what you may, is it relevant that we pay them homage through our referencing? So, this is a question I ask myself, and I ask others. And, Mari what you are now raising, I had no idea. Sinfree needs to be acknowledged, because he brought Roy Harris into my life. I had no idea about him until a couple of years ago. And I relate to Roy Harris' work. I think I picked up, I bought 10 of his volumes. And whatever I put my fingers into, I relate to them. And that's because of the kind of theorizing I met as a doctoral student in the 80s and the 90s. So, I don't know anything about Roy Harris' personal life, but I'd like to understand a general principle: Is it just the history of a particular area that we are reproducing? Don't we then become complicit ourselves? So, I think what Mari is raising goes beyond just this particular person. And I can take up some other references in other fields, in the field of democracy for instance, where my colleagues in Sweden pay homage to perpetrators in the Nazi regime because they have happened to have written fantastic philosophical texts. And I find it very hard to reference them when other people who I happen to have also read say exactly the same things. So, I just want to make that point. It is, why, why take that particular road, when others have said…?

> **Comments from the chat box**
>
> **Cristine Severo:** And we all know that our struggles against oppression should also cover institutional and structural issues. Individuals also reproduce larger patterns of domination that have been reproduced and naturalized by our institutions (and vice-versa).

Adrien Ngudiankama: Interesting discussion. By training, I am a theologian and anthropologist. Our relationship with co-creatures is central to theological and anthropological thinking. We can reference Luther's idea of 'Coram' here, discussing his theological anthropological discourse of 'humanity as a relational being'. As well, we may also refer to Scottish theologian Thomas Torrance's work, as well as J.S. Mbiti's ontological anthropological dictum, 'I am because You are, since You are therefore I am.' Throughout the history of science, mankind has been proved to be animals, as Thomas of Acquinas thought. In your talk, you imply that animals have a universal language, a universal way of communicating. I'm not sure how valid it is. Having grown up in rural and urban settings, I would doubt it. My communication with pigs was different from that with dogs while hunting, even goats, and even the chickens in our backyard. I tested this in my native DR Congo, in England, and even in the United States, where I have lived for some time. Yet any form of communication with animals implies the notion of 'power' in the Foucauldian sense. The animals must be domesticated. The power mechanisms have to be imposed on them. Power is not excluded from the ethical ontological bond between animals and humans. Contrary to Foucault, this is not an oppressive or repressive power. The challenge for us as humans is that we cannot know how animals think even if we developed an objective phenomenology of how they communicate. I don't know your thoughts on this.

Rafael Lomeu Gomes: Some of you might be interested in checking out the video of the session we had with Monica Heller and Bonnie McElhinny in which we discussed issues related to power hierarchies in sociolinguistics: https://www.youtube.com/watch?v=ouZb4zRhr2I

Salikoko Mufwene: I recommend the following recent book on language evolution that connects human language(s) to animal communication: *From Sign to Symbol*, by Ron Planer and Kim Sterelny (2021).

Mari Haneda

May I just jump in? I just wanted to reinstate what I said. So, pay homage to the history of a discipline, but with an eye of, you know, like, a caveat. So, you have to make an effort of, like, John Gumperz's seminal work in India is now pronounced as a manifestation of colonial project that we shouldn't follow. So, it's not really reproducing, but studying it with a critical eye. So, there's a difference of just tracing, but with sort of, like, what we can learn and what we probably shouldn't do. So, it's not really as docile, submissive, tracing that I am advocating, or ignoring problematic, underlying issues that surrounds that individual. We shouldn't circumvent that; we should really confront it. I just wanted to follow up on it.

> **Comments from the chat box**
>
> **Ashraf Abdelhay:** Sinfree, I remember that you once argued that human language should be viewed as related to animal language as a way of decolonizing racist social Darwinist linguistics which excludes African languages as premodern. Can you elaborate on this when your turn comes up. Thanks, David, for the very interesting talk.

Rafael Gomes

Thank you for your interventions, Mari and Sangeeta. There are more people who would like to ask questions or make comments. I see here on my list. There is Salikoko Mufwene and Ashraf, Magda, and there is one just posted now. Now, Salikoko, if you would like to make your comment or ask your question, please.

Salikoko Mufwene

Yes, it's not a comment. David I'm very grateful that you accepted Sinfree's invitation to speak to us. The presentation has been powerful, well-articulated, well put together and really on target for everything that you said.

David Bade

Thank you! [*Warm laughter*]

Salikoko Mufwene

I'm a professor of linguistics at the University of Chicago, and it's a shame that we never met. [*Warm laughter*]

David Bade

I was going to say, I saw your name, and I even got a mass email from you once, but I never met you.

Salikoko Mufwene

Yes. And, so, I'd like to point out that linguistics has its roots in the colonial enterprise. And it's probably not by accident that the rules of linguistics lie in genetic linguistics. Incidentally, when Sir William Jones hypothesized that Indic languages were related to European languages, hence the Indo-European language family, people reacted negatively to that hypothesis in part of the 19th century, because they said Indians are inferior to Europeans. European scholars said, 'Indians are inferior to us.' There is no way that the languages they speak can be related to Latin, to

Greek, and the like, which were put on the top of the pedestal, of the scale. Then you got people like Schlegel, trying to rank languages in terms of the complexity of the grammatical structures and so forth, putting European languages at the top of the scale and non-European languages, either Chinese, or African languages, or Native American languages, at the bottom of the scale. Later on, when linguistics in America developed – and there is an interesting book. I don't know if you can read the title there, in the comments. That was published recently.

David Bade

Native Tongues, yeah.

Salikoko Mufwene

Native Tongues by Sean Harvey in 2018. And it shows to what extent the American government sponsored linguistics for the purpose of determining how primitive Native American languages were, and to justify why they should be confiscating land from Native Americans and push them to reservations, and so forth. And, when you put it in the big picture, you also realize that linguists in the early 20th century wanted to find out how different non-European languages were in relation to European languages. But, along with that, when you put things in perspective, is teaching non-Europeans to study non-European languages from the perspective of European languages, and not do things the other way around. To what extent, what we learn about non-European languages should prompt us to question some of the established approaches to, some of the established interpretations of, how languages work. And that is something that I believe remains in linguistics up to this day: that it is too Western-centric, leaving very little room for non-Western perspectives to influence the development of linguistics. And that is very serious. In the same way that some Europeans complain that linguistics is too Americano-centric, or Anglocentric. A number of us non-Europeans complain that linguistics is really too Western-centric. And for people like me that have published extensively, people can say how can you complain? You have made it. Well, I complain because I struggle every time for every publication to convince a reviewer: 'There is something you are missing. There is an alternative way of looking at things, and so forth.' And that isn't happening fast enough in linguistics. You know? Yes, linguistics has been emancipated somewhat from that colonial tradition, but in my mind, not really enough and not fast enough. And things can really move faster and evolve for the better. You mentioned Robert Lees – I met him. And I'm grateful I met him because in formal settings, he taught me to question what I was reading about generative grammar and the like. And I'm fortunate that at the University of Chicago, where I was trained by people like Jim McCawley, I was really encouraged to think independently, out of the box. And that has helped me. And Braj Kachru is also very important in that particular context, and so forth. I think I will close by saying, thank God all White linguists don't fit the mold of generative linguistics, that not all generative linguists really follow Chomsky closely. But you were right on target when you put your finger on Universal Grammar. It doesn't help us to deal with linguistic diversity, you know...

David Bade

Least of all, a Universal Grammar based solely on English! [*Laughs*]

Salikoko Mufwene

That's right. That's right, and that's where you find a lot of colonialism. Because, especially when you are non-European and you question the value of Universal Grammar, and so forth, it's very hard to get published. But what's wrong with Universal Grammar is that it doesn't work. Part of what is wrong, is that it doesn't tell you what real universals there are. And those universals, are they consequences of the way the mind works? Because some of those principles you can find them outside language! Or are they consequences of the materials that the languages are made with? Okay – and things like that. So, I'm glad – really grateful that you gave this presentation, because it gives us a lot of food for thought. Thank you.

Rafael Gomes

Okay, everyone. Yes, David?

David Bade

I would like to back up just a minute to Mari Haneda and Sangeeta's comments on the issue of how to listen to and acknowledge people who, in their personal lives, have attitudes and ideas that we cannot agree with. That's a major issue. That's a big issue. That goes back a long way, political correctness movement in the United States in the 80s and 70s. I don't know how far back. But I'm inclined to not want to read people whose lives as it is known to me, offend me, but at the same time I have had experiences where... I would like to just relate one such experience which kind of stops me in my tracks, whenever I dismiss a thinker. Namely, when I was in graduate school, and this would have been 1978 or 79, right before I left, I was terribly broken-hearted because a certain woman that I was madly in love with married somebody else. That really left me in quite a state of turmoil. I was terribly depressed. And I went and I talked to a fellow linguistics student. Now, he was in fact kind of a renegade, and ostracized in the department – and I enjoyed associating with outcasts. But in fact, he was one of the nastiest, meanest, vicious intellectuals I have ever met. And never had a career, and I don't know what else I should say, except that he ranks at the top of people I would not want to associate with since. I did it as a foolish, young student because he was a bad boy. But I told him about my unhappiness, and that I had even thought about killing myself, I was so unhappy. And he looked at me, snarled, was just completely contemptuous, and said, 'If you really loved her, you should make her proud of you,' and then he stomped off and I didn't see him for years. In fact, that was the conversation that saved my life, turned me completely around. And it was the meanest, wickedest, stupidest, nastiest pseudo-intellectual I've ever met. Now, what has that to do with Roy Harris and John Gumperz? Perhaps a lot.

But I always remember that when I get ready to dismiss someone for not having the right political attitude, for being a feminist, or a not feminist, or whatever it may be. I remember that conversation, that he had the right word that I needed to hear at the right time. And that's all I can say. Roy Harris spoke to me really powerfully. And Heidegger I've never read because I just couldn't get over his attitudes, but probably I should read him. But there you have it. There are people we don't read for many reasons, and there are people that we do read and learn from. But definitely, if we don't read someone, we're never going to learn from them.

Rafael Gomes

Thank you very much, David. Unfortunately, we're reaching the end of the formal session of our conversation today. So, I'll hand over to Makoni for his final considerations before we move on to the after party.

Sinfree Makoni

Anisa, you wanted to comment.

Anisa Caine

Yes. Thank you. First of all, I can't thank you enough. This was just music to my Being. So many golden threads for us all to take away with us. I've been looking for someone like you to listen to. I think you are at the hub of what our forum is about, listening to understand and connecting beyond human borders.

David Bade

Well, I was trying to write for the forum! [*Laughs*]

Anisa Caine

You have brought so many valid arguments that often lie dormant. There is so much I would like to share. I see that the main thing here is that superiority is the enemy of trust. As soon as one species puts itself above another, trust that is essential for understanding and connecting vanishes.

David Bade

Exactly.

Anisa Caine

Whether it be male/female, animal/human, tree/insect, two nations, superiority is the enemy of trust. I went to Edinburgh to study applied linguistics with many questions and a hope for understanding of language and communication. Most of my hopes were met. There was a *lot* of emphasis on methods and methodology, and validated knowledge, but nothing on trust. Language is about communication, and linguistics is to do with language, but there was nothing on trust. When I spoke about my time with the Ituri Forest Pygmies and said that they could communicate with other species, I was told the only non-human communication that is recognised is in bees during the bee dance. So, I kept all the really valuable knowledge that I learned at the university regarding linguistics, and moved on in search of multi-disciplinary, multi-intelligence and multi-sensory knowledges, knowledges beyond theory but not excluding logic. In search of experience and heightening instinct. And I see now, from what I'm hearing today, that other ways and waves of knowing are thriving.

The greatest ecological disaster is the lack of trust. Trust requires spiritual intelligence. If we want to understand animals, maybe we should also understand the people who *do* understand animals. Now, I want to share a brief story. When I moved to the Scottish Highlands, one of my first friends was a shepherd who had lost half of his brain in an accident. And he had total communication with sheep. He taught me so much about how to connect with sheep. It was all about love and trust. And thank you so much, because you've brought so much trust here, and you've moved us all forward. Thank you.

David Bade

Talbot Taylor published an essay a few years ago (Taylor, 2013) It was Meredith Williams, a book about Wittgenstein. It is a marvellous piece where the issue that comes to the fore is that trust is essential for children to be able to learn language. They can't go at it with the intellectuals' critical, dissecting, analytical attitude. They have to believe that you're speaking to them and that you have something to say, and that their response matters. It's a profound essay. I wish I had the title of it. But it's by Talbot Taylor and it's about Meredith Williams' book, and the basic part is how much children have to have a world of trust, or they cannot learn language. I was really impressed with the essay. I mean, so much so that I'm gonna have to read Meredith Williams if not Wittgenstein.

Anisa Caine

Yes. Wittgenstein is amazing on the correlation between learning and trust. For all relationships trust is the key force. You cannot have any meaningful and connecting experience without trust. As soon as superiority walks in, trust walks out.

David Bade

Well, as soon as Hobbes' attitude that knowledge is power orients our learning, then we have already decided that the knowledge that enables domination is the only knowledge that is knowledge. I reject that completely. I think the only way to know your children or your sheep is to be madly in love with them and wish them their own life. Not a life that follows my desires and my demands, but something which will allow them – as Rosenstock-Huessy said, in male/female relationships, it's got to be a world that we can each say 'yes' to. Which means we each have to be a part of making it.

Anisa Caine

Trust and understanding. In his *Ethics*, Spinoza identifies three kinds of knowledge, defined by the methods by which they are obtained (De Spinoza, 1996). They are knowledge from imagination, knowledge from reason, and knowledge from intuition, and he thinks the last one is superior to the others. To access wider knowledge, we should apply all three to get the widest picture, and this requires trust in self and others. (Many thanks again, David, for your contribution to that wide approach.)

David Bade

Well, I haven't read Spinoza either; I'm sorry. I've only lived 63 years. I just can't read everything.

Sinfree Makoni

Rafael, you said Ashraf had a question that he wanted answered. Ashraf, what is the question?

Ashraf Abdelhay

Actually, first I should say thank you to David for the interesting presentation. I heard you once, Sinfree, talk about, or make an argument that we need to consider human language as part of the animal language as a strategic way of combating the social Darwinist conception of African languages as premodern. I heard you argue it.

Sinfree Makoni

Yes. I think what I was trying to say was that if you think of human language as part of animal language, it liberates and enables you to see more about what animal languages may provide and how that may enrich your own understanding of what constitutes human language. If you think of animal language as completely separate from human language, you may then tend to fall into the trap of thinking of animal language as being inferior to human language. But if you think that human language is part of animal language, then the distinctions between us and animals really are inconsequential. You are liberated to see more things than you would if you saw the two as completely different. This, to some extent, goes back to the point that Sangeeta was making: that the distinction between animals and humans is not consistent across the globe. In some cases, animals and humans intermingle in a single pot. We're all part of the same species. That's what I think I was trying to get at. But we need to revise this whole thing. It ties to what Sali was saying; the critical question to pose is, 'What would English, French, Spanish, etc., look like if they were to be analysed and framed from the perspective of African languages?' What is it that the analyst who studies English would learn about English if they looked at the world starting off from the perspective of African languages, Arabic, etc., or Native American languages? That, I think, is an interesting question to pose, even for the specialist in English. They can never have a comprehensive analysis of English until they see how English looks like from the perspective of African languages, Native American languages, indigenous American languages. Because that perspective, it's not there.

David Bade

Ashraf, while you're still here, let me just say I really enjoyed your essays that I happened to read while editing Sinfree's book. You've got a wonderful topic and written quite a few really nice things. I was really happy to read your works. Thank you.

Sinfree Makoni

David, the part of your work I like best is when you say that you remember this Romanian girl who had such an impact on you, even though she said 'No', and that linguists are bad at falling in love. I thought that was the most articulate statement I've ever heard about linguists. [*Laughter*] Right. Any other questions? Okay, Sali says that he recommends the following book that connects human languages to animal communication: *From Sign to Symbol* by Ron Planer and Kim Sterelny. Thanks a lot. Višnja, do you have any questions?

Višnja Milojičić

So, all of these comments actually inspired me, as I was thinking through these issues. And I think a lot of these questions are coming up of how to make more horizontal, critical practice. And how to go about thinking about things critically and from a decolonial perspective. And I was thinking, also, of Dr Bade's comment about how we should find a world in which both men and women can live with. And just taking that, even extending that, to think of how can we, not just find a world in which men and women can live with, but how can we look at, like – Dr Makoni, you said looking at European languages from the perspective of African languages. So, how can we look at the world from the perspective of female scholars? How can we look at the world from the perspective of African scholars? Like, through their lenses, and not just agreeing to disagree on certain things – but how can we actually start looking at the world *through* those lenses, if that makes sense?

David Bade

Well, first of all, I think I have to listen to you if I want to know what a woman thinks. I'm not gonna figure that out myself. And as far as African scholars, it's why I read Ashraf Abdelhay and Sinfree Makoni. My own delight in discovering my world in the library, was that all of those voices can come together. No one was excluded. That's why I could work in the library much more happily than I could stand in front of a classroom and tell people what I thought was what. I was very, very uncomfortable in that role, and never will be comfortable in it. When Sinfree asked me to talk here, I told him 'Sinfree, I really... What does a white boy from Central Illinois got to talk to an Africa Forum?' But, in fact, it is the conversation that we need, and it's a conversation we need, not me giving people the voice of science. I refuse to speak in the name of science. I speak as somebody who's interested in what all of you have to say. And, I think that multi-perspective conversation is the only way we'll get beyond that narrow-minded view of the English-only America, you know, science... Every adjective you put on there – English, America, Science – you just narrow the world so far down, that all you've got left is that knowledge is power, and a world that you're destroying. I want knowledge that is more of a, well, as I would put it – I think it's impossible to have justice without love. I don't think it's possible to know the world, if you hate it. If you love the world, you can, it can affect you. It can change your life. If you hate the world, all you can do is kill it. That's it.

As I've mentioned, the experience of falling in love as a teenager, as a college boy, has profoundly oriented my attitude towards theory. And it was because she was real. She was not a fantasy. She was not a theory. She wasn't just something I'd been told about. And, for the rest of my life, I've sought to meet the world in that fashion: to appreciate it, to know it, to love it for what it is – not for what I wish it would be.

Sinfree Makoni

Did you ever meet that woman again?

David Bade

Did I what?

Sinfree Makoni

Did you ever meet this woman who turned you down?

David Bade

No, I left her alone because I thought it would make her happiest. No, really, if you're a woman and some crazy guy in love is after you, it could be horrible. I'm sure it is something she worried about. I mean, women have to deal with stalkers and all sorts of crazy things. I don't want her to think I'm...

Sinfree Makoni

One of them.

David Bade

I've never forgotten her, that's for sure. I mean, but I leave her alone because I think that's what is best for *her*.

Sinfree Makoni

Thanks a lot. Thank you very much.

Notes

(1) For those unfamiliar with Rosenstock-Huessy's writings on language, many are collected in his *Die Sprache des Menschengeschlects: eine leibhaftige Grammatik in vier Teilen*. Heidelberg, Verlag Lambert Schneider, 1963 (two volumes). For an introduction to his philosophy of language in English with a discussion of his linguistic philosophy in relation to the Integrational approach of Roy Harris, see my essay 'Respondeo etsi mutabor: Eugen Rosenstock-Huessy's Semiological Zweistromland' *Culture, Theory and Critique*, 2015, 56, (1) 87–100, or its earlier and longer version presented at a conference in 2014, 'Respondeo etsi mutabor: Eugen Rosenstock-Huessy and Linguistic Theory' available here: http://www.erhfund.org/wp-content/uploads/BADE-Respondeo-etsi-mutabor-Eugen-Rosenstock-Huessy-and-Linguistic-Theory.pdf
(2) The as yet unpublished lectures were circulating in typescript at that time; they were later published as: Chomsky Noam. *Lectures on government and binding. The Pisa lectures.* (Studies in generative grammar, no. 9) Foris Publications, Dordrecht and Cinnaminson, N.J., 1981.
(3) That review was published in *Language Sciences* 1995, 15 (4), 379–382.
(4) Chomsky's 1955 dissertation, first published under the same title in 1975 by Plenum Press, New York.
(5) Noam Chomsky, based on Conversations with Mitsou Ronat, *Language and Responsibility*. Pantheon Books, NewYork, 1979.
(6) Harris' imaginary conversation between the bald talking heads in Saussure's famous diagram appears in the epilogue to *The Language Machine* (Duckworth, London, 1987), one of several books by Harris that I read in 2002.
(7) See especially Roberts' first book *The Man who Listens to Horses* (Random House, New York, 1997) and his later book which explores the relevance of his work with horses to relationships among people, *Horse Sense for People* (Penguin Books, New York, 2002).
(8) The reader should understand that this remark and the remarks which follow in this paragraph reflect my own memories of my all too brief experiences of being taught Chomskyan linguistics and generative semantics during the years 1975–1979. It is true that we were never taught any other theoretical perspectives nor encouraged to explore other approaches apart from a brief flirtation with Relational Grammar on the part of some faculty. What my professors knew of the history of linguistics I cannot honestly say for I do not know; what I can say is that what they taught and all that they taught was Chomsky and Chomsky's followers, even though some of those followers did not fare well in the subsequent development of The Standard Theory.
(9) For the reader who wishes to pursue this matter, see Savage-Rumbaugh *et al.*, 1998.

References

Bagga-Gupta, S. (2022) Editorial introduction: Contemporary issues of languaging, participation and ways-of-being. *Bandung Journal of the Global South* 9 (1-2), 1–20. https://doi.org/10.1163/21983534-09010001

Bandung (2022) *Journal of the Global South*. Double Special Issue theme: Languaging, Diversity and Democracy. Contemporary issues of participation and ways-of-being across the global North-South 9 (1-2). https://brill.com/view/journals/bjgs/9/1-2/bjgs.9.issue-1-2.xml

Byung-Chul Han (2018) *What is Power?* Cambridge: Polity.

Chomsky, N. (1956) Three models for the description of language. *IRE Transactions on Information Theory* 2 (3), 113–124.

Chomsky, N. (1957) *Syntactic Structures*. The Hague: Mouton.

De Spinoza, B. (1996) *Ethics*. Part II Proposition XL. London: Penguin Classics.

Harvey, S.P. (2018) *Native Tongues: Colonialism and Race from Encounter to the Reservation*. (Harvard Historical Studies). Cambridge, MA: Harvard University Press.

Roberts, M. (2014) *From My Hands to Yours: Lessons from a Lifetime of Training Championship Horses*. Solvang, CA: Monty and Pat Roberts.

Said, E. (2003) *Orientalism*. 25th anniversary edition. New York: Vintage Books.

Savage-Rumbaugh, S. Shankar, S.G. and Taylor, T.J. (1998) *Apes, Language and The Human Mind*. Oxford: Oxford University Press.

Taylor, T.J. (2013) Calibrating the child for language: Meredith Williams on a Wittgensteinian approach to language socialization. *Language Sciences* 40, 308–320.

Wiener, N. (1948) *Cybernetics: Control and Communication in the Animal and the Machine*. New York: Wiley.

2 An Iconoclast's Approach to Decolonial Linguistics

Salikoko S. Mufwene

Salikoko S. Mufwene

I thank Sinfree for inviting me to speak to this forum. I take it as a distinction. Having listened to so many brilliant presentations before, I'm a little bit nervous. I hope I will not disappoint you. Before I continue, I would like to acknowledge some friends that took some time to come and listen to me. I noticed John Baugh is here; and Raj Mesthrie, of the University of Cape Town is here; and my colleague John Goldsmith is here. And I seize this opportunity to make a correction: I'm no longer the Frank J. McLoraine Distinguished Service Professor at the University of Chicago. Now, I am the Edward Carson Waller Distinguished Professor of Linguistics and the College. The latter was John's title, a higher distinction than mine. After he retired, it was passed on to me, effective January [2021]. And John also has the distinction of having co-authored with a colleague, Bernard Lacks in Paris, a voluminous book titled *Battle in the Mind Fields*. It's now the complete reference where you can find the history of our discipline. And I'm sure you'll be ready to correct me if I make a mistake today in talking about colonial linguistics and its practitioners. I would like to also recognize Michel DeGraff, at MIT, with whom I have collaborated since the 1990s on many things regarding creoles and now about using mother tongue in formal education.

So, let me now explain why I use the term 'iconoclast' in the title, not to characterize anybody else but myself. Michel, he knows that I used to refer to myself as a heretic. But, in 2011, I was a fellow at the Institute for Advanced Study in Lyon (France), and its director encouraged me to apply for funding to do research on language endangerment around the world. It was an ambitious proposal because the plan was to recruit experts around the world that could tell us stories about language – not just language endangerment, but language vitality in their parts of the world, because I complained that there was too much of a Western, and especially American, perspective in the way that people deal with language endangerment today. I was not funded, not because the proposal was bad, but because they thought that I had asked for funding to develop an institute, which was too much. One of the reviewers characterized me as an iconoclast whose views are difficult to refute. It reminded me that that is the kind of thing that I have usually done in creole studies, and in some other work regarding African languages. So, I have accepted the characterization with pride, and that is why I use it in the title.

Regarding decolonial linguistics, I want to point out that I'm just jumping on the bandwagon, because other people, including Sinfree Makoni and his colleague Alastair Pennycook, with whom he published a book called *Innovations and Challenges in Applied Linguistics from the Global South* (2020) paved the way. And the book is a wonderful contribution to decolonial linguistics as a way of questioning some of the working assumptions that evade our discipline, expose the bias that we have inherited from the colonial period. It is this historical context that shaped some of the founding principles of linguistics as a discipline. And this is why we have to question some of those working assumptions.

There is also a wonderful book, edited by Ana Deumert, Anne Storch and Nick Shepherd titled *Colonial and Decolonial Linguistics* (2020) to which I noticed that Sinfree Makoni also contributed a chapter, along with myself. While contributing to the book as a commentator, I noticed that not everybody that claims to do decolonial linguistics really does decolonial linguistics. This is not just a method of saying there are so many studies and the largest proportion of them have been conducted by Westerners, by people from outside the former European colonies. It's a method of sorting things out, checking what are genuine mistakes in the works, in current publications, in the state of the art. What are the true European biases and what are just honest mistakes that anybody could make, and so forth.

It doesn't amount to saying, 'Well, such and such topics were not approached before; I'm going to deal with that kind of topic; and therefore this is decolonial linguistics'. No, that is not necessarily decolonial linguistics. Finding a new topic of interest is just something that is quite independent from decolonial linguistics. So, it's delicate work that we are engaging in, in which we have to resist the danger of throwing the baby out with the bath water, and that is part of what I'm going to talk about.

Allow me to share an anecdote with you from the early stages of my career. I submitted a paper to a journal. It was about Gullah; and I noticed that the structure of Gullah was quite different from what I had learned about English grammar. This had to do with the intersection of the count/mass distinction – with how you use articles: definite article, indefinite article, or no article. While working on Gullah, I noticed that some of the differences actually arose from English itself, but in ways that the school grammars that we learn have not been able to explain clearly. Here, Gullah was helping me come back to English, to question whether we have dealt adequately with the count/mass distinction in English itself. I argued that the opposition is not as a lexical property, but part of the grammar that goes along with strategies of specifying reference.

The editor wrote me and said, 'Well, you are not a native speaker of English. There are too many subtle distinctions there that you, as an outsider may not grasp'. At that time, we didn't correspond by email, so it took time, and I wrote back and I said, 'That doesn't really speak very well about linguistics if you think about it, because the vast majority of languages around the world have been studied by Europeans, and the Europeans that wrote about these languages were not native speakers of these languages, and yet they are the ones that have developed the paradigms that we are following.' That was the end of the discussion. The editor was gracious enough to take back his comment and to publish my submission. In other words, there are a number of people that are open-minded enough to revise their positions. It's a matter of how we articulate our points of views and how we address their objections. There is ample room for change. It encouraged me to do many more things, and the editor and I actually became good friends; he encouraged me to submit more articles to his journal.

So, what I want to start with is pointing out that linguistics as a discipline started in the 19th century. We credit Ferdinand de Saussure as the father of modern linguistics, and I know there are other people that think that Chomsky is the father of modern linguistics, so it really depends on whose perspective you consider. But, for me, as far as Western linguistics is concerned, we can trace it as far back as the 19th century. Other people will go to Sanskrit, but I wouldn't go that far. We can go all the way to the beginning of the 19th century, and this is also the time when Europe was developing a strong interest in Africa because, in the colonization venture, the primary interest had gone to the New World, where Europeans had developed settlement colonies. The Portuguese were interested in Africa for trade, and they went all the way to East Asia, but they didn't penetrate the interior of Africa until the 19th century. For Asia, it was the same. The Europeans did not penetrate the interior either. But what happened is that there was a British judge, Sir Lawrence Jones, who went to India, and he developed an interest in Sanskrit. He discovered that Sanskrit had a number of features that it shared with European languages. At that time, people did not speak of the Indo-European language family yet, just about European languages, and you compared those languages with Latin, and Greek, and so forth.

This did not sit well with people that wanted to colonize Africa and Asia in order to 'bring them civilization.' To them, people of Africa and Asia were inferior to Europeans and less evolved than Europeans. You find this thinking in the work of Charles Darwin too, in *The Descent of Man* (1871), where he characterizes Africans and Native Americans, and non-Europeans in general, as people that are less evolved. You will be surprised to find this characterization of non-Europeans as less-evolved in the work of Otto Jespersen too. In my book, *Language Evolution: Contact, Competition and Change* (2008), I report the early Western reactions, according to which Indians couldn't possibly speak languages that share features with European languages. Inferior people couldn't possibly speak languages similar to those of superior, more evolved populations! This was the first reaction to the idea of the Indo-European language family as including also Indic languages, before Europeans changed their mind. The objections that I report here are objections that were formulated in 1875, and that is quite striking. So, we have come a long way towards admitting that people who are not of the European stock can share the same language family as Europeans and form a group called the Indo-European family.

The 19th century is the century of 'la mission civilisatrice'. In British English, it was referred to as 'the white man's burden' to bring civilization to us. We have to beware of the legacy of this colonial approach. Modern linguists have now emancipated themselves from that kind of prejudice, but there is a difference between emancipating one's views toward particular people, and not paying attention to the consequences of some of those biases that we have to undo, because they may otherwise continue.

Another feature of research in the 19th century, and we find it in the work of Frederick von Schlegel, is the comparison between different morphosyntactic patterns around the world, for instance the fusional pattern of many European languages (regarding, for instance, the expression tense for verbs and number for nouns) vs the isolating morphosyntax of, say, Mandarin. For people who are not linguists, for instance, instead of saying 'John came', in an isolating language you say 'John', and then the marker of past tense as a separate word, and then 'come'. In Mandarin the marker of aspect precedes the verb and the marker of tense is actually an adverb following the verb. In the phrase 'John came', you have the fusional morphology. If you speak an agglutinating language, you would have in one word the marker of person, the marker of number, the marker of tense... all of them packed in one word. But, in European languages, you do it differently. In the mid-19th century, Frederik von Schlegel had his own idea. At that time, he was familiar with Chinese, and he thought Chinese to be a primitive language. According to him, it was languages with either the isolating morphosyntax or with an agglutinating system that were primitive.

Nobody would think that there might be something odd with European languages in not doing things like these languages. People rarely thought of typological variation in neutral terms. Nowadays, in my work, I say we can think of languages as technologies: that is devices or strategies that you develop to solve problems. One of the problems is how to package information when you are communicating with each other. Different people solve problems in different ways, and there is no significant reason for saying that one way is less evolved than the other. You can accept variation and try to explain the patterns of variation. But, for Europeans in the 19th century invested in *la mission civilisatrice*, they could not resist the temptation of hierarchizing European languages at the top (like they did with the European or White race).

There is an interesting book that has been published recently titled *Native Tongues: Colonialism and Race from Encounter to the Reservation* (2018), by Sean Harvey. The subtitle is quite telling in the sense that it articulates how precursors of linguists in the United States, in the 19th century, studied Native American languages. They did it with the purpose of determining ethnic, or in their terminology, tribal groupings and how to manage the dispossession of land from Native Americans on the basis of language and push people to reservations in groupings that made sense to them (the colonizers). Among the arguments in the book by Sean Harvey – he is a historian but did a lot of work on philology and historical linguistics – there is a recurring theme that Native American languages are allegedly primitive, and nobody should make an effort to learn them. Ironically, the people that gave us ideas about Native American languages are people that married into the Native American population and learned Native American languages by immersion. But, at that time, the attitude was that whatever is considered too difficult for Europeans to learn, must be primitive and inferior. So, it is not just about Africa and Asia, but about all these territories that were being colonized.

The point here is that we need to be cautious when we investigate these languages that are unfamiliar to us. The danger resides in approaching them from the point of view of grammars familiar to the authors, like those of Indo-European languages, especially Western European languages. To what extent are we projecting categories in the object languages that may not exist in them? Remember, you are dealing with typology. If you think of languages as technologies, they can vary in a number of ways, and perhaps in ways unfamiliar to the investigator. The only constraint is what the mind is capable of processing, and what the mind may not be capable of processing. But otherwise, we are subject to prejudices that we may want to avoid. In a short while, I will get back to what I mean by these prejudices.

Something else happened in the 19th century, and here is where the work by Michel DeGraff and by myself comes in. In the late 19th century, when the exploitation colonization of Africa, Asia and the Pacific was in place, the Europeans started noticing the ways in which the European languages had been modified in the colonies. They came to acquaint themselves with creoles, and they came to acquaint themselves with pidgins. It was obvious to them that the European languages had been modified because of contact with non-European languages.

So, you would expect, as a rational reaction, that somebody would ask, 'Did anything go wrong with how we accounted for the speciation/diversification of Indo-European languages?' Because, the speciation, the diversification of the Indo-European languages and the idea of the Stammbaum, or cladogram in modern terminology, was based on the comparative method. You compare lexical items, you compare morphemes that come with those lexical items, and you determine which languages are more closely related to one another. But, as pointed out by Antoine Meillet in the early 20th century, when the languages show such correspondences, it could be for any number of reasons. One of them is inheritance from the same protolanguage, an idea that is very much cherished in genetic or genealogical linguistics. Another reason is that the same languages could have borrowed items from similar languages (other than the putative protolanguage) and would be modified in similar ways. And this is where we deal with language contact. Another reason could be homology that, by independent evolutions, they would wind up with similar things.

In other words, you do not jump to the Stammbaum or the cladogram without embedding your research in social history. But, the reaction of the European genetic linguists, at that time we characterized them as philologists, was that the modified languages in the colonies are 'bastard tongues.' When you read, in particular French philologists such as Lucien Adam, Charles Baissac and Julien Vinson, they say, 'Well, it's not a surprise that those who speak inferior languages are incapable of learning the sophistication of European languages. That is why our languages have been modified to such an extent that we cannot recognize them anymore.' That's the legacy of colonial linguistics.

This legacy has survived in creole studies; thus Michel DeGraff came up with the term 'Creole Exceptionalism' in his endeavor to debunk it. When we verify history, a notion such as 'break in the transmission of the lexifier' – the lexifier is the language that gives the overwhelming majority of the vocabulary to the creole or to the pidgin – quite a bit of the grammar comes from the lexifier because the language varieties to which people in and from Africa (around the Atlantic), in the Pacific and in Asia were exposed were not standard varieties of European languages. The

Indo-European language family was constructed on comparing written varieties of European languages, not the non-standard varieties of European languages. So, we have a partial history in the reconstruction of the Indo-European languages. Thus, in a way, the discovery of creoles and pidgins was an opportunity for people doing Indo-European linguistics to re-examine things in order to do better genetic linguistics. There are people, currently, who are invested in this kind of work about a century and a half later. But we have to go back to the late 19th century where prejudices toward populations in the colonies prevented Europeans from doing something better than they were doing.

There were exceptions such as Hugo Schuchardt, who argued that creoles and pidgins are telling us how the Romance languages must have evolved. For instance, Vulgar Latin would not have been transformed into so many diverse languages if it had been uniform (which it was not) had not come in contact with the Celtic languages in the colonies (the provinces of the Roman Empire). When you put things in perspective, in the case of the Romance languages, the Celts gave up the Celtic languages, shifting to the colonizer's language, just like the Africans did in the Caribbean: giving up the African languages and shifting to the European languages. Moreover, this was in settings where the people shifting languages were in the overwhelming majority, just like on the plantations, taking into account the fact that the Celts were at home, but the Africans were not. These are things that we have to take into account.

I can go on and on, but at some point, for those of us that are interested in genetic creolistics – concerned with how creoles emerged – these are some of the biases that we still have to fight against. For instance, when it comes to creoles, unless the transmitters were Europeans, linguists have jumped to the conclusion that there must be a break in the transmission of the language. But the European languages need not be transmitted by people of the same race as the heritage speakers. A language need not be transmitted by its heritage speakers only. We talk a lot now about English being a global language. Who are the people that have played an important role in spreading English around the world? It is not just the Europeans. In the case of Asia, in 2015, I gave a lecture in New Delhi, and the title of my paper was 'How India too made English a world language.' I focused on the role of India in spreading English in especially Southeast Asia.

It is often people like me, from the Congo, who have contributed to spreading English in places not colonized by the British. When I go back to the Congo (DRC), I become the model of an English speaker even though I may not be an impressive one here in North America. But, this is how things evolve. If you take the plantation settings, the people who really played an important role in the transmission of the European languages were not necessarily their heritage speakers. They were people like the European indentured servants who were not necessarily native speakers of these languages, the Black Creole children who were born locally and learned the lexifier as a mother tongue. These people became the transmitters and spreaders of these colonial languages.

So, how could people stick to the idea that there was a break in the transmission of the lexifier when the evidence is there that there could not have been a break in the transmission of the lexifier? In the work that I am doing about the emergence of pidgins in Africa, I have encountered surprises. There were so many unions between Europeans and Africans on the coast of Africa, and out of these unions were born children. There was also a category of women called the 'Signares' in Senegal and 'Nharas' in Ginea Bissau; they formed unions with the European traders and became bilingual in European and indigenous languages; and their male Mulatto children, native speakers of their fathers' heritage languages, were the people that carried on the trade in the interior. There could not have been a break in the transmission of the lexifier in the trade forts/settings of Africa and Asia. You cannot reconstruct situations in Africa and Asia where, because they could not communicate with Europeans, the Natives created a pidgin out of thin air. The trade that produced pidgins was global trade on the model of trade today between, for instance, Microsoft and its customers in Germany, or Belgium, or any other country. For instance, trade between the merchant companies and the rulers of the Ghana Empire, or the Mali Empire. These trade partners exchanged commodities through brokers, and the brokers are the people that had expertise in the local languages; and there was never a need for a pidgin for the trade to take place, especially when large quantities of highly prized commodities were involved. Pidgins are later inventions of probably the early 19th century (if not the middle of century), when the European languages spread locally as lingua francas among indigenous people.

It is not by accident that the European philologists and colonizers noticed the emergence of pidgins in the 19th century. There is no evidence of any pidgin in the 15th century or the 16th century. The earliest evidence of anything that we find approximating a pidgin comes in the 18th century. When you look at the texts, those texts are closer to European languages as they were spoken, non-standard European languages mind you, than they are to the pidgins that we know today, which are more divergent from European languages. The way the emergence of creoles and pidgins has traditionally been explained, in different ways, bears the colonial legacy of non-Europeans considered as incapable of learning the European languages.

The other thing that I want to mention here regards the identification and grouping of languages in Africa, and this is where Sinfree Makoni may step in. How did Europeans group African languages? Missionaries played an important role, because for the missionaries, it was a matter of how to group people in the territories in which they were going to proselytize. They found a language that they thought was widely shared in a geographical area so that they did not have to learn so many different languages. They then grouped these languages according to their convenience, not really doing it like the Indo-Europeans did in applying the comparative method. Of course, there are people like Karl Meinhoff in the 19th century who tried to classify African languages into language families.

But, for missionaries, it was a case of practicality. 'What are the languages that we have to capitalize on so that we can do our job well or easily?' And so the colonial administrators piggybacked on the work of missionaries and started identifying particular ethnic groups. This was also the time that coincided with Europe redefining itself politically in terms of one-nation-one-language ideology. And so, this was particularly significant to them.

So, we find groupings of languages in Africa that are sometimes at odds with how people determined their ethnolinguistic identities. Some people have been ascribed ethnic identities that are not real to them. Where I come from, there is a particular language called Kikongo. This is a construct that corresponds to no reality! What exist are varieties like Kiyombe, Kiladi, and Kimanyanga (among many others) that have been lumped together into one language. These languages are as mutually unintelligible as the Romance languages are among themselves! For instance, it is like me and Cécile traveling to Brazil, and when we wake up in the morning, people are speaking to us in Portuguese and Cécile is a native speaker of French. I then turn to her and ask, 'Can you understand?' And she asks me back, 'Why did you ask me if I understand Portuguese? That's not my language.' But this is the kind of assumptions that Europeans carried over to Africa when they were grouping these particular languages. Why it was this way, I don't know. I found out that something similar happened with the group of languages identified as Quechua/Kichwa in South America, and there are similar cases in many places around the world.

Approaching languages outside Europe with a European lens can be dangerous in the sense of leading us to wrong analyses. One example is how many textbooks have described the noun-class markers in Bantu as articles. Well, if they really are articles, then they would be doing the kind of job that articles do in French or in English, but this is not what noun-class markers do in Bantu languages. Noun-class markers in Bantu languages do not tell us anything about definiteness. You have to express definiteness by using a demonstrative, but not by the noun-class marker alone. It is difficult to tell the count/mass distinction just by the noun-class marker. There are dedicated markers such as the plural marker in class 6. The same marker in class 6 is also used for things that come in pairs that do not correspond necessarily to the count/mass distinction. If you pay attention to the noun-class markers, you find that they also have a derivational function. For instance, in some languages, the word for family is related to the word for parent, and it is related to the word for giving birth. So, you use the same stem, but by changing the noun-class marker, you convey a different kind of meaning and so forth.

There is something troublesome about defining a noun-class marker as a kind of article because it sets the analysis in a different kind of frame that is misleading about what you want to investigate. It even keeps you away from discovering how things work in that particular language. The other thing that caught my attention, for instance, and this was when I started working on creoles and people were talking about Verb/Predicate Clefting, something like, in Gullah, *da talk he duh talk* 'he is really talking'. (*Da* and *duh* are both pronounced with a schwa; the former is the definite article and the latter marks the progressive.) In this example, *da talk*, for instance is the way that he is speaking. Here, the construction changes the verb *talk* into a noun, with the definite article, and you put it at the beginning of the sentence. Because it is similar to clefting in English, and most of the studies about this have been in English, the construction has been called 'Verb Clefting.' But in English, you cannot put a verb in that position. This has led to people saying 'See, creoles are just so different, and they will use even a verb in that position.' But creoles happen to have an isolating morphosyntax. They do not have these inflections, as in *It's singing that he does best*. You have to deal with the zero or null morpheme. You can nominalize without putting anything on the verb in that particular position. In the creole construction, the article before the nominalized verb/predicate should give you a hint that you are not dealing, really, with the verb there. Even adjectives can be used in this construction too, as *da tall he tall* 'he is really tall'.

You are dealing with something different. And when you think about it, the verb or predicate in that focus position is nominal. Then, you will see that in English there are verbs that occur in that position, but they must be nominalized by assuming the gerund suffix. For instance, *it's his singing that I don't like*, just like *it's his voice that I don't like*. When you put a verb there, you have to change it into the gerund, and a gerund is a form of nominalization. When I went back to Bantu languages, that is precisely what I found. There are two ways of nominalizing a verb in Bantu languages: one of them is to add the so-called infinitive noun-class prefix, so the infinitive is nominal in Bantu languages, unlike the infinitive in English. The other way is to just use the stem without a prefix, just another form of nominalization.

So, there is really no Verb or, more accurately, Predicate Clefting in creoles. What you have is Clefting, and then you have to deal with what really happens when you put a verb in that position. The other thing here, we have to recognize are adjectives. The category 'Adjective.' For instance, consider examples like *the beautiful boy* or *the strong woman*. In Bantu languages, this does not work. The items that fall in the category of adjectives are really a small set. In many ways, you use something that is similar to a relative clause. In Bantu languages, a sick person is a person that has sickened or is sickening, a ripe fruit is a fruit that has ripened, etc.

When you read a lot of grammars in which researchers are calling certain words 'adjectives', you start to wonder, what is the essence of an adjective? What are we learning about the language typologically? These are some of the challenges. Another phenomenon to consider is serial verb constructions. We talk about serial verb constructions while they are opposed to subordination. Are they also opposed to complementation? That's really not a question. The one thing about serial verb constructions is that you have a sequence of verbs without a conjunction or a preposition between them. For instance, in Gullah, *Uh tell dem come,* which means 'I told them [to] come'. For instance, *Uh aks um come kyah me to da hospital,* which means 'I asked him [to] come [and] take me to the hospital'.

When people define serial verb constructions, the usual explanation that I have found in the relevamt literature is that in serializing languages you describe with many verbs what is expressed in English as 'an/one event'. How do you know that the event boils down to the way the relevant information is packaged in English, and not the way that things are formulated in a serial verb construction? So, in English you can say 'I cut the meat with the knife', but you also can say 'I took a knife and cut the meat'. Which one is truer to the notion of event? Or is it just a matter of variation in how the relevant information is packaged?

It is dangerous to just take the lens of an English grammar and project it onto another language and then present differences noticed in the other one as a deviation from the English grammar rather than as instances of typological variation in the ways that people package information. For instance, in the case of serial verb constructions, what you may want to express in English as an event is not just one single event to the eyes of somebody else, and they express it as more than one event. Even in your own language, English, you do have this option, why do you dismiss it? For me, working on different languages is an opportunity to go back and forth. There are these languages I know, and I want to see how they work. Is it possible that that language may send me back to the language that I already know, and I may have to revise my analysis? This is a step that has usually not been taken; and I think that is a facet of colonial linguistics.

To my last point: English has been claimed to be the 'killer language' par excellence; it is accordingly about to kill all the other languages in the world. L'Organisation Internationale de la Francophonie has taken advantage of this claim and is trying to form partnerships with African governments to fight the spread of English. But La Francophonie is silent about whether or not French may be a threat to African languages, because France is there to promote French as a superior language. But then, you travel around the world, and in Africa, you notice that English is not threatening indigenous languages, French is not endangering indigenous languages. As a matter of fact, as you go around the world, you notice that everything is not proceeding the way it has in Europe or the way it has in the Americas and in Australia. You notice that things are evolving in different ways. In Africa, it is some African languages that may endanger some other African languages. In some cases, if you step back and notice the way in which things are evolving, you may develop the impression that French may not have much of a future in the Democratic Republic of Congo or Senegal. Because, in Dakar, Wolof is becoming dominant, and people are becoming more and more interested in Wolof and less and less interested in French. In Kinshasa, Lingala is becoming dominant, and people are taking more and more pride in speaking Lingala and less and less pride in speaking French in many domains of the public sphere. You can go to Nigeria, and Nigerian pidgin English, which is an indigenous language in Nigeria although it is lexified largely by English, is becoming dominant, which may be to the disadvantage of English. These are the kinds of things that we also have to pay attention to. What has struck me, which I voice in my publication in *Language* (the journal of the Linguistic Society of America) in 2017 is that there is too much of a Western, Anglo-Saxon bias that is preventing us from learning language evolution from the point of view of language vitality. What are the factors that really matter? Like economic power or popular culture? My argument is that in Africa, English and French are doing poorly because there is no, or little, economic development to be associated with these foreign languages.

You shouldn't trust reports of economic growth. Economic growth does not mean anything when the people that are farmers, those that have been disenfranchised from the European style economy, are not partaking in the payoffs of economic development. It's because they are frustrated, they have no interest, or little interest in French and English that they won't learn or speak them. Then people say: 'what if China is going to replace English'? Wait a minute. For every 100 people learning Chinese, there are millions of Chinese learning English, and, as Nicholas Ostler has expressed in his book, *Empires of the Word* (2005), it's the buyer's language that prevails.

Follow the market language practices. American companies trading with China are not trading in English, they are trading in Chinese. Americans trading in Japan are trading in Japanese and not in English, and other countries are doing it the same way. So, how do things balance out? We really don't know. So far, English has benefited from places like India that count as Anglophone even if only 30–40% of Indians speak English, but you see it in terms of close to 1 billion people living in India. People trading with India are investing in English instead of investing in Hindi. This is favoring English. While there are millions of Chinese and millions of Indians invested in English, there are only smaller numbers of non-Chinese and non-Indians invested in Mandarin or Hindi. Moreover, the dynamics of coexistence between indigenous and non-indigenous language in Africa are quite different from those in the European settlement colonies. The local dynamics in India are quite different too. In the end, all evolution is local, subject to local ecological factors.

It is time for us to step back and realize that the population structures of different parts of the world are not identical, and we have to go and investigate things locally and not make projections from far away in the United States or Australia, because the colonization histories of these particular territories are not the same as in the rest of the world. So, the question is who practices colonial linguistics? It's not just Europeans, or people of European descent. All of us trained in the European research paradigm may be applying colonial linguistics too. So, my message here is not a discourse against linguists of European descent. There are many of them that are doing decolonial linguistics too. My discourse is for all of us trained in the Western paradigm and the need for us to step back and put things in context and re-examine our analyses. So, I think I am going to stop here by saying again we have to be cautious not to throw the baby out with the bath water. Thank you for your attention.

Comments from the chat box

John Baugh: China is investing heavily in the spread of Chinese in many African countries, coming in the form of trade agreements, building schools, hospitals, and roads. The spread of Chinese is a clear goal.

Cécile Vigouroux: China has been in Africa for a very long time. When you go to many parts of sub-Saharan Africa, Chinese traders speak African vernaculars. I think we shouldn't confuse the extent of an economic market with the spread of a language. Ethnographic work shows that dynamics are much more complex.

Magdalena Madany-Saá

Thank you so much, Dr Mufwene. Really, time flew with your fascinating lecture. Before I hand over to Dr Makoni, two interesting comments. I don't know if you want to refer to them, Dr Mufwene, about the last topic you've been mentioning, the spread of Chinese trade and the spread of Chinese language. So, one is from Dr John Baugh and the other from Dr Cécile Vigouroux. I don't know if you can- did you read it?

Salikoko Mufwene

Yeah, China has been in Africa for a very long time. This is from Cécile? When you go to many parts of sub-Saharan Africa, Chinese traders speak African vernaculars. We should not confuse the extent of an economic market with the spread of a language. Ethnographic work shows that dynamics are much more complex, and that is very true.

Cécile Vigouroux

And yeah, I was responding to John before. You need to look at John's message. China is investing heavily in the spread of Chinese.

Salikoko Mufwene

Yeah, China is investing heavily in the spread of Chinese in many African countries coming in the form of trade agreements, building schools, hospitals, and roads, and the spread of Chinese is a clear goal. I can respond to this. Actually, it is related to what I read from Cécile Vigouroux in the sense that even here the principle of buyer's language applies, and the Chinese in Africa are interacting with the Africans in African languages when they can learn them. Or people at the low level of the system actually learn African languages and they speak them very well.

But people at the higher level of the system, they invest in the official language of the country, like French in the Congo (DRC) and in Senegal. In Zimbabwe, they practice English. But, the reason why there are so many Confucius institutes is because Africans want to go to China, and they are going to need Chinese when they go there. So, that's really the way it works. The difference between Europeans and the Chinese is that the Europeans, probably because of colonial history, did not invest that much in African languages, and they thought that it was enough to teach African the European language. But they did it also in a strange way.

European colonization in Africa and Asia proceeded by intermediaries. The late William Samarin used to speak about colonial auxiliaries. And the colonial auxiliaries, the low-level administrators and teachers who were indigenous, and people in the police force (though they were not officers), and so forth. These are the people that interfaced between the local population and the European colonizers. So, a lot of European colonizers didn't really interact directly with the Africans, and there are a lot of places in Africa where people don't have a clear idea of what European culture is.

'European culture'? This is really a terrible over-generalization. But one can speak of French culture or of Belgian culture. So, the similarity is really in the process, and that's why when you study Africa, you will find out that the proportion of Africans that speak European languages has been very low. It hardly exceeds 20%. There are a couple of exceptions like Gabon and Angola. Gabon goes up to 80%, but because they never developed an indigenous lingua franca, Angola goes up to close to 50% for reasons that I don't know. But, everywhere else it's really around 20%. And when you consider the fact that African countries have been independent for over 60 years now, and education has been in European languages, you wonder how much money and how much time have been wasted because in over half a century, the proportion of people learning and becoming competent in and practicing European languages has remained very low.

Magdalena Madany-Saá

Okay, thank you so much for this answer, Dr Mufwene. I see Dr Sinfree Makoni's ready to ask his question. I also see Dr John Goldsmith raising his hand. I don't know if your comment, Dr Goldsmith is about the last comment, or is it a different question?

John Goldsmith

Yes, my comment was more general. Salikoko, that was such a wonderful talk, and I'd like to emphasize how much your work over the last 25 years has spoken to the importance for linguists of looking at the history of the times in which we live and over the past 100 or 150 years. It's so important to understand the political, the economic, and the social history of these times – because they have a deep impact on the way we do linguistics. Most linguists aren't teaching it, and they're not teaching it because they don't understand it – they don't know it, I imagine. But your work has always, over the last 25 years, underscored that.

And especially in the book that you mentioned, *Battle in the Mind Fields*, which I wrote along with Bernard Laks, we tried to emphasize the same way of looking at 19th century linguistics. I think it's helpful to understand that, from the European point of view, the 19th century was the century of history. And the reason it was a century of history (people at the time even called it that) was because of the rapid change in the economic and political nature of Europe. We could begin with the French Revolution, and then Napoleon (the Napoleonic era was obviously a development out of the revolution as well. Napoleon marched out on the rest of Europe in the first decade in the 19th century in an effort to break down feudalism, in an effort to break down the Holy Roman Empire. And the result of that was the effort on the part of many people in Europe to create new nations, and linguistics was a very important tool in the creation of a national consciousness so that languages, which today seem like standards, were anything but. They were vernaculars spoken by normal people, hardly thought of as anybody's standard – nobody in a serious professional situation could even think of Czech, for example, in a context like that, early in the century.

So, the concept of evolution, as you see in the work of a philosopher like Hegel, who was looking out at political revolutions around him, and he integrated the revolutions into his philosophy. Evolution was on everybody's mind, and in the third generation of linguists, which was the generation of neo-grammarians, in the 1870s, things were changing because of the rise of laboratory psychology, as in Leipzig, where Wundt had his laboratory. And for the first time, people started to think about language as reflecting a universal species-specific way of thinking. And so, this new way, this kind of structuralism – the term wasn't used at the time, but starting with the Neo-grammarians, and then Saussure, and into the 20th century, the rise of cognitive approaches to languages – this was in turn a response to what, today, we would call a evolutionary view of things.

But there were certainly anthropologists like Franz Boas and others in the 20th century who reacted against the evolutionist bias which declared there was a single ladder which all cultures and societies had to climb up, and the reaction was to say, no, that's not the way it is. More in line with, as you put it, Salikoko, at the beginning of your talk, we need to recognize and appreciate the variety across human cultures. So, I just want to thank you for emphasizing the importance for all linguists of thinking seriously about the historical context, both in which they work, and also in which the peoples and languages they're studying have evolved.

Salikoko Mufwene

Thank you very much, John. All I can say to complement your underscoring what I was doing is that it is thanks to Saussure that we could do language typology. Because, by focusing on structure, then people could really see how, synchronically, the structures could vary so much from one language to another. Thank you.

Sinfree Makoni

Okay. Let me jump in then. I have two questions, Sali, that I want to ask. The first one is a very general question that kept bugging me as I read your work and as I was writing some of the material that I'm currently working on, on language in the Global South. I kept coming back to your work on decolonial linguistics, and I want you to help me think this through. What is the nature of the relationship that we are positing, or that you think might emerge, between theories of language from the Global South and notions about decoloniality? Why I'm asking is that, at least in my writing, I tend to move between these two different frameworks, and I'm not yet sure what exactly are the connections between the two. So, I thought perhaps you might help me clarify these two sets of ideas.

Salikoko Mufwene

Have you finished?

Sinfree Makoni

Yes, I've finished, yes. I just want you to help me think these ideas through, whether in actual fact they are related, or are they completely different?

Salikoko Mufwene

I think they are related. I tend to talk about theory and the growing diversity of languages being investigated as an expansion of opportunities to create a dialogue between hypotheses and facts. And so, since the 1950s with Noam Chomsky, we have become very much interested in universals of language. But Noam Chomsky developed his hypothesis on universals not so much on the model of Joseph Greenberg, but mostly in terms of language and the mind, how the mind works, and largely on his knowledge of English. And a lot of people were fascinated by Chomsky's ideas and went on to investigate a number of languages. And when you follow the track, you will find out that this is where you'll find a lot of colonial linguistics, because a lot of people out there were just trying to see to what extent their language did some of the things that Chomsky had pointed out about English.

If you take *Syntactic Structures* in 1957 and then *Aspects of the Theory of Syntax*, I think, in 1965, and then you come to the principles-and-parameters approach, this is in the early 1990s – how long did it take people doing linguistic theory to become sensitive to the idea of typological variation? And Greenberg had already talked about this in the early 1960s. And so, I think the message that I want to convey is that people have to put their feet on the ground and say, 'Wait a minute, this is not the way it's working in my language.' There are probably universals, but we would like to have a clear idea of how to talk about universals, and this is what we should be doing from the Global South.

One thing that has struck me particularly is how the Japanese talk about the reflexive pronoun (*zibun*) in Japanese. The item that they identify as a reflexive pronoun is nothing like a reflexive pronoun in Bantu languages; it's not a reflexive affix. It is not like a reflexive pronoun in French, because you can find the Japanese so-called 'reflexive pronoun' in the subject position, and that's not the place for the reflexive pronoun in languages that have a reflexive pronoun. And what people identify as a reflexive pronoun in Japanese actually means referring to the nearest antecedent, and the nearest antecedent may be in the preceding sentence in a discourse. This is a discourse phenomenon. It is not subject to the same constraints as the so-called 'reflexive pronoun' in English, for example.

John Baugh

Salikoko, I'm going to jump in, and I apologize for doing so, but I'm mindful of the time. And my question is related. First, I apologize because I am not as well-versed in many of these issues as you are, and your work and Michel [DeGraff]'s work has been strongly influential in my own thinking. And so, I have a very naïve question as someone who is not a Creole scholar. But, it seems to me that Derek Bickerton tried, in his formulation of the bioprogram, to wrestle theoretical linguistics into a place where the serious consideration of Creole languages was also taken seriously. I think you do a much better job than he did in some ways, but I don't know if the bioprogram has been debunked or refuted. Is Bickerton's work, in any way, connected to the same mission that you're pursuing?

Salikoko Mufwene

Yes. Bickerton actually got me thinking, because when I started my research on creoles, Bickerton is the person that I found the most convincing. But, Bickerton made no allowance for substrate influence. In more or less the same way Robert

Chaudenson in France insisted very much on the legacy of the lexifier but made no allowance for substrate influence either. I convinced Robert Chaudenson to think otherwise, and he did. But, Bickerton and I, we kept locking horns to no clear end, except that in his last book before he died, he gives me some credit for something. I think that Bickerton deserves the credit of getting us to think harder. But, he made the mistake of saying that it's only children that have access to the bioprogram. And the bioprogram plays no more role when you become an adult. It's like saying, 'Oh, my computer is working, let me go and take away the underlying language.' If you do that, you know what will happen to your computer. You won't have a computer.

So, I kept saying if there is a bioprogram, it must stay alive throughout a speaker's life. Otherwise, that person won't be able to speak or sign. And the other thing is that he was very Chomskyan, and very much frustrated that Chomsky didn't recognize him. He claimed that we find in creole grammars the pristine grammar, but that is not true. A lot of features that Bickerton would associate with the bioprogram, you find them more systemically used in languages such as Chinese, and they are not so systematically used in creoles. And creoles just reflect that hybridization of features coming from different languages. People have criticized me of not underscoring the role of Africans enough in the inventions of creoles. Au contraire, what I have said is that creoles wouldn't have become different from their kin non-creole varieties developed by Whites in the colonies if it hadn't been for the influence of African languages.

Even the principle of selection, as I have hypothesized in my feature pool model, factors African languages in, because they determine which features you are going to favor in the lexifier if you don't introduce any more features. My objection to the extreme substratist view regards the suggestion that Africans must be incapable of learning anything European. And that's why we find all this. That is as terrible as what Bickerton was suggesting in arguing that children shaped the new vernaculars where their parents failed to do so. And I had a bad exchange with him when I reviewed his book. What was the title of the book again? *Language and Species* (1990). But I said Bickerton talks about Africans as adults living bestially on the plantations without any linguistic communication and waiting to have children, and the children made the language for them.

John Baugh

Ouch, bro. Wow.

Salikoko Mufwene

Yes, and then he got very upset about it too. So, these are the kinds of things that we have been trying to wrestle with him. So, as far as I am concerned, Bickerton's language bioprogram hypothesis is dead. But, you have to go and talk to somebody else that doesn't believe me.

John Baugh

Okay, thank you Sali. Nice job. Great talk.

Salikoko Mufwene

Thank you.

> **Comments from the chat box**
>
> **Oyeronke Oyewumi:** Prof, isn't vernacular a derogatory word?
>
> **Sangeeta Bagga-Gupta:** Thank you for your provocative and interesting talk! I have two questions: **Question 1:** While your point about the bandwagon of 'Decolonial lingustics' can hold, there is important work that is being done to raise awareness about specific erasures and hegemonies, I'd like you to comment on the difference between Decolonial and Colonial linguistics; **Question 2:** In your 2021 commentary text you raise important issues regarding a difference between what you call true western biases and mistakes. Can you give a couple of examples of these?

Magdalena Madany-Saá

Thank you. Dr Makoni, if you agree, we have Oyeronke that put a message and also has the hand up, and also we have a question from Sangeeta. So, after that, we could finish the formal session with your last comment, Dr Makoni.

Oyeronke Oyewumi

Good morning, everyone! And thank you, Professor Mufwene, for that wonderful lecture, very informative for me. I'm not a linguist, and so, my question will not have all the razzmatazz, but I'm just happy to have such a renowned linguist in front of me. My first question, I have put it there. I said, 'Professor, isn't vernacular a derogatory word?' I would like you to answer that.

Salikoko Mufwene

No. Well, I'm glad you asked that question because, yeah, vernacular has been used in cultural studies in a slightly different way. Vernacular in linguistics means the language that you use for day-to-day communication, especially in the family environment, and with your close friends, and so forth; this is a vernacular. You can compare it to the attire that you put on at home in order to feel comfortable instead of the suit or the highly-styled dress that you put on when you are in the street.

Oyeronke Oyewumi

Okay. But I never hear people talk about European vernaculars today.

Salikoko Mufwene

Well, I did in a different way by referring to non-standard varieties in order to explain why creoles are the way they are. Creoles did not evolve from the standard varieties that people insist on comparing them with. In my work, I prefer to call the latter 'scholastic varieties.' A lot of us non-native speakers will learn European languages in school, not at home. We learn scholastic varieties, and when we communicate well in them, then Heritage speakers deride us and say, 'You speak bookish English or bookish French,' or something like that, or your French is too flowery, of course, because we learn it from *les belles lettres* or literature. We thought that people speak like that, but they don't speak like that. But yes. When I write, I also mention European vernaculars.

Oyeronke Oyewumi

Okay, let me ask my main question. I appreciate your reminding us again that language is a technology for storing information. I am a gender scholar, and I have been interested in the whole question of gender and language. And so, when you talk about language as a technology and that different languages approach that in different ways, I wonder whether, at this point – and I don't know whether in linguistics people have debated this – I wonder whether scholars have revisited what I used to know as the Sapir-Whorf hypothesis, to enlighten us as to why some languages focus on certain things and not others. I wondered whether, in your work, you have addressed such a question. Then, my other question, which is a very short one, and that of a very layperson: I get the impression that, generally speaking, the place we've designated as Europe, had fewer languages. Maybe at a particular point in time, let me say the 16th century, Africa and Asia seemed to have so many more languages. Could you speak to that, please, as a linguist? Thank you.

Salikoko Mufwene

Okay, I'll start with the last one. I'm writing a book now on the subject matter. It is so subversive that I'll be lucky if it is published in time. But Europe has so few languages because of its history of colonization. We don't really think of Europe as a territory where there was colonization. In my approach to language evolution, I say this. Since the exodus out of Africa, the history of mankind has been one of layers of colonization. And you have to interpret colonization here in two ways: one is just 'to settle another territory', and the other one is the one that we are more familiar with: you settle in another territory, and you subjugate the population that preceded you in that particular territory. The first definition is less controversial, but that's the one that you find in population genetics, for instance.

But the second one that we are more familiar with: we don't think of the Roman Empire as a form of colonization, but it *was* a form of colonization. We don't think of the Hellenic Empire as a form of colonization, but it *was* a form of colonization. We don't think of the Germanic populations invading England as a form of colonization, but it *was* a form of colonization. So, there's been a lot of internal colonization. Actually, when you approach things like this, you even develop a better understanding of the diversification of the Indo-European language family because it's a consequence of those migrations, population movements, and layers of colonization.

So, nobody tells us about how many Celtic languages died because of the emergence of the Romance languages, because the Celts were shifting to Latin. And after that, how many neo-Latin varieties actually emerged? And then they competed with each other until the French of Île-de-France, the Parisian French prevailed as the language of France. And in Spain, it's more or less the same thing. And by the time the colonization of the New World starts, actually, Spain didn't exist yet. Spain arises as a country around the same time as New Spain emerges. That is the colonies in the New World that people retrospectively have called *New Spain*. It was Castile, Galicia, Catalonia, and the like that merged into Spain. These are the political spaces that existed.

But, you see, to put things in perspective, these have been in competition with each other and so forth. And Catalonia doesn't want to be superseded by Castile. So, you put things in this perspective, you realize there's always been colonization, and that colonization has been at a cost, at the expense of something, and one of those is the loss of the Celtic languages and the endangerment of languages like Sami in Norway. And you wonder how Basque has survived for so long. So, that gives us an idea of what happened in Europe, and it happened earlier than the kinds of changes that would take place in the New World, where Native American languages have been disappearing because they are being replaced by English, French, Spanish or Portuguese.

It doesn't really make much sense when you put things this way. You have to discuss them in terms of economic development, in terms of political pressures, and in terms of population structure, whether the population is segregated or not segregated, whether the dominant population is culturally assimilationist or not assimilationist. And that's why you can understand why there are so few languages in Europe because Europeans in Europe have been traditionally assimilationist when they spread to relocate in new territories. And they did the same thing – they have done the same thing (I should put it in the present perfect) – they have done the same thing in the New World and Australia, which has resulted in the endangerment or loss of the indigenous languages.

And, by the way, it's not just Native American languages that have been displaced. It's also other European languages that were not dominant. So, German is no longer alive, Italian is no longer alive in North America. Dutch is no longer alive in North America and so forth. And Europeans actually started losing their languages before Native Americans started losing their languages. It tells you a whole lot about segregation and discrimination in the New World and the marginalization of indigenous populations. I'm not counting here cases where Native American languages died because of ills introduced to the population from the Old World or because of genocides committed, for instance, by the Spaniards in Central America and in the Caribbean. So, you get an idea of why there is little linguistic diversity in Europe.

I use a less developed, unsophisticated typology of colonization to make a distinction between trade colonization and settlement colonization such as in the Americas and Australia, and the exploitation colonization of Africa, and Asia, and the Pacific since the 19th century. And exploitation colonization was grounded in segregation between the indigenous people and the colonizers. And it was non-assimilationist because the main purpose of the exploitation colonization, according to me, was to fuel the Industrial Revolution in Europe. And Europeans were better off with Africans not becoming fluent in European languages and not understanding a whole lot of what was going on. So, that more or less answers your question.

But, about the Sapir-Whorf hypothesis: yes, the idea of languages as technologies is quite consistent with the Sapir-Whorf hypothesis, because the representation systems that different people develop needn't be the same. First of all, the natural ecologies in which they live are not necessarily the same. The adaptive responses to these natural ecologies need not be identical. I can make things a little bit more complex. If you take two or three individuals and you put them in the face of the same challenge, they are not going to react necessarily in identical ways. And there is variation.

And what happens in a population is that we keep comparing ourselves with others. And we can give up our own solution and adopt the solution of somebody else because it works better. Or they can do the same. Eventually, we converge to where we're doing things in similar ways – never in identical ways. And so, when we describe world views and so forth, the way that Edward Sapir and Benjamin Lee Whorf did, when we speak of those world views, we are over-generalizing and overlooking variation within. Otherwise, yes, I think that this perspective can give us stronger motivation for pursuing the Sapir-Whorf hypothesis. However, the fundamental problem that remains is whether the Sapir-Whorf hypothesis is deterministic or non-deterministic. So, deterministic means you have mindsets that have been fixed, and from which it could be difficult to emancipate.

And then the non-deterministic position tells you we don't really know what the nature of the language of thought is; we don't really know how conceptualization works, and so forth. However, when we communicate, there are some convenient ways in which we package information. And we have to package information in ways that make it easier for each one of us engaged in communication to interpret each other very fast and effectively. And I have been in favor of the non-deterministic approach to the Sapir-Whorf hypothesis. But there are people that suggest otherwise, and we may agree to differ, or we may continue to fight and try to convince each other.

Comments from the chat box

Oyeronke Oyewumi: Thank you Prof Mufwene!

Yamina EL KIRAT EL ALLAME: Thank you for a very insightful talk. May I ask you to get a copy of Prof. Mufwene's book and other publications of his? I am looking at the presence of foreign languages in Morocco, and the spread of English now as a form of linguistic imperialism. I would love to get some references in relation to the fact that Morocco is still linguistically colonized.

Magdalena Madany-Saá

Thank you for this answer. We are already actually in our afterparty time, but we had Sangeeta waiting for a long time to ask her question, so please Sangeeta, go on. And Lynn Mario, in the after-party, please feel free to ask your question or make your comments.

Sangeeta Bagga-Gupta

Given the time, I would love to comment on some of the things you have said, but I'll stick to the two questions I put up in the chat. So, I'm a bit concerned about the way in which everyone is in this decolonial linguistics bandwagon, and you started your talk with that. My question is related to – 'How do you differentiate between decolonial linguistics and colonial linguistics?' So, that's question one. And perhaps, related to that, in your 2021 commentary, you raise interesting issues regarding the difference between what you call Western biases and what you call mistakes. And you're commenting on a particular number of chapters in this book. Can you give a couple of examples of what you mean by Western biases and what you mean by mistakes?

Salikoko Mufwene

The Western bias, it has to do with, for instance, imposing categories of one language onto another language before you really have examined the data. It's the data that should be suggesting what categories are going to work, and not your knowledge of another language that should determine what categories you have to work with. That's the Western bias. So, I gave an example with the noun-class system in Bantu, how it is different from the article and gender system in European languages. They don't do the same jobs. And this is related to the question about the Sapir-Whorf hypothesis. There are certain things that are more important to some people than to other people. And so what is considered less important is not really packaged in the information that you convey to the other. Or if it becomes important, you have to use a different kind of strategy. I don't know if this answers your question.

The difference between decolonial linguistics and colonial linguistics is, you have to interpret decolonial linguistics more or less the way like Jacques Derrida speaks of deconstruction. It's not necessarily to reject things; it's to see how the paradigm that has been offered works and to see what can be changed in it, or what *must* be changed in it, in order for it to help you analyze other languages adequately. And the converse of that is how can you enable the new language that you are investigating to talk back to your theory and suggest how the theory can be adjusted, can be modified so that it will do a better job. That's really a short way of answering your question.

And so, as I said at the beginning of my presentation, coming up with a subject matter that has not been dealt with before is not necessarily doing decolonial linguistics. If you find something interesting in a language, and you notice the theories or hypotheses that you know have not dealt with that particular subject matter, and you start dealing with it, that is just a contribution to the research paradigm. It is not necessarily decolonial linguistics. Or if somebody made a mistake, even according to the paradigm that they have used and you are not necessarily changing the paradigm, you are just making a correction to somebody's research.

So, I gave the example of the count/mass distinction in Gullah; it's because I noticed, for instance, people can say, 'I go to boy store,' and this was on an occasion where people were mocking somebody because he had no children and there was nobody to celebrate him on Father's Day. And so, his friends were teasing him. And his friends told him, 'You should go to boy store and find a child there'. So, 'boy' is used here as a mass noun, and according to the grammar that I had learned, you cannot use 'boy' as mass. Then I checked – and then you hear somebody say in English, you arrive at an intersection, and there was a car accident. And you say, 'Boy, there was car all over.' Does it make sense to you? It's very English. There was car all over, and you are using car as if it were a mass noun. I call this mechanism 'non-individuation.' And that's how I started checking whether there were things that were not really adequately explained in English itself, before I could make sense of what was going on in Gullah.

So, there's a story, for instance, in one of Gullah Animal Tales, Brother Patridge is asking Brother Wolf, 'How you gwine ['going'] kill me? With knayf?' That's the pronunciation of 'knife,' like in Australian English. So, when you take 'with knayf,' in English you would ask 'with a knife,' right? But it turns out that, in the grammar of Gullah, there's a difference between 'knayf' used without an article and 'a knayf.' You say 'kayf' (without the indefinite article) when you don't really know what particular knife is going to be used. You say 'a knayf' when there is a knife somewhere that is available and it is specific for you, or the addressee in this case.

And so, the question, you get that kind of difference in Jamaican Creole between *Im a teacha*, *Im a wan teacha*, and *Im a di teacha*. You translate the first two the same way in English: 'He's a teacher' or 'She's a teacher', whereas the latter is just like in English: 'He/She is the teacher'. But there's a difference; one of them describes the profession, and the other one identifies the individual that assumes this profession in a specific group that the speaker knows. So, in the end you realize that creole grammars – too bad John Baugh is already gone; he asked me the question about Bickerton. You find out that creole grammars are not as simple as you would think they are. They just have been restructured in ways that display different patterns and different systems. I call the change 'typological realignment.' Not all the rules are different, but you get these other nuances in creoles that you wouldn't have thought of just by studying them from the point of view of the lexifier, English in the present case.

Sangeeta Bagga-Gupta

Thank you. I think I was coming from somewhere else. So, from a performative angle, and I think the previous question or set of questions on gender studies, for instance, also are hinting this, that there is a time-space difference. So, I wonder whether we would agree that it is not the languages of the Global South but languages everywhere that can be approached through what is being called decolonial linguistics. And I'm reminded of my colleague, Catherine Hoppers, who was decorated in my previous university in Sweden.

About 15 years ago, she was invited as a keynote for the Swedish Research Council's annual dialogue meeting in Umeå. And she made a very provocative statement which a number of my colleagues and I particularly were very, very shaken up by. She was not talking of linguistics or language, but the positionality of bodies across spaces. And she had argued that dogs from outside Europe are now situated and barking in Europe. And it was only in the dinner at this particular event that we could talk about what Catherine was saying. And Sweden is a very specific geopolitical space since we had not been allowed to talk about racism here, in an attempt to not recreate racism.

So, what Catherine pointed out, then, is very close to the title of your talk, which is why I raised this issue of how do *you* differentiate between decoloniality and coloniality in linguistics? And I think, for me, linguistics is much more than just the grammars and different languages and the places in which languages have existed. And digitization, for instance, opens up to questioning of place.

Salikoko Mufwene

Yeah, you are very right. Linguistics is about more than the grammars of languages, and even so, I think it depends also on how you define grammar, whether you just say it's syntax, morphology, and semantics, and so forth, and don't include pragmatics, or whether you include pragmatics. But I have another retired colleague who has said he doesn't like the term *sociolinguistics*, and the reason is that there is no linguistics without sociolinguistics. And his point to me was, language must be grounded in its population, in its history. So, there is a whole lot that comes with that.

I think that if you come from a former colony, it's cute to use the term 'decolonial linguistics', or if you empathize with people that have been colonized, it's also cute to use the term 'decolonial linguistics'. And I think this goes along with Sinfree's term, the Global South, and the title here, *Applied Linguistics from the Global South*, in the sense that people from the Global South must stand up and voice their views. That's really what it means. It's that political dimension that we have to bring into it. If we had all been equal, we wouldn't need the term 'decolonial linguistics'. We would just need Derrida's notion of deconstruction. And that would just do the job. That's my point over here.

And finally, to conclude, decolonial linguistics speaks not just to Westerners, but to everybody. We have to step back and question ourselves and see whether we are doing the right thing. So, Sangeeta, you are correct. Maybe we don't need the term 'decolonial linguistics', but sometimes it helps to have this political perspective, that a person from the Global South coming to study in the Global North is more likely to be influenced by views of the Global North than the other way around, where a person from the Global North relocates in the Global South – especially during the colonial period. There are a whole lot of things that developed this way because colonization was very influential. And the message simply is that we have to emancipate ourselves from mental slavery, as Bob Marley said. I have a sign in my office, and the words from Bob Marley is, 'Emancipate yourself from mental slavery'. It speaks to what you are saying.

> **Comments from the chat box**
>
> **Oyeronke Oyewumi:** The question of power is always a part of this especially when our systems of knowledge are continually subjected to subjugation and epistemicides in the academy!

Sinfree Makoni

Thanks a lot, Sali. My view about this, I think, is fairly simple. My view is that what we are engaged in at the moment in decolonial linguistics is an exercise in epistemological and ontological framing of what we think we are trying to do. So, for example, one way of thinking about decolonial linguistics might simply be to say to yourself, okay, 'How do I carry out linguistics, for example, if I seriously consider issues about land as interlocutors – if I ask completely different questions?' So, what decolonial linguistics provides you with is at least some freedom to ask questions which are not obvious to linguists who are not operating in a decolonial framing. In decolonial linguistics, I may seriously consider land as an interlocuter.

So, I then ask myself, 'How do my practices as a linguist shift if land is seen as an interlocutor?' Then the other thing that comes from all this is decolonial linguistics provides you, also, with an opportunity to reimagine other more critical ways of being and talking about language. So, for example, the argument that Sali was making was that some of the categories that we use in linguistics, for example, force us to see language in a very specific way, thus rendering us blind to other workings of language. So, what a decolonial linguistics does is to force us to get back to the metalanguage and say that the metalanguage itself should be a way, and an important project that we should be engaged in.

Then the last thing that I would like to say is that what a decolonial linguistics should seek to try to do, among other things, is to redefine language using indigenous epistemologies. But, having said that, I'm not claiming that there are untainted, untouched indigenous epistemologies out there which can try and help us rescue, like Jean Comaroff would put it, an overheated metropole. But you are simply creating some space for other epistemologies, by being cautious enough to realize that, yes, these epistemologies do not provide you with a solution, but simply an indicator of where you might go. Thanks. Thanks a lot.

Acknowledgment

We would like to thank Chanel Van Der Merwe for assisting with the revision of this chapter's transcript.

3 Giving Jack His Jacket: Linguistic Contact in the Danish West Indies

Robin Sabino

Chanel Van der Merwe

Today, I have the honor of introducing Dr Robin Sabino. Dr Robin Sabino is a Professor Emerita in the English Department at Auburn University. Her research interests include linguistic contact, variation and change and the working of language in the human brain. Previous published work includes a chapter in *Integrational Linguistics and Philosophy of Language in the Global South* (2021), *Languaging without Languages: Beyond Metro-, Multi-, Poly-, Pluri-, and Translanguaging* (2018) and *Language Contact in the Danish West Indies: Giving Jack His Jacket*, also (2012). A forthcoming book chapter on the US Virgin Islands will appear in the handbook of *Caribbean Language and Linguistics*, and some of Dr Sabino's honors include Auburn Alumni Association 2014 Minority Achievement Award, and also the Auburn University Research Award in the Study of Diversity. Today, Dr Sabino will speak on *Giving Jack His Jacket: Linguistic Contact in the Danish West Indies*. Dr Sabino, the floor is yours.

Robin Sabino

Thank you. Welcome, everyone. To give Jack his jacket is a double entendre. Broadly, it means to give credit where credit is due. More narrowly, it refers to paternity. In the Danish West Indies as elsewhere in the Caribbean, Africans and Europeans experienced the displacement and challenges of plantation economies in profoundly different ways. The monograph (Sabino, 2018) I'm discussing today provides a linguistic history of the colony focusing primarily on the agency and rich cultural resources of the West African persons forced to make the small, arid island of St. Thomas their home. In doing so, my argument lays bare a crucial link between identity formation and linguistic choice.

Spanish, British, French, Dutch, Latvians, Danes and Swedes established Caribbean colonies. Europe's re-peopling of this part of the world produced the largest coerced population movement in human history. Communities of indigenous peoples were decimated, the lives of tens of thousands of Europeans, and twelve and a half million Africans were permanently altered as were untold, others were left behind. The monograph has its deepest roots in my 1990 dissertation, which grappled with the phonological variation in field recordings of conversation with the last speaker, and a collection of texts published in the 1920s (Jong, de Josselin, 1926). Like the dissertation, the monograph assumes documentation of Virgin Islands Dutch Creole was composed of three varieties: Negerhollands, developed by Africans and their descendants, Hoch Kreol developed by the Euro-Caribbean settler population, and the Liturgical Lect created by missionaries. I still understand the colonies' linguistic development in terms of inter and intra speaker variation that initially developed as Africans' incorporated heritage linguistic resources and input from their oppressors into a means of communication and self-identification. I also continue to hold that linguistic differences in data from the 18th, 19th and 20th centuries reflect the settings under which they were produced. Crucially, however, I no longer believe in creole languages as autonomous bounded systems, because I see the individual as the only locus of human linguistic activity. Thus, I'm not going to talk about creole varieties. Instead, I will discuss how Africans, Europeans and their descendants entrenched, conventionalized and vernacularized linguistic resources.

Let me briefly explain these terms as I understand them. Memories are entrenched as an individual encounters linguistic material under conditions that allow it to become part of his or her repertoire. Following Bybee (2010), I understand linguistic memories to be stored as a neural network of auditory patterns, kinesic activities, grammatical patterning, previously negotiated linguistic and sociocultural meanings, details of the context in which use occurs, and inferences derived from communication in those contexts. With each encounter, the network is updated, producing and modifying probabilistic responses to future discourses.

Conventionalization, although it has the appearance of group activity, also occurs as a result of individual activity as probable alternatives circulate within a sociocultural group. Overlapping associations develop in the brains of multiple individuals. Importantly, similar expectations for the deployment of available linguistic resources also develop because deploying one's linguistic resources is agentful and fundamentally transactional. Crucially, despite overlapping expectations, linguistic choice is characterized by moment-to-moment unpredictability. Nevertheless, individuals often choose high-frequency patterns. Crucial to what happened in the Danish colony, conventionalization can occur as entrenchment progresses; form/meaning potentials not only conventionalize, they reconventionalize over time producing linguistic change. Because identities are situated and interactively constructed, as we enact our sociocultural affiliations and stances, we create categories that make identity performance and perception possible. Indexes link variant choice to identity positions. In parallel to conventionalization, vernacularization, which is also individual, occurs when multiple individuals entrench similar indexes. And like conventionalization, vernacularization plays a role in what has been studied as language learning and linguistic change.

History records something of the lives of colonists, soldiers, government and church officials, but next to nothing about subaltern populations, whether indigenous, indentured or enslaved. As a result, although we know that contact transformed cultural systems exactly how and under what conditions today's vibrant Caribbean linguistic resources developed remains a subject of debate. Evidence of early linguistic practice in the Danish colony was produced by German and Danish missionaries, a local grammarian, a Danish physician, and when only a few users remained, by linguists. Believing that Africans were intellectually incapable of grasping the structures of European languages, instead of celebrating African linguistic accomplishments under debilitating conditions, Europeans believed Africans were bastardizing European tongues. Racist assumptions and an understanding of linguistic change as decay motivated the view that Caribbean creoles were corrupt reductions of European targets, a view I rejected.

Bickerton provides a witty example of concerns about the integrity of the data collected from the last speakers in the former Danish colony. He writes, '… although languages, like people, die, they do not like some people drop dead. On the contrary, like Charles II, they are an unconscionable time a-dying. And since we know that in language death, languages become severely distorted, but do not know at what time the process started, there is no way in which we can be certain what any text represents, whether the full flush of the language, the earliest concept of decrepitude, or the final phases of decay, in which key terms are lost or worse, replaced by forms from competing languages and dialects.' (Bickerton, 1975). Taking what den Besten and van der Voort characterized as a 'rather radical' (den Besten & van der Voort, 1999) approach, I assumed there was considerable undocumented linguistic activity from the beginning of colonization. *Giving Jack His Jacket* explores who would have spoken to whom under what conditions. I conclude that the emergence of Afro-Caribbean linguistic resources in the Danish colony reflects subaltern negotiation of a virulent, exploitive environment.

In seeking to demonstrate the legitimacy of this perspective, the first chapter explores Western hegemonic ideologies that legitimated centuries of exploitation and limited inquiry into the origin and nature of Afro-Caribbean communities by underestimating non-European agency. By the end of the 17th century, when Danish settlement began, Europeans viewed Africans as physically deformed, naturally uncivilized, lazy, linguistically limited, sexually promiscuous, idolatrous, cannibalistic, duplicitous, fiendish and as having developed only rudimentary political organizations. Despite geographic proximity and material interdependence, cultural asymmetries emerged at the beginning of colonization.

The second chapter draws on psychological and sociolinguistic research focusing on identity and the conventionalization of linguistic resources in asymmetric social situations. I also explore archaeological and ethnographic studies and historical sources in order to characterize African and Afro-Caribbean responses to what Hall (1992) calls 'hubristic eurocentrism'. Following Christie (1983), I argue that in St. Thomas clashing African and European ideologies resulting in psychosocial distress, distance and the emergence and maintenance of oppositional communities. Those who survived capture and transport faced permanent residence in the colony. Brutally separated from family and community, as they reconstituted their social selves, transshipped Africans developed Caribbean linguistic resources. Olwig (1985) points to developing network ties by the early 18th century. In contrast, Europeans initially saw residence in the colony as temporary, desiring to return to their homelands as soon as possible. As a result, linguistic indexing of local identity was delayed for this group.

Chapter 3 discusses the colony's history and demographics. Denmark began transshipping Africans in the 1650s. The first colonists, free or indentured Europeans, arrived on St. Thomas in 1672. Of the 190 persons landed, fewer than 30 were alive after seven months. Death rates remained high, with replacements rather than births contributing to the colony's population for the next 15 years. The first slave ship arrived one year later in 1673, adding to a very small population of enslaved persons brought from other Caribbean islands. This year also saw the arrival of Dutch planters. In 1680, there were 156 free persons primarily Dutch, Danish and English, and 175 enslaved persons, including one indigenous individual, living on St. Thomas in three resident types: European only, African only and mixed. I contend that African entrenchment occurred both in African only and mixed households, but that the latter is particularly relevant to the colony's linguistic history.

By 1690, survival rates were increasing, first in the Euro-Caribbean, and later in the Afro-Caribbean population. Beginning in 1700, enhanced economic opportunity and substantial improvements in infrastructure made permanent residence attractive to the colony's elite. Increasing wealth produced large domestic staffs of enslaved persons. Personal attendants became common in these households. St. Thomas' agriculture peaked in 1725, thereafter trade dominated. In 1718, Denmark settled the island of St. John from St. Thomas. Plantation activity expanded to that island. In 1733, Denmark acquired St. Croix. The flat, fertile terrain of that island and the devastating St. John uprising in the same year, in which 150 Amina held the island for more than six months occasioned a second population shift. By the 1730s, a small, free urban Afro-Caribbean population exists in St. Thomas. A century and a quarter after the arrival of the first cohort of Africans, more than one-third of the free Charlotte Amalie population was of African descent. By the 1780s, St. Thomas' commerce is dominated by Americans. The colony is occupied by the British in 1802 until 1805 and again between 1807 and 1815. By this last date, the colony's free Afro-Caribbean population had surpassed the Euro-Caribbean population. Slavery is abolished in 1848. In 1917, the colony is purchased by the United States and becomes the US Virgin Islands.

These historical events have linguistic implications. The Danish West Indian company was formed in Amsterdam, and it is likely that Danish and Dutch linguistic resources remained in circulation. For example, early government documents are written in both Danish and Dutch. But if Dutch linguistic resources were not available initially, the arrival of Dutch settlers would have increased available Germanic variants. For Africans entrenching new linguistic resources, this environment would have been highly variable. Warfare on the African coast suggests that in early decades, the Danes transshipped primarily Akan, Ga and Ewe people. Enslaved persons would have expanded their linguistic repertoires to some extent during capture and on the transatlantic passage. Once landed in the colony, survivors would have entrenched necessary linguistic resources in use in the households to which they were attached. There also would have been entrenchment of African, non-maternal linguistic resources, but ultimately, the colonial environment impeded their transgenerational transmission. I estimate that within 25 years of the colony's founding, for locally born members of the Afro-Caribbean community, the functionality of locally conventionalized resources would have superseded the functionality of those developed in Africa.

In the colony's first decade, communication across plantations was limited by isolation and the rigors of survival. As survival rates increased in the late 1680s, Afro-Caribbean community formation began with networks extending across plantations. Crucially, the colony's exploitive social and material arrangements and asymmetric power relations provided minimal benefit from cultural assimilation to Africans and their descendants. This was one factor limiting entrenchment to much more than the lexical resources of those who exploited them. Thus, in spite of attempts to impose European definitions of culture on the colony's residents, members of the Afro-Caribbean community conventionalized and vernacularized shared heritage linguistic patterns. The creation of large domestic staffs in elite Euro-Caribbean households increased opportunities for the entrenchment of linguistic resources developed by the colonies two communities. Individuals with interests in both groups encountered a wider range of linguistic resources more frequently than did those whose interactions remained isolated within their respective groups. Within the Afro-Caribbean population, proverbs that warn against hanging your hat higher than your head imply some movement towards Euro-Caribbean norms. In parallel, Euro-Caribbean adolescents indexed local variants to island as opposed to European identity. Among these individuals was Magens. Born in 1715, he would later author a New Testament translation and an 18th-century prescriptive grammar of Euro-Caribbean linguistic resources.

Moravian missionaries arrived in 1732, 50 years after the colony's founding, again expanding the colony's linguistic resources. According to Sensbach (2005), initial Afro-Caribbean response to the cultural alternatives the Moravians offered ranged from bewilderment to resistance. Eventually, missionary persistence bore fruit, in part due to the advantages promised by Christianity, particularly literacy.

With the move to St. John and then to St. Croix, the linguistic resources conventionalized and vernacularized on St. Thomas expanded to those islands. By the middle of 18th century, European cultural influence was waning in the urban areas. (There are no urban areas in St. John.) The growing cultural influence of missionaries and the emergence of a free Afro-Caribbean community prompted the creation of identities that were intermediate between enslaved plantation workers and rich planters and merchants. To encode these identities, individuals drew on positively indexed features of Euro-Caribbean speech and the missionaries' evangelical texts. With the incursion of linguistic resources from the United States and the British colonies, those initially conventionalized by the Afro-Caribbean community became indexed to rurality and enslavement. By the 1870s, those linguistic resources are dominant only among the oldest generation on St. John. By the 1930s, their use is limited to older adults concealing information from children.

Hubristic eurocentrism not only undergirded the re-peopling of the Caribbean, it laid the foundation for Creole linguistics. For example, in 1933, the Dutch linguist Hesseling uses the terms '*Negerhollands* and *Bastaardhollands*' to describe Afro-Caribbean linguistic practice. Hesseling (1933 in Markey and Roberge 1979: 56, 57 and 58) regards the earlier texts as representative of 'a much purer creole' and describes the 20th-century data as revealing the 'gradual downfall of the language' pointing particularly to 'erosion,' 'confusion' and 'simplification.' Half a century later, den Besten *et al.* (1996) see the colony's language as only really flourishing during the period it was written by Europeans. Using Moravian mention of a creole on St. Thomas in 1736, scholarship initially drew on 18th- and 19th-century text created by missionaries and a member of a prominent Euro-Caribbean family. When the language use documented in the 20th century was compared to these texts, it was found wanting because of internal differences and because of perceived Anglophone lexical corruption. Having argued that resistance, not linguistic decay, motivated Afro-Caribbean communicative practice, I reconsidered the ways in which the scholarly literature had interpreted the available record, focusing on the cultural frames and linguistic knowledge of those who produced the documentation. The influence of language standardization, grammatical prescriptivism and racist assumptions about cultural context and linguistic capacity were consistent with my position.

Consideration of the nationalities, ethnicities, nativity and legal and social statuses of the colony's residents points to a heterogeneous linguistic environment. For example, in 1688, 44% of the Euro-Caribbean households for which nationality is identified, contained persons born in different countries. Moravian missionaries, whom Graves (1997: 50) describes as 'secondary speakers who tampered' with actual practice, were influenced by notions of grammatical correctness and concerns that the Afro-Caribbean linguistic resources were not suitable for worship. Nevertheless, when proselytizing in Dutch failed, they began to make use of local words and grammatical elements. The syntax of their text is unlike linguistic practice anywhere in the Caribbean. Magens' grammar prepared for Lutheran teachers and missionary ministers, was published in 1770. He announces at the beginning of his grammar that his focus is on the linguistic choices of the Euro-Caribbean community, since he too found those conventionalized by Africans and their progeny to be deficient. As Sprauve (1997: 44) puts it, his aim was to 'alert those who would learn the language to African linguistic features and to denounce them.' Denmark established trading relations with the American colonies very early in 1715. By the 19th century, the linguistic impact of American financial interests and discussions of abolition circulating on nearby British islands were such that the colonial government argued for English instruction in public schools. Pontopiddan, a Danish physician serving in the colony from 1876 to 1881 documents the oldest St. John residents using linguistic resources developed by the Afro-Caribbean community. In the 20th century linguistic documentation appears.

The lack of 17th-century data necessitates examination of situational variables to determine how transshipped Africans would have coped with linguistic contact prior to population stabilization and the emergence of community. Several factors favor the persistence of heritage linguistic features: age of arrival, sex, trauma and anxiety, and intentionality and investment. Conversely, a positive attitude towards expanding one's linguistic resources and the previous entrenchment of non-material linguistic resources favors the entrenchment of new linguistic patterns.

Like other cognitively driven functions, the ability to entrench linguistic resources diminishes across the lifespan. Lexical learning remains intact, but the processing of inflectional morphology, number, gender, case agreement, word order and lexical exceptions is diminished for older learners. Age is also a particularly good predictor of phonological attainment with youngest learners most likely to achieve target-like pronunciation. Although the Danes did transship children, in 1680, 80% of the colony's enslaved population were adults. The preponderance of adult learners in the colony does not predict early entrenchment of European input. It is, however, consistent with the persistence of heritage linguistic features. There is not a lot of research on sex and language learning, but there is some evidence that estrogen enhances learning requiring verbal and declarative memory. Given the demands of infrastructure building, it is not surprising that in 1680, the ratio of enslaved adults, females to males, is 0.66 to 1. In mixed households, where I think the resources emerged, it is even lower: 0.38 to 1. The persistence of unnatural sex ratios into the 1740s, well after population stabilization, also predicts the retention of heritage linguistic resources.

The earliest stages of entrenchment require substantial cognitive processing and working memory. Because competition for cognitive resources inhibits one's ability to direct in attention to input, trauma and anxiety negatively impact learning. Historical evidence indicates that many who arrived in the colony had suffered physical and mental trauma during capture and transshipment. Once bound to Euro-Caribbean households overwork, periodic starvation, inadequate housing, disease, generalized stress and psychological, sexual and physical brutality negatively impacted longevity and the accrual of linguistic resources at the level of the individual, and thus, at the level of the group. Although attentional demands decrease as learning progresses, focus on form is needed to achieve target-like performance. For this reason, an early 18th-century report that the colony's enslaved, trembled and shook when asked to do something similarly predicts early learning challenges. Learners' intentions, and the effort they invest in expanding their linguistic resources, correlate with attainment and demarcate linguistic targets. Evidence suggests that an integrative orientation, coupled with the perception of permeable social boundaries enhances investment, increasing the range of strategies used to expand linguistic resources. The Danish colony's social hierarchy, based as it was on the legal status and ethnicity, was largely impermeable.

Investment is particularly relevant when input is limited, as it would be when interaction with members of another group is avoided. The psychosocial distance engendered by brutality and cultural clash would have motivated the development of strong in-group network ties and the avoidance of outgroup members. Considering intentionality and investment also points to the maintenance of African linguistic features. In contrast to the factors just described, an aptitude for the accrual of linguistic resources and non-maternal linguistic experiences are associated with learning success. Aptitude is particularly relevant to phonological learning. Owomoyela (1985) suggests that oral societies encourage attention to the nuances of communicative events, and the development of 'strategies for learning, preservation, and appropriate use'. This would seem to provide a learning advantage comparable to what has been studied as aptitude. Consistent with this, Goodman (1964) references a 1659 document describing Africans as attentive observers. In the Danish colony, Oldendorp

(1987) describes Africans' general aptness for learning languages. There is also evidence that the prior entrenchment of heterogeneous linguistic resources enhances subsequent learning. LaCharité (2007) points to the Ga and the Akan, two groups subject to Danish slaving operations as particularly valuing the ability to deploy multiple discursive practices, observing that historically and contemporaneously there is evidence that these groups positively view non-maternal linguistic resources.

On its own, a culturally valued propensity to expand one's linguistic resources raises the possibility of substantial early learning in the Danish colony. In contrast, the effective age of arrival of, sex, trauma and anxiety, and, intentionality and investment, make it likely that during the decade and a half it took to achieve Afro-Caribbean population stability, survivors negotiated common solutions to communicative challenges, achieving only the initial effortful stages of entrenchment with respect to the European input they encountered.

Because learners negotiate communication in specific contexts, social relations crucially determine the nature and frequency of interaction. Focusing on the early settlement period when entrenchment is most effortful, I next considered what research predicts about input processing, negotiation, and output in light the colony's sociohistorical context. Initially, African shared little to no linguistic resources with the colony's European population. Survival necessitated some degree of entrenchment in cross-group communication. However, typological differences, the heterogeneous input produced by Europeans primarily from Denmark, the Netherlands and the British Isles, psychosocial distance and minimal opportunities for negotiation would have likely limited entrenchment to lexical items. In contrast among Africans, shared cultural and linguistic knowledge as well as similar typological features and aerial patterns, common goals and, following Peirce (1995), the ability to impose reception provided for the negotiation of comprehensible input and output. It is reasonable to assume that in the culturally heterogeneous colony, individuals encountered input that differed both qualitatively and quantitatively and that they differentially attended to and process the input they encountered.

Initially, there would have been instability and idiosyncrasy, as individuals isolated in European households struggled on their own. Later arrivals who were domiciled with surviving members of the early cohorts would have had the benefit of a linguistic buffer between themselves and those who exploited them. The first generation of locally born children encountered the linguistic resources circulating in the emerging Afro-Caribbean community, widely shared and highly regarded features, whether retained, adapted or adopted would have had the greatest probability of continued use. Those features from whatever source that resonated with the greatest number of survivors became part of the Afro-Caribbean community's linguistic repertoire. As conventionalization progressed, features were indexed to sociocultural identities. Positively indexed elements had an enhanced likelihood of persistence across the generations, despite external cultural pressures from the Euro-Caribbean and, later, the American communities. Over time, conditions ameliorated and the financially independent segment of the Afro-Caribbean community increased in size and in wealth. Linguistic practice in the colony reflected these changes, but evidence of its African linguistic heritage remains in the 20th-century documentation.

The three chapters on phonological, morphological and syntactic variation also speak to the results of a pressing need for in-group communication and communal identity, resistance to oppression and pressures for assimilation to European cultural norms. In all three instances, the 20th-century material is closer to African heritage linguistic patterns, consistent with effortful adult learning. Magens' 18th-century material shows both evidence of retained European heritage features and borrowing from the linguistic resources developed by the colony's Afro-Caribbean community. Due to time limitations, I'll highlight a few areas of influence. The influence of heritage linguistic resources is greatest when frequency of use exceeds that of use of a target. The chapter on phonology reveals the operation of Afro-Caribbean developmental patterns and adoptive strategies, as would be the case if the data in the 20th century reflected limited early learning. Syllable structure reveals retention of a West African syllable pattern.

Adults whose heritage syllable patterns are less complex than those of a target community proceed through developmental stages, the first of which reflects a heritage linguistic structure. Among the Twi, Ga and Ewe, the preferred syllable structure is consonant-vowel. In contrast, the Danes, the Dutch and British prefer syllables ending in consonants. The 20th-century material shows a wide range of syllable types, including those found in European languages. However, the most frequent syllable is composed of a consonant and a vowel. Comparisons with lexical source material reveal learners employed several strategies to reshape syllables in the input. These included reanalysis, vowel insertion, consonant deletion and metathesis. The frequency of consonant-vowel syllables in Magens' material was intermediate between that of the 20th-century data and European lexical items consistent with the proposal that Euro-Caribbean adolescents selectively indexed features of Afro-Caribbean speech to encode local identity while carefully maintaining distinctions that signals social distance. Word-final vowel copying – a type of vowel insertion – provides insight into conventionalization during negotiation within the Afro-Caribbean community as it satisfies the requirement of harmonic feature sharing, regardless of a user's linguistic background. For example, among the Ga, vowels other than [e] or [o], must agree in orality or nasality, while among the Akan, harmonic vowels share the feature plus/minus advanced tongue root position. The compromise copies a vowel from a lexical source onto word-final position. For example, Afro-Caribbean *futu* 'foot' corresponds to *fod* when used by Danes, *voet* when used by the Dutch and to British *foot*. There was also evidence of direct retention of African heritage phonetic features. For example, in the 20th-century material the front and high back vowels: [i] ~ [I]; [u] ~ [U] are non-contrastive. This is also a feature found in conventionalized resources used by Twi and Ewe people. However, Dutch has only [i]. [I] and [u], while in Danish or English there is contrast. For example, in English *seat* [sit] and *sit* [sIt], *fool* [ful] and *full* [fUl] are different words.

Plural marking in the 20th century similarly shows affinity to plural marking in Africa as it does throughout the Caribbean. It differs from that used by Europeans in three ways. First, the same form is used to encode third-person plural (*they* in English), the additive plural (*goats* in English) and the associative plural (*mamma and them* in Southern US English.) In Northern Europe, when associative plurals appear, they are periphrastic. A second characteristic is the semantic features that constrain plural making. For example, among the Akan, a plural suffix is used with human referents (e.g. *boys* but not *boxes*). Among the Ga, the plural suffix is used primarily with animate nouns (e.g. *boys* or *bulls* but not *boxes*). The second pattern occurs in the 20th-century material. The third characteristic is the pragmatic determination of plural marking. In the 20th-century material, plural marking is optional on definite nouns. Indefinite nouns are not available for plural marking. This pattern is partially replicated in Magens' material: although he marks indefinite nouns, their frequency of marking is less than that of definite nouns. Additionally, the semantic features that trigger marking are different. In the 20th-century material, the marking of definite and non-human animate nouns is the same while Magens' marks definite and inanimate reference. As with syllable structure, the similarity between Magens and the 20th-century material is attributed to partial borrowing of features developed by the Afro-Caribbean community; differences reflect heritage linguistic patterns. There is minimal overlap between the plural forms used to encode plurality by members of the Euro-Caribbean and Afro-Caribbean communities. For the former, plural markers are limited to heritage forms by standardization. For the latter, a profusion of forms emerges from innovation and unrestricted use.

In the 20th-century data, coordination, subordination, complementation, clause chaining and verb serialization are used to express complex events. Serial verb constructions are monoclausal, occurring under a single intonation contour with no overt markers of coordination or syntactic dependencies. Serial verb serialization is an old, highly diffusible feature documented in use among the Akan, the Ewe and the Ga. Both asymmetrical and symmetrical serial verb constructions are documented in the 20th-century material. It is likely that this feature originates in discourse organization and information packaging strategies that emerged as Africans negotiated processable input and output within their group. Here are some examples of serial verb constructions from the 20th-century material. The bolded items are the verbs:

(1) di   difi   sini   am   a   kan   **goi**   mais   mi   ris   **gi**   sini
    the   dove   pl   3sg   past   can   throw   corn   and   rice   recipient   them
    'the doves, s/he could throw corn and rice to them'

(2) dan   am   a   **lo**   **rapo**   **ne**   en   steki   mes
    Then   3sg   past   directional   gather   take   a   piece   knife
    'then s/he went and picked up a piece of a knife'

(3) ju   no   **wɛl**   **antut**   mi
    2sg   neg   want   answer   1sg
    'you don't want to answer me' (MSA 5B)

(4) nu   di   kiniŋ   no   a   **wet**   se   dʌ   man   a   ka   **ma**   en bot   zeil bo di   lan
    Now   the king   neg   past   know   comp   the   man   past   can   make   a boat   sail on the land
    'now, the king didn't know that the man could make a boat sail on land'

Often, but not always, the verbs are sequential. Two verb sequences are the most frequent, although longer sequences as in *lo rapo ne* 'go and gather' are also possible.

The chapter discusses 10 serial verb constructions, four appear in symmetrical constructions, **ma(k)** 'make', **maŋke** 'want', **stat** 'start', and **wɛl** 'like.' Serial verb constructions contain major verbs which also function as main verbs. In symmetrical serial verb constructions, these are unrestricted by semantic or grammatical category, except that they cannot be copulas or existential or state of verbs.

The remaining six verbs occur in asymmetric constructions: **gi** 'give', **kaba** 'finish', **ko(m)** 'come', **lo** 'go', **ne** 'take', **se** 'say.' Asymmetrical serial verb constructions consist of a minor verb and a main major verb. Minor verbs are drawn from restrictive classes. The two types of serial verb constructions have different developmental trajectories. Asymmetrical serial verb constructions grammaticalize, as when *gi* 'give' and *ne* 'take', come to signal benefactive and instrumental or commutative cases, or when *se* 'say' becomes a quotative or a complementizer. They also participate in grammatical chains. For example, *lo* 'go' begins as a main verb then develops into a serial verb, then a progressive marker, an aspect marker and a modal. Similarly, *kaba* 'finish' begins as a main verb and becomes a serial verb, then an aspect marker and a transitive causative. Alternatively, symmetrical serial verbs lexicalize. Parkvall speculates that serialization can emerge within 19 years of a colony's founding. This maps well onto the stabilization of the Danish colony's Afro-Caribbean population in 1688. Early use of verb serialization is also predicted by the situational constraints which point to a period of early effortful learning, during which communicative imperatives would have led to persistence of African heritage linguistic patterns. Magens' material also demonstrates the retention of a heritage feature. One superficially resembling verb serialization. However, unlike serial verb constructions, bare infinite title complements such as *go get* as in *go get your sister*, display syntactic dependency that emerges with third-person subjects, as in, *she always goes to get her sister* or *she always goes and gets her sister*. There are 10 two-verb sequences in Magens' dialogue with exact parallels in European input. The exception is *lo slap*, which means go to bed, go to sleep, sleeping or asleep. This would have been learned from Afro-Caribbean caregivers.

The monograph also contains a conclusion and three appendices. These are translations of two 19th-century articles by Pontopiddan and a glossary of variant forms illustrating the phonological alternatives available to the colony's residents. The online version contains more than 300 sound files of the last speaker.

In summary, drawing on strands of evidence from a number of humanistic disciples, *Giving Jack His Jacket* identifies agency and identity as key to linguistic resource development in the Danish colony with implications for the survival of cultural influences throughout the African diaspora. The cultural assumptions that propel the Caribbean's repopulation render the creation of new linguistic resources opaque. Consideration of subaltern agency and the role of linguistic choice and identity construction reveals how conflicting worldviews and cultural practices impacted entrenchment, conventionalization and vernacularization in the Danish colony. The colony's history begins in privation, suffering and death. Its system of exploitation and oppression begot resistance, ensuring psychosocial distance between Africans and those who held them in bondage. Initially, Africans deployed their existing linguistic resources, adding only what was needed for survival. Population stability in the late 1680s was a precursor to community formation and the conventionalization of linguistic resources.

Around 1700, prosperity increased cross-group ties and the diffusion of linguistic features, fostering the indexing of some features of Afro-Caribbean speech to Euro-Caribbean local identity. The Danes acquired St. John long before the variants favored by the missionaries emerged. The economic conditions on St. John facilitated the persistence of early linguistic features into the 20th century. In contrast, on St. Thomas, social conditions ameliorated as miscegenation, the emergence of an Afro-Caribbean middle class, and abolition blurred the lines between social groups. The positive indexing of variants developed by the Euro-Caribbean community and the missions led to the creation of intermediate variants documented in the 19th century, even as American and British cultural economic influence encouraged the adoption of Anglophone linguistic resources.

Research on adult linguistic resource expansion provides insight into the colony's linguistic history, refuting earlier explanations rooted in hubristic eurocentrism. Examination of situational variables suggest that despite a cultural orientation towards linguistic resource expansion, age, sex, the psychological and physical duress of captivity, and the effects of intentionality and investment, argue for only the initial effortful stages of development. The colony's social structure was such that intergroup communication was limited while communication within Afro-Caribbean community allowed for the negotiation of comprehensible input and output.

As community emerged, communication patterns were conventionalized and vernacularized. Insight from linguistic practice, agency and identity, and the entrenchment of linguistic resources by adults, demand that in rejecting hubristic eurocentrism, we give Jack his jacket.

Chanel Van der Merwe

Thank you so much, Dr Sabino. It was a highly detailed, informative and interesting talk that you've given us. Over to you, Prof Makoni.

Sinfree Makoni

Thanks, Robin. I've been struggling with two things. I'm trying to answer the following question for myself. Let me start off with the easy one. Last week, we spent some time talking about relational ontologies, for example, that people do not live in a single container universe, that there are different realities, etc. We had some discussion about domestic life, etc. So, what I've been trying to do for myself is this: I've been saying, if I were to take the analytical apparatus that Mastin Prinsloo was talking about from Barad (2001), the quantum feminist physicist, for example, and then apply it to your data, what happens? Was there something similar happening?

Robin Sabino

I think so. Certainly at the level of the individual, it's exactly what happens. As we live our lives and interact with others, we perform different selves. Linguistically, we enact different values, assumptions, beliefs, ideas, emotions and communicate demographic and sociocultural identities, ideological stances, alliances, affiliations and sympathies. But we don't function only at the level of the individual. Transhipped Africans were stripped of their social identities, removed from family under terrible physical conditions. They were isolated linguistically and brutalized. A natural impetus is to make connections. Even on shipboard as the terms *mat, kabe* and *kontri* 'shipmate, countryman, fellow, companion' show, people developed relationships. For example, there is a story of a woman of on St. John who buried a woman who came over with her mother on the slave ship. People would have been desperate to reconstitute social and psychological identities within community, even as they attempted to protect themselves from others.

Sinfree Makoni

If that is the case, then, that to some extent your argument partially supports Barad's argument, that what you fundamentally find in individuals is the desire to establish relations, what she calls 'relational ontologies'.

Robin Sabino

Well, I think the conditions were so awful, they were most interested in trying to survive.

Sinfree Makoni

Yes, so the relations then were the consequences of people trying to survive, right? The issue that I want to talk to you about, is one of different realities within the same space. You kept talking about the Caribbean, the Ga, the Ewe, and all these different communities. Are you therefore arguing that what you were analyzing are people who were living in the same geographical space, but situated in different realities altogether?

Robin Sabino

I think part of survival in this environment was (re)establishing personal identity and reconstituting relationships. With respect to different realities in the same space, I don't think that can be different altogether because of the brutality of the setting. I mean, if people did not acquiesce to demands, there were horrific punishments that were meted out. At least superficially, there had to be some appearance of unity, but I think that it's been greatly overestimated. In the book, there is an excerpt from one of Magens' dialogues of a woman and her body servant – and the woman is getting dressed, and the exchange shows very clearly that the enslaved individual just doesn't talk, both probably because she's not invited to talk and probably because she didn't want to talk. And when she does talk, she simply meets the woman's demands and nothing more. There is a semblance of shared reality, but like the woman who said she jumped up and cheered for herself that we heard about last time, there's consistent division, I think.

Sinfree Makoni

How did you intellectually, more or less, move from talking about creoles to ending up in your other recent book, adopting the position that languages may not exist, at least in the form in which we think they do?

Robin Sabino

Rejecting the idea that language death was responsible for the variation in the material I was working with arose from my encounter with Kretzschmar's research on human language as an emergent system. Figure 3.1 provides an example from the Virgin Islands data I worked with illustrating that positing a shared grammar is simply invalid.

The data in the figure are from Mr Joshua and Mr Roberts who were recorded in the 1920s and Mrs Stevens who was a last user of these linguistic resources. The words on the bottom – *bo, abo, abobo, obu, bono, op*, etc. – are the forms that mean 'above'. You can see that these speakers use these forms at quite different rates. As I discuss in *Languaging without Languages* (Sabino, 2018), Mr Joshua's most frequent choice, *bo*, represented 69% of the data, suggesting it is his most strongly entrenched variant. Mr Roberts patterns similarly to Mr Joshua for *bo, abo* and *obu*. However, he differs in his use of *abobo, bono, op, ^bo*, and produces no tokens to *bu, ^bobo* or *aobu*.

In contrast to Mr Joshua and Mr Roberts, *bo* represents a smaller % of the forms produced by Mrs Stevens. Instead, her most highly entrenched form is *abo*. She produces *abobo* and *bono* at frequencies similar to those of Mr Roberts. However, she produces *op* at a frequency nearer to Mr Joshua, and like Mr Joshua but unlike Mr Roberts produces tokens of *bu, ^bobo* and *aobu*. There are many words that exhibit this type of variation. Looking at language behavior from this perspective forced me to conclude that these three speakers have' have different but overlapping and thus comprehensible linguistic systems.

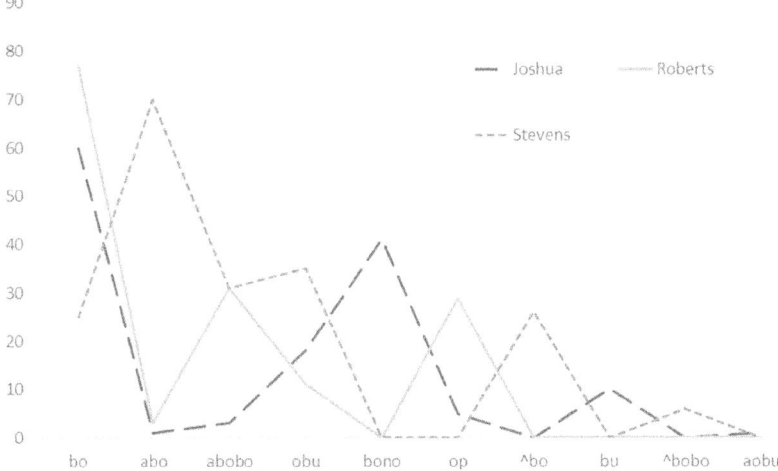

Figure 3.1 Frequency distribution of variants for 'above' used by three Virgin Islanders

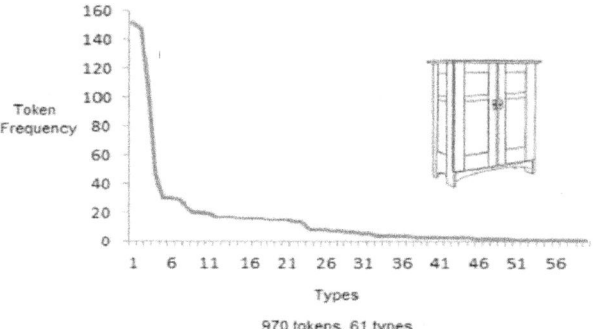

Figure 3.2 Distribution of terms 61 names self-identified Alabamians used for a piece of furniture

Figure 3.2 provides a second example. It shows the distribution of a substantially greater number of terms for the piece of furniture pictured in the figure offered by respondents to a series of surveys.

Of the 970 names for the furniture item that were recorded, w*ardrobe* and *armoire* were the most highly conventionalized responses. Each of these terms comprised 26% of the total. *Cabinet* accounted for an additional 9% of responses. However, many of the furniture terms were offered by single respondents. Again, given that this type of variation is typical of human language, it makes it difficult to write a unitary grammar.

Let me give you one more example. Figure 3.3 shows a number of variants for the modal + *have* construction.

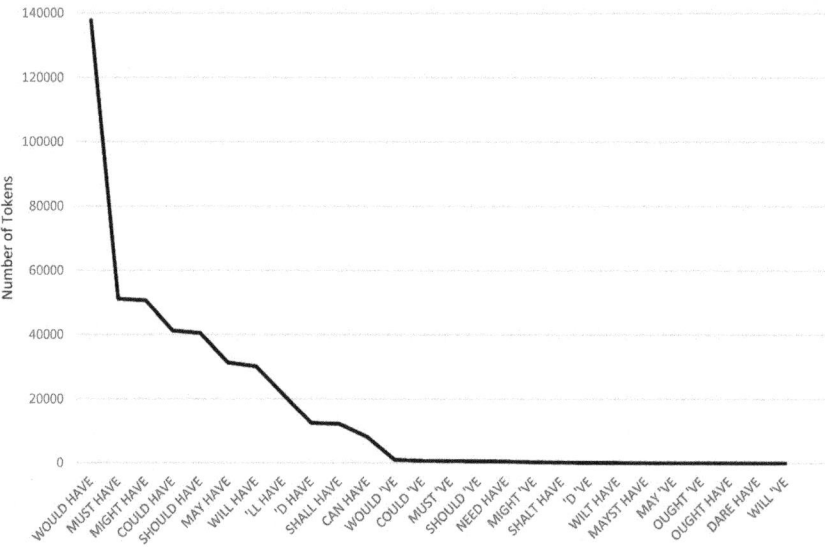

Figure 3.3 Variants of the modal + *have* from the Corpus of American English

Again, we see substantial variation with only a couple of variants widely used. The remainder are far less frequent, and a number of the are used by only one or two persons. While there are several that I doubt I have ever used, I believe that were I to hear them in context I would understand them.

Kretzschmar argues that this pattern, which he calls the A- (for asymmetric) curve, is the only pattern that exists in human language. So, if you look at actual usage and do not get trapped by language standardization (which reduces variation to its fewest and most prestigious variants) then you cannot write unified grammars. And by extension, the things that those grammars describe, languages, simply don't exist.

I honestly think linguistics can be a science, I think it's going to be a neuroscience, and I think to be seriously a science, you can't work with imaginary elements like languages.

Sinfree Makoni

I support the argument that linguistics does not need to postulate the existence of language as bounded entities for it to make progress. That's my own take, but what you are providing, I think, seems to be the case. You find it, for example, even in 19th-century African linguistics, when you read some of the textbooks, some of the early grammars, or the narratives by people who were putting together these grammars, they complain and say with a lot of frustration that, 'I went and I asked this guy what is the meaning of this word, and he gave me this word; then the following woman gave me a different one, and I met somebody else and they come up with a totally different one' – meaning, that there was such wide variation, but it's possible that the variation was subsequently controlled through language standardization. I liked your concept of 'hubristic eurocentrism.'

Robin Sabino

Yeah, I liked it so much I had to steal it from the Jamaican historian Neville Hall.

Sinfree Makoni

What is the difference between conventionalization and vernacularization?

Robin Sabino

Conventionalization is the linguistic patterns. The syntagmatic and pragmatic patterning. Vernacularization is the linking of linguistic forms to stances and identities. For instance, before I moved to Alabama, I used to talk about [pikæns], and now I speak about [pikans]. In doing so, which choice I make immediately signals either my origin or whom I'm identifying with.

Sinfree Makoni

I want to get you back to the other argument about languages and idiolect. Your argument, then, is that we should focus on the speaker and not primarily on the language.

Robin Sabino

No, there's actually also – there's a nice piece of work done by one of Obama's press persons, and he tracked him over three years, and there is a difference between patterns of speaking and patterns of hearing. It's not just the speaker, and that's why I found the term 'languaging' in John Joseph's work and adopted it, because you have to, I think, consider the totality of linguistic practice. For instance, my vernacularized indexes may not be the same as yours. We may both hear something and interpret it quite differently.

Sinfree Makoni

So, you are arguing that one of the limitations in linguistics is that it is too much focused on the speaker.

Robin Sabino

That's one of them, yes. But I do want to consider the locus of languaging the individual even though I recognize that languaging is by its very nature transactional. Individuals do not language in isolation. It is interaction with others that prompts us to conventionalize and vernacularize linguistic forms.

Sinfree Makoni

In a universe in which you are studying how languaging occurs in terms of hearing, it would be a fascinating experience, to see how do different individuals *hear* the same sound. linguistics tends to be speaker biased.

Robin Sabino

Yeah, and ironically, in the Danish West Indies case, it was focused on written texts, because that was done primarily by Dutch scholars who could actually read these things because they were so Dutch-like.

Sinfree Makoni

The general framework you have been using is also relevant to an analysis of contemporary urban African vernaculars. But, if that is the case then what is the relevance of phonological and morphological analyses when you're trying to carry out research in a highly fluid situation?

Robin Sabino

I think it depends on whether you're looking at where things come from, or where things are going. For instance, there was some work done in Britain by Cheshire (2013). Looking at the word *man* developing into a pronoun form. I haven't experienced any of these environments, but my guess is that there's a lot of really interesting, innovative conventionalization going on, so things turning into grammatical elements being used in very interesting ways. And that, for descriptive linguists, that's something that you might indeed want to track. You might want to see how it develops over time, you might want to try and figure where it came from.

Salikoko Mufwene

Hi, Robin. I'd like to –

Robin Sabino

Hi, Sali. How are you?

Salikoko Mufwene

Fine. I'd like to thank you and congratulate you for such an elaborate and detailed presentation of how creoles emerged.

Robin Sabino

Yeah, sorry.

Salikoko Mufwene

No, but it's what we have always needed in talking about the emergence of creoles, whether or not we accept that creoles are a special category of languages. I really agree with you, we shouldn't insist so much on the term 'creole', but see – focus on how language naturally evolves under specific ecological conditions; and you really get into various details showing how things really evolve normally, in the sense of naturally what any other person under similar conditions would have done, and not particularly because these are people of inferior mental capacity – presumably – not because people are assumed to have inferior mental capacity or inferior anatomical endowment. The citations you gave us are very much reminiscent of things that – those of us, for instance, that read about the emergence of creoles have reported from 19th-century French philologists, such as Lucien Adam, Julien Vinson, Charles

Baissac and the like. And they literally started with saying, you know, these Blacks, these Africans are inferior to Europeans; they are less evolved than Europeans, and the European languages were just too sophisticated for them, and they couldn't acquire them and so forth. And the picture that you present is really much more plausible to recreating the circumstances of language transmission.

I'm grateful that you clarified the way in which you used 'vernacularization,' because as you were speaking, I interpreted it in a different way. Vernacularization is the stage when the language is no longer serving just as a lingua franca, but as a variety for day-to-day communication. And this is quite consistent with how these patterns emerged, and so forth. One thing that I'm trying to sort out here is the way in which you used the word 'Euro-Caribbean', 'Afro-Caribbean', since you have avoided the term 'creole', but creole is also being used in the literature; and actually, before it was used for language variety it was used for people, locally born, that were not indigenous to their territories. Now, the confusion for me is whether you are using 'Afro-Caribbean' and 'Euro-Caribbean' as locally born people of African descent or locally-born of European descent, or whether you are referring to people of mixed unions, say, between Africans and indigenous people, or European and indigenous people. Can you clarify it for me, please?

Robin Sabino

Let me say that – the point you make about vernacularization is an important one, because I use the old meaning in the book, but I have now rejected that meaning and created a new meaning. Years ago, I rejected the notion that you would insightfully deal with these communities by talking about blacks and whites. I just thought that skin color says nothing about language behavior, and so I rejected it. In looking for a way to encode likely language linguistic behavior, I came upon Afro-Caribbean from Mervyn Alleyne, and created Euro-Caribbean on the pattern as an inclusive cover term, trying to capture people who were linguistically and culturally influenced by heritage behaviors. They're very broad terms. There is very little information I came across about miscegenation. I mean, it was there. The governor had a mistress, but there's really nothing I can do with that.

Chanel Van der Merwe

Thank you, Dr Sabino.

References

Barad, K. (2001) Re(con)figuring space, time, and matter. In M. DeKoven (ed.) *Feminist Locations: Global and Local, Theory and Practice* (pp. 75–109). New Brunswick, NJ: Rutgers University Press.
Bickerton, D. (1975) *Dynamics of a Creole System* (p. 75). Cambridge: Cambridge University Press.
Bybee, J. (2010) *Language, Usage and Cognition.* Cambridge: Cambridge University Press.

Cheshire, J. (2013) Grammaticalization in social context: The emergence of a new English pronoun. *Journal of Sociolinguistics* 17 (5), 608–633.
Christie, P. (1983) In search of the boundaries of Caribbean Creoles. In L.D. Carrington, D. Craig and R.T. Dandaré (eds) *Studies in Caribbean Language* (pp. 13–22). St. Augustine, Trinidad: Society for Caribbean Linguistics.
den Besten, H., Muysken, P., van Rossem, C., Stein, P. and van der Voort, H. (1996) Negerhollands[:] An Introduction. In C. van Rossem and H. van der Voort (eds) *Die Creole Taal* (pp. 1–44). Amsterdam: Amsterdam University Press.
den Besten, H. and van der Voort, H. (1999) Negerhollands and the Atlantic English Creoles: Comparative Remarks. In P. Baker and A.A. Bruyn (eds) *St Kitts and the Atlantic Creoles: The Texts of Samuel Augustus Mathews in Perspective* (pp. 387–418). London: Battlebridge Publications.
de Jong, de Josselin J.P.B. (1926) *Het Huidige Negerhollandsch (Texten en woordenlijst)*. Amsterdam: Koninklijke Akademie van Wetenschappen te Amsterdam.
Goodman, M. (1964) *A Comparative Study of French Creole Dialects*. The Hauge: Mouton.
Graves, A.V. (1977) The present state of the Dutch Creole of the Virgin Islands. PhD dissertation, University of Michigan. Ann Arbor, MI: UMI.
Hall, N.A.T. (1992) *Slave Society in the Danish West Indies: St. Thomas, St. John, St. Croix*, B.W. Higman (ed.). Baltimore: John's Hopkins University Press.
Hesseling, D.C. (1979) Papiamentu en Negerhollands. In T.L. Markey and P.T. Roberge (Trans. and eds) *Dirk Christiaan Hesseling, On the origin and formation of creoles: A miscellany of articles, and Hugo Schuchardt, The ethnography of variation: Selected writings on pidgins and creoles*. Ann Arbor, MI: Karoma. Original work published in 1933.
LaCharité, D. (2007) Multilingualism in Creole Genesis. *Journal of Pidgin and Creole Languages* 22 (1), 159–164.
Magens, J.M. (1770) *Grammatica over det Creolske Sprog: Som bruges paa de trende danske eilande, St. Croix, St. Thomas og St. Jans i America: Sammenskrevet og opsat af en zaa St. Thomas hedföd maed*. Copenhagen: Giese Salikath.
Oldendorp, C.G.A. (1987) *A Caribbean Mission*. J. Jakob Bossard (ed.) and A.R. Highfield and V. Barac (trans.). Ann Arbor, MI: Karoma Publishers, Inc. Original work published in 1777.
Olwig, K.F. (1985) *Cultural Adaptations and Resistance on St. John: Three Centuries Afro Caribbean Life*. Gainesville, FL: University of Florida Press.
Owomoyela, O. (1985) Proverbs: an exploration of an African philosophy of social communication. *Ba Shiru* 12 (1), 3–16.
Peirce, B.N. (1995) Social identity, investment, and language learning. *TESOL Quarterly* 29 (9), 9–31.
Sabino, R. (2018) *Languaging without Languages: Beyond Metro-, Multi-, Poly-, Pluri-and Translanguaging*. Leiden: Brill.
Sabino, R. (2018) *Language Contact in the Danish West Indies: Giving Jack his Jacket*. Leiden: Brill.
Sensbach, J. (2005) *Rebecca's Revival: Creating Black Christianity in the Atlantic World*. Cambridge, MA: Harvard University Press.
Sprauve, G. (1997) Chronological implications of discontinuity in spoken and written Dutch Creole. *Journal of the College of the Virgin Islands* 5, 40–57.

4 Challenging the Dominance of Mind over Body in the History of Language Analysis

John Joseph

The brief from Sinfree Makoni for my talk was to discuss my book, *Language, Mind and Body: A Conceptual History* (Cambridge University Press, 2018). I won't go through it chapter by chapter, but will explain what it's trying to do, then focus on aspects that are particularly relevant to this Forum. I work in a School of Philosophy, Psychology and Language Sciences that's been one of the centres for what's known as 4E cognition – embodied, embedded, enacted, extended. Unfortunately, the terminology is not used anything like consistently. The key thing is that five basic approaches to locating language are current in the literature:

(a) Language is in the brain (intracranialism).
(b) Language is in the neuro-muscular system, with the brain as its centre (internally extended cognition).
(c) Language extends not just through the neuro-muscular system but to devices beyond the body that are as available and reliable as internal cognition is (externally extended cognition).[1]
(d) Language extends beyond the individual to include other people (distributed cognition [sometimes called 'extended'], situated cognition).
(e) Language has no location, because it lacks extension.

Approaches (b) to (e) share a determination to move beyond conceiving knowledge of language as a collection of representations stored in some module of the mind or location within the brain. It seems clear enough that what we call having or not having, knowing or not knowing a particular language involves something physical in us, given that a stroke or other damage to the nervous system can make us lose it. There are certain regular correlations, observable across individuals and languages, between damage to a particular part of the brain and loss or weakening of particular structures or functions, known since the 19th century. But, as the appropriately named David Braine (2014: 53) has put it, intracranialism leads to abstraction away from physical reality when it proceeds 'as if one can assume that it is possible to consider language separately from speech and the hearing of speech, sight separately from eye and head movement and exploratory activity, and the brain and nervous system as operating without interdependence on other systems within the body'.[2]

For my colleagues in Philosophy, including until recently Andy Clark, extended mind meant getting cognition out of just-the-brain, to extend through the whole nervous system, which to say the whole body, and possibly outward to devices which are used seamlessly with bodily cognition. The classic example is, not the smartphone, but the blind person's white cane, which we already find in Descartes. Within linguistics, 'embodied cognition' was strongly associated with Lakoff and Johnson's work on 'metaphors we live by', and to a lesser extent with Wierzbicka's theory of semantic primes (Lakoff & Turner, 1989; Wierzbicka, 1972). Some linguists and psychologists were also pursuing work on synaesthesia which they sometimes cast as falling into this vein.

There was a scattering of papers exploring how 'extended mind' in the philosophers' sense could be applied to knowledge of language, but nothing that had really made a splash. When extended-mind philosophers talked about language, they, and I'm thinking particularly of Clark, treated it as something given, just there, which they could use to account for 'distributed cognition', knowledge conceived not as something stored in an individual, but created and recreated in interaction. Some of these philosophers were also tracing the historical lineage of these ideas, but again with any consideration of the role of language absent or at least marginalised.

So, my book sets out first to show linguists, both theoretical and applied, what might be gained from rethinking knowledge of language in a 4E perspective, building on work already done, and also establishing the venerable pedigree of this perspective. Well, not always venerable – because the long tradition of tying the shape of languages to the bodies of their speakers has played a significant role in the development of pseudo-scientific racism, work cast in a superficially scientific vein and aimed at establishing the basis of racial differences. Understanding how it was possible for linguistics to play a role in this is a vitally important historical task, because it's not clear that linguistics has entirely washed its hands of this legacy. Some will say it's quite clear that it hasn't.

It didn't start out that way. In this translation of the opening of Aristotle's *On Interpretation*, I put additions drawn from other Aristotelian texts in square brackets:

> What is in the [unarticulated] voice [uttered by humans and animals] symbolizes the passions of the mind/soul [viz. passion, gentleness, fear, pity, courage, joy, loving and hating, in all of which the body too is involved]. Articulated words symbolize what is in the [unarticulated] voice. Just as articulated speech is not the same for all people, neither are [unarticulated] voices the same. But what these things are primarily the signs of, the passions of the mind/soul, are indeed the same for all people. Likewise, the objects [which provoke the passions, and] which [therefore] the latter are images of, they too are the same. (*De interpretatione* 16a3-9, my translation)

Aristotle implies that articulated words developed out of unarticulated speech, but doesn't speculate on how it happened. A generation later, Epicurus makes breath the cornerstone of a significantly different account of language from Aristotle's, not directly contradicting him on most points but drawing out possible readings of his texts on language:

> And so names too were not at first deliberately given to things, but men's natures according to their different nationalities had their own peculiar feelings and received their peculiar impressions, and so each in their own way emitted air formed into shape by each of these feelings and impressions, according to the differences made in the different nations by the places of their abode as well. (Epicurus, *Letter to Herodotus* 75)[3]

Emitting air – breath – spirit – differing by the feelings and sensory impressions peculiar to each *ethnos*. This answers a big question Aristotle left tacit: why do different languages exist? On one point, Epicurus does directly contradict Aristotle. When he says that *pathē* 'feelings' or 'passions', and *phantasmata* 'impressions' or 'images', differ ethnically, this can't be reconciled with Aristotle's belief that the *pathēmata*, passions of the mind/soul, are the same for all. Epicurus offers a dramatic increase in explanatory power, a framework for understanding languages as direct expressions of the national or racial soul, rather than merely different ways of encoding thoughts that are universally human.

It seems like a lot of benefit at little cost, but at stake is the conception of a common humanity. Epicurus lays out what will be enduring themes in the bodily approach to language outside the medical context: the central place of breath and the organs that produce it; the effect of racial difference, temperament and complexion; the roles of innate nature and environmental experience; compulsive action at the first stage of language, and reasoned choice at the second. But the Christian and Islamic Middle Ages will forget Epicurus; for over 1000 years 'The Philosopher' meant simply Aristotle. And for Aristotle language is both mental and bodily, but without the body being conceived of ethnically.

Over these long centuries distinct theories of mind developed in medicine, philosophy and theology, insofar as the latter two can be separated. Theologians got very exercised over how it is that beings without bodies can speak, as they are represented as doing in the sacred texts. Angels were a particular worry: hearing prayers when they have no ears, choirs of them singing when they have no throats or lungs.[4] Mediaeval theologians weren't ready to accept any fantastic construct on the grounds that God is omnipotent; the universe needs to be coherent. Outside the monasteries and mosques and later the universities, religion wasn't separate from medicine, and in every town street vendors sold obleys, iron-cooked wafers on which to write Latin 'charms'. Eating the Latin, taking the sacred language into the body, would bring healing. For an example, see Amsler, 2011. Or you might write it, or have it written, on a strip of cloth or paper, and either ingest it or lay it atop a wound or a tumour. That's embodied language at work. And we find a very bodily representation of grammar in the 13th-century poem *Laborintus* by Eberhard the German, a contemporary of Thomas Aquinas, with lactating Lady Grammar, her breasts 'full of milk' from which the future *magister* 'suckles all grammatical knowledge'. The *magister*, the master or teacher

> Imprints an 'a' on his mind while sucking the first breast:
> The entire grammatical herd is summoned and follows each in its proper place.
> He sucks out how many types of syllables there are,
> How many are the parts of speech, which create each gender; ...
> He sucks out which parts are located in the anterior brain,
> And which in the posterior;
> He drinks from the remaining breast (which offers even greater nourishment)
> Through what meaning each word may take a bride. (Translation adapted from Cestaro, 1997)

The reference to the anterior and posterior brains evokes the conception of knowledge found both in St Augustine of Hippo (354–430),[5] and, five centuries later, in the great Persian medical authorities, Rhazes, Haly Abbas and Avicenna. Dante Alighieri (1265–1321) will also bring in the wet nurse, but doesn't fail to notice that, unlike lactating Lady Grammar, it's not Latin she speaks, but the vernacular which we learn 'without any formal instruction, by imitating our nurses'.[6]

It's been argued that print culture contributed to the disembodying of language and mind by removing language from direct bodily representation in handwriting (see, for example, Mulholland, 2013). Maybe; we should be sceptical of such historically deterministic explanation when it isn't corroborated by contemporary testimony, which I haven't seen adduced. But printing did allow for wider circulation of ancient texts, and the writings of Epicurus, and of the Roman Epicurean Lucretius, provided an intellectual pedigree for Renaissance empiricism. Empirical knowledge is acquired bodily, by the senses, as opposed to being implanted by God, or transmitted through quasi-angelic communication, as per the *doctor angelicus*, St Thomas Aquinas (1225–1274). The revival of Epicureanism began with Lorenzo Valla's (1407–1457) *De voluptate* of 1431, and the ancient tension we saw in Aristotle and Epicurus is played out again in the 17th-century debate between René Descartes (1596–1650) and the Neo-Epicurean Pierre Gassendi (1592–1655), who address other semi-facetiously as O *Ame!* 'O Mind' and O *Chair!* 'O Flesh'. In his objections to Descartes' *Meditations*, Gassendi argues that the bodily senses suffice to account for all the knowledge a person has, up to and including the idea of God. The passages of the *Meditations* which most excited or upset readers include the statement that 'my essence consists solely in the fact that I am a thinking thing ... I am really distinct from my body, and can exist without it' (Cottingham *et al.*, 1984: 54). Although the definition of a human being as *res cogitans* was traditional, Descartes' use of it captured attention to such an extent that other passages were overlooked, for instance: 'Nature also teaches me, by these sensations of pain, hunger, thirst and so on, that I am not merely present in my body as a sailor is present in a ship, but that I am very closely joined and, as it were, intermingled with it, so that I and the body form a unit' (Cottingham, 1984: 188–189). His last major work, the *Passions de l'ame*, maintains that 'the soul is really joined to the whole body, and that we cannot properly say that it exists in any one part to the exclusion of the others' (Cottingham *et al.*, 1985: 359, Art 351).

Baker & Morris argue that the supposedly 'Cartesian' concept of disembodied mind that became the core of philosophical debate for the next three centuries doesn't accurately represent Descartes' view. They call it the 'Cartesian legend' (Baker & Morris, 1996).[7] The account of language in *Passions de l'ame* doesn't divide the mental from the bodily, any more than Aristotle does. When I will something, this causes a particular movement of the pineal gland, pushing some of the animal spirits it contains into the pores of the brain (Cottingham *et al.*, 1985: 341, Art. 34). Imagination operates through these animal spirits opening the brain pores in such a way as to represent the thing imagined (Cottingham *et al.*, 1985: 344, Art. 43), and memory by the spirits going to the same brain pores where they were when the thing remembered was previously represented, and where they've left traces (Cottingham *et al.*, 1985: 343–344, Art. 42).

Across the Channel, the idea of 'associationism' would be sketched out by Thomas Hobbes (1588–1679) and John Locke (1632–1704) before being fully developed in the mid-18th century by David Hartley (1705–1757). In Hartley's theory, all knowledge is acquired and retained as 'vibrations' in the nervous system. The example he gives is a cross-sensory one:

> For this is fact; a child has the idea of the sound *nurse* often presented to the ear, at the same time with the visible appearance of the nurse herself in the eye, and by this frequent conjunction it comes to pass, that the visible appearance of the nurse shall itself excite a faint image of the sound nurse in the ear; and the sound nurse in like manner shall excite a faint image of the visible appearance of the nurse in the eye. And all this seems to be effected by the mutual influence which the motions in the optic and auditory nerves, constituting seeing and hearing, have upon one another according to the laws of matter and motion. (Hartley, 1837: 68-69)

Hartley's 'faint image of the sound nurse in the ear' is akin to what in the Middle Ages was called the *verbum cordis* – the 'heartly' word, funnily enough – and in more recent times 'inner speech.'

Hartley's contemporaries saw the potential of his theory for explaining differences in racial sensibilities, and national differences in culture and thought that were continuous with language differences. Like Epicurus, Montesquieu (1689–1755) doesn't try to separate intrinsic ethnic difference from the effect of environment: his *Essai* reasons that a hot or cold climate has a direct physical effect on the nerve endings, which can account for national minds (Montesquieu, 1892). Later, Johann Gottfried Herder (1744–1803), Friedrich Schlegel (1772–1829) and Ernest Renan (1823–1892) are among those who essentialise a Semitic versus Indo-European difference along body versus mind lines, sometimes, as with Herder, to assert the superiority of Hebrew poetry. Renan asks, 'Isn't the religious and sensitive race of the Semitic peoples painted stroke by stroke in these totally physical languages, in which abstraction is unknown and metaphysics impossible?' (Author's own translation. See Renan, 1858: 190). This perception of Semitic languages as physical endures: commonly cited examples include the fact that Hebrew uses the same word for *nose* and *anger*. But English uses *heart* to mean *courage*, and *courage* itself derives from a word for heart. This 'Orientalism' is the dark side of the neo-Epicurean heritage.

A question I take up in my book is how different people in Shakespeare's audience for *The Merchant of Venice* at the end of the 16th century would have answered Shylock's series of questions about Jews. The first three all compel a 'yes':

if you prick us do we not bleed? if you tickle us do we not laugh? -f you poison us do we not die?

But the next one is more contentious:

and if you wrong us shall we not revenge? – if we are like you in the rest, we will resemble you in that.

And then follow questions about diet and physical reaction to climate where we might expect different responses from the common folk in the pit and some of those who paid for a seat in the stalls. The former shared the mediaeval Aristotelian heritage with the middle-aged folk among the well-off. But the young urbane set were hip, man, to the neo-Epicureanism coming over from the Continent, and wouldn't necessarily have answered Shylock's questions in the same way as the Aristotelian *hoi polloi* and uncool. Epicureans might have pointed to stereotyped racial differences. Aristotelians might accept that Jews and Christians have physical sensations and eating and violent reactions in common, but that these things are also shared by dogs, which isn't the enlightened answer we want to hear either, particularly as *The Merchant of Venice* is filled with references to the 'dog Jew'.

By the mid-19th century, associationism was no longer of central interest to philosophers in Britain, who instead were arguing over various continental theories, including Auguste Comte's (1798–1857) positivism, and the eclectic Victor Cousin (1792–1867). But way up north in Aberdeen, Alexander Bain (1818–1903) was undertaking a scientific modernisation of associationism. It treated memory as a physical phenomenon, with a description that prefigures the 'connectionism' of a century later: currents of force passing through nervous circuits create 'specific growths in the cell junctions' (Bain, 1875). The stronger the original force, the more vivid the impression left on the circuit, quite like the 'weights' of connectionist analysis.

After Bain, this view of linguistic knowledge as being at least partly neuro-muscular was lost from sight. When Chomsky resuscitated enquiry into language and mind in the late 1950s and early 1960s, it was very much in the older, intracranial mode. He insisted that knowledge of language must be autonomous from other modules of the mind/brain, which is to say closed off from them – his argument being that a speaker's knowledge of the world is entirely detached from his or her linguistic knowledge as a native speaker. Chomsky also made it explicit that knowledge of language is a physical part of the brain – in his term, a language organ. In later work Chomsky refers to his research programme as 'biolinguistics' and describes its aim as the 'discovery of the [...] internal mechanisms that generate linguistic expressions and determine their sound and meaning. The whole system would then be regarded as one of the organs of the body [...]' (Chomsky, 2007: 12). In contrast, Bain took the internal mechanisms to be spread through the sensorimotor system, including the brain as its centre, but emphasizing how much of language, from learning to production and understanding, cannot be reduced to purely cerebral functions.

The 1970s and 80s saw applied linguistics still attempting to accommodate its models of second-language acquisition to the 1960s-style Chomskyan version, notably in Krashen and Terrell's (1983) so-called 'natural approach' in language teaching (Krashen & Terrell, 1983). There was no widespread will to do otherwise, so strongly were applied linguists, like their theoretical counterparts, under the sway of the concept of 'native speaker', which was the basis of Chomsky's linguistics. How do you recognise whether or not someone is a native speaker? There's a surprising dearth of research on the question. My experience suggests that I and others don't need to hear someone say very much before we make the decision. Except in rare cases, a few syllables suffice; sometimes just one, in which case I'm not making the decision based on their knowledge of syntax or lexicon or morphology, or even phonology, but fine-grained phonetic clues. In ordinary parlance: an accent, although that term is used to cover more than just phonetic features, which makes it too imprecise for our purposes. Phonology is the system of sounds as they exist in the mind – the systematic differences that distinguish one word or form from another; phonetics is about the sounds as produced in the mouth and perceived by the ear. An accent *can* involve phonological differences, but it's the phonetic ones that give the first clues as to native or non-native speakerhood. The mouth and ear are obviously body parts; the mind isn't. So I usually recognise a native or non-native speaker from their speaking body. If I can see them, that may prime me for certain expectations: if the person doesn't 'look Chinese', I won't expect them to be a native speaker of Chinese, although there's no logical reason for them not to be. Primed by visual indices, I'll need few phonetic data to confirm or falsify my presumption – not always accurately, but powerfully.

My late colleague Alan Davies (1931–2015) exposed the native speaker as a 'myth' with dangerous, quasi-racist consequences for language teaching and above all testing, which was his specialised area (Davies, 1991, 2003, 2013).[8] It's mythical because in reality there's no clear boundary between native and non-native speakers. Some people learn a language to such a level of competence, even starting well after puberty, that they're indistinguishable from native speakers. Whatever fine differences in their grammaticality judgements a psycholinguist may detect belong to the research laboratory, not to everyday life. In Davies's view, the native speaker myth sends learners the message that, however strong their motivation, however great their efforts, they can never reach the ultimate goal of foreign-language teaching, by virtue of their birth and other conditions beyond their control. It's thus an unjustifiable form of social exclusion, which applied linguists should combat rather than reinforce. My comment about the priming effect of a person's visual appearance should make clear too why this matter is quasi-racist, though as the definition of 'racist' broadens, the 'quasi' may have to go.

During the second half of the 20th century the idea of cognition as a process of working out algorithms, done by a mind/brain increasingly conceived on the model of a computer, attained a dominance that linguistics helped to back up. The first widely-felt tremor to shake this view came with work in Parallel Distributed Processing, based on an approach I mentioned earlier called connectionism (Rumelhart *et al.*, 1986). It rejected the computer model of the brain and its chains of binomial switches, replacing them with 'neural networks,' still metaphorical but approximating more closely to the known physiology of the brain. The network consists of multiply interconnected neurons whose connections vary in 'strength' or 'weight' accordingly as they are activated and reinforced by exposure to patterns, following the basic principle established decades earlier by Donald O. Hebb (1904–1985) (Hebb, 1949). In this way the network is able to learn; and its recursive action allows it to teach itself how to learn – to write its own learning programs, as it were – with sufficient exposure to data, and starting with minimal cognitive 'hardware'. Connectionism allowed for a more central role to be allocated to environment (broadly defined) in a person's cognitive development than the algorithmic model of cognition did.

Also worth mentioning in this context is 'situated cognition,' an approach with roots in the ecological psychology of James J. Gibson (1904–1979) and the enactivism of Maturana and Varela (Gibson, 1996; Maturana & Varela, 1987). It shares with distributed cognition the impulse to move away from thinking about mind as something stored in the individual, in favour of looking at how cognitive elements are constructed in particular instances by multiple actors.[9] In applied linguistics, James Gee has contributed significant work with a situated/affective dimension (Gee, 1992, 2004).

The classical model of mind can only accommodate the social by turning it into a feature or image in the mind of the individual. For Freud it's represented by the super-ego; but the Freudian subconscious is effectively absent from the contemporary discourse on mind and language. Distributed and situated cognition treat the individual perspective as the dominant view that needs to be resisted. Extended cognition is more about expansion of than resistance to the individual, and in that regard comes closer to the concerns of Pierre Bourdieu (1930–2002), who focused relentlessly on the problem of reconciling a belief in real agency with the fact that, as agents, we nevertheless make and carry out our choices within the contexts and constraints of a social world. Yet it's rare to encounter Bourdieu's name in the literature on cognition, perhaps because in the Collège de France he held the chair of sociology, although all his training was in philosophy, and his research is close to ethnology.

Bourdieu adopted the classical concept of the *habitus*, 'a set of dispositions which incline agents to act and react in certain ways' (Thompson, 1991). On the meaning and background of *habitus*, which also figured in the work of Max Weber, Marcel Mauss, Edmund Husserl, Norbert Elias and Merleau-Ponty, see Joseph, 2020). The word is connected to *habitare* 'inhabit', how the world we inhabit is reflected in us; it's not to be confused with 'habits', involuntary reflexes, conceived in a mechanical way. The dispositions of your habitus have sedimented within you through social interaction from childhood onward, becoming a physical part of your nervous system and generating practices that are regular without being governed by any 'rule'. Bourdieu was indebted to Merleau-Ponty for his rehabilitation of the body as the support for the historical incorporation of knowledge and the contribution of the emotions to language (Lescourret, 2008). The habitus is inhabited by an active human agent who engages in exchanges of symbolic power with other agents, each of whose habitus is linked to the rest in the shared field. The problem Bourdieu was addressing is how to explain the actions agents undertake that are not deliberate, and the cases where they undertake a deliberate course of action but find themselves unable to achieve it because of their own strong dispositions.

Bourdieu applies this form of analysis specifically to language, and how the quasi-choice of a particular way of speaking 'challenges the usual dichotomy of freedom and constraint. The "choices" of the habitus (for example, using the "received" uvular "r" instead of the rolled "r" in the presence of legitimate speakers) are... dispositions which, although they are unquestionably the product of social determinisms, are also constituted outside the spheres of consciousness and constraint' (Bourdieu, 1991: 51).

The concept of native speaker as it has figured in applied linguistics has been grounded in the intracranial view of cognition, and specifically in its Chomskyan version, where linguistic knowledge constitutes an autonomous mental module with an innate basis. The importance of the innateness is intensified through its echo in the etymologically-related *native* of native speaker: both terms tie the individual's language to his or her birth. It's often pointed out that 'native speaker' is a solecism, since one isn't born with a mother tongue, but learns whatever language he or she is exposed to when growing up. Despite considerable evidence from developmental psychology that fœtuses are already sensitive to their mother's language *in utero*, (DeCasper & Spence, 1986) a child of a Thai-speaking mother given up for adoption at birth to a Cambodian-speaking family doesn't grow up speaking Cambodian with a Thai accent. Within linguistic theory, the continued use of 'native speaker' subtly strengthens the contention that innate Universal Grammar defines the underlying reality of every language (to the point that Chomsky thinks that a visiting 'Martian scientist might reasonably conclude that there is a single human language, with differences only at the margins') (Chomsky, 2006: 7).

Any link of native speaker to birth implies a correlation with other sites of discrimination, particularly race. Chomsky always linked Universal Grammar with every child's infinite linguistic creativity in an anti-racist way. But when the context is switched to that of the language learner being assessed against the criterion of the native speaker – in colonial and post-colonial settings where the learners are of a race that suffers discrimination in various forms, some of them bound up with a perception of intellectual inferiority – the intracranial native speaker becomes conceptually problematic.

Does anything change if intracranialism is abandoned in favour of extended and distributed cognition? In exploring this I shall focus on Bourdieu's habitus, because he applied it to issues involving language to a greater degree than more recent psychologists and philosophers of extended mind have done, and attempted a fuller reconciliation of social and individual aspects of language than distributors have so far managed. Extended/distributed cognition frees us from a conception of language limited to representations stored in the brain, and from a research programme that simply assumes a brain born with a particular structure for storing such representations, that develops in an automatic way with minimal exposure to input data. This in turn frees us from any obligation to forget that the acquisition of our first language was a long apprenticeship occupying nearly all our waking moments during the first three or four years of our lives, and that has continued since.

In the course of this childhood apprenticeship, the knowledge we acquire becomes part not only of our memory but of our entire nervous system – our extended mind – which is to say part of our bodies. My first language doesn't set limits on what I'm capable of thinking or doing, but it makes some things come more easily than others, makes certain inclinations more natural, while others require greater effort. To be a native speaker concerns an individual's position in the distributed cognition of language as it reflects the historical facts of his or her extended cognition, or habitus, the set of dispositions, schemata of action and perception that individuals acquire and incorporate through our social experience.

Thus, the native speaker can be redefined without recourse to his or her linguistic competence. Instead, competence becomes a by-product of habitus. As Bourdieu put it, 'The habitus – embodied history, internalized as a second nature and so forgotten as history – is the active presence of the whole past of which it is the product' (Bourdieu, 1990a: 56). One can, with greater difficulty for some people than others, attain later in life a competence indistinguishable from that of a native speaker, without going through the whole apprenticeship which produces the native speaker's habitus. So long as the second language learner doesn't display the entire habitus that one expects as the accompaniment of native competence, he or she may remain native-like in the judgement of others, though it depends on the others with whom linguistic knowledge is distributed in a given context.

Bourdieu's work is on the rise again after a couple of decades of an 'ebb tide' effect, caused by a perception that the concept of habitus is deterministic, ignoring agency in favour of structures. Bourdieu himself argued over and over against this misperception, and described his approach as 'refusing to reduce *agents*, which it considers as eminently active and acting (without necessarily doing so as subjects) to simple epiphenomena of structure' (Bourdieu, 1990c: viii) '[T]he notion of habitus expresses first and foremost the rejection of a whole series of alternatives into which social science (and more generally, all of anthropological theory) has locked itself …'. But, he laments, 'Unfortunately, people apply to my analyses – and this is the principal source of misunderstanding – the very alternatives that the notion of habitus is meant to exclude, those of consciousness and the unconscious, of explanation by determining causes or by final causes' (Bourdieu, 1990b: 10).

Davies was right to insist that it cannot be an objective or neutral move for us to make the native speaker the implicit goal of language teaching and the yardstick for assessing the proficiency of a non-native speaker, so long as the concept is bound up with the Chomskyan mind/brain of an idealized individual in a speech community where everyone is linguistically the same, combined with the political-ethical belief in native speaker equality. The intent may not be to oppress any non-native speaker, but we don't assess policies based on intentions, only on their results. The result of taking native proficiency as the implicit goal of language teaching and testing is that the effort to learn a language is doomed to failure, in the sense that, however good a learner you are, you will never measure up to even a speaker of the most socially stigmatized non-standard form of the target language. That's not only absurd but self-defeating.[10]

If, on the other hand, we redefine native speaker in the bodily terms of habitus, with all that it captures concerning extended cognition, at least intra-corporally, does that actually help with the oppression problem? I believe it does, the reason being that habitus does not carry the conceptual baggage of the 'standard language', as grammatical knowledge does, nor the link with intellect, and certainly not the lingering traces of Chomskyan Universal Grammar. Extended cognition implies that a language proficiency assessment isn't a measure of the amount of information stashed in a cerebral closet, to use Bain's disdainful phrase. It measures the adaptation of a person's whole nervous system, whole sensorimotor system. And distributed cognition implies that the assessment is a measure of something *beyond* the person being projected *back into* the person. It forces us to admit the artificiality of such measurement, while extended cognition, as habitus, likewise forces us to face the absurdity of giving a mark to a person's embodied history.

I'll end with a couple of recent developments within applied linguistics which you're familiar with, and which are pushing forward the agenda of extended and distributed cognition and language. One is the concept of *translanguaging*. For García,

> when describing the language practices from the perspective of the users themselves, and not simply describing bilingual language use of bilingual contact from the perspective of the language itself, the language practices of bilinguals are examples of translanguaging [...] [T]ranslanguagings are *multiple discursive practices* in which bilinguals engage in order to *make sense of their bilingual worlds*. (García, 2009: 45, italics in original)

García's implication, Blackledge and Creese note, is that 'bilingual families and communities must translanguage in order to construct meaning' (Blackledge & Creese, 2013: 127). The concept challenges, though it doesn't contradict, the concept of compartmentalised language knowledges. The multilingual brain could have separate grammars which it draws upon in its multiple discursive practices; but the very fact that multilinguals don't neatly separate their discursive practices by language is evidence that their knowledge of languages isn't compartmentalised. And that sits more comfortably with languages being embodied in habitus, as well as with it being distributed – because translanguaging depends on not just one speaker's linguistic knowledge. It occurs in a context where all or at least several of the discourse participants comprehend what is said in what traditional analysis would separate into different languages.

'Extended' cognition is used by some people to mean getting out of the skull and into the whole body, and by others to mean getting out of the body. That 'distributed' cognition isn't necessarily conceived in a bodily way, and when it is, the bodies taken into consideration aren't necessarily limited to human bodies. Zoosemiotics or biosemiotics has challenged the human-animal dichotomy since at least the work of Jakob von Uexküll in the first decade of the 20th century, and more recently 'posthumanist' theory has extended cognition to non-living bodies – in Bruno Latour's words, 'the parliament of things' (Latour, 1993; Von Uexküll, 1909). Posthumanist applied linguistics looks at how the things talked about, or included in the context but *not* talked about, play a role in the linguistic production that transpires in a given setting – such that their role, and the roles of speakers and hearers, cannot be neatly separated into agentive and non-agentive (see Pennycook, 2018). If something – some thing, or animal – in the situation compels an utterance, is it not the agentive subject, under which the speaker is acting in something like a passive way, or blurring subject and object roles?

Zoosemiotics: well, we've come full circle. You'll recall that the story began with Aristotle describing what aspects of language are shared by humans and animals. And he also mentions 'the objects which provoke the passions'. He's right up to date. As we pursue an understanding of what, if anything, it means to be a native speaker, or to engage in translanguaging, we'll eventually have to come to grips with what, if anything, it means to be human. Maybe it doesn't mean so much as we self-obsessed humans have always thought.

Thank you all for your patience. I know that not everyone finds these historical odysseys as intoxicating as I do; but I put to you that, in linguistics, the past is a second South – the place most linguists avoid, except for an occasional holiday to bring back souvenirs, or open a mine, a data mine, for nuggets they'll use to confirm that their North, the present, represents the universal, and is all we need to attend to seriously.

Discussion

Chanel Van der Merwe

Thank you so much, Professor Joseph, for a very insightful talk. Professor Makoni, you have the floor to start the conversation.

Sinfree Makoni

John, thanks a lot. I have a couple of questions but before I do that, I want to read back to you the first paragraph – the opening paragraph in your paper 'Extended/distributed cognition and the native speaker', because that, I think, captures what I am going to be talking about (Joseph, 2017). You write: 'Every concept, model, and technique devised by theoretical or applied linguists has its limits in terms of applicability and shelf life. It is futile to assess them simply as right or wrong. In the long run, to paraphrase Keynes, they're all dead wrong. What needs to be asked is: right or wrong for what? What does the concept, model, or technique make it possible to do, and, at what cost? Could an alternative one do it better, or at less cost?' That, I think, is the critical way of thinking about this. That, for example, if we say the native speaker, what is it intellectually that the native speaker allows us to think about, which other terms might not? Bearing in mind that we will come to a phase where we need to move beyond some of these terms, let me get back to issues about, let's say, translanguaging.

The interesting thing, given what you are talking about is this: is it possible that the notion of native speaker and translanguaging are incompatible? Is it possible that we now need to begin to think of the intellectual phase beyond translanguaging? Because as sure as the sun rises, there will come a time when we will forget that there was a discussion about translanguaging, in as much as we have forgotten that there was a phase we were all stuck up with communicative language teaching and all that. So, my first question to you is, is the notion of translanguaging and the notion of native speakers – are they compatible? Then I'll move on to the second set of questions. Thanks, John.

John E. Joseph

It depends which universe we're having this conversation in. Because in the universe of linguistics, the concept of native speaker has been shaped by a Chomskyan view that had – even before Chomsky, too; the structuralist view – that had no place for multilingualism. Multilingualism is marginalized, swept under the rug. It's a problem; we don't want to go there. So, the whole concept of native speaker is so strongly tied, historically, to a monolingual norm that – within linguistics – within theoretical linguistics, the answer to your question 'Are translanguaging and native speaker incompatible concepts?'; I think the answer is yes. They have to be. In applied linguistics, we've been more at the forefront of moving beyond that. Of course, we've been at the forefront of – you were actually Alan Davies' student, were you not?

Sinfree Makoni

I – yes, I was. [*Laughs*]

John E. Joseph

Indeed, yes. And so, you know how passionately he was trying to break that whole concept down, and I think succeeded to a large degree, so that applied linguistics is conflicted when it comes to the concept of native speaker. Because on the one hand, we have this legacy from theoretical linguistics that is very monolingual-focused, and on the other hand, applied linguistics is, by its nature, multilingual in focus. So, I think there's a kind of – more of a cognitive dissonance than an incompatibility.

Sinfree Makoni

Let me continue with you on this one. The issue, I think you're right, is that the notion of native speaker in applied linguistics, there's a bit of ambivalence there. Because, for example, Alan Davies would keep reminding me that you can't be sceptical of the notion of a native speaker, but still try to do research in second language acquisition. His argument was that the two just don't go hand in hand. Second language acquisition, somehow, he said – his argument was – buys into the notion of a native speaker. He then would argue that politically, then, second language acquisition as currently practiced, can only be oppressive. If, for example, you can never be a first language speaker, you can never succeed in becoming a native speaker. So, his argument would be, why then have, in a discipline like applied linguistics, an enterprise founded and indications of a sketchy nature from earlier centuries, but really, you have to get up until, well – I have to explain to my students at the beginning of every semester that, if they hear me say 'modern', I probably mean the 17th century, and if I say 'recent', I probably mean the late 19th century. But, it's absolutely the case: from the time that we have any indications of sign language, the bodily semiotics that's so central to sign language, is – how it's related to the semiotics of spoken language, is extremely interesting. There are clear points of overlapping contact, and I think, clear differences. But it can be controversial to talk about that because some people who work in sign language get nervous about talking about the differences, the unique features of sign language, while other people want to celebrate them, but it's a hugely interesting thing – aspect of this whole question, for sure. And I'm sorry that – you know, trying to plan this talk to fit within a 50-minute slot, I omitted to make any reference to it. I should have, though.

> **Comments from the chat box**
>
> **Maya Alkateb-Chami:** Thank you for this great presentation. Q: In the space of multilingual education, and certainly for those advocating for the teaching of children's first language before English or another dominant language is taught, the theories of interdependence of language development between different learned languages, and of common underlying proficiency are used. Could you situate the theories of interdependence of language development against the trajectory of the field that you shared with us?

Rafael Lomeu Gomes

Thank you. I will just include a comment, or call your attention to a comment, made by Miranda Anderson with a potentially relevant reference related to this question; and I'll move on now to ask the question posed by Maya. 'Thanks for the great presentation', and asks, 'In this place of multilingual education, and certainly for those advocating for the teaching of children's first language before English or another dominant languages taught, the theories of interdependence of language development between different learning languages plus of a common underlying proficiency model are used. Could you situate the theories of interdependence of language development against the trajectory of the field that you shared with us?'

John E. Joseph

Twenty years ago, I remember colleagues of mind who do second language acquisition having huge arguments about whether a bilingual person has one grammar or two grammars in their mind, or in their brain. And, again, because of the dominance of that Chomskyan native speaker model, they almost had to answer – if they were theoretically inclined, they almost had to answer – well, there have to be two separate grammars. And, to me, this seemed quite an expensive construct, as Sinfree read that quote for me, you have to judge a concept or a theory based on what it can do for you, but also on what it costs in theoretical terms, how expensive it is, how much faith it requires to sustain it, to keep it up in the air, and that idea of non-interdependence of language development, of separate language development, seemed to me to be one like the Hindenburg, you know, that Zeppelin that couldn't stay up, that finally fell to the earth. So, I think that, yes, the theories of interdependence of language development fit much better with models based on embodied or extended mind, and extended language and distributed language, than they do with the concepts that are still dominant in linguistics, that are based on the idea of a native speaker with a knowledge of language that's completely intracranial. I hope that's addressed the question.

> **Comments from the chat box**
>
> **Busi Makoni:** If experiences matter, can we then say we are a 'native' speaker of a gendered variety of the language you speak.

Rafael Lomeu Gomes

Then there is an intervention by Busi Makoni. 'If experiences matter, can we then say that you are a native speaker of a gendered variety of the language you speak?'

John E. Joseph

Well, I'm trying to get away from native, but I know what you mean. So, are there gendered varieties? I mean, should we talk about women's English? Men's and women's English? Is that the kind of thing you mean, Busi?

Busi Makoni

I don't know about English, but I know that in Nguni languages, there are gendered varieties like women's language of respect, or Isihlonipho, which is a women's variety. This is a variety which women use to show respect. And, as you transition into speaking other languages, I find, personally from experience, that it's almost constrained – what you can say – even in English.

John E. Joseph

I would say that – this is a difficult territory these days, because when I was growing up – where I grew up – the situation I grew up in, there were quite separate cultures of men and women. And there were language differences that were very clear, and I think that on the one hand, those cultural differences have shifted. And, again, as I was saying before, with people talking about sign language, taking strong stands either in favour of the differences with spoken languages or against there being any differences in spoken languages, I think it's a similar situation now when we talk about language and gender, and so, I'm reluctant to get into this off the cuff without thinking about it quite hard first. But insofar as you have experienced yourself these differences in language, does it make more sense to think of them as being something that connects to intracranial knowledge, or to embodied experience, something like habitus? I would say absolutely the latter. So, yeah, I mean, I think there's a story to be told there as well, about not just gender differences, but any sort of difference that can be related to experience and to culture, in terms of the body and the entire nervous system, and that that opens up potential for a much richer account.

> **Comments from the chat box**
>
> **Celeste S Kinginger:** Hello John! Thank you for the wonderful talk. The Bourdieusian perspective on learning that you describe seem quite consistent with the Vygotskian genetic approach to development in which, according to our Jim Lantolf 'the method is history' in various domains such as sociocultural history, life history/ontogenesis, and moment-by-moment learning. Do you see a link here?

John E. Joseph

And Celeste Kinginger. I see a message from Celeste Kinginger, whom I've known since we were children.

[*Warm laughter*]

Celeste Kinginger

Hello, John. It's so great to see you.

John E. Joseph

Hi, Celeste. And thank you; and yes, Vygotsky is somebody else who figures in my book quite prominently with references to Lantolf and others, as well.

Celeste Kinginger

The first time I heard of Bourdieu was in the Jiménez Hall of the University of Maryland, where we worked together.

John E. Joseph

Is that right?

Celeste Kinginger

And I met Lauretta Clough, your student who was translating the great work.

John E. Joseph

Yes, a student of mine translated a book by Pierre Bourdieu, and she went to see him in Paris with a long list of words. She was worried about translating them directly from French into English. And so, she sat down with her list and went through it, and he said, 'I don't care! What does it matter? You just do whatever you want to!' [*Laughter*] John, could you comment a little bit further about the resurgence of Bourdieu in your view? I'm aware that people generally turned away from him for the reasons that you have mentioned. I wonder if you could give us a sense of how you see the historical context for resurgence of interest.

John E. Joseph

There's a very interesting article that David Cram from Oxford wrote. I think it was 2007 in *Historiographia Linguistica* about 'ebb tides' in the history of – not just the history of language study, but of any scientific field, where when somebody's work makes a big splash and becomes controversial, then almost inevitably, there's a falling off (Cram, 2007). That's the 'ebb tide', and it's predictable that, over time, the things that were appreciated in that person's work will be revisited and reappreciated. So, I think that's a large part of it. I think the other thing is that the reaction against Bourdieu was also driven by a very particular context having to do with Marxism. Bourdieu considered himself a Marxist, and he said, if Marx were writing today, he would argue against Marx. He would argue with himself, and he would look for new positions, and he was a person who looked at the world around him and took account of how the world changed. But for the Marxist establishment, they weren't having that; they wanted their Marx 'pure'. And that created a very strong rejection of Bourdieu in his native country, but also in many other parts of the world – and over the nearly 20 years since his death, a lot of that has changed; a lot of that has abated, and I think that's a part of it.

But a couple of years ago appeared the *Oxford Handbook to Bourdieu* (Medvetz & Sallaz, 2018) and you know that whenever one publisher publishes a handbook of something, every other publisher does as well. So, that's the part of why I think there's a resurgence happening, of interest in him; and I hope a revisiting because I meet so many people who 'know' – who think they know Bourdieu, having made up their mind about Bourdieu years ago. And they made up their mind about why they don't want to go there; and I say to them, 'Just try to forget what you "know", and go back and reread, and you might be surprised.'

Rafael Lomeu Gomes

Thank you. It's great to see how this forum brings people together that go way back. Next up, there is someone with the screen name 'Salikoko Mufwene', but I suppose it's Cécile Vigouroux.

[*Laughter*]

Cécile Vigouroux

Thank you. Yes, obviously, I'm not Salikoko Mufwene.
[*Laughter*]

Sinfree Makoni

Not yet.
[*Laughter*]

Cécile Vigouroux

Not yet. I'm not sure I will ever reach that point. Anyway, so, thank you very much, John, for your wonderful talk. I've got one comment and one question. So, regarding Bourdieu, I think we need to acknowledge that the ways in which his work has been received in the English-speaking world has been influenced by the ordering in which his books have been translated. And if you look carefully at the ways in which his work has been translated in English, this hasn't been done in the order in which the books were published. So, that's why, when you follow the order in which the books were published, actually, you see how his model developed; and there is no contradiction of the kind that people have generally claimed; and that's one of the big problems. So, my question is about habitus: I agree with you that there is agency in the habitus, but one of the problems that people, especially sociologists, have raised about habitus is that it doesn't account for the ways in which the habitus can change social structures. Okay? So, of course, there is agency, but if you take habitus and apply it to language as social practice, how do you account for the fact that habitus may actually be a vector of change for language? And how do you reconcile that?

John E. Joseph

Well, I would say that – but is there any less of a problem if you take a mental grammar approach to knowledge of language? Does that make it easier to answer that question? About how – is this not Saussure's problem that, you know, language change, Saussure says, begins in *parole* – happens in *parole* – and some of them get into *langue*. Through this mysterious process that no one understood, and no one still understands. And I think that, given that the idea of a mental grammar has had 60 years or more, well, let's say 100 years, to try to give us the answer to that question, and has failed, why don't we give habitus a chance? Because, as I say, linguists have not really used it much. They've not applied it much to that sort of problem. I don't know that it will help with that really fundamental and intractable problem, but I just don't see this as better than the alternative. The other thing is – I mean, you said that sociologists make this objection, and again, Bourdieu wasn't really a sociologist. He did read sociology once he got appointed to a chair of it, but he found more things to reject or to contest than to follow.

But particularly, I think, what I find him saying is, before we try to answer questions, before we try to think about social structures, before we try to really understand social structures, we need to understand ourselves first of all. We need to look – the direction has to be from understanding the individual to understanding the social structures, and that's not what your average sociologist does.

Cécile Vigouroux

Yeah. No, I – just a follow up: I'm fully in favour of habitus, and I've been using it in my own work. I'm just trying to see what kind of limits it may have imposed on understanding language dynamics, including language ideologies and stuff like that, but I'm fully in favour of habitus as a meta-term. Thank you.

Comments from the chat box

Maya Alkateb-Chami: The distancing away from Bourdieu might also be linked to his inferred disengagement with colonialism in his work. Recently, some scholars have been re-reading Bourdieu's work from a postcolonial perspective; for example, Edward Said on Bourdieu:

> The Arabs of *La Peste* and *L'Etranger* [by Albert Camus] are nameless beings used as background for the portentous European metaphysics explored by Camus... Is it farfetched to draw an analogy between Camus and Bourdieu in *Outline of a Theory of Practice*, perhaps the most influential theoretical text in anthropology today, which makes no mention of colonialism? (Said, 1989: 223, as cited in Go, 2013: 49)

John E. Joseph

There's a comment from Maya. There are a couple of comments about colonialism. I'm puzzled by this, because Bourdieu's work actually comes out of colonialism; it's all about colonialism and particularly his experiences in Algeria and the war in Algeria, and his early work is all about that. It figures in everything – in all the work that he did. I think *Outline of a Theory of Practice* – I'll have to revisit it. I mean, Edward Said, of course, would not make a mistake like the one indicated in Maya's comment.

Maya Alkateb-Chami

I agree that in his early work, he spent some years in Algeria and wrote about the colonial context, but then in his more theoretical work around capital, symbolic violence, etc., he does not really centre colonialism, which I think might have caused – or been part of the cause of this reaction of distancing away from Bourdieu. He also had an interesting tension with Fanon. I've recently come across some scholarship trying to resituate Bourdieu from a post-colonial perspective and talk about his trajectory. I'll put a reference in the chat.

> **Comments from the chat box**
>
> **Maya Alkateb-Chami:** Go, J. (2013) Decolonizing Bourdieu: Colonial and postcolonial theory in Pierre Bourdieu's early work. *Sociological Theory* 31 (1), 49–74.

John E. Joseph

Please. Please do. Yeah. I just want to say – I'm sorry, I'm looking up my paper here, just to see – all right. The opening chapter of the – I thought it was *Outline of a Theory of Practice*, but maybe it's another book. One of his most famous books from the end of the 60s, the whole opening chapter is about colonialism and Algeria. And so, I'll go back and check on this and send you a message as well, but thanks for that reference. I think the other thing that he does is to – I think he tries to show how a colonial mentality – how colonialism also exists within the global north. And he was doing that at a time when other people *weren't* doing it – within France, even, between the north and the south. So, my initial reaction is that this is an unfair charge that's being laid against him, but I will follow these things up and get back to them.

> **Comments from the chat box**
>
> **Robin Sabino:** The Arawak are said to have provided an extreme example of linguistic gender differences.
>   **Cristine Severo:** Thanks a lot for this fascinating presentation. One question: do you see the possibility of framing this discussion differently if we consider the existence of other genealogies of knowledge. For example, African, Asian or Indigenous concepts of mind or consciousness?
>   **Desmond Odugu:** Thanks, John, for this helpful conversation. Could you say more about Cristine Severo's question about other genealogies of knowledge? (Thanks, Cristine!)

Rafael Lomeu Gomes

Thank you. We're reaching the end of our talk, so I was thinking of perhaps asking the three final questions/comments, and then John can select how to go about them. So, I'll start from the question asked by Christine, which can be somewhat related to this last topic. 'Thanks for this fascinating presentation. Do you see the possibility of framing this discussion differently if we consider the existence of other genealogies of knowledge? For example, African, Asian or indigenous concepts of mind or consciousness?' So, this would be one question, and then a comment from –

John E. Joseph

Let me answer that. Yes. Absolutely, and hugely important – hugely important work, too. Go ahead.

Comments from the chat box

Diane E Larsen-Freeman: I think part of the problem in Applied Linguistics is the use of the term 'second language acquisition,' which among other things reflects a commodification view of language. I have suggested 'second language development' to challenge the NS endpoint of the interlanguage continuum.

Rafael Lomeu Gomes

Yes. A comment by Diane Larsen-Freeman: 'I think part of the problem in applied linguistics is the use of the term "second language acquisition", which among other things reflects a commodification view of language. I have suggested "second language development" to change the native speaker-as-endpoint of the interlanguage continuum.' Would you like to comment on it?

John E. Joseph

I totally agree, and I try to do the same and sometimes cite you on that, Diane. It's an important thing to do. It's one of those things, though, you know, where you've got a field that is established under that name, so it's not as if you can't actually use the term – set the term aside completely.

Diane Larsen-Freeman

Yes, but it is habitus, and if we work together, we can in fact change it. For example, my colleagues at the University of Pennsylvania accepted my request to rename their course, 'Second Language Development.'

John E. Joseph

All right, all right. I hereby resolve that I will no longer use the term 'language acquisition'. Just 'language development'.

Diane Larsen-Freeman

I'm with you, John. Thanks for the talk.

John E. Joseph

But we have – our master's program in that area is the MSc in Developmental Linguistics, so language development is mostly what we do – but there are some journals that need renaming. Maybe that ought to be the battle front. *Second Language Acquisition*, and so on.

Diane Larsen-Freeman

Yes. Yes. Happy to have you join me in the campaign.

John E. Joseph

All right, all right.

Rafael Lomeu Gomes

I mentioned there were three interventions, but another one just came up. So, there are two now. One is from Deyanira Sindy Moya Chaves, who asks: 'How can we understand variation within a language itself from your lens?'

John E. Joseph

I think – let me look for the question here. Sorry.

Rafael Lomeu Gomes

It's 4:13. Well, my time. It's 14 minutes ago.

John E. Joseph

Okay. I don't see it, but that's okay. So, um, variation. Language variation. I think that sociolinguistics has always struggled — I'll be interested to hear what Salikoko Mufwene has to say about this — I think sociolinguistics struggled from the beginning with trying to reconcile itself with an intracranial, universally based grammar concept of language. And there's been very interesting work on Labov's various attempts over the years, to try to stay in line with that conception, even when some of his most prominent students were trying to move away from it. And there was an article by a former student of mine in *Language & Communication* a couple of years ago, Johannes Woschitz, which I can recommend to people; it's a very good study of that particular angle to the question. I think that when we're talking about – you know, variation – the word variation is like acquisition. It's a problem in itself. Just talking about variation suggests that there is something that is core and solid – you know, theme and variations – that the variations are not what's ultimately real.

And yet, it's a tough term to get away from, again, so we try to talk about variability of language, rather than language variation. And again, I think that a move towards an experience-based – maybe distributed cognition approach to language opens up new ways of thinking about what gets called language variation, new ways of analysing it, that get us out of some of the corners that you get painted into when you're working from the theoretical concept of an intracranial grammar. And I see a hand up.

Rafael Lomeu Gomes

Mufwene?

John E. Joseph

Yes.

Salikoko Mufwene

Yeah. Now, this is Salikoko Mufwene. Thank you very much for a thought-provoking presentation. I just want to articulate a rejoinder to your answer about variation. I think that in sociolinguistics, two kinds of variation have been conflated; the variation within the individual when they speak and the variation across individuals. And sometimes, people try to keep the variation between the individuals clear, but there are times when people overlook the fact that variation within the individual speaker is not tantamount to variation across individuals. And if you become a dialectologist, then you add another kind of variation: variation across groups, and these are things that have been difficult to sort out. But I think part of this is the fact that variation in sociolinguistics itself is predicated on the notion of communal grammar, which, in fact, Chomsky has also conflated into one – that if you study one individual, you have studied the whole population – but that is not necessarily true. And somehow somebody has to sort these things out. My own attitude has been that – unfortunately, this is all a consequence of linguistics being developed at the time of Newtonian physics, and not at the time of the theory of emergence – that if linguistics had developed at the time of the theory of emergence, people wouldn't have rushed to, for instance, interpret competence as system. And I think that's one of the things that you highlighted in the beginning in contrasting competence with habitus.

But then, that would take me again to the question – the comment that Cécile made, and you answered it adequately – whether if you substitute one term for another, you would explain why things happen. And Chomsky has not told us how competence develops, and that – you deal with habitus – Bourdieu didn't have to explain how habitus develop. And you read Chomsky, you wonder whether Chomsky really meant that it must be constant, immutable. And the same question arises with habitus. Does it have to be constant, immutable? And these are open questions, and I think that the more we pay attention to the theories of emergence, the more we realize that these notions can be questioned and rearticulated differently, and maybe there is a way of bridging them. I don't know. Because people focus on different facets of language and they talk about – they emphasize some aspects of language, but not all relevant aspects of language. That's the contribution I want to make. Thank you very much.

John E. Joseph

Thank you. I would just say on that one question – Bourdieu is very clear that habitus is not constant, that habitus changes as we go through life, even if there's a sort of intense period of sedimentation early on. Whereas, with Chomsky, you're a native speaker from the age of four, and anything that happens thereafter is trivial. So, there is, I think, a big difference there. Maybe it's a difference of degree rather than kind, but it is a difference.

Salikoko Mufwene

Well, my take is that the competence that you develop as a child and makes you a native speaker of a language must differ from the competence that a person develops in a language as an adult, because if you already speak a particular language, when you learn the next language, there are transfers that you may make from the previous language, and it's not going to be the same thing. But what Chomsky didn't factor in at that time, or he didn't talk about, first of all: if you acquire two languages concurrently and you are therefore a native speaker of two, are the systems separate? (That's another issue that you brought up.) Or do they overlap? And my hunch is that, if at the time people discussed these issues, instead of doing linguistics on paper they had done it on a computer, then people could have thought of a tagging system. The same system, but you have tags that tell you, 'This goes with this domain; this goes with this other domain. You're talking to this individual.' And things like that. So, these are things that we really haven't revisited well enough to be able to take clear positions on them.

John E. Joseph

Yeah. Yeah.

> **Comments from the chat box**
>
> **Susan Coetzee-Van Rooy:** Yes. If the systems overlap – where does that leave one with concepts of second language, variation etc.
> **Salikoko Mufwene:** The overlap does not entail concomitance.
> **Susan Coetzee-Van Rooy:** What would it mean if genealogies of knowledge across people are the same? What would it mean if genealogies of knowledge across people are different?

Rafael Lomeu Gomes

Thank you. And as we are passing a great time and phasing into our after-party, there are just two more questions. I face this dilemma all the time during the discussions because the discussions get richer and richer and – 'I can't stop it now, sorry.' So, there is Ashraf who would like to ask a question himself. And also, there is Desmond Odugu, who asked if you could say more about Christine Severo's question about other genealogies of knowledge.

Ashraf Abdelhay

Hello. Thank you so much, Prof Joseph, for this very interesting presentation. I remember when I was doing my PhD under the supervision of John, I was met with the following dilemma: how to deal with the notion of language rights without falling into the trap of the 'native speaker' as it is conceptualized in the mainstream linguistics? And I remember John directed me to a way which was very productive, and it involved addressing the issue of language rights not through the construct of the 'native speaker' but through the notion of habitus. Rethinking the issue of language rights from the perspective of the habitus was a turning point, because I ended up with a different understanding of language rights: it is a very interesting way of de-essentializing the link between language and ethnicity, particularly in contexts of conflict.

The point here is that we need to delink the notion of native speaker from the individual's mind and race, and to reframe it from the perspective of social practice and experience. Conceptualizing the 'native speaker' in this way could help us settle many contradictions outside the Global paradigm of language. For example, in the Arabic traditions of language the construct of 'the native speaker' is not viewed as oppressive because it is entangled with social practice. In fact, in the Arabic classical tradition of language, the term 'native speaker' does not exist. It is not there at all. Most importantly, the 'standard language' itself was constructed mainly by non-native speakers. Sibawayh, who is now considered the 'founding father' of Arabic grammar, is of a Persian origin.

John E. Joseph

Thank you, Ashraf. And, I agree, and that's very enlightening. And I just wouldn't go so far as to say it solves it – but offers a path out of that trap.

Rafael Lomeu Gomes

Thank you. Before passing on the word to Makoni to wrap up the conversation, Desmond, would you like to – ?

John E. Joseph

Sorry. Was it Cristine who wanted me to say more about framing the discussion differently if we consider the existence of other genealogies of knowledge, Africans

– ? Again, the answer is absolutely, yes. I do. I do some of that in my book. I don't do as much as I would like to do, and there's a lot to be done. I'm trying to – when students look for projects to do, this is the sort of thing, sort of direction that I push them into, particularly if they come already with the knowledge of the genealogies in question, because it's not something that you can pick up easily or readily, and my own is – I have a smattering of knowledge in some of these areas and not I think enough to do serious work on the African, Asian, indigenous concepts of mind and consciousness that needs to be done. And when work appears that is doing that, I'm delighted to take the first opportunity to look at it. And there is some work of that nature in not only the book Sinfree is co-editing, to which I contributed the preface, but the other 300 books that Sinfree's co-editing or writing at the moment. The work that you're doing, Sinfree, is, I think, contributing hugely in that regard. But I think I'm being asked to give an example of something, and I would like somebody else to do that for me who is more qualified, more deeply knowledgeable of this, to give me an example of how an African or Asian or indigenous concept of mind and consciousness could help us in reframing these questions in another way.

> **Comments from the chat box**
>
> **Cristine Severo:** Actually, 'Yes' is definitely an inspiring answer.

Rafael Lomeu Gomes

Did you raise your hand, Desmond? No? Okay.

Sinfree Makoni

Desmond, do you want to ask your last question before we wrap up?

Desmond Odugu

There is no additional question here. Thank you, Professor Joseph, for reawakening my earlier sojourns in philosophy. This is interesting. Thank you.

Rafael Lomeu Gomes

I saw that Sangeeta raised her hand.

Sinfree Makoni

Okay, Sangeeta.

Sangeeta Bagga-Gupta

I thought I was the last one on the planet to have learned that in Sanskrit; there is a word and I've forgotten it. So, this is a big apology, but this is what you do when you say 'mind' [*places hand on heart*]. I was thinking of that when you were talking of how cognitively we are framed, and this is the mind [*places hand on heart*], so that also helps you kind of trouble the very essentialistic and Eurocentric way of understanding the dissociation between mind and body, but I'm not an expert. I just came across this a couple of months ago, and I thought that was very enlightening.

John E. Joseph

This is in my book as well, but it's also part of the Greek tradition as well, because Aristotle, whose father was a physician and Aristotle himself took part in dozens, if not hundreds, of anatomical dissections of not only human corpses, but of living animals – vivisections, to see the operation of the body. And through all of that experience, Aristotle determined that the mind is located in the heart. Plato, who never had any medical knowledge whatsoever, never saw inside the human body, determined that the mind is in the brain. And people found that hard to believe because the brain is a cold organ. Aristotle's reasoning was that the heart, because it is warm, and sends fluid throughout the body, the heart must therefore be the mind: it must be the center of it all, where the things that we think or desire, then get translated into muscular action. The brain has fluid in it, but it's all contained, and so on. But it's ironic that the Western tradition, both medical and philosophical decided, at some point, about not quite 2000 years ago, that it is the brain.

Sinfree Makoni

To sum up, this is what we are going to be doing moving forward. The first five sessions by Chris Hutton, John Boughey, Monica Heller and Bonnie McIlhinney and Kwesi Prah are going to appear in a volume that we have edited, published by Multilingual Matters. So, as far as the publication of this series is concerned, we are just starting. So, at least, we now have one volume that we are going to be handing over to Multilingual Matters at the end of the month. Then we'll move on to another set, so that ultimately you'll have the YouTubes, you'll have the transcripts, and you'll have the volumes from all these conversations. Then we also have a series of books that are coming out soon; there's a handbook on Language and the Global South that is more or less complete now. We are just waiting for Boaventura de Santos and my other friend, Ana Deumert, to write the concluding note and the preface, but we have got most of the chapters ready and a couple of other projects that are more or less finished. For example, Ana Deumert and myself have finished now another volume called – I can't remember the title – *Decolonizing Sociolinguistics*, which is more or less finished.

So, in a sense, this is going to be quite a bit of reading that is coming out from all these activities, and I must say that it has really been exciting to work on all these projects and to engage with all of you. John, thanks a lot for your wonderful presentation. And I'd like to thank everybody else for their participation.

> **Comments from the chat box**
>
> **Rafael Lomeu Gomes:** Thanks everyone for your very interesting and generative questions and comments!

Notes

(1) Variants of (c) and (d) which take the internal part to be intracranial rather than internally extended are logically possible and may be held by some, but I have not encountered them.

(2) Two powerful correlations between parts of the brain (Broca's and Wernicke's areas) and types of language loss were established in the 1860s and 1870s and still have to be memorized and reproduced by first-year linguistics students today. In so doing, the students continually re-establish the faith that language is located in the brain and is further localizable within it. But linguistics is not such a historically-oriented discipline that students would be made to memorize these 19th-century discoveries if there were more recent ones of a comparable generalizability. The exceptional nature of Broca's and Wernicke's areas is camouflaged by the paedagogical role accorded to them, which matters because the idea of brain localization adds greatly to the scientific allure of linguistics, as it already did when Saussure made a point of including Broca's area in his lectures on general linguistics (see Joseph, J.E. (2012) *Saussure* (p. 575) Oxford: Oxford University Press). The actual messiness and unpredictability of what happens where in a single brain, let alone across brains, needs to be swept under the rug if one is to persuade funding agencies and university administrations that unprecedented progress is being made in scientific understanding of language and the brain, which implies findings that apply to everyone – whence some of the resistance to extended and distributed approaches, though not all of it.

(3) Trans. from Cyril Bailey, *Epicurus: The Extant Remains* (Oxford: Clarendon Press, 1926).

(4) An example is St Thomas Aquinas (1225-1274), *Summa theologica* 1, 107, 4: 'The angel's speech consists of an intellectual operation, as is apparent from what has already been said (1, 107, 1–3). The angel's intellectual operation is entirely abstracted from place and time: for our intellectual operation too takes place by abstraction from the here and now, except accidentally through phantasms, which do not exist in angels' (my translation).

(5) Augustine, *De Genesi ad literam* (Literal meaning of Genesis).

(6) Dante, *De vulgari eloquentia* 1.1: 'We learn the vernacular without any formal instruction, by imitating our nurses' (my translation).

(7) They are right, although arguably the 'real' Descartes is the more widely-held legend rather than the textually accurate one. Baker & Morris accept that it is the Cartesian legend that matters historically.

(8) Davies's was a rare voice articulating demurral from the Chomskyan consensus; his efforts were perhaps more hindered than helped by the idiosyncratic, self-published Thomas M. Paikeday making similar arguments about the quasi-racist undertones of the native speaker concept (*The Native Speaker Is Dead! An Informal Discussion of a Linguistic Myth with Noam Chomsky and Other Linguists, Philosophers, Psychologists, and Lexicographers*, Toronto & New York: Paikeday Publishing, 1985).

(9) In addition, situated cognition aims to create a balance between cognition as computation and what it calls the affective dimensions of mental/bodily experience. Some of those working in situated cognition, like those in extended mind, draw inspiration from Maurice Merleau-Ponty (1908–1961), as do others discussed in the next paragraph.

(10) The instrumental vs integrative motivation distinction established in the 1960s was a way of saying that the chances of success in L2 learning increase as the learner feels the L2 as part of his or her *identity*, rather than just as a tool to be used for communicative purposes (see Bonny Norton, *Identity and Language Learning: Extending the Conversation*, 2nd ed., Clevedon: Multilingual Matters, 2013). Casting it in terms of instrumental vs integrative is a reductionist way of putting it, because the dichotomy is often a false one: is a person who is striving to master English in order to get into Harvard Medical School doing this for instrumental purposes, if in fact her projected self as a future physician holding a prestigious degree is central to her personal identity? But the point remains that the 'classic' conceptualization of the native speaker turns the integrational/identity-based drive, the key to success in language learning, into a mug's game. Learners can't win it, though to add injury to insult they can potentially come close enough to the goal to let them turn into oppressors, or accessories to oppression, of other L2 learners who are not quite as good at the mug's game as they are.

References

Amsler, M. (2011) *Affective Literacies* (pp. 270–272). Turnhout: Brepols.
Wierzbicka, A. (1972) *Semantic Primitives*. Frankfurt: Athenäum.
Bain, A. (1875) *Mind and Body: The Theories of their Relation* (p. 91). New York: D. Appleton & Co. (Orig. publ. 1872.)
Baker, G. and Morris, K.J. (1996) *Descartes' Dualism*. London: Routledge.
Blackledge, A. and Creese, A. (2013) Heteroglossia in English complementary schools. In J. Duarte and I. Gogolin (eds) *Linguistic Superdiversity in Urban Areas: Research Approaches*. Amsterdam: John Benjamins.
Bourdieu, P. (1990a) (orig. version 1980) *The Logic of Practice* (trans by Richard Nice). Cambridge: Polity, in association with Blackwell, London.
Bourdieu, P. (1990b) *In Other Words: Essays towards a Reflexive Sociology* (trans. by Matthew Adamson). Stanford: Stanford University Press.
Bourdieu, P. (1990c, orig. version 1994) *Practical Reason: On the Theory of Action* (trans. by Randal Johnson *et al*). Cambridge: Polity, in association with Blackwell, London.
Bourdieu, P. (1991) *Language and Symbolic Power* (ed. by John B. Thomson trans. by Gino Raymond & Matthew Adamson). Cambridge: Polity in association with Basil Blackwell.
Braine, D. (2014) *Language and Human Understanding: The Roots of Creativity in Speech and Thought*. Washington, DC: Catholic University of America Press.
Cestaro, G.P. (1997) Dante, Boncampagno da Signa, Eberhard the German, and the Rhetoric of the Maternal Body. In B.D. Schildgen (ed.) *The Rhetoric Canon*, 175–197 (p. 186). Detroit: Wayne State University Press.
Chomsky, N. (2006) *New Horizons in the Study of Language and Mind*. Cambridge: Cambridge University Press.
Chomsky, N. (2007) Of minds and language. *Biolinguistics* 1, 009–027 (p. 12).
Cottingham, J., Stoothoff, R. and Murdoch, D. (1984) (Trans.) *The Philosophical Writings of Descartes*, vol. 2. Cambridge: Cambridge University Press.
Cottingham, J., Stoothoff, R. and Murdoch, D. (1985) *The Philosophical Writings of Descartes*, (trans. by J. Cottingham, R. Stoothoff & D. Murdoch), vol. 1, Art 351 (p. 339). Cambridge: Cambridge University Press.
Cramm, D. (2007) Shelf life and time horizons in the historiography of linguistics. *Historiographia Linguistica* 34, 189–212.
Davies, A. (1991) *The Native Speaker in Applied Linguistics*. Edinburgh: Edinburgh University Press.
Davies, A. (2003) *The Native Speaker: Myth and Reality*. Clevedon: Multilingual Matters.
Davies, A. (2013) *Native Speakers and Native Users: Loss and Gain*. Cambridge: Cambridge University Press.
DeCasper, A.J. and Spence, M.J. (1986) Prenatal maternal speech influences newborns' perception of speech sounds. *Infant Behavior & Development* 9 (2),133–150.

García, A. (2009) *Bilingual Education in the 21st Century: A Global Perspective*. Oxford: Wiley Blackwell.
Gee, J.P. (1992) *The Social Mind: Language, Ideology, and Social Practice*. New York: Bergin and Garvey.
Gee, J.P. (2004) *Situated Language and Learning: A Critique of Traditional Schooling*. London: Routledge.
Gibson, J.J. (1966) *The Senses Considered as Perceptual Systems*. Boston: Houghton Mifflin.
Hartley, D. (1837 ed.) *An Enquiry into the Origin of the Human Appetites and Affections, shewing how each arises from association, with an account of the entrance of moral evil into the world. To which are added some remarks on the independent scheme, which deduces all obligation on God's part and man's from certain abstract relations, truth, andc. Written for the use of the young gentlemen at the universities*. Lincoln: Printed by W. Wood, and sold by R. Dodsley, at Tully's Head, in Pall-Mall 1747).
Hebb, D.O. (1949) *The Organization of Behavior: A Neuropsychological Theory*. New York: John Wiley & Sons.
Joseph, J.E. (2017) Extended/distributed cognition and the native speaker. *Language & Communication* 57, 37–47.
Joseph, J.E. (2020) The agency of habitus: Bourdieu and language at the conjunction of Marxism, phenomenology and structuralism. *Language & Communication* 71, 108–122.
Krashen, S.D. and Terrell, T.D. (1983) *The Natural Approach: Language Acquisition in the Classroom*. Hayward, CA: Alemany Press.
Lakoff, G. and Turner, M. (1980) *Metaphors We Live By*. Chicago: University of Chicago Press.
Latour, B. (1993, orig version 1991) *We Have Never Been Modern* (trans. by Catherine Porter (pp. 142–145). Cambridge, MA: Harvard University Press.
Lescourret, M.-A. (2008) *Pierre Bourdieu: vers une économie du bonheur* (p. 139). Paris: Flammarion.
Maturana, H.R. and Varela, F.J. (1987, 2nd edn 1993) *The Tree of Knowledge*. Boston: Shambhala.
Medvetz, T. and Sallaz, J.J. (eds) (2018) *The Oxford Handbook of Pierre Bourdieu*. New York: Oxford University Press.
Montesquieu (written c. 1734-9, first publ. 1892) Essai sur les causes qui peuvent affecter les esprits et les caractères. In Mélanges inédits de montesquieu. Bordeaux: G. gounouilhou; Paris: J Rouam & Cie.
Mulholland, J. (2013) *Sounding Imperial: Poetic Voice and the Politics of Empire, 1730–1820*. Baltimore: Johns Hopkins University Press.
Pennycook, A. (2018) *Posthumanist Applied Linguistics*. Abingdon: Routledge.
Renan, E. (1858) *De l'origine du langage*. (1st ed., 1848). Paris:Mitchel Levy freres
Rumelhart, D.E., McClelland, J.L. and The PDP Research Group (1986) *Parallel Distributed Processing: Explorations in the Microstructure of Cognition*. Vol. 1: Foundations; vol. 2: Psychological and biological models. Cambridge, MA: MIT Press.
Said, E.W. (1989) Representing the colonized: Anthropology's interlocutors. *Critical Inquiry* 15 (2), 205–225.
Thompson, J.B. (1991) Editor's Introduction. In P. Bourdieu (ed by J.B. Thompson) *Language and Symbolic Power* (trans. by G. Raymond and M. Adamson) (pp. 1–31). Cambridge: Polity.
von Uexküll, J. (1909, orig. version 1991) *Umwelt und Innenwelt der Tiere*. Berlin: Julius Springer.

5 Keywords for India: A Conceptual Lexicon for the 21st Century

Peter de Souza and Rukmini Bhaya Nair

Peter Ronald de Souza

There's this wonderful critique by Chinua Achebe of Joseph Conrad's *Heart of Darkness*[1] where he highlights the contrast in Conrad's description of travel down the two rivers, the one in England and the other in Africa (Achebe, 2016).[2] What were purportedly just descriptions of people, places, activity and nature were in fact, perhaps subconsciously, descriptions that reinforced the subconscious bias of the white man's burden, between the savage and the civilized., that we have to struggle with. The second is invisibilization. A lot of what the post-colonial has to deal with is that their stories and their narratives, have disappeared from dominant discourses, have been invisibilized. Much of this happens because of the practice of historical erasure. The colonial authorities erased records, erased practices, erased cultural memories. There's this classic book by Ian Cobain, *The History Thieves* (2017) that details how the records of colonial rule in large parts of the colonial world, this particularly refers to English rule, were ordered to be burnt or dumped in the ocean so that they would be unavailable as testaments of the brutality and disingenuity of colonial rule. So, erasure and amnesia were instruments of colonial rule. I come from Goa, which was part of the Portuguese colonial that had to endure the Portuguese strategy, within the larger civilizational landscape of India, to connect us with Europe. Disconnect us from India, connect us with Europe. Erasure. And, of course, this whole process – this multi-pronged attack of the colonial state in the colonial period – resulted in what a Bengali philosopher K.C. Bhattacharya has famously called 'the enslavement of minds' (Bhatttacharya, 1954). Now, it is *this* 'enslavement of minds' that we need to fight because it persists. Even though political colonialism has ended, intellectual colonialism persists. It persists, as Said says in his book *Orientalism* (1978) through the hegemony of certain frameworks. It persists in terms of the dominance and the persistence of the epistemology of the North.

How does one respond to this formidable fortress of intellectual domination? I mean, your platform is one attempt at breaching that fortress. It's a formidable fortress. Just a few books and a few articles here and there don't really do very much: we have to breach that fortress. And I certainly see – and I'm sure Rukmini shares my view – that one way of breaching that fortress is through language. So, when

Rukmini invited me to be part of her project – this was *her* conceptual [project]; *she* conceptualized it – when she invited me to part of the project, I joined in because I saw, okay, this was an opportunity to, in a sense, use language to breach the fortress of hegemony of the Global North. And we did that by identifying concepts. So our book, even though its genealogy links it with Raymond Williams' (1976) work, has this uniqueness. It has 200 contributors, submitting 250 entries, organized along seven rubrics. And the concepts range from high-level concepts to mid-level concepts, to fun concepts. And you will see from the Table of Contents, which has been circulated, that what we have done is to identify and include a set of concepts that don't meet at the conditions of the high table of conceptual discourse in the Humanities and Social Sciences. These are not concepts that appear in discussions at international seminars or when we go to give great books lectures, or when we discuss the canon. These are concepts that are rooted in certain cultures. These are concepts that are rooted in certain histories. These are concepts that carry a baggage of meanings, which we think needs to be made available, not just to an Indian audience – because remember, we are hegemonized by English – but needs to be available to a global audience. Why not? Let me give you an illustration.

There's a word *jootha* in our *Keywords* book (Nair & de Souza, 2020). *Jootha* means food which is contaminated by the touch of a person considered inferior. It's a terrible, very offensive word in Indian cultural practice. But if you have access to that word, you can, in a sense, through that word, come to understand the whole structures of domination and exclusion and oppression that has been a part of the Indian cultural landscape. Take another example, a fun word like 'time pass.' Now, it seems like an English word; I'm sure to audiences all over the world it would sound like, 'What does 'time pass' mean?' Time pass, in the kind of everyday cultural space in India, is about just spending time doing very little... Perhaps gossiping. So, we've got that as well, in our lexicon. Now, how do we do this? So, if one way of breaching the fortress is to think of language, and to use language as a sort of battering tool, and to do that by identifying a set of concepts from our linguistic spaces – like, I suppose, if you were from Africa, you would talk in terms of Kagisano in South Africa, you would talk of Ubuntu in Southern Africa. So, there are concepts all over the world which need to be brought into the seminar room of Humanities and Social Sciences to flatten the asymmetry of power.

How did we do this? We did this by adopting a four-part strategy. We did this with a very clear idea that we will infiltrate the comfort zones of the hegemonic conceptual universe of German, French, English, Latin. We'll do that by introducing into that hegemonic world concepts from the Indian linguistic space, concepts which are high-value concepts, such as *swaraj*. I mean, it hasn't acquired the same kind of conceptual weight as the concepts of freedom or liberty and yet, it has a nuance which needs to be uncovered because it has many layers of meaning. *Swaraj* merits the same degree of analytical scrutiny, to uncover these meanings, as liberty and freedom have received over the centuries in the Western intellectual history. When that it done it will receive its merited place in the global philosophical lexicon. Or, take for example another rich concept, *izzat*, which means honor, dignity. Again, it comes from the Persian linguistic zone, from where it enters through Urdu into the Indian cultural space. It too covers a range of meanings that I think Humanities and Social Sciences need to use because, I want to suggest, the HSS space does not adequately represent us, our philosophical and cultural world if such representation is only in the European languages. It does not capture the meanings that we think are significant. So, *infiltrate* is strategy number one. Strategy number two is to *elevate*: to take concepts from our world and give them respectability. So, for example, *jhanjhat*. *Jhanjhat* means troublesome. Our strategy is to give it respectability. Why do we have to always use English or French words when we have words that enjoy wide currency in India like Jhanjhat.? Third, is to *appropriate* words which have the provinence in English, or Portuguese, and give them Indian meanings. So, from Portuguese would be *susegad*, or *saudade*. But see how they have new meanings in the Goan landscape. Similarly, from England, you would take a word like 'tension', or 'file', and infuse it with Indian meanings. You will see that in our lexicon, I hope. Some of you had an opportunity to see that. And the fourth strategy is to *populate*.

So, if we *infiltrate* the conceptual universe with Indian concepts, if we *elevate* Indian concepts to a certain respectable status in the Humanities and Social Science discourse, if scholars begin to use Indian phrases – instead of saying, for example, 'It was a Herculean task,' we could say, 'It's a Hanumanian task.' Now, those of you who know one of the great Indian epics, Ramayana, will know that Hanuman was this very powerful, very strong devotee of Lord Ram. So, one can begin to complicate and challenge the comfort zones of Northern epistemologies if we *infiltrate*, *elevate*, *appropriate* concepts from there and make them Indian concepts such as tension. Tension is a wonderful word. It has an English origin, but it is used in *all* the Indian languages. *All* – and you know, India is a very pluralinguistic space – and it has the same meaning in all the languages, because it has now acquired a kind of folk ownership of the concept. Then we will be able to, in a sense, get the community of Humanities and Social Sciences outside their comfort zone. I believe this may be happening. This may be happening in North America. I mean, let's call it – if I could use a metaphor, let's call it, you know, a certain kind of jazz radicalism in language. Can we make language break out of the classical formats, one is trained into, in terms of idiom, vocabulary, grammar, and make it speak to the lives that we come from? I'll end on that note and hand it over to Rukmini.

Rukmini Bhaya Nair

Like Peter, I want to begin by thanking Penn State for inviting us to speak at this African Studies Global Virtual Forum on Decoloniality and Southern epistemologies. Peter has already spoken to you about the various strategies for decolonization, and the way in which he sees our recent collaborative work in *Keywords*. As he's just pointed out to you, this work drew on the scholarship, enthusiasm and expertise of a *very* large collective of over 200 Indians – who were not all academics, but who were all deeply absorbed in the history and the epistemology of words that they wrote on. But, speaking for myself, I have to admit that when I saw the Penn State 'African Studies Virtual Forum' rubric for the first time, I asked myself, 'What on earth can someone like myself, whose life and whose experiences of language are so vastly different from that of, say, speakers of Swahili or Xhosa, let alone a phalanx of other languages and cultural heritages on the African continent, have to contribute to an Africa-led debate on decoloniality?' There was already so much richness present in the African critique. So, I was puzzled enough to go back to the drawing board and ask myself: 'What is the epistemic state of decoloniality? Is it, in fact, a state of mind, a social process, or some species of complicated hybrid production?' Now, asking myself these sorts of naïve questions in the bold and bare-faced way that I've just posed them has for me, at any rate, something of the absurdity, but also the imaginative, fantastical stretch, of that old Superman formulation: 'Decoloniality? It's a bird, it's a plane. No, it's Superman!' And, in my view, a view that I've strongly advanced in the Indian *Keywords* volume we are discussing today, is that we should never, as theorists, repeat the colonial trope of thinking in terms of any sort of 'civilizing mission' – even if it's one in which we deeply believe. Taking on the omniscient, rescuing role of a Superman is not just accepting a *trope* – it's entering a *trap*. Decoloniality cannot afford the guise of a Superman – or even a Superwoman! Indeed, as I maintained long ago in one of my books, *Narrative Gravity*, as far as I'm concerned, even Nietszche's towering ur-Superman is actually a fragile construct of affixes –subs, -metas, trans-es, alters, pseudos, -uns, -semis, etc. So, my first proposition today, in trying to discuss the idea, not of post-coloniality, but of *de*coloniality or decolonization is, unsurprisingly, that we need to make a concerted attempt to consider subjects and objects that have long been – via powerful hegemonic social strategies such as those produced by colonialism or caste – just part of our *peripheral* vision.

For example, consider our current political stances in India where the rich histories of the Mughal period, from the early 16th to the 18th centuries in our subcontinental history, are being erased and confined to exactly such a peripheral vision; and, as a consequence, tremendous insights from our syncretic pasts are being lost.[3] For example, I've recently been reading the Akbar Nama, a detailed court history of the reign of the Mughal emperor Akbar by the scholar Abul Fazl ibn Mubarak (1897-1910), whose ancestors hailed from Yemen right across from the Horn of Africa. Abul Fazl[4] tells us that Akbar conducted a remarkable linguistic experiment back in the 16th century. What Akbar wanted to find out, perhaps partly because India was just so linguistically multifarious: what would be the first language in which infants spoke? So, what he did was to not so much imprison as keep locked up (a fine distinction, I know!) a group of babies, complete with wet nurses, food and everything else. However, he instructed their wet nurses never to *speak* to the children because he wanted to find out what that 'first language' might be. After four years he then went back to the Gan Mahal, or the 'Dumb House' as it was called, on the 9th of August in 1582. And the next day, the 10th of August, he went to what's was also interestingly referred to in Fazl's record as 'The House of Experiment'. But no cry, says the text, came from that house of silence, nor was any speech heard there. 'In spite of the four years, they heard no part of the Talisman of speech, and nothing came out but the wailing of the babies.' Now, a tale like tells us a lot about the history, the complex linguistic history, within which we undertook a project like *Keywords*. Of course, it goes without saying that we cannot conduct such experiments today – but I want to maintain that there's much that we can learn from this past experimental spirit with regard to language and culture – if only we *looked* in these directions. I believe such retrievals from a historically peripheral vision are an important aspect of decolonization. Colonial regimes have always tried to live by strong forms of structural binarism: self and other, ruler and ruled, illiterate and literate, savage and civilized and so on. And this is absolutely to be expected because these categories are so seductively obvious, their combinatorial properties so marvelously well-ordered. The difficulty with the structuralist paradigm has always been its seemingly 'neutral' binarism and this is precisely where critical race theory and other such theories could provide us with valuable lenses to look at, for example, apparently impartial legal structures that nevertheless erase the long histories of suppression and subjugation to which Peter has already drawn our attention.

It is this crucial idea of *context* that we need to bring back into the discourses of decoloniality. Part of my own argument concerning decolonization, one which I've discussed at length in many other places, is that the contextual materials neatly left out, excised from structural analysis, including narrative analysis – the Nietzschean subscripts, the paras- and alters- as it were – have turned out to be far more cognitively instructive than one might reasonably expect. Thus, when our publishers asked me a few years ago if I had a book in mind for them, I said to them – yes, I did indeed! But rather than yet another self-authored book, perhaps we could take a risk and invest in a multivocal 'keywords' book – a book that paradoxically combined focused vision with peripheral sight. Further, we could *only* engage in building such a collaborative volume if the contributors were mostly Indian – not for chauvinistic reasons, but because these were people who were the long 'subalternized' masters of the Nietzschean subscripts.

Our contributors had the experiential basis, that interior knowledge of emotional residues, that could only come from living within the day-to-day common rooms of vocabulary that the subcontinent experimented with on a quotidian basis. Peter has mentioned many of these words, like 'tension' and i*zzat* and *jootha* to you. It was in fact through such a granular process that we were actually able to include, in our *Keywords* book, categories and words that had never before been included in any keywords volume, including Raymond Williams' absolutely amazing book.

For instance, we were able to introduce the three categories I'll mention here: one, *material culture words* such as *chulha, balti, chappal*. *Chulha* means an oven of sorts – a 'wood-oven' which poorer women across India routinely cook on but which can severely damage their eyes and lungs. *Chappal* means slipper – but in India, cultural custom often decrees that you leave these everyday objects outside the door when you enter a home. So why are chappals left outside in this culture– is it for reasons of hygiene, to mark an inside-outside boundary, to show respect? My point is that even though such everyday material culture words seem insignificant at first, they actually come packed with all these small hidden subscripts, these tiny cultural notes that open up huge interpretive apertures.

We were also able to include *acronyms* such as VIP/VVIP – which I know is one of Peter's favorite entries! In my view, acronyms of which there were few in the pre-modern world, but which really came into their own with, among other economic forces, the spread of multinational corporations in the 19th and 20th century, are great indicators of what 'modernity' is – its hidden economic and social subscripts. Today, every society has its own acronyms. A third category not included in earlier 'keyword' books, were commonplace *borrowings* from the English, alongside the 'high value' words that Peter mentioned such as 'democracy', 'climate change' and 'social media'. This third category constitutes a tactic, if not a high-level strategy, for democratizing the linguistically colonized, dominated by English, hierarchy of languages that we still have in India. We have, that is, English at the apex of the postcolonial language pyramid, then we have the high classical languages of India – and then we have a large base of languages that constitute an oral-continuum that aren't well documented at all. Ideally, documenting this flux of oral forms that show up as 'subaltern' material culture words; as acronyms; and as incoming borrowings across the Indian languages such as the recent words 'tension', 'gym', 'adjust' and 'beauty parlor', enables a whole new take on what sort of a phenomenon the 'postcolonial' is.

I have argued elsewhere – and not entirely in jest! – that when the British departed India, they left us with three morally ambiguous gifts with whose effects we're still struggling in our attempts to decolonize. These were what I call the 'Magic Mirror of Pakistan' a distorting glass into which we still look and witness our emotions not always accurately reflected; the 'Seven-League Boots of the English Language' that allow us to travel vast distances across the globe, but which still burn up the soles of our feet; and lastly the 'Wondrous Labyrinth of the Indian Bureaucracy'! Now, Peter and I were both born into a newly independent India, which was in the throes of reimagining itself as a nation state. Given this odd history of inheriting a colony governed in English for the past century or two, one of the first acts of the newly minted Republic of India was to redo the map of India as a conglomeration of linguistic states, each with its own language (today we have 22 official languages!). Their vision then was to retain English just for 15 years until these 'other' languages of India regained the strength sapped by the dominance of English. Well, that has conspicuously not happened. English is still around as an 'official' language 75 years after India gained independence in 1947. As I see it, this is one of the great ironies of our subcontinental history – and I wish we could compare this to other postcolonial histories in various parts of the globe! – that we now have to grapple with. How we should deal with the aspirational role that English plays in our country today as a lifestyle, a lifeline and, some say, 'a killer language'?

So, just to summarize after this long-winded opening salvo, I would like to offer my own linguists' list of four tentative, deliberately small-scale, tactics for decolonization. The first of these is to try and retrieve the meanings that attach to the *fragments of language* that often escape our attention. Such 'ordinary' fragments that have long belonged to our extraordinary peripheral vision but have almost been erased by the hegemonic power of English and an excruciatingly hierarchical social system might include words like *maya*, *tamasha* and *gaon* (all in our *Keywords* book) and their vast collocational ranges – affixes, presuppositions, prepositions, complements etc. These words can be retrieved through the forensics of sharp-eyed grammatical analysis. It is important to embark on the details of this 'local' investigation in all decolonizing societies to retrieve our twin senses of longing and belonging. A second tactic would be to attend closely to discourse forms that are part of the *orality-literacy continuum* in India but that have largely been ignored in conventional linguistic theorizing – forms such as narratives, riddles, proverbs, conversational conventions. Third, the pair of tactics suggested above would, I believe, give us excellent training in *listening* to others with care. Such listening in to the debates in other 'decolonizing' cultures with humility, with respect and with patience, is likely to enable reliable and trusting cooperation in the long run. In short, we need to train ourselves, via a myriad, small acts of decolonization, to persistently knock on the doors of languages *other than* the superior colonial languages of 'the west' – or, as Peter would say, the Global North. Fourth, we have to be *diachronic* in our stances. That is, we have to remind ourselves that each word, each 'key' word, encapsulates innumerable spooled threads of memory. At the same time, synchrony should remain an important aspect of our theory of decolonization especially at a time like the present when we are in midst of a major technology-driven communication revolution. I've talked a lot about this in my introduction to the *Keywords* volume – about the technological genie released into the world that now seems to have the power to alter our embodied forms of being and our cognitive processes, to force all of us to reassess the intricate relations between language and memory, interaction and emotion.

Well, those are some prescriptions – but I want to end on a personal note now, with a childhood memory that came back to me when we received the poster for this seminar just a few hours ago. The poster announced clearly that it was the aim of the present forum to 'challenge the notion of universal truth'. This reminded me of the work of the 'ordinary language' philosopher J.L. Austin who is a founding figure in my own field of linguistic pragmatics – and this is what he wrote: *Under the heading 'truth', what we have in fact, is not a simple quality nor a relation, indeed, any one thing, but rather a whole dimension of criticism* (Austin, 1962). So, as 'decolonizers', we have, of course, to study the canon, keywords etc. in our postcolonial settings, but we should also perhaps look at the work of people like Austin, comfortably ensconced in their Oxbridge ivory-towers, who were also, ironically, trying to build arguments against a monolithic understanding of 'truth' in their particular cultures. Austin goes on to say: *there's a lot of things to be considered under the dimension of truth: the facts, yes, but also the situation of the speaker, his purpose in speaking, his hearer, questions of precision, and so on.*

So here again, we return to the theme of the *fragment*, this time the *fragments of truth* as they are to be recovered in postcolonial circumstances. As it happens, I'm currently working on a book on deception, that other face of the truth, and I wanted at this point to briefly tell you the story of my 'first lie' because I think it brings out some crucial features of what decolonization ought to imply. When I was about four years old, I was sitting outside in the verandah (another word of Portuguese origin included in our book) with the person who helped around the house, Medina. My parents were inside the house playing scrabble in English. Meanwhile, we had an argument, Medina and I, about whether the time of the day was the evening or night. Now, I said it was night, and Medina said it was evening. To resolve our dispute since neither of us had more than a smattering of English, Medina suggested: 'Why don't you go inside and ask your parents who actually know English?' So, I did this, and my parents said: 'Well, of course, it's evening.' But I went back and told Medina that they'd said it was night! This, to my mind, was a specifically linguistic story about vocabulary substitution – *and the guilt of it has never left me*. All the emotions of guilt and moral ambiguity; of language hegemony – my parents spoke English, we did not; of class; of historical inheritance; of memory; of unequal power and access – neither Medina or I knew English but we both sensed its overweening importance; of alienation; of the 'inside' versus the 'outside' – all these chilling effects were something that could be visited even on a four-year-old child and her adult interlocutor in a postcolonial state. And I sincerely believe that some of these dilemmas remain with us still, which is why bringing together our 'keywords' was like an adventure, a wonder, a voyage of discovery that made us see the world anew in terms of these basics of language categorizations. Thank you – and I'm breathlessly done for now!

Magdalena Madany-Saá

Thank you so much, Dr Rukmini Bhaya Nair, and thank you, Dr de Souza. So now, I invite you to ask questions to each other about things that *haven't* been said, and maybe things that you were not even expecting in this question, right? So, let's enjoy this moment of interaction.

Rukmini Bhaya Nair

I see. Should I go first?

Magdalena Madany-Saá

Of course.

Rukmini Bhaya Nair

Thank you. Let me begin with a very small question, some fragmented thoughts – and then we can build up to a real fight! By the way, one of the things I most enjoyed about putting together this book was the forceful arguments Peter and I had throughout. Anyhow, I wanted to ask Peter about the very first word that he mentioned today – *jootha*. He explained this word as one where you don't really eat from a plate or drink from a glass which has been used by a lower caste person. True enough – but we need to understand who that 'lower caste' person is in our society. And then we need to understand whether the system of caste, the structural system of caste is general enough to be applied elsewhere as well – in America, for example. As some of you will know, the American journalist Isabel Wilkerson has recently written a bestselling book starkly titled *Caste,* in which she has claimed that 'caste' is perhaps the most apt framework to discuss the positioning and historical humiliation of black people in the USA. Here she seems to be in agreement with Louis Dumont, who studied the phenomenon of caste in India and declared: *Caste is a state of mind*.

What is this state of mind and how does it pertain to decoloniality? It is in this connection that I wanted to say to Peter: for me, *jootha* means drinking from anybody's glass, or eating from anybody's plate – it could be an American's, it could be a child's. *Jootha* does not necessarily imply eating or drinking from the vessel of a lower caste person. The constraint is more universal. It applies to all humans. In my own case, I was trained from childhood not to touch anything touched by the lips of another. Caste is part of this, but it's not necessarily the main constraint. There is a larger, deeper pollution complex at work across Indian culture. Peter made his interpretation of this word caste-related – and he is not wrong. What's interesting to me, though, is how the powerful idea of caste has, to use Peter's word, 'infiltrated' all these other practices which may be independent of caste and has somehow made them even more lethal, more dangerously hegemonic. In short, even a concept like *jootha* which is to found everywhere in Indian culture can be interpreted very differently, can provide the grounds for varying and foundational arguments about meaning. Peter thinks of the meaning of *jootha* essentially in terms of caste; I don't. I think of it as a still underanalyzed practice that's part of an overarching pollution schema relating to embodiment. Can Peter now explain to me why he explained this keyword in terms of caste?

Peter Ronald de Souza

Okay. Thank you, that's a good entry point for us to have a friendly quarrel. Right? Now, I chose the word *jhootha* quite deliberately because I wanted to signify to the community that's listening to us that through that word, one can enter the structure of social stratification in Indian society. The system of social stratification carries with it, not just a system of superior and subordinate social terms, but carries with it deep cultural meanings, and those cultural meanings constitute relationships of power. Those cultural meanings inferiorize. Those cultural meanings make some superior, make some inferior. And therefore, they have created a whole body of practices and spaces in which people are located and are expected to remain. So *jhootha*, largely used in the context of food and water, basically refers to this cultural edifice of domination and inferiorization. In that sense, it shares a commonality with cultural domination and exploitation in other societies as well. You know, race – it shares a commonality with race, it shares a commonality, say, with the segregation of towns and cities. So, having said that, the description that you have given, is you've referred to it as, in your mind, being primarily or being significantly or predominantly hygienic –

Rukmini Bhaya Nair

No – *polluting.*

Peter Ronald de Souza

But polluting, with reference to cleanliness, with reference to – that if you drink from somebody – that is not the case, because remember, there are cultures in many parts of the world where everybody eats from a common plate. You know, in West Asia, in large parts of the world, people eat – I mean, there's a common plate and everybody's joining in and sharing. So, why does the concept of polluting carry such a traction in India? It carries traction in India because it comes from a certain structure of social stratification and its accompanying cultural practices, which then get embedded and then acquire a certain fixity in social life. Because it's not a universal truth. It's not a universal practice. So, I think that's the point – and then it gets glossed over with hygiene, and cleanliness, and other things. But it's ultimately a cultural practice of domination and exclusion.

Rukmini Bhaya Nair

That's a really enabling thought about the cultures of West Asia – and also many communities in India – where people all eat from the same plate. Still and all, Peter, I just wanted to say that when I chose this word initially for our *Keywords* book, I did so because I thought that it shared an important intersection with the idea of *truth* which I was talking about earlier. Now, this is a linguistic point which is to do with the phonology of two words that sound very close to each other. The first is is *jootha*, which is the word we've been discussing so far at great length, and the other word is *jhoota* where the aspiration is on the first syllable – and this very common word means 'untruthful' as you well know. So, even mispronouncing the word *jootha* slightly leads you to a grave moral conundrum. It's just a phonological difference, a tiny phonological difference – but how interesting is it that *jootha*, which involves the pollution complex and – of course, as you, Peter, have rightly reminded us, a social hierarchy – is just a phoneme's breath away from *jhoota* which mean a *liar*! And, to me, Indians are able not only to understand the pollution complex and the hierarchies associated with it – whether it originated with the high caste, or wherever it originated – but are able to reflexively *play* with this pair of terms. They are able to pun with it. They are able to use them to reflect on the notion of truth. This a huge advantage in any culture. And that is why I think that being an insider within languages, and knocking on the doors of languages which are not our own is so important – because we are then able to see how delicate and malleable and trans-mutant the being of language is across cultures. In talking about 'keywords', I think we need to always bear in mind that there's a huge, enabling element of play, of phonology, of lexicology, of parallels, subscripts and so on in the process of unravelling them. So, Peter, now you can ask me a question. As for me, I think it truly rewarding that this discussion about the simple word *jootha* has brought us to important ideas about pollution, caste and sociality as well as to another really important word – untruthfulness.

Peter Ronald de Souza

I think it's wonderful that you've made that wonderful distinction between pollution and untruth. You know, in that sense, it underscores once again the value of our keyword project, which is what we were trying to do. You know, that – if you were to just use the word polluted and untruth, you wouldn't be able to capture all the meanings. And therefore, as an anthropologist or as a sociologist, if you want to describe India, it would make more sense to use the words *jhootha* and *jootha* than to use the word untruth or pollution. So that point, I think, has gone home. Now, let me ask you another question, because, you know, since we are speaking to this very interesting platform. Mine is not a derivative question, mine is: do you think our project, do you think something that we've attempted – because, you know, there were moments when we thought it was an impossible project – you know, trying to get entries from all the Indian languages, the recognized Indian languages and from different cultural zones, recognizing that it will be non-representative and could never be comprehensive. But we have succeeded; we've got a volume out. We've got something that the world can see, and hopefully, be excited by and maybe even replicate. Do you think other language zones – like regions of, say, East Africa or West Asia – do you think they could do something similar? Do you think this project can travel? Because why should it be seen as just an exotic Indian exercise? Why can't we have this global collaboration, which can really shake the citadel of dominant languages?

Rukmini Bhaya Nair

That's an important observation, but there have been so many keywords books, right? This is by no means the first one. So, one of the things we have to understand is that the idea of a keyword has itself traveled extensively from when it was initially mooted by Raymond Williams. Williams, as I say in my Introduction, did *his* keywords project because when he came back from the war – World War II, that is – one of the things that he noticed was that people were using words like 'democracy' or 'freedom' quite a bit. But he remarked – he was talking to a friend as this thought came to him – that while people were still using the same words, they were using them in a *completely different way* from the way they were used before the war. And that – that mapping of the moment in language when things change radically was very important – and continues to be so. For example, I started noticing in the 1990s, that people globally began to use words like 'outsource' and 'public-private partnership' and 'liberalization'. These were words that were then unfamiliar to my ears. A few years later 'outsource' was linked to 'crowdsource' and such other forms. Then, the word 'meme' started to be extensively used. This was a term I was actually familiar with from Dawkins' 1970s work in evolutionary studies – but it was not then in the common sphere (Dawkins, 1976). Suddenly, though, the word 'meme' was everywhere. This is a simple example of how words are incorrigible travelers, boundary crossers. India, of course, has a huge lexicon of words borrowed from the English, and English has taken in hundreds of Indian words. Likewise, the cultural lexicon that we have presented in our keywords project has already traveled. Today, it's traveled to Penn State! What we have to really think about now is whether our sort of experimental project can really travel even further to nations, societies and cultures which are currently seeking to decolonize. And if they can, what are the particular features that our book has to offer that add up to something more than a scholarly record of shifts of meaning? Broadly, I think our book is equipped with the wings – or wheels – to get to others interested in such verbal experiments for three or four reasons – and I highlight the idea of experimentation here in line with what I said earlier in this discussion about Emperor Akbar's 16th-century language project.

The first experiment has to be one, as we've both emphasized, in *cross-cultural communication*. Can we bring together groups of people just to discuss sets of words, as you have so kindly allowed us to do today in this Penn State forum? Also, can we borrow Peter's notion of *elevation* to bring into everyday usage humble words like *chappal* alongside 'big' words like *ahimsa* (non-violence) which Gandhi made so famous and Martin Luther King and others conceptually borrowed in the form of non-violent resistance? *Chappals* (slippers), for example, have to be left outside the house, as I mentioned, in Indian homes – so at another level of analysis, do they also contribute to a 'deep' notion of pollution? Or take the word *sari*. Everybody associates this word (which we have in our volume) with the women of India – but do they know its etymology? Do they know its structure? Our keywords book pulls at these skeins. In short, we have collaboratively gathered and folded these everyday material cultural words into our book hoping they can generate a deeper discussion about the meaning of cultural decolonization. This is so because words like these are a measure of the everyday lived experience of societies which are uniquely different those inhabited by the colonizing nations. Borrowings are particularly critical in this respect because then we can compare them across all the societies colonized by a particular power, say the British. The last thing I wanted to mention in this connection was what Fanon (1963, 1993) said, looking again at the Hegelian master–slave relationship. Fanon insisted that what the colonial master wanted from his slave was not the 'recognition' that Hegel craved, but *work*, sweated labor. So, you know, we could argue somewhat arrogantly that the nature of labor – intellectual labor – is being a little bit rewritten through projects like ours. If we can come to some sort of agreement about the types of labor we put into future keywords projects, the types of words which we might want to concentrate on, the types of collaboration we want, I think this project will travel, will spread its wings. Otherwise, I think – maybe not. And so, we live in hope and anticipation – and also with nervousness, if not fear. We don't really know what's going to happen. All that can be said at the moment is that we've put our effort out there – and it does contain provocative elements which no other keywords book contains. Perhaps *this* could be a deliberate decolonizing move, a work of travelling theory...

Peter Ronald de Souza

Now the discussion can travel to Makoni. I think we've taken up enough time.

Magdalena Madany-Saá

Yes!
[*Laughter*]

Sinfree Makoni

I have a couple of comments but let me begin by thanking you for putting together these keywords from all India. When I was reading your work, my favorite words were the word file and the word call, because I could, from an African perspective, understand the notion of file – that if you go to a bureaucratic office, if your file is not there, it's more or less like you don't exist, so to speak. So, in a sense, what I'm trying to make, at a very pedantic level, is that, yes. What you have got are keywords from India, but it's possible that they may overlap with certain conceptual meanings in other geographical regions, as well. So, it would be quite interesting to have a follow-up project which uses some of your concepts but tries to see how those words play themselves out in a different region, for example. Because, at the moment, by focusing on India only, you by default create an impression that this is just uniquely an Indian phenomenon, but if it were to be a decolonial project, it would be interesting to see whether, in actual fact, these words and meanings have similar meanings in different parts of the world. In West Africa, for example, Southern Africa, or even in South America. Then, the other part that I found quite interesting, which I wanted to discuss with you, is this: let me quote the statement that was made by Peter towards the end of his epilogue. He says this: 'We see our book as belonging firmly in the literature or the politics of knowledge, as it seeks to partner many attempts to flatten the knowledge asymmetries between the North and the South. It has subversive intent, it seeks to disturb the regular vocabulary of Social Sciences and Humanities and to disrupt the flow of communication between the North and the South.' Right. Now, my question is this – then you proceed: 'It seeks to upset the complacency of scholars within their language is adequate to the task of representing their world of inquiry. It seeks to suggest that the language is deficient, and that new words and concepts are required.' My question to both of you is, how far successful did you think you got? To what extent were you successful in accomplishing these noble objectives?

Rukmini Bhaya Nair

Peter, you made that claim, so now you must be the defender of the faith!

Peter Ronald de Souza

Well, see. First of all, the exercise has just begun. The book is only a year out, and COVID has overtaken its dissemination, but having invitations like yours – and we have had the opportunity to discuss the book in Basel, Switzerland, and in three locations in India. So, what we have attempted here is new even to India itself. So, it's already beginning to give a sense of confidence to scholars who come – and I'll use a metaphor – scholars from outside the metropolis, and by metropolis, I mean, those who have studied within the language zones of the dominant languages. That's beginning to happen. You know, democratization of knowledge in India has brought in scholars from language areas where there is no English, where there is no French, where there is no Portuguese; and they are beginning to offer idioms, they are beginning to do things with grammar that were earlier frowned upon, and earlier treated as inferior, and now they are beginning to get respectability. I mean – how successful? It's a long project; and that's why I deliberately asked Rukmini the question.

Hopefully, we can hand over the baton to you and *you* can run with it within *your* community, because I think this has to be a collaborative exercise. Ours was the first. 200 authors – you said it gives the impression that it only works for India, but you must remember, India is a subcontinent. It pretends to be a nation state, but it's much more than that. So, when these words are introduced into the cover of a book, people in other language zones get quite excited. So already – if you want to measure success – we have requests from two language zones in India, who want to do something similar in their language zone. In Northwest India, there has been a request that – 'We'd like to come up with 100 words, which cover both India and Pakistan. [This is the kind of Punjabi-speaking area of West –] And we'd like to come up with the keywords for that region.' A similar request has come up from South India, from a region Karnataka, saying 'We'd like to do something similar.' Now it's not a – and we are nobody to give permission. We only have produced this book, and we know that this is just a showcase, that it is possible. So, if other regions of the world, whether Latin America – I can see my friend Lynn Mario over there; 'Hi, Lynn.' So, if he picks it up and runs with it in Brazil, we'd be delighted.

Sinfree Makoni

That would be good.

Peter Ronald de Souza

You know, I mean – that's it. It's the beginning of what I hope – when I say, we'll force the dominant Humanities and Social Science community out of their comfort zones, I was hoping that when we go to seminars, we will use words without translation. You know? So that they are expected to know these words. If they are going to be writing about India, I don't have to say Jootha and then put [polluted], or jhoota and put [untruth.] They must know these words. It must be part of any seminar presentation initially of India but later, hopefully, of the world. That's the point I want to make.

Sinfree Makoni

Okay.

Rukmini Bhaya Nair

Can I add something?

Sinfree Makoni

Yes, you can add something. Then I will ask another question, and then we can move on.

Rukmini Bhaya Nair

The only thing I wanted to add here – Peter has already spoken about how people have been enthusiastic within India about participating in this project, and we do hope that the model can spread – but the other thing that I worked at quite hard in this volume was to set up a kind of template for *how* to write a keyword. Raymond Williams hardly touches on any of this practical stuff, nor do other keywords volumes. In our book, though, we offer a step-by-step guide to writing a possible entry beginning with the vexed notion of 'etymology'. Then, we set up these seven rubrics such as 'Emancipatory Imaginaries', 'Economic Mantras', 'Cultural Intimacies' and so on. Here again, is a potential chance to discuss matters of decoloniality at both the 'micro' as well as 'meta' levels of enquiry. That is, we should be able to clarify whether our template for writing a keywords text works in other cultures. If it does not, why not? There is a heuristic here, a working process for understanding the valence of words that we have tried to think through in this book. If we use terms of reference which are not word-related, but structure-related – or theme-related – could this help collaborative cross-cultural ventures in the future? This could be important when we think of keywords ventures in relation to processes of decolonization. I'd want to remind ourselves that templates, categories, heuristics, these sorts of low-level things are also important when discussing the viability of a keywords project in any society.

Sinfree Makoni

Okay. If I can continue with that, when I was reading your keywords, one of the key issues that kept coming back to me was that, frequently, the contributors will try and attribute the origins of some of the words to Sanskrit, for example. As I tried to apply that framework to another context, I kept asking myself, 'What about in contexts in which you don't have a language that might have the same status of Sanskrit? What rubric or template would you give your contributors?' How would you ask them to write the etymology of these words? In India, because of the presence of Sanskrit, you could eventually go back to Sanskrit, so to speak. But there's no language that occupies a similar slot, like Sanskrit, in Africa, that I know of at the moment.

Rukmini Bhaya Nair

Can I answer this question?

Sinfree Makoni

Yes, sure. Yes.

Rukmini Bhaya Nair

When we embarked on this book, I thought very hard about whether to include in our template the notion of etymology as Raymond Williams had so meticulously done for each of his keywords. In our case, I think about half the words in our book *don't* have a Sanskrit etymology. So, of the 250 or so words we have included, maybe over 100 don't have a Sanskrit etymology. And here, again, one has to return to the notion of hierarchy – namely, that some these high-level words have a Sanskrit etymology. But on the other hand, a word like 'democracy' does not, and democracy – the entry is by Peter – is a central word in our book. So, you know, we've included lots of non-Sanskrit, even non-Indian words. *Tax*, which comes from the Latin, does not have a Sanskrit origin; VIP does not. So if you actually make lists, and I did make several for this project, many of our words come from, let's say, a Portuguese origin like *verandah* or *susegad* – or from some other non-Sanskritic origin.

Back now to the question of etymology: when children learn language, Sinfree, as you know well, they have no idea of the etymologies of the words they are acquiring, right? This does not deter them in the least, they acquire language anyway. But when we get into academic garb, we realize that a word, as I said earlier, is encapsulated memory. People often want to know: where does this word come from? – just as they are hungry for answers to the evolutionary question: where did *we* come from? But the deeper problem you raised, Sinfree, is what if you don't *have* etymologies at the ready. or simply cannot access these origins because they are 'off-record'? I think that's a critical observation – what if we can't track a word back? To which I say, 'So what?' Children learn words without etymologies. We acquire languages, new languages, without etymologies. I think etymologies are fascinating, but they are probably the least important of the social moorings of a word. Many of the European languages track back to Latin or Greek; we in India can sometimes return to the Sanskrit – but that is simply what I'd call contingency or happenstance. I don't think that etymological rootedness is part of the core meaning of any word. The core of a word lies in its semantic import, its everyday pragmatics, its contextual nuances in terms of language negotiations, its capacity to provoke the sort of vital, public disagreements that Peter and I had today over the word *jootha*. The bottom-line for me is no, it's not so important. If you don't have an etymological spoor for a word – well, leave it out.

Sinfree Makoni

Leave it out. Okay. Let me stop there because I'll come back later on. Who is coming in next? Lynn?

Magdalena Madany-Saá

Yes, thank you, Makoni. Lynn Mario, over to you. Thank you for having a question.

Lynn Mario de Souza

Thank you, Peter and Rukmini. I think it's wonderful, what you've done. And considering your last comments, I'd like to recuperate something from Rukmini's introduction, which is linguistic incontinence, Rukmini. Which I think is an important notion to us in language, as many of us on this platform are looking at. We're trying to decolonize linguistic theory, which has imposed – which is basically Eurocentric and has imposed on us notions of language as bounded phenomena. And, Rukmini, it's curious – this is something which relates to Peter, as well – when I was at the IIAS, Peter, thanks to you, I discovered the work of Lachman Khubchandani, which the IIAS has published; and one of the things that – he makes a critique of Eurocentric sociolinguistics by saying that multilingualism in Europe has got nothing to do with multilingualism in India. Multilingualism in Europe sees languages as $1 + 1 + 1$. He gives us arithmetical formula, and he says in India it's more like $1 \times 1 \times 1$. So, the sum of $1 \times 1 \times 1$ is 1, meaning no languages – the languages are indistinguishable, whereas $1 + 1 + 1$ gives 3, which is a European notion of multilingualism. Meaning they are distinguishable distinct languages. So I think that linguistic incontinence is extremely important as a decolonial strategy.

And, as you said, Rukmini – you wondered if decoloniality is a state of mind – I would say, from a Latin American perspective (my colleagues here on this platform may be speaking from different, African perspectives, for example); from a Latin American perspective, in which colonization involved settlers coming in and then taking over as natives, we have this whole notion of culpability. So, culpability, here, is part of our decolonial strategy; it's where the dominant class in Brazil, which sees itself as colonized, are also the colonizers. So, the first step in decolonization in Brazil is to recognize oneself as an agent of colonization, right? *Before* you can embark on any decolonial activity here. Now, coming back to the linguistic incontinence, the two things which also appear in the work of Khubchandani, when he talks about the plurilingual ethos in India: he says the plurilingual ethos in India involved two aspects; one is synergy, which means collaboration, and the other is serendipity, which involves chance. So, both of these together – and, Rukmini, I'm not sure if it was you or if it was you, Peter, who gave the example of when you're in a chai store, listening to what's going on around you?

Rukmini Bhaya Nair

I did – in my intro to *Keywords*.

Lynn Mario de Souza

It's these two things which come into play. There has to be a collaboration in wanting to understand what the other person is saying. Right? And, the second aspect of serendipity is chance. There's nothing that will guarantee whether you do understand or not. But, when you don't understand, you *pretend* to. Because the important thing in collaboration is the sentiment, the feeling, right? And this is something we have difficulty, in linguistics, in dealing with. And this brings me back to the idea of the keywords themselves. So, keywords, unlike dictionaries, are not instruments of normatization. Right? Dictionaries were. So, when you mentioned if etymology should come in or not – etymology definitely comes into standardizing dictionaries, normatizing dictionaries. Right? And what my reading of your – and I'd be interested to see if you agree or not – my reading of your keywords is that – is this play? It's as if you're reversing the colonial strategy in India of the Brits wearing mufti and going native, right?

Rukmini Bhaya Nair

Yes. 'Matthew Arnold in a sari', we used to call it. [*Laughs*] Yeah.

Lynn Mario de Souza

What you're doing in English is exactly the opposite, right? You're going mufti in the corridors of Buckingham Palace. So, what's happening there is you're offering your keywords, not as an instrument of normatization, but an opposite. You're saying, in spite of the fact that we are giving explanations to these words, which you probably don't understand, you're introducing a level of opacity in their hegemony, which is saying that, look – and this is a decolonial strategy, especially in Latin America – we are not trying to, as what post-colonialism did, we are not trying to simply substitute a more truer representation, or a false representation which the colonizers had of us. What we are trying to say is that all representations are produced in context.

Rukmini Bhaya Nair

Yes.

Lynn Mario de Souza

So, there are localized bodies behind the representations. So, what you are trying to do is basically, what I call, mark the unmarked. You're trying to denormatize the whole process of existent hegemonic normatization. I'm not sure if you agree with me or not. Thank you for listening.

Sinfree Makoni

Thanks a lot.

Rukmini Bhaya Nair

I'm dying to say lots of things, but Peter, if I start, I won't stop! Would you like to go first? But I really do want to respond when you're done.

Peter Ronald de Souza

Rukmini, you go ahead. I think I'd be happy to listen to you. I'll say something towards the end.

Rukmini Bhaya Nair

Okay. First of all, thank you, Lynn, for picking up on the 'incontinence' idea, which I think is really important – or was at least important to me – in playing around with ideas of decolonization and subversion. And I am very grateful, too, for the way in which you have expanded it; but beyond that, let me respond to your mention of Lachman Khubchandani. Khubchandani, for those in this audience who are unfamiliar with this work, did among other things, this excellent, original linguistic research on the Census of India which of course was first set up by the British and had a powerful role in bolstering the colonial mindset. But he also made a more recent and very interesting distinction when he presented a keynote paper at the International IPRA Conference we organized in Delhi in 2013 which had about 800 or more delegates from about 30 or 40 countries that is extremely relevant, to my mind, to our present session on 'plurilingual' decolonization.

The distinction Khubchandani (1991) made was between 'language professionals' (linguists who practice their scholarly craft within the stated bounds of academia) and what he called the 'language planners' or 'language visionaries'. So, professionals versus planners – what does this distinction imply? As I discussed the subject with him, I noted that Khubchandani was quite upset with the idea that we academics had all apparently turned ourselves into 'suit-boot' professionals. We never wore mufti in the corridors of power, as you put it, Lynn – we stayed within our lanes. And I have since noticed that in much of Western academia, this is the dominant paradigm. You have to stay in your lane. So, if you're working on linguistics, you certainly shouldn't be writing poetry. Put all such illegitimate, polluting, activity aside, banish it to the zone of peripheral vision, as it were! But in India we have not been very good at maintaining these strict separations, these intellectual silos. We seem temperamentally inclined to stray into each other's lanes. We are not professionals, in that sense. In our *Keywords* book, for example, we have historians, doctors, lawyers, engineers, philosophers, talking, cross-talking, to each other. And that enriches the idea of the person who thinks ahead with language. This is a summary of Lachman Khubchandani's insightful distinction between the language planner, the language visionary and the professional.

One other intriguing thing he also said was that language professionals want to remain *anonymous*. Even if they are interested in certain causes, they don't want to show their hand, they want to stay in their safe zones; whereas language planners have this enthusiasm about planning for their country, and they come bravely out of the woodwork, risking public humiliation, even annihilation. I think this is quite a useful distinction to bear in mind when we're thinking of further phases of this project. You also talked about the Brazilian situation – and I – you know, my brother lives in Brazil; I go to Brazil to lecture there, and so on. So, I know the country, and one of the things that really engages me are the linguistic relationships on display between groups – between the urban people and the indigenous people and others such as the Portuguese and the Japanese who populated Brazil at various stages in its very complex development. This is a very different history from the story of the Indian subcontinent from which I believe we all have much to learn. So, you're saying, I presume, that under the local circumstances of Brazil, the powerful elite there, the rulers, still have to decolonize – not in the sense that they shouldn't think they were never colonized but, rather, that they should think of *themselves* as the current colonizers. I think that is a very astute observation for us today discussing *Keywords*, because despite the differences between our societies, India is still a *highly* 'colonial' state in that sense. Coming back to Sinfree's point, the role that Sanskrit – and English, today – have played in creating new grammatical 'colonies' is also very pertinent here.

So, the matter of 'internal decolonization' has to be carefully decoded. Without attention to that internal decolonization, we do not have a viable 'decoloniality' model. These are important points that you've made today and there are many others that I would like to talk about. For example, in the words we've picked: have we been far too influenced by our own contexts and backgrounds? How biased is such a positioning? Because Peter and I, like everyone else, are inevitably situated, mired in context. We see what we see with the eyes that we see; we cannot exit this gaze, get rid of it. We are intrinsically embodied as selves, colors, 'races'. So, that's why I think we need to look, also, at 'race theory' – how it remains a cognitive filter today. In a biological sense, we know that we are all natural genetic twins, we are 99% similar: age, sex, color – each of these parameters is encoded in the tiniest jiggle of a chromosome. Yet our cultures seem to function as vast magnifying glasses; they blow up these tiny fragments of difference and makes them overwhelmingly huge. So, when we valorize the role of culture, as Raymond Williams did, one of the things we tend to forget is that distinctions between people are really very, very, very small. I find it difficult myself, as a linguist, to parse at the same time these two facts – about the twin roles that nature and culture play in the production of 'key' words. I confess I have to think much harder about how to bring these insights into visualizing the next steps towards 'decolonization' via our keywords project!

Peter Ronald de Souza

If there's no other question, then I'll sort of also briefly respond. I saw Lynn Mario's intervention more as a comment than a question to us. And therefore, I just want to add to that one small detail and give you some background as to the production of the book. The detail is – we thought very strategically that the first release of the book would be in the House of Commons in the UK, because the book was published in England, and we had actually an event planned and everything was fine, but then COVID disrupted everything. It was exactly around the same time, because we wanted to go right into the heart of the colonial power and defend our book. But, unfortunately, that didn't happen. Secondly, now that the book is out, one gets the impression that we had a roadmap of how to produce this book. We didn't. It was – serendipity worked a lot. You know, we had long lists of words that we wanted. We tried to find contributors – we couldn't. We bullied friends and colleagues, they promised, 50% of them only delivered. When you go through the book, you will notice that there's no single philosophical or political perspective from which all the entries are written. It's very plural, because we gave a structure, a template, but we did not insist on a perspective.

So, the book, in that sense, is very plural, and each entry speaks about the location of the author – not of the editors. So, that we were able to get 250 entries itself, if we did nothing else – that would merit us a place in history. As any of you know, getting people to contribute to an edited volume is itself an impossible task; to get 200 authors to contribute 250 entries was very difficult. We were hoping for more. And then, of course, reducing the length of the entries because the publisher said only 200,000 words. We had 300,000 words. This was the difficulty. Now what looks like a very clear, very philosophically worked out manuscript was actually something that emerged through a lot of struggle and a lot of luck, and a lot of goodwill and prayer – towards the end of it, a lot of prayer.

[*Laughter*]

Magdalena Madany-Saá

Thank you so much, Lynn Mario, for your great question and great comments. So, we are actually about to wrap up the formal part of our session. If you still have time, please stay with us for the after-party so that you can still ask questions to Rukmini and Peter, or to other people in the forum. Dr Makoni, do you have anything to say before I wrap up and stop recording?

Sinfree Makoni

Yes, I do. When I was listening to the conversation, I kept going back to my understanding of African pragmatics in a decolonized form. And I asked myself, 'What would be the axioms that underpin African pragmatics?' And I identified, I think, at least five. One, it would be opaqueness. The second one would be obscurity. The third would be ambiguity. The fourth would long-windedness, and the fifth would be circuitousness. Why I'm mentioning that is that in any decolonial project, I think it's important to realize that the world that you want to describe will be completely different from the world of Western scholarship. The axioms that I have identified here are completely different from what would be the axioms in, let's say, speech aids and in pragmatics. In other words, if you're going to describe African pragmatics in its own right, you have to assume that it might be completely different from the conversational principles that guide pragmatics in Western scholarship.

Having said that, when I was listening to the conversation, and you were identifying some of the principles that should underpin decoloniality, I then added three more. I added innovation, animation and transgression to your notions of infiltration, elevation, and appropriation and population. What I was trying to say is that what your book has done, at least to me, is to force me to ask a very practical question: conceptually, how would you go about trying to decolonize linguistics? What are the procedures that you would set in motion in order to realize that? Then I realized that in order for that to take place, I need to identify the analytical and philosophical principles that I think I would want to deploy in order to create this vision of a new linguistics that I am interested in. That's my view – but this is a wonderful book. I'm telling you, Peter, we're going to have our own keywords for Africa soon; and I will invite both of you as consultants.

Magdalena Madany-Saá

Thank you so much for wrapping up, Dr Makoni.

Notes

(1) Joseph Conrad 'Heart of Darkness', a novella first published in 1899 and which served as the inspiration for Francis Ford Coppola's film *Apocalypse Now*.
(2) Chinua Achebe, 'An Image of Africa' is a lecture he gave at University of Massachusetts at Amherst in 1975. It is a critique of Joseph's Conrad's 'Heart of Darkness' where Achebe finds a racist framing in his descriptions of land and people.
(3) In this Penn State conversation, I have drawn attention to the possible 'erasure' of the Mughal records in the present-day educational and social discourses of our times. A couple of months later, as this transcript goes to press, the following article has now appeared in the Indian press concerning topics 'dropped' from the class 10 and 12 syllabi of Indian senior schools https://www.ndtv.com/india-news/cbse-drops-democracy-and-diversity-mughal-courts-poems-by-faiz-and-more-from-syllabus-2913024#pfrom = home-ndtv_bigstory Ironical, is it not?
(4) Oddly, it will be found that a single work represents *both* Emperor Akbar and Abu'l Fazl in the References section below. This is because (a) it was customary for the Mughal Emperors to have *nama* (the word is cognate with 'name') 'officially' written by court scribes to record/commemorate their reigns in detail; (b) Akbar is widely reputed to be the only one among the 'Great Mughals' who was formally non-literate, so Fazl's voluminous court records are critically important among the extant, contemporaneous primary sources we have on the life and times of Badshah Akbar.

References

Achebe, C. (2016) An image of Africa: racism in Conrad's Heart of Darkness. *The Massachusetts Review* 57 (1), 14–27.
Austin, J.L. (1962) *How to do Things with Words*. Oxford: Oxford University Press.
Bhattacharya, K.C. (1954) Swaraj in ideas. *Visvabharati Quarterly* 20 (2), 103–114.
Cobain, I. (2017) *The History Thieves: Secrets, Lies and the Shaping of a Modern Nation*. London: Granta Books.
Dawkins, R. (1976) *The Selfish Gene*. Oxford: Oxford University Press.
Fanon, F. (1963) *The Wretched of the Earth*. New York: Grove Press.
Fanon, F. (1993) *Black Skin, White Masks*. London: Pluto Press.
ibn Mubārak, A.A.F. (1897–1910) *Akbar Nama* (Vol. III) (H. Beveridge, Trans.). Asiatic Society of Bengal: Series Bibliotheca Indica.
Khubchandani, L.M. (1991) Evaluating language planning in the Indian context. *Bulletin of the Deccan College Post-Graduate and Research Institute* 51, 303–312.
Nair, R.B. and de Souza, P.R. (eds) (2020) *Keywords for India: A Conceptual Lexicon for the 21st Century*. London: Bloomsbury Publishing.
Said, E.W. (1978) *Orientalism*. New York: Pantheon Books.
Williams, R. (1976) *Keywords: A Vocabulary of Culture and Society*. Oxford: Oxford University Press.

6 Queer Anger: A Conversation on Alliances and Affective Politics

Tommaso Milani

Thank you, Makoni. I have to say that I feel quite intimidated by the group here. Many people whom I respect highly are in the audience. I thought it would be just a small reading group. So, I am quite overwhelmed, but also very happy. I just want to begin by saying that my presentation is going to be quite personal, and I am happy to go on record about it. Instead of talking *about* my articles, which you have access to and which we can discuss during the Q&A session, I want to speak *to* them, looking back *at* them, from the perspective I have now. I'll take a little bit of distance.

The two articles I sent you could be read together under the umbrella term of 'queering multilingualism' (Milani & Levon, 2019; Milani & Levon, 2017). So, if I look back at them, or if I look back at anything I do, they are informed by affect, more specifically by anger. I'm always angry. I'm angry at a *lot* of things. And, we know that anger has been used in a variety of movements, including the queer movements of the 80s, during a specific time when HIV and AIDS became increasingly handled in quite a bad way, especially in the US and in the UK, and the rest of the world too – but the US and the UK were particular contexts because of Reagan's presidency in the US [and Margaret Thatcher's prime ministry in the UK], which had an immense impact on the rest of the world. So, when I look back at those years, I was an adolescent, and I was characterized by one specific emotion: rage, and this is something that I have been carrying with me since then, a sort of queer rage. A writer that has always influenced me is Michael Warner (1991: 16), who describes queer as a 'stance that rejects minoritizing logic of toleration or simple political interest-representation in favor of a more thorough resistance to regimes of the normal.' If one wants to turn this quote into a motto, one could say, 'Not gay as in happy, but queer as in fuck you!'

That's more or less what characterizes *every*thing I do. I do not necessarily want to be accepted. I do not want to be tolerated, as a human being or as an academic, but I try to go against the grain as much as I can. What is this anger about, especially at this specific historical juncture? I'm often angry about politics, about the injustices of anti-queer politics, especially in the context where I live now, Sweden, we are experiencing huge backlashes against what we *thought* we had achieved over many decades of LGBT and queer activism. To take a recent example, a professor of philosophy published an article in one of the main Swedish dailies, saying that dispossessed groups have become the new saints. In saying so, he *bemoaned* the fact that queer scholarship has become increasingly more vocal in Sweden. Needless to say, he is white, and heterosexual, and middle class, and so on. And he's very annoyed by all critical scholarship – not just queer scholars, but also critical race scholars; he's angry about any form of critical research. But I'm also angry about this professor's oversimplification of a complex power situation. I'm also angry against those forms of politics that have co-*opt*ed LGBT rights into nationalism. So, in a sense, I am angry about countries like Israel – but also the Netherlands, Sweden, the US – that use LGBT rights to create new forms of discriminations against other groups. And I'm sure for those of you who have read my work about Israel and Palestine, you are aware that Israel markets itself as a 'heaven' in the Middle East for gay and lesbian rights. Of course, Israel is, to a certain extent, very progressive with regard to LGBT rights, but the question is, how is it used then to downplay or even erase the discrimination against Palestinians?

Having said that, I'm also angry about those who have done work on Israeli *homonationalism*. Why? Because, as Sa'ed Atshan has written in a wonderful book that has just been published, and I strongly recommend you to read – *Queer Palestine and the Empire of Critique* (Atshan, 2020) – critical scholarship on Israel-Palestine has constructed what he calls an *empire of critique*, a form of scholarship that is so quick to issue a verdict of 'guilty' against those who refuse to take one side and instead seek to unveil the complexities of the Israeli-Palestinian situation. So, I'm very much in line with what Sa'ed says: '[A]ctivism at the intersection of LGBTQ and Palestinian rights can reveal the potential of what sociologist Eve Spangler calls the "more Mao than thou" trend in many leftist circles. Because progressives see themselves as challenging power and oppressive forces, they can become self-righteous to some degree and thus think that they have a monopoly on truth and morality' (Atshan, 2020: 23). Although his book appeared in 2020, a year after Erez Levon and I published the article 'Israel as Homotopia' (Milani & Levon, 2019) in Language and Society, his argument resonates well with what we sought to do in that article, namely, we were trying to say that we should avoid issuing a verdict of 'guilty' against *some* queer Palestinians who are drawn to Israel. Instead, we should try to capture the *complexities* in which queer Palestinians find themselves in, and seek to understand what kind of negotiations of *belonging* they perform.

Finally, I am angry about research on multilingualism, because this scholarship has produced an *immense* body of work talking about ethnicity, more recently race, social class and all possible factors that play an important role in the lived experiences of multilingual speakers, but sexuality is never *really* engaged with properly. A notable exception is Holly Cashman's fantastic book, *Queer, Latinx, and Bilingual* (Cashman, 2018).

So, how do I channel all this anger analytically? Because one should always seek to channel emotions towards things so that these can hopefully become productive. My main channeling, not just in these two articles, but in all my work, is by looking at incoherences, ambivalences, double-binds. Looking back, I feel that my work has been influenced by an experience I had when I had just finished my PhD in 2007. I went to AILA in Essen, Germany, where I attended a panel, in which a very important scholar gave a commentary along these lines: 'Oh! What brings together all the papers in this panel is coherence. The coherence of narratives.' And I was thinking, 'There's nothing coherent about what the papers are saying. Moreover, there's no coherence in the *actual data*.' Coherence was something that had been superimposed by that scholar in order to try and find what they wanted. I believe that the most important aspect of my work is to show how human beings are *deeply* incoherent, even in one and the same sentence, and it's okay, because we are constantly juggling between very different opposing ideologies that take us towards different directions.

I would say that we (human beings) are always in the midst of a magnetic field of forces that push and pull us towards different directions at the same time. And my role as an analyst is not to try and put order but to show those ambivalences, double-binds and incoherences. In this respect, I find Foucault's notions of *heterotopia* and *heterochrony* particularly appealing to capture those incoherences, those double-binds, those ambivalences. As Foucault argued, heterotopias are 'real places – places that do exist and that are formed in the very founding of society – which are something like counter-sites, a kind of effectively enacted utopia in which the real sites, all the other real sites that can be found within the culture, are simultaneously represented, contested, and inverted. Places of this kind are outside of all places, even though it may be possible to indicate their location in reality. Because these places are absolutely different from all the sites that they reflect and speak about, I shall call them, by way of contrast to utopias, heterotopias' (Foucault, 1986: 24). And Foucault would go on to say, and this is a very powerful image: 'Everyone can enter into heterotopic sites, but in truth, it is only an illusion – we think we enter and yet we are, by the very fact of having entered, excluded' (Foucault, 1986: 8). This is, to Erez Levon and to me, the crux of the matter for the queer Palestinians who are part of the documentary 'Oriented,' which we analyzed in the article, 'Israel as Homotopia.' Because, in a sense, they get attracted to Israel. They get *pulled* to Israel – Israel is a magnetic field of force that attracts them. But as soon as they enter the space, they get de facto excluded, and that's what we called 'vicious belonging,' to be attracted to something that ultimately is going to exclude you and kick you out.

To conclude, I think that part of the anger and the complexity that I try to capture in my analysis about other people, as well as the complexities, the double-binds, in which *I* find myself in as a human being can be captured through Michael Rothberg's very recent book, *The Implicated Subject* (Rothberg, 2019). In this book, he suggests the notion of *implicated subject* as a way to complicate too simplistic distinctions between victims, perpetrators and bystanders, and captures 'the fact that most of us feel torn by our relation to divergent, intersecting histories – in this case, histories of antisemitism, genocide and occupation' (Rothberg, 2019: 19). He states that the category of the 'implicated subject allows us to retain our sense that situations of conflict position us in morally and emotionally complex ways' (Rothberg, 2019: 19). And I have to say that I am morally and emotionally caught in very complex ways with regard to Israel-Palestine where, on the one hand, I strongly recognize the right of Israel to exist as a sovereign state. At the same time, I also strongly support the movement for Palestinian justice. I'm going to close on this.

Sinfree Makoni

Tommaso, thank you very much. I've enjoyed your presentation, and I've enjoyed reading your work over the years. But I have a couple of questions, and some of my questions arise from reading your work, and from listening to Busi talk about your work. So, there won't be anything completely original in these questions that I pose, but I can assure you I didn't share my questions with her before this. This focus on the issue of queering multilingualism – I want to focus on the issue about queerness. Are you framing queerness, in this case, as a universal representation of sexuality? Or are you saying that queerness is a reduction of the world's queer representation? Which direction are you taking there? Is it a universal representation of sexuality or a reduction of the world representation?

Tommaso Milani

No, I see 'queerness' as a very complex subject position that cannot be necessarily captured by the categories gay, lesbian, and so on and so on, but it's in many ways an anti-categorical way of seeing oneself and one's own sexuality. I'm not saying that people should not use gay or lesbian. People can use whichever categories they want. It's just that queering, both as an academic project and as an activist practice, is always trying to show and argue for the complexity of identities, and also the double-binds of identities, and the constraints that identities always bring with them – they become like straitjackets. And so, we need to see the limit of what identity can bring to us, both as analysts and as activists.

Sinfree Makoni

So, if that is the case – if queerness is a multi-layered, ambivalent category – my question then is this: Within the world of queer/lesbian scholarship, what are the debates that occur within it? What are the tensions? What are the fault lines within that particular universe of scholarship or of activism?

Tommaso Milani

That's an excellent question. And I could speak for days about the debates in queer scholarship. Just to keep them very short, the most recent ones are about the *whiteness* of queerness, because we know that queer scholarship has been produced in the northern hemisphere. Although there is, of course, burgeoning queer scholarship in the south of the world – in Brazil and in South Africa, for example. And one of the critiques that are being moved both from South Africa and from Brazil at the moment is precisely about how queer scholars in the north relate to, engage with, or better, do *not* engage with scholarship in the south of the world. This is an important topic that is being currently discussed in queer scholarship, and in the field of language and sexuality. For example, wonderful scholars like Rodrigo Borba and Branca Falabella Fabrício in South Africa, Thabo Msibi in South Africa, have advanced important southern critiques of queer work on language (Lewis *et al.*, 2014; Msibi, 2014).

This is, to me, the main debate. The other debate, which emerged as a result of a special issue published by Robyn Wiegman (2012), in the feminist journal *Differences*, is about normativity, or better, the normative *anti*-normativity of queer theory. They argue that queer theory and academic work influenced by it has nurtured an anti-normative attitude that has become a normative engine that underpins queer scholarship. It's an interesting debate because it forces us to discuss what queer theory would look like if we took normativity, or better, if we took *anti*-normativity out of it.

Sinfree Makoni

Okay. Right. Let me then continue the conversation; I'll ask one or two more questions, and then I'll give up to Rafael to open up the conversation. I agree with you that there is a sense in which queer scholarship is methodologically white. The limited literature I've read on the topic gave me the impression that it sets up white experience as a universal category, and everybody else's experience is, to some extent, identity politics. So, from a southern perspective, I would prefer the whole situation to be the opposite, right? In a sense, to explore how southern experiences can become the norm against which white queer scholarship or white queer sexual practices are assessed. To turn the world completely upside-down, so to speak. That's one way which I would be interested in pursuing. That leads me to the second issue – if I were to borrow the terms by Boaventura de Santos, the question becomes, 'From your perspective, what are the sociological absences? What are the topics that are not raised currently in queer scholarship? In other words, if you had to use the notion of *sociology of absences*, what is absent at the moment, from that world of queer scholarship?'

Tommaso Milani

Yeah, it's a tough one. Talking about what's absent is always a bit difficult. I would want to see more work coming from the south of the world, by scholars who are from the south of the world, and who are based in the south of the world, really speaking back to queer theory and telling us what aspects of queer theory do not work in the specific context that they are analyzing. So, say, how we can speak back to queer theory in a way that we can contribute to a more complex, more nuanced theory production from the south. People like Thabo Msibi and University of KwaZulu-Natal and colleagues from Brazil *have* started this work. It's just that because of the geopolitics of publishing, their research does not often appear in more mainstream journals. That's why in *Language in Society*, Susan Ehrlich and I are welcoming *more* scholarship from the south. I mean – not to say that people should not publish in small local journals, they absolutely should. However, I would want to see *more* influence from the south on the key debates, published in international journals read by many academics.

Sinfree Makoni

Okay. Then, my last question is, given the way in which you do work, both in queer scholarship and activism, how do you seek to build into your work three dimensions: issues about resistance, disruption and disobedience? If one were to borrow from Walter Mignolo, how do you build that into your work and, as an individual scholar, into your professional responsibilities? In other words, you in your totality, how do you build into yourself these three different dimensions: resistance, disruption and disobedience?

Tommaso Milani

Yeah, excellent. Really excellent point. I think I have been influenced over the last years by Luiz Paulo da Moita Lopes's notion of *undisciplined applied linguistics* (Moita Lopes, 2009). I am undisciplined. I'm always *very* disorderly. I'm a very contrarian person. I try to go against the grain whenever and wherever I can. I try never to conform, both in terms of *how* I write, my style, and *what* I write, the content. Obviously, I need to underscore that I can do what I do; I can write what I write, because of the privilege I carry with me, because of the fact that I'm a full professor, that I am established… And so, although I certainly want to encourage more junior scholars to also be disobedient, to always be defiant, they need to be aware of the risks connected to non-compliance. Currently, I *can* be disobedient, I am allowed to be disobedient, because of the structural power I have.

Sinfree Makoni

Okay. Thank you very much. Thanks a lot. We can continue the conversation later on, but let me open it up to other people.

Comments from the chat box

Mantsoaki Moorosi: Good afternoon everyone, Mantsoaki Moorosi from Lesotho.
   Brett Diaz: I do have some questions about the readings :)
   Busi Makoni: I would like to comment on 'rage' and injustice in scholarship.

Rafael Lomeu Gomes

Thank you for initiating the conversation, Makoni. So far, two people have written in the chat box, saying that they wanted to either ask questions or make comments, and the first one is Brett Diaz.

Brett Diaz

So, I really enjoyed the readings quite a lot. And it was really refreshing for me to see work incorporating, as you put it, more queer and sexual identities that go across different spaces in different areas. And especially for multilingualism, not just being understood as a thing that people do, but also the way people form who they are and express themselves. And so, one of the questions I had relates to my background, which is especially focused on affect and emotion. That was also very refreshing, because the turn to affect has been quite interesting to me over time. Not quite sure how I feel about it overall (but, here I am.) So, when I was reading the two works, I had a specific question, which was if you could expand a little more on how you use and understand emotion or affect, depending on how you want to use it, at the time: how do you understand it in your work, especially as a discourse analyst? Because I can see the thread with Sara Ahmed's work (2004) in your work, but one of the problems I tend to have with that more cultural or critical theory approach to it is that I miss some of the substance. I miss some of the how it's done, or what is being done, in that way. And I think a critique of that would be, a lot of the times I find that those constructions of emotion tend to be very WEIRD – 'capital' WEIRD: western-educated, industrial, those sort of conceptions of emotion – which can erase a lot of the nuance and a lot of what the practice is potentially trying to accomplish.

And so, I was hoping you could expand on that a little bit. And as an addendum to that, as you were talking, I really appreciated your mentioning the incoherence, because a lot of work in stance (that takes on affective stance) sees it as very unidirectional and very static. And I patently disagree with that, and my work has focused right now on using discourse-analytic structures to find incoherence. So, finding ways in which people, as you say, conflict with themselves and are incoherent with their own statements, even minute-to-minute, even though the subject hasn't changed. Sort of like you showed with Luiz, for example, using these different affective positions as he's talking about the same thing – sometimes in the same language, but his identity shifts at times – and the affect is one of the fluid parts of that. And so, I would really appreciate it if you could expand on that a little bit, maybe concretize it a little bit for me. Thank you.

Tommaso Milani

Thank you. And thank you for reading my work so thoroughly. Yes. So, I have to say, I also want to add that I identify as a critical discourse analyst. So, another reason for the anger I've had over the years against critical discourse analysis has been the focus – obsession even – that critical discourse analysis has had on rationality, the Habermasian idea of the public sphere and deliberative debates. This has led CDA scholars to concentrate on the ways in which people try to convince each other in a democratic society. I was at the conference a couple of years ago, where Norman Fairclough gave a talk in which he argued that argumentation is the locus of CDA analysis. My plenary instead made the opposite argument, 'No, no, no. It's *affect*. We cannot understand politics without affect.' So, I've tried to add an affective element to CDA. In this respect, I find the work by Sara Ahmed particularly relevant. However, I agree with you that for discourse analysts, it's sometimes difficult to operationalize Ahmed's theories. I found help in the work by Margaret Wetherell (Wetherell, 2015), who is a discursive psychologist; and although I do not identify as a discursive psychologist, she really gives a very clear indication about how to apply Ahmed's concepts to different forms of discourse analysis, including multimodal discourse analysis.

In this respect, I want to take the opportunity to mention a special issue of the journal *Social Semiotics*, which I recently edited together with John Richardson (Milani & Richardson, 2021), dedicated to the topic of discourse and affect. In the special issue, the contributors offer different perspectives on how affect can be analyzed through discourse analysis and semiotic analysis. For me, it's always a matter of trying to ask oneself the question, 'What lies beside identity?' This is what Eve Kosofsky Sedgwick (2003) said many years ago: 'Too much focus on identity does not make us see what lies beside it.' And what lies beside is, in this specific case, affect gluing together the interactions. Analytically, of course, I'm sure that you want to know how I go about it. It's complicated. It's tricky, because it's not just a matter of finding words, or verbs, or nouns that are 'affective'. Ultimately, any word can be affective. One needs to understand the affective loading in a specific context. And – because I'm not a conversation analyst, but I'm ultimately a critical discourse analyst, it's always about trying to bring your ethnographic knowledge about the context, about the political situation, about the specific *loading* that certain words may have in a specific context. When analyzing Israel-Palestine, I always co-write with people who are either Hebrew and/or Arabic speakers, and who live or have resided in Israel-Palestine. So, it's always a teamwork in the analysis.

Brett Diaz

So, if I could just add one thing, I really appreciate you mentioning Margaret Wetherell. That was actually going to be my question on that particular line – whether you had looked at her work (Wetherell, 2012). And one of the things I've found really fruitful about taking her affective practices approach is the use of what's currently called the 'constructed theory of emotion,' and this way of seeing emotion as an experience of different forms of raw affect that combine and create complex emotional expressions – but it's always situated and put into a particular context with particular speakers, with particular actions, like sort of on order. And so, in my work, the thing that I've done most recently is trying to find how you can locate those different incoherences that you mentioned, like connotative inversion. Because, you know, you might present yourself, as Luiz does, as Palestinian, but he is also pushing against that by saying, 'No, I'm Israeli. I was born to have this card, that card…' And what you find is that that particular example – the card or the being, or the whatever – are charged along affective dimensions.

As opposed to this, you will not usually find someone say, 'I'm angry about this, because I feel that I am X or Y or Z.' You find them using their phonetics, their sociophonetics, using their discourse. And that's where I find that these evaluative elements come in. And so, I wondered if you had thought about that as a way of disentangling, as you said, the identity from the expression itself. Because from my perspective, as you said, the affect is the fluid on which the identity rides. You know, you don't find someone say, 'This is who I am: blah, blah, blah, blah.' It's expressed along these – and it becomes charged semiotically through – the affect. And so, I didn't know if you had anything to say about that, or some specific examples you might have come across that you could find a way to operationalize in a concrete way? And then I'll get off of this high horse and other people can talk.

Tommaso Milani

Absolutely, I totally agree. As you say, there are specific markers. In your case, what you look at is language, but the markers could also be visual. The markers could be other things. They could be gestural, or the use of a specific color. So, as you say, there are always some markers, and those markers are always tiny. They're never big – they're never glaring at you, unless you're looking for them. Right? And that's why a substantial portion of research that has focused on identity – and, I mean, I've contributed immensely to the work on identity, and I'm saying that we should definitely continue working on identity – but I'm also saying that work that has focused exclusively on identity has sometimes *missed* that there were other things *alongside* identity, And it is these things that made those identities quite salient in particular ways.

Brett Diaz

Thank you.

Rafael Lomeu Gomes

Thank you. Next up is Busi Makoni, who would like to make a comment on rage and injustice in scholarship.

Busi Makoni

Okay. What I wanted to say was, I do understand Tommaso when he expresses this idea of queer rage. As a black woman in scholarship, and an African, I am also experiencing a lot of rage. While I cannot call it 'queer rage' as such, this rage also emanates from my experience of injustice, particularly injustice towards black African women in scholarship. Our work as black African women is not published or rarely published. The idea of, you know, the geopolitics of publication has already been mentioned. Yet, even when we black African women publish, we're rarely ever cited. We're rarely ever called upon to be in editorial boards for the premier journals in our disciplines. We are not *visible* in scholarship, to the extent that we feel as if we're completely erased from scholarship, even if, in terms of our bodies, we are present. So, this experience on its own leads to a lot of rage. I, to some extent, feel that

Tommaso is in a better position, because he can at least *use* his position of white privilege to exercise that disobedience. He can express that rage. If *I*, as a black woman, express any form of rage, then I would be dubbed an 'aggressive, angry black woman' and fall into the stereotype of the Sapphire. So, for me to avoid the stereotype of the Sapphire, I must walk a very thin, fine line to keep myself in check. And, in keeping myself in check, I am falling into the trap of what Audre Lorde views as *keeping silent*, to which she also says, 'Your silence will not protect you'. After all, keeping silent makes you complicit with the system that is discriminating against you. In as much as silence is a shield from being viewed in negative terms – i.e. viewed as angry, aggressive, and all that – it also leads to a simmering rage inside. I have had moments to think very deeply about this issue because, like I said, I also am experiencing that element of rage, a simmering rage that might explode at some point.

During this period of lockdown, I really had a lot of time to think about a lot of things. And it also didn't help to experience George Floyd being murdered in the glare of the international media, and we saw it repeatedly played in our eyes. During that time, I read the book *Sister Outsider* by Audre Lorde (2012). I also read this book by Gloria Hull, Bell Scott and Barbara Smith titled *All the women are white, All the blacks are men*, something to that effect (Hull et al., 1982). One of the things that struck me, which I had never really thought about seriously, was that in colonial times the idea or the category of a 'black woman' did not actually exist as all blacks were, presumably, men. The question this raises in my mind is, 'If all the women are white and all the blacks are men, then who are the black women?' So, it seems our invisibility is 'natural' or is the norm, at least in my view, to foreground that aspect that we have – actually, even in colonial times, have been sort of a sidebar, a nonexistent category. So, if that be the case, then it sort of makes sense that the question Sojourner Truth posed is, 'Ain't I a woman?' This question is very poignant for us black African women because in as much as there is a lot written in scholarship about sexism, the sexism that is being written about is about '*the* women', i.e. white women, being excluded in scholarship. Yet, the women – the bodied but nonexistent ones – that are being entirely erased from scholarship are black African women. However, if we take Gloria Hull, Bell Scott, and Barbara's Smith's assertion into consideration, because the category 'black women' does not exist, the absence of black African women and their silencing is to be expected – we don't expect that which does not exist to be present and have a voice. The absence of black African women is often never raised because it is not an issue, after all we don't exist. So, this is the impetus for the rage in me.

The question to my good old friend Tommaso is, 'How do I, as a black woman, ever express this rage, this anger, and become disobedient without falling into the stereotype of being the quintessential Sapphire?'

Tommaso Milani

Honestly, I don't have words, because I am overwhelmed by what you said, because I completely understand. And that's why what you're saying makes me even angrier, and that's why I said what I said – that the disobedience that I can perform is *allowed* because of my being white, male, cisgender, and middle class. And I think it would be out of place of me, as a white man, to tell a black female academic what to do. Somehow, I do believe that I understand what it means for you to fall into the category of the disobedient black woman, and what that would mean. But, at the same time, I believe, actually, that we need to forge more solidarities among angry academics, whether it's queer anger, whether it's black anger – and especially for those of us who find ourselves in a position of power, me in particular also being the editor of an international journal – I think we need to create the space for this solidarity to take shape. So, my point, I'm not sure whether it's going to help or not, is that we need to talk more, and we need to link our academic activisms together.

We might have different perspectives, and we might want to have different foci, but I think that we have so much more in common about fighting injustices. Therefore, we should not be split, but we should forge more global solidarities: North, South, queer, black, and so on and so on. Because that's the only way we can actually push our disciplines forward, at the same time as we fight back in these horrible times characterized by the return of the Nazis in Sweden. We can only fight if we are in solidarity with each other, and with a common goal: fighting against injustices, both out there and in the academic world. In this respect, we have to remember that there is a huge return of positivism. So, my work is *constantly* being questioned from specific strands of multilingualism research, or from specific disciplines in the humanities, that say practically that my work is just some form of glorified journalism, because I do not measure things. So, there's also *that* fight that we have to carry, and that's the fight for the *legitimacy* of queer activist inquiry.

I really hope to have made it clear that it's easier for me to be angry as a queer man than angry + other identity categories. Even if queer scholarship hasn't often engaged with intersectionality, I've been one of those who argues that there is so much to gain from bringing queer scholarship into a dialogue with intersectionality research. On the one hand, intersectionality has often seen their queer peers as 'threatening', because queer scholarship questions identity categories. But that doesn't necessarily need to be the case because queer scholarship has *also* pointed out that identity categories can be used and should be used, as long as we are aware of their *limitations*.

On the other hand, queer scholarship hasn't really considered intersectionality, because the starting point of queer inquiry has always been sexuality rather than race, but I believe that we should go beyond that impasse. The question is not so much whether it's first sexuality, then race, or it's first race then sexuality. Instead, we need to try and understand how these patterns of oppression intersect with and mutually constitute each other. Therefore, I do believe that queer and intersectionality can and actually *should* be brought into a very productive dialogue if we want to move on.

> **Comments from the chat box**
>
> **Brett Diaz:** Solidarity can have quite different discursive baggage in different regions and modes of thought, though… one wishes it didn't.
>
> **Cassie Leymarie:** In some circles of Critical Discourse in the US, there is discussion of LGBTQ rights only existing and gaining momentum, especially transgender recognition/rights, because white men were leading the movement.
>
> **Busi Makoni:** Injustice to one is injustice to all!
>
> **Cristine Severo:** I agree that the focus is not 'lack of' Southern production (people have been producing a lot in other languages as Spanish, Portuguese) but about the politics of publication and dissemination of knowledge. There is an intense scholarship and activism taking place in Southern contexts. One powerful example that mixes scholarship and activism is the International Seminar Fazendo Gênero (Doing Gender) that takes place in Brazil since 1994.
>
> **Javier García León (he, him, his/él):** Yes, the politics of publication as well and the politics of citation. Many works in Spanish and Portuguese are not cited in journals that mainly publish in English.

Rafael Lomeu Gomes

Okay. Magda and I would now like to ask Cristine Severo to perhaps make a comment about what you wrote in the chat box in relation to the mixes between activism and scholarship in southern contexts, or more specifically in Brazil, because we feel that this connects very well to what has just been talked about now. Cristine, would you be willing to talk about this?

Cristine Severo

That was just a comment on how southern contexts have been producing a lot in Portuguese and Spanish, even – scholarship in terms of activism. And one example is this international seminar called *Fazendo Gênero*, doing gender, that attracts people from all parts of the world. And I agree that the main issue is related to the politics of publication and dissemination. Yes. Thanks.

Tommaso Milani

Thanks, Cristine. *Fazendo Gênero* is a *fantastic* conference. I know it. Unfortunately, I've never been able to attend it, but my good friend, Carmen Caldas-Coulthard was part of the organizing committee when it was at University of Santa Catarina in Florianopolis. And I think that a lot of the inspiration I get is precisely from scholars in the Global South, or from scholars who produce work about the Global South.

So, for example, in the African context, I've been inspired by queer scholarship in Uganda, in Nigeria, in South Africa, in Zimbabwe, in Botswana. There is substantial queer rage , and there are different types of queer activism in African contexts. The problem is that this rage and activism is not seen or *read* enough in many parts of the world, unfortunately. Moreover, there are very problematic discourses circulating among northern academics. When the Board of the International Gender Language Association (IGALA) discussed the proposal of the IGALA conference being hosted in Gaborone, some otherwise very progressive scholars reacted against having the conference in the capital of Botswana because they were afraid of homophobic attacks against the participants. Some of us had to say very firmly that there are very established queer academic and activist environments in Botswana. We reassured the IGALA Board that nothing bad was going to happen to the participants. Fortunately, the conference did take place in Botswana, and the Vice Chancellor gave the most *touching* speech I've ever heard. You know, vice chancellors always open conferences and they're typically extremely boring. Their speech is about how successful the university is, or how amazing the university is, and so on and so on. It's their job.

In contrast, the Vice Chancellor at the University of Botswana did not do that; he had actually read very carefully what the conference was about – namely, gender, language, and sexuality; his speech focused on transgender experiences and rights, and the importance of transgender lives in Botswana. We were all in tears, realizing that the Vice Chancellor had prepared such a beautifully crafted, powerful speech. Interestingly, many of the delegates were slightly surprised that a Vice Chancellor from an African university gave such a speech. I was quite pleased that they actually realized that all the reservations against having IGALA in Botswana were unfounded.

Comments from the chat box

Ofelia García: Good morning everyone, from early NYC. Unfortunately, I have to leave around 9.15, so I apologize now!

Hilary Janks: Can Tommaso speak more about queer multilingualism specifically as, say, opposed to queer linguistics? Hilary Janks.

Rafael Lomeu Gomes

Thank you. Next up, we have Hilary Janks who wrote in the chat, 'Can Tommaso speak more about queer multilingualism specifically, as say, opposed to queer linguistics?'

Tommaso Milani

Yeah. I mean, it's not so much that it's opposed, it's just that queer linguistics, which is a fantastic body of scholarship on language and sexuality, has historically been quite monolingual. I mean, there are always exceptions, and the main exception is Holly Cashman's monograph on *Queer, Latinx, and Bilinguals* in Phoenix, Arizona. But yes, I would love to see more work on language and sexuality that takes a queer perspective to engage more with multilingual data, because it feels like they haven't really done so enough. So, I would say that queering multilingualism is part of queer linguistics, but bringing a multilingual perspective to it.

Rafael Lomeu Gomes

Thank you. Ashraf, you have a couple of questions about queerness and revolutions in the Arab world?

Ashraf Abdelhay

Yes. Thank you so much. I first need to thank Tommaso for the presentation, which I learned a lot from. I need to raise a couple of questions. The first question is about the relation between people with queered orientation and the largely heteronormative revolutionary dynamics and the protests in the Arab world. We know that since the end of 2010, there has been a series of revolutions in the Arab world. So, have you thought about the position or the contribution of the people who have an anti-normative attitude in these situations, particularly, the complexities and the contradictions inherent in these contexts? People there are fighting for establishing a democratic system using the traditional framework of the nation-state, which is very exclusionary of people with, using the language of the system, 'abnormal sexual orientations.' So, how can you deal with that contradiction? The dominant argument goes as follows: Let us have a democratic system in place first and then through that system everyone can have a voice. However, marginalized groups (including women) reject this linear thinking because for them a democratic system as we experienced it is itself patriarchal and its very structure does not allow any alternative voices. So, how do you react to this point?

A related point is about the way we talk about these sexual issues. From the way you talked about these issues, the automaticity of your performance should make me flag up the significant point that talking about sexuality is a very seriously situated business. In the Arab world, for example, if you talk about sexuality in the way you do, it becomes a matter of life and death. So, for this reason, the interpretation that this discourse which you use is White discourse is rationalized. The second question is related to our book on *The Sociolinguistics of Protesting*, and I think this question was touched upon by Busi and Sinfree: Have you thought about the vocabularies which you use to talk about sexuality? Have you tried to think through non-western vocabularies of talking about sexuality and sexual relationships? Thank you very much.

> **Comments from the chat box**
>
> **Sangeeta Bagga-Gupta:** @ashraf: the work on the hijras in India may be of interest here (on vocabularies).

Tommaso Milani

Yeah. Thank you for your questions. I mean, I don't think I can talk about the Arab world in its entirety. And it's always difficult for me to talk about the relation between sexuality and the politics of nationalism in the Arab world. And I do understand the double-binds that you are emphasizing. I just want to refer you to the work of a very important Palestinian activist collective called Al Qaws, 'the rainbow,' and especially the work by Haneen Maikey, who is the director of Al Qaws (http://www.alqaws.org/articles/Queer-Politics-Haneen-Maikey?category_id=0). Haneen has written and spoken extensively about the double-binds of Palestinian queer resistance within the context of establishing a Palestinian state. So, I do not want to answer your question, not because I *can't* answer it, but because other people should answer it, namely, Palestinian queer activists. I can, send you the links to her publications, statements, and YouTube videos. So, I think you will find a compelling argument from her about how queer movements *can* be part of broader struggles for the establishment of an independent and democratic nation-state.

When it comes to vocabularies, yes. Definitely. I mean, vocabularies that are not Western vocabularies – yes, definitely – in my writing on Brazil together with Rodrigo Borba and in my work on South Africa inspired by South African scholars, local vocabularies have always been an important component, in order to capture things that could not be grasped with concepts that have been created in northern or western contexts (Borba & Milani, 2017; Milani, 2014).

Comments from the chat box

Brett Diaz: Could Tommaso explore a little bit the borders between nationalism (imagined identity) and citizenship (a norm or mode of conduct)? I am very curious about this because of Butler's work on norms and conduct, and its (damaging) reifying effects on gender, sexuality etc.

Desmond Odugu: To the distinction between identity and emotions: is the target of your analytic arrows partly the tension between competition for inclusion on one hand and the quest to dismantle the underlying hierarchies that is the fundamental legacy of imperial politics on the other?

Ofelia García: So, I have to leave early, and I'm feeling a bit of rage about what it feels as silencing Busi's rage. Not by anyone in particular, but because we haven't sat long enough with the discomfort and the pain of what she expressed.

Ofelia García: So, I don't want to leave without reminding all of us that Tommaso talked about Queering. The 'ing' requires a body for the performance, bodies that have different emotions depending on how they have been radicalized and sexualized and minoritized, so I think Tommaso and all of us would say that we have to be careful about keeping the ambivalence and the double-bind.

Eunjeong Lee: Such an important point about embodiment and experiences in unequal realities!

Rafael Lomeu Gomes

Thank you. We have three more people who have signalized that they want to ask questions. Let us start with Ofelia.

Ofelia García

Oh, thank you. I was just writing something in the chat, and I'm going to send it, even though it's not coherent, because I didn't think I was going to have a chance to see all of you. First of all, Tommaso, it's good to see you again.

Tommaso Milani

Likewise.

Ofelia García

And, you know, I had felt very uncomfortable about our reaction, collectively, to Busi's rage, because I think that there is so much going on these days, and I felt Busi's pain, and somehow I don't think we grappled with it. So, that is my main concern: that every time that a black woman raises this rage that they *absolutely* need to express, and that takes so much courage to be able to say – because we all know Busi's work; we all know how powerful it is, and yet how silent she has been – and she has now really taken on this voice. And I thought we needed to be mindful of that. And then, I wanted to just say that I think that Tommaso's approach to talking about queer*ing* – the *–ing* part of it – I think has to remind all of us that we all have different bodies, and our emotions are embodied in us, and that the way in which we perform and the way in which others see us makes our experiences different. So, I think that, you know, queering is also something that is felt differently by a lesbian, by a white person, by a black woman, and I think we have to be mindful of that. [*Kisses hands and gestures outward*]

Tommaso Milani

Absolutely.

Ofelia García

So, thank you, Tommaso, for making me think about these things. Bye-bye. [*Waves*]

Tommaso Milani

Thank you, Ofelia! Bye. [*Waves*]

Busi Makoni

[*Claps hands*]

> **Comments from the chat box**
>
> **Hilary Janks:** I don't know enough about the new theories of 'love,' but I wonder if that is not one of the ways in which black academics in the US have found an alternative way of dealing with affect as opposed to rage.
>
> **Mari Haneda:** Hilary, I concur with your assessment of the use of love by US black scholars.

Rafael Lomeu Gomes

Thank you. And the last comment, then, by Sangeeta?

Sangeeta Bagga-Gupta

Thank you, Tommaso. You bring such a fresh breath of air to disobedience. I have one question and a couple of comments. And the question is – of course, it shouldn't sound rhetorically, but given that we are in Sweden, can one be complacent and not be angry as a scholar? So, that is my question, and I mean it seriously. And, of course, it is the shared Swedish space that I draw upon.

So, my comments are related to where the field of Southern theories (in the plural) are going. I sometimes get to feel in your responses that there is the staticness of who is and where one can position a researcher. So, instead of someone being in the north, or bringing scholars from the south, given our contemporary lives, don't we need to look at *gaze*, which is mobile? So, I'm reflecting a lot about these issues of the *mobile gaze* in much of my writing, and I just wanted to throw that out. And then, Sweden is a periphery in the Global North. And I think that is one way in which I grapple with this *obedience* that all white Swedish scholars seem to have. And in that sense, when you came back from South Africa to Sweden, you brought this breath of freshness with you. So, on social media, we become allies because we see that things are so quiet. And I think this needs to be also recognized, that spaces like Sweden are very, very complacent. I was in lockdown during the pandemic and couldn't get myself back home, and so from a distance, I could see what was happening with Black Lives Matter all over the globe, but *nothing* was happening in Sweden. So, that is just one way of understanding this.

And I completely agree with you that having a position of a senior scholar in a place like Sweden allows us to do certain things, but it also is a very, very precarious situation because you get *immediately* branded as perhaps being foolhardy. I remember getting my chair when I was just 44, and I was not aware of the foolhardiness that was required. And so, it was good to get branded very young, because then you have no other place to go to. But I'd like you to reflect on this complacency: 'Can research, whether it is in the area of queer studies, or functionality, or other areas of marginalization – *can* we not be enraged?'

Tommaso Milani

Thank you. Sangeeta, who is my ally on social media, and in the academic world, especially in Sweden. For those of you who are listening from all over the world, I want to say this: if you believe that Sweden is a multicultural paradise, then you're wrong. It's a good place in many ways, but it's a very *complex* place insofar as there's a lot of falling in line. So, there's alignment, and people like me who are not aligned, or try not to be aligned – we get marked as the 'troublemakers.' And it's okay. Before I answer your question, I really want address an important point you're making, namely, the gaze. I wasn't trying to reproduce a too facile distinction between scholars in the south and scholars in the north. But, at the same time, I also want to emphasize the importance of scholars who are from the south and who still live in the south and work in the south compared to, say, Mignolo and others who *are* from the south and whom I thoroughly respect, but who are in the north and can reap other types of institutional privileges than, say, a scholar at a rural university in South Africa or Brazil, can't.

So, I totally agree with your point that it's important to look at gaze; it's a way of seeing, it's a way of analyzing the world. At the same time, I *am* at times a bit unsettled by the fact that discussions on southern theories and southern multilingualism are being carried further by white scholars from the north, based in the north, or white scholars in the south. What I'm trying to say is that we need to negotiate our positionalities. And I'm not here to cast any verdict of guilty. I'm just saying that whatever we do, it's important to have a different gaze. Right? But we cannot possibly write about southern theories or southern multilingualism or southern perspectives without actually spelling out our own positionality *in relation to other* positionalities. So, I completely agree with you, Sangeeta. I certainly do not want to place people in too-easy boxes, but I still want to underscore the importance of the work done by southern scholars from the south who stay and work in the south, because their labor is performed under very different conditions in terms of structural support to that we have in the north. Obviously, there is also the south in the north, the north in the south, and so on and so on.

When it comes to complacency, Sweden is a place where one can become easily complacent for two reasons. On the one hand, we have institutional wealth. We have support. There are grants. There are possibilities. On the other hand, there are forces within the Swedish academic world that want us to get aligned and not to be disobedient. I feel it every day. I can see it when I sit in committee meetings. I look myself around and I'm the only non-Swede at the table. And I say, 'Oh! Not only am I the only non-Swede, but also, there's only one woman!' And it's like, 'Oh, good grief! Sweden is supposed to be the most gender-equal society in the world!' And the committee only consists of men plus one woman! And I say 'I think there's something wrong here! Where are the women? Where are the people of color?' And then, people start rolling their eyes and start cringing. They wiggle in their chairs. They look down. I don't want to essentialize Swedes as non-confrontative, but it's like, 'Oh, my world. Did I just say something wrong?' And then I say, 'Okay. Let's not look at race. Let's just start from gender. How is it possible that we have committees where men still dominate the scene?' This is Sweden. I don't think I will ever be complacent. If I ever become complacent, Sangeeta, you have to tell me, because at that point, there's something wrong with me. But yes. One can be complacent, but I hope I will never be.

> **Comments from the chat box**
>
> **Brett Diaz:** Sweden has a certain paradise-like look for those of us who have the equivalent of *Sverigedemokraterna* allies in the White House, though. Not to diminish other experiences of similar traumatic politics.

Sangeeta Bagga-Gupta

Thank you. I've lost the thread, but yes, I quite agree with your comment on the mobility issue. It's very right. My point was just that instead of north-south, we need to talk about mobility, as making it much more complex than it is in contemporary times, because this boxing-in then creates other kinds of issues. So, there can be double- and triple-marginalizations.

Tommaso Milani

Absolutely.

Sangeeta Bagga-Gupta

Sure. Thank you.

Rafael Lomeu Gomes

Thanks to everyone who asked questions, made comments, and enriched our discussion. Makoni, would you like to bring together some of the topics that have been discussed?

Sinfree Makoni

Okay. Let me try and do that and move the discussion further. I understand the issue of north-south, etc. and the dynamics about positionalities. I think the key issue here is the importance of self-reflexivity about where one is, in terms of the epistemological orientations and political positions that they may take. But I think we need a much more global view that also includes post-Soviet Republics, because there's a tendency to exclude scholarship from the former/post-Soviet Republics in any discussions about north-south. However, if you include that particular geographical region, I think we will have a much richer understanding of whatever south or northern scholarship is all about, because the post-Soviet Republics bring with them certain challenges about being on the periphery, but not being on too much of the periphery, so something like semi-periphery. So that, I think, is an important issue to consider. Then I think the general discussion left me with the impression that issues like sexuality and queerness are, to some extent, ambiguous and ambivalent terms. And the form that they eventually may take may depend very much upon the bodies to which they are enacted, which means in some contexts, you might need to link up sexuality with patriarchy, or sexuality with matriarchy, etc. in order to understand what is taking place there.

Then, there was a very important discussion that took place about affect. My own response is that: in as much as I am sympathetic towards that scholarship, it is important to bear in mind that the categories like affect, cognition, attitudes, etc. are not natural categories. They are categories that are an artifact of particular analytical ways of thinking. And I think Kurt Danziger put it very neatly, that the tendency is to think the categories which one uses are the natural categories, and the categories which everybody else uses are not natural categories.

So, if there is anything valuable about southern scholarship, it is that it should lead northern scholarship to question some of the basis of their assumptions. For example, is affect a category that is different from cognition? Or is affect a product of a Western mind thinking about the world in particular ways? Then, I think the most important part which we need to think about as we go along is the statement that was being made about the nature of what *disobedient scholarship* means. And ultimately, I think the extent to which you're going to be disobedient, or the form that your disobedience will take, may depend very much on the stage where you are in terms of your own career trajectory, and what are the options that are left open to you. Having said that, now I'm going to give over to Ashraf and Cristine to wrap up.

Cristine Severo

Thank you, Tommaso, for the great, great talk today.

Ashraf Abdelhay

Thank you, Tommaso. Thank you very much.

> **Comments from the chat box**
>
> **Joey Andrew Lucido Santos:** Thank you, Tommaso! You've delivered a very inspiring talk. I hope, as a graduate student, I'll be able to write something from the Southeast Asian perspective.
> **Hilary Janks:** Great webinar. Thanks, Tommaso. Miss you. Hilary
> **Ari Sherris:** Thanks Tommaso and everyone for bringing so much fresh thinking around the challenges of queering, rage, protest, and the biased framings by the Global North of the Global South. I am left wondering if heterotopias challenge us more than intersectionality to bring a more dynamic sense of our relationships and entanglements, alliances, and radical love(s).

Acknowledgment

We would like to thank Merel Lobo for assisting with the revision of this chapter's transcript.

References

Ahmed, S. (2004) *The Cultural Politics of Emotion* (1st edn). New York: Routledge.
Atshan, S.E. (2020) *Queer Palestine and the Empire of Critique*. Stanford: Stanford University Press.
Borba, R. and Milani T.M. (2017) The banality of evil: Crystallised structures of cisnormativity and tactics of resistance in a Brazilian gender clinic. *Journal of Language and Discrimination* 1 (1), 7–33.
Cashman, H. (2018) *Queer, Latinx and Bilingual: Narrative Resources in the Negotiation of Identities*. New York: Routledge.
Foucault, M. (1986) Of other spaces: Utopias and heterotopias (J. Miskowiec, Trans.). *Diacritics* 16 (1), 22–27.
Hull, G.T., Bell Scott, P. and Smith, B. (eds) (1982) *All the Women are White, all the Blacks are Men, but Some of us are Brave: Black Women's Studies*. New York: Feminist Press.
Lewis, E.S., Borba, R., Fabrício, B.F. and de Souza Pinto, D. (eds) (2014) *Queering Paradigms IV: South-North Dialogues on Queer Epistemologies, Embodiments and Activisms*. Peter Lang AG, Internationaler Verlag der Wissenschaften.
Lorde, A. (2012) *Sister Outsider: Essays and Speeches*. Toronto: Crossing Press.
Milani, T.M. (2014) Querying the queer from Africa: Precarious bodies – precarious gender. *Agenda* 28 (4), 75–85.
Milani, T.M. and Levon, E. (2017) Queering multilingualism and politics: Regimes of mobility, citizenship and (in)visibility. In R. Wodak and B. Forchtner (eds) *The Routledge Handbook of Language and Politics* (pp. 528–540). New York: Routledge.
Milani, T.M. and Levon, E. (2019) Israel as homotopia: Language, space and vicious belonging. *Language in Society* 48 (4), 607–628.
Milani, T.M. and Richardson, J.E. (2021) Discourse and affect. *Social Semiotics* 31 (5), 671–676.
Moita Lopes, L.P. (2009) Da aplicação de linguística à linguística aplicada indisciplinar. *Linguística aplicada: um caminho com diferentes acessos*. São Paulo: Contexto.
Msibi, T. (2014) Is current theorising on same-sex sexuality relevant to the African context? The need for more African voices on same-sex desire in Africa. *Pambazuka News*, 667.
Rothberg, M. (2019) *The Implicated Subject: Beyond Victims and Perpetrators*. Stanford: Stanford University Press.
Sedgwick, E.K. (2003) *Touching Feeling: Affect, Pedagogy, Performativity*. Durham, NC: Duke University Press.
Warner, M. (1991) Introduction: Fear of a queer planet. *Social Text* 29, 3–17.
Wetherell, M. (2012) *Affect and Emotion: A New Social Science Understanding*. London: SAGE Publications Limited.
Wetherell, M. (2015) Trends in the turn to affect: A social psychological critique. *Body & Society* 21 (2), 139–166.
Wiegman, R. (2012) *Object Lessons*. Durham, NC: Duke University Press.

7 Identity and the African Storybook Initiative: A Decolonial Project?

Bonny Norton

Magdalena Madany-Saá

I think we are all very excited to have Professor Bonny Norton with us. We have as I can see already over 60 people that have joined this session. So, let me very briefly, I know that the majority of you, you are here because you are familiar with Professor Bonny Norton's work. So, just to read one paragraph about her, she's a University Killam Professor and Distinguished University Scholar in the Department of Language and Literacy Education, the University of British Columbia in Canada. As research advisor of the African Storybook, and Project Lead of Global Storybooks, her research addresses identity, digital storytelling and open technology. She is a Fellow of Royal Society of Canada and the American Educational Research Association. Thank you so much, Professor Norton, for being with us. As I said, it's an honor, and we are all looking forward to your presentation and to talking to you and to having a conversation with you. So, the floor is all yours.

Bonny Norton

Thank you very much, Magda. What a delight it is to be here, and what a privilege it is to be part of this Penn State family that has been growing for a number of years now. And I want to acknowledge Sinfree Makoni's initiative in bringing us all together across time and place. And even though some of you on the West coast arrived at nine o'clock this morning, Eastern Time – we're all trying to manage these different time zones – it's wonderful that people have made the time to join this conversation. I am speaking to you from the traditional, ancestral and unceded Territory of the Musqueam people here in Vancouver, but I'm originally from South Africa, and also acknowledge the African lands I had the privilege to grow up on.

I want to note that I'm dedicating this presentation to two remarkable women who have been very active in the African Storybook, one being Tessa Welch, who was the project lead of African Storybook for many years, whom we lost a number of years ago, and also Dr Juliet Tembe, who was the Ugandan coordinator of African Storybook, and in fact, did her PhD with me at the University of British Columbia. It's wonderful that Magda did, in fact, open the session with a recognition of Átila Calvente, and his contribution to this conversation. We stand on the shoulders of giants, we learn from one another and these conversations continue. It's important to recognize the many contributions that people have made, those who are perhaps not with us at this time, and those still to come.

I'm going to share my screen and then begin my presentation. I've titled my talk 'Identity and the African Storybook initiative: A decolonial project?'

When I began preparing for this talk, I was reading quite a lot on linguistic citizenship, but I began to realize how the current research on decolonialism is also relevant to my work. So, my invitation to conversation is:

- What is the relationship between identity, linguistic citizenship and the African Storybook initiative?
- To what extent are the African Storybook, and the derivative Global Storybooks, decolonial projects?
- Can we define a decolonial project as one that seeks to expand the range of identity options for decolonial subjects?

This is an interest of mine that I've had for many years, and I hope to make the argument that expanding the range of identity options could be seen as a potentially decolonial initiative. I begin with the work of Christopher Stroud on linguistic citizenship. Christopher Stroud makes the point that, 'The concept of linguistic citizenship is a Southern and decolonial concept that arose out of the contradictions surrounding programs and practices of mother tongue and bilingual education in the 1990s in the context of the geopolitical south' (Stroud, 2018: 18). In some of his earlier work (Stroud, 2001: 353) makes the case:

> The concept of linguistic citizenship permits multiple (democratic, participatory) approaches to citizenship issues, based on the idea of language as a political and economic 'site of struggle,' on respect for language diversity and difference and on the deconstruction of essentialist understandings of language and identity.

In many ways, Stroud's theory and this definition of language resonates very much with the ideas on language that I've used in my work and certainly is associated with most poststructuralist theory (Norton, 2013; Norton & Morgan, 2020). Stroud argues further that linguistic citizenship highlights the importance of language practices that vulnerable speakers themselves exercise precisely to avoid the othering that comes with linguistic imposition. In sum, he argues, 'When speakers exercise linguistic citizenship, they also forge decolonial subjectivities' (Stroud, 2018: 7–9).

Following on from this research is the important work of Pennycook and Makoni (2019: 100), on *Innovations and Challenges in Applied Linguistics from the Global South*. As they note:

> We are acutely aware that under the broad umbrella of decolonization, there are many potential paradoxes, disagreements, diverse images of decolonial futures, and possible strategies for arriving at these different futures… We are trying to make a case for the bigger picture here, one where decolonizing applied linguistics is not just an issue for critical educational projects but a much wider set of concerns about knowledge and research.

More recently, there's been a great deal of research that's been coming out on these topics, and Finex Ndhlovu and Leketi Makalela (2021) talk in their book on *Decolonising Multilingualism in Africa*. [*Holds up book title*] What perspective do they bring to this project? They argue, 'Our position is that the standard language ideology, the mainstream understanding of multilingualism is pre-eminently colonial and needs to be decolonized' (Ndhlovu & Makalela, 2021: 17). They use the concept of 'coloniality of language' to describe the ways in which notions of language and multilingualism in postcolonial societies still remain colonial (Ndhlovu & Makalela, 2021: 17).

Most recently, Pinky Makoe (who I think is actually on our Zoom, so welcome, Pinky, great that you could join us!) has been writing about coloniality and decoloniality in Carolyn McKinney and Pam Christie's book *Decoloniality, Language and Literacy* (McKinney & Christie, 2022). I found Makoe's definition of colonialism and coloniality very helpful.

> In contrast to colonialism, coloniality refers to the establishment of a colonial matrix of power that continues to be reproduced even in the absence of direct colonial administrations… (Maldonado-Torres, 2007: 243). Based on this context, the nexus of decoloniality and ideology… enables us to problematize the privileging of European knowledge, language, subjectivity, and the invisibilisation of non-European forms of knowing. (Makoe, 2022: 49)

So, I'm setting my work in conversation and in dialogue with scholars who are grappling with notions of linguistic citizenship, with notions of coloniality and decoloniality, and I thank them for inviting me into this conversation, and for helping me to think through my ideas.

To this end, I work with an amazing group of students and colleagues here at UBC. I began my research when invited to Uganda in 2003, working with my colleagues Maureen Kendrick and Margaret Early here at UBC. We worked with a remarkable group of graduate students, predominantly from Uganda, but also from the Canadian and international context. These graduate students include Doris Abiria, Sam Andema, Shelley Jones, Harriet Mutonyi, Elizabeth Namazzi, Lauryn Oates, Monica Shank Lauwo, Espen Stranger-Johannessen, Juliet Tembe and Carrie-Jane Williams. We were interested in looking at research, practice and policy on African language and literacy in the African context. We also worked with policymakers, because one of the things that we have learnt, working not only in the African context, but many other contexts, is that if you don't work *with* policymakers, it's very difficult to make change at institutional level.

In the context of the digital, we were very interested in how digital technology could help us in grappling with language and literacy education in the African context. And another book that's come out, and my work is represented in there (Norton, 2021), is by Leketi Makalela and Goodith White, *Rethinking Language Use in Digital Africa* (Makalela & White, 2021). I love this image that was taken by Willy Ngaka in Northwestern Uganda. It's an image of a keyboard that is made of clay. Even if people don't have electricity and running water, they are highly invested in the digital for their future hopes and dreams, and are making digital clay keyboards to practice typing, so that when the digital does enter into their communities, they will hit the ground running.

So how then do poststructuralist theories of language resonate with theories of language that Christopher Stroud and others have proposed? What I've argued is that structuralists conceive of language as having idealized meanings and linguistic communities as being relatively homogenous and consensual; poststructuralists, on the other hand, take the position that the signifying practices of society are sites of struggle, and that linguistic communities are heterogeneous arenas characterized by conflicting claims to truth and power. How then do we think about poststructuralist theories of language and identity? What I've argued is that identity is how a person understands his or her relationship to the world, how that relationship is structured across time and space, and how a person understands possibilities for the future. I think it's the future that is such an important dimension to language and literacy education. We clearly learn from the past, but also, what are our hopes for the future? Where are we going? And I'm thinking for example of Theo, a Ugandan teenager, who says:

> I want to spread technology about, over the village and then, if time goes on, even the world in general. Because there are many of people in our villages that don't know about using the computer. And they cannot read, but if I train them how to use the computer, you never know. they can use it. (Norton & Williams, 2012: 323)

What is very interesting are the shifting identities as people engage with technology. If we look here at Henrietta, for example, who works very hard in her local Ugandan community, works domestically in her village, carries a lot of water to and from the wells. But when you put a computer in her hand, you shift her identity in relation to herself and her community. She can actually go into a police commissioner's office and take a photograph of a police commissioner, because she is seen as a person who has resources or knows people who have resources. And this final image was taken, actually, in an internet café, in southwestern Uganda. Many of the students who live in this larger community had never *been* inside the internet cafe. And after having access to some digital knowledge and technology, they went into that cafe and said, 'Today is our day.'

What we see here is that there is a very interesting relationship between digital identity and language. And in fact, some of the research on *new materialism* would pick up this fascinating connection between the material and the non-material world. This connects to questions of investment here: What are people's investment in the digital, and digital technology and digital discourse? I've argued, 'If learners invest in a language, they do so with the understanding that they will acquire a wider range of symbolic and material resources, which will in turn increase the value of the cultural capital and social power' (Norton, 2013: 6). I've argued that a learner may be a highly *motivated* language learner, but may nevertheless have little *investment* in the language practices of a given classroom and community, if it is, for example, racist, sexist, elitist or homophobic.

I've worked with Ron Darvin, who is also on our Zoom today, on developing the construct of investment more fully by looking at theories of capital, drawing

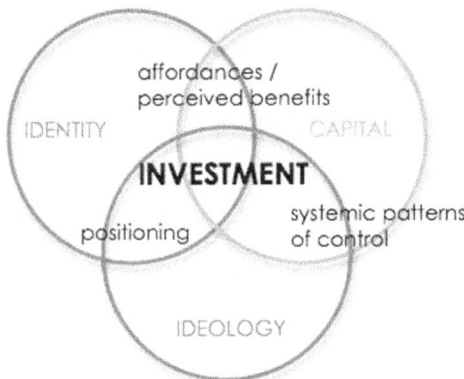

Figure 7.1 Darvin and Norton's (2015) model of identity and investment. *Annual Review of Applied Linguistics*, Cambridge University Press.

particularly on the work of Bourdieu and issues of ideology that we are all grappling with, see Figure 7.1 (Darvin & Norton, 2015, 2021).

If we look at these questions, in relation to Henrietta, we ask:

(1) How is the learner **positioned** by others, and how does the learner position her interlocutors? How do these positions shape her investment?
(2) What does the learner perceive as **benefits of investment**? How can the capital she possesses serve as **affordances of investments**?
(3) And, very importantly, how do **systemic patterns of control** (policies, codes, institutions) constrain or enable investment?

We look here at Betty who's a Ugandan school teacher who says:

I feel very powerful like a man because I had never held a camera in my life. I have always seen only men carrying cameras and taking photos in big public functions like may be independence celebration, political rallies and wedding ceremonies. But now as I move in the community taking pictures with my camera, I feel I am also very powerful, like a man... *I am now a learned person!*. (Andema, 2014: 91)

I find this data to be very bittersweet because we know that well before Betty picked up a camera, she was a learned person. She went through a very rigorous education, she became a schoolteacher, she ran a home and family – but only when she puts a camera in her hand, she feels a learned person, she feels powerful 'like a man'. This is data that comes from Sam Andema, and his PhD research (Andema, 2014).

How do we connect this with the issue of literacy and language internationally? We see that over 750 million youth and adults still cannot read and write, and 250 million children are failing to acquire basic literacy skills (https://en.unesco.org/themes/literacy). We have asked, 'What is the promise of the digital and open technology in providing access to materials and resources to promote multilingual literacy in both African communities and the global community'? An organization called Saide in South Africa – a remarkable organization – set about developing the African

Storybook. This is all free open access stories available on the site, africanstorybook.org. What Saide has done is to provide open access to picture storybooks in the languages of Africa, for children's literacy, enjoyment and imagination.

Working with a remarkable team, we find in 2022 that there are now over 225 languages on the site, over 3500 storybooks, and nearly 7500 translations. We at UBC have been active in this African Storybook project because I've served as the research advisor on this project. And you see me working here with Tessa Welch at the launch of the project in 2013 in Cape Town; here we have a picture of Juliet Tembe working with teachers in Uganda; we have Sam Andema in Northwestern Uganda, working with children; and we have Espen Stranger-Johannessen who I know is with us today, who worked actively on research and development of the site and is now in Norway.

What we have done at the University of British Columbia is to see the potential of leveraging these free open access stories on the African Storybook for additional resources within and beyond the African context. And we developed, with the remarkable technological skills of Liam Doherty and others, the original Storybooks Canada site. We drew on 40 stories from the African Storybook and have been translating those into multiple languages for use in other sites. As we note on the home page (storybookscanada.ca):

> Storybooks Canada is a free open educational resource that promotes literacy and language learning in homes, schools, and communities. Part of the Global Storybooks project, it makes 40 stories from the African Storybook available with text and audio in English, French, and the most widely spoken immigrant and refugee languages of Canada.

And from this one site, we now have over 50 sites that are freely available throughout the international community (Norton *et al.*, 2020). I've worked with a remarkable team, Sara Davidson, who's at Simon Fraser University, Monica Shank Lauwo, who's here today, Asma Afreen, Ingrid Schechter, Liam Doherty, as well as the continued work with Espen Stranger-Johannessen and others. What is very interesting is the work on parallel texts. What we've done in that translation of 40 stories is to create parallel texts, so that people can utilize a language that is familiar to them to learn other languages as well. Here is some data from a story called *Magozwe*, which is one of the many stories on the Global Storybooks site (globalstorybooks.net). We also have an Indigenous Storybooks site, which draws on open access stories from the Little Cree Books. And there is also the Storybooks African Languages site that I'd like to share with you at the end of my talk.

I wear many hats, as a researcher, and also a practitioner. We have many research questions that arise from the research that we've done with the African Storybook and our Global Storybooks project. I'd like to share three of those research projects with you, to demonstrate how many questions arise from these open access stories. For example:

- Can school teachers use Global Storybooks to promote multilingual literacy?
- What are diverse students' investments?
- Can Global Storybooks promote multilingual identity?

- How can we develop home/school connections?
- What challenges do translators face?
- To what extent do the parallel texts in Global Storybooks promote language learning?
- How helpful is the toggle feature?
- Is translanguaging productive for language learning?
- To what extent can Global Storybooks promote multilingual language awareness?
- How do stories travel from one region of the world to another?

Our first study, with Espen Stranger-Johannessen, takes place in three Ugandan schools, and focuses on a teacher, Monica (Stranger-Johannessen & Norton, 2019). Our questions were as follows: *What is Monica's investment in the African Storybook? How does this investment provide insight into her language teacher identity?* What is very interesting here is that on the African Storybook, people can contribute their own stories, and one of the things that Monica did was to contribute some poetry to the African Storybook site. It was very interesting that Átila talks about poetry as a powerful resource; this was a story that Monica wrote about insects and mosquitoes. Monica summarizes the impact on her as follows,

> When I see my name in there, online, I'll be very happy, I wanted my name to appear such that people, people come, I mean, people begin to look for me, who is this woman who writes the story? But when they reach here, they will want to know who Monica is.

One of the stories on the African Storybook site is *Andiswa Soccer Star*. It's a wonderful story about a young girl who wants to play soccer, but soccer in the school is only for boys. When one of the boys gets sick, Andiswa is allowed to go and play soccer, and scores the winning goal. What the teacher Monica says is,

> Such stories really helped me, it changed the attitudes of boys, where they could think that a girl is not supposed to play football, but this time when I go for my physical education lesson, when I prepare a lesson about football, they don't complain, they don't pick the ball away from the girls, they just play together like that, this time they've started attitude change instead, it helped me a lot.

It's very interesting to see that Monica has been able to draw on the African Storybook, and this particular story, for transformation, in a sense, both of her identity as a teacher, but also the identities of the boys and girls in her class.

In the second study, I've done work with Rahat Zaidi and Robin Metcalfe on French immersion classes in Canada, and the extent to which they can use Storybooks Canada, and African Storybooks, for French immersion purposes (Zaidi *et al.*, 2022) This story is one of the stories called *Counting Animals*. I was intrigued by this data from one of the teachers Victoria. And what she says is (2022: 78):

> In my class, we did *Counting Animals* (Buthelezi *et al.*, n.d.), and one of my students was particularly really happy about it because she comes from Pakistan. And she was like, 'Oh, well, I see lots of different animals that maybe you guys never saw before,' and she started to talk about these different animals. And then the other one just added on about different animals…I think it makes them more secure to talk about

it because, well, 'We saw these animals that are in Africa, so I come from another place, and I saw other things. So, I can talk about it like everybody is talking about the bears.'

The point here is that because the material in the African Storybook introduces children to other animals that children may not be familiar with, children from different parts of the world feel that they can talk about the animals in their own countries such as Pakistan, Brazil and Iran. It now becomes legitimate to talk about animals, not only in the Canadian context, where there are bears, but animals in other contexts as well. This data brings me back to Bourdieu's work on legitimate discourse. What constitutes legitimate discourse in classrooms? This student felt it was legitimate to talk about animals in Pakistan, because now that she'd seen animals in the African context, she could be seen as a legitimate speaker, as opposed to an imposter in her French immersion classroom.

In the third study I've worked with Liam Doherty and Espen Stranger-Johannessen on the identity of the translator (Doherty *et al.*, 2022). In our analysis, we have worked with two divergent theorizing of translanguaging, one which recognizes the strategic usefulness and importance of named languages, and the other which recognizes the importance of drawing on the full range of linguistic repertoires available to individuals, groups and communities in the construction of meaning making. Ofelia García and Li Wei and others have been grappling with the issues of translanguaging, and I know one of the conversations that we had here at the Penn State Virtual Forum concerns the role of named languages, and certainly this is the work of Pennycook and Sinfree Makoni and others. How do we work with the full range of linguistic repertoires that students and learners bring to a given classroom?

What we found in our project is that we were working with two theorizations of translanguaging, which includes named languages, and also the full range of linguistic repertoires. This brought us to the identity of the translator, who works with texts from a formal and a functional perspective (Afreen, 2022). What we also found in our research is that there are many people who are active in the translation process, not only the translator, but the proofreader, the editor, the narrator; they are all active in translation and they have a different relationship to the target language and the source language. They may in fact not speak the target language – it may be L1, L2, L3 for them. And similarly, in relation to the source language, people may have little access to the source language, or they may speak it as a first, second or third language. So, we're looking at the complexity of translator identity. What we see here in this wonderful data that we've collected, is a debate by different participants on how we would translate, for example, Swahili (see Figure 7.2). In trying to make these stories into parallel texts, there's a great deal of conversation about translation.

The key questions I ask are, 'Do the African Storybook and Global Storybooks projects expand the range of identities available for teachers, students and translators? To what extent do these initiatives promote linguistic citizenship for vulnerable people? To what extent can these initiatives be perceived as decolonial projects?' What I'm going to do before we open this up for conversation is just take you to one

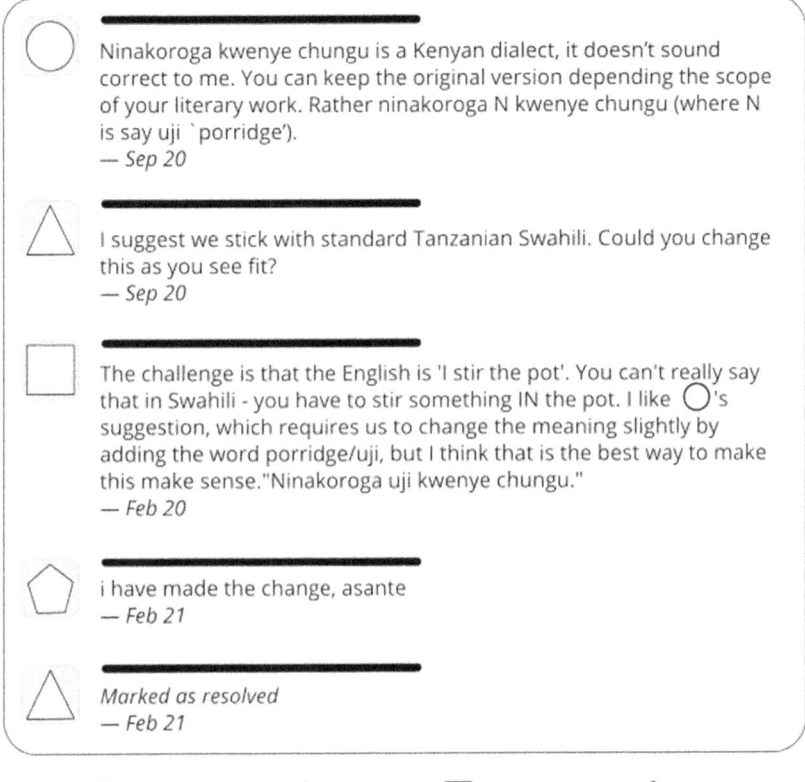

Figure 7.2 Debate on the Swahili translation of 'I stir the pot' in the story, Lazy Little Brother

site on our Global Storybook site. I'll just pull this up here, I hope you can see that everybody. So, this is the Global Storybooks portal. [*Begins screen sharing*]

We can see that we have a range of sites from Afghanistan to Brazil, Central African Republic, East Timor, Haiti where we have Haitian Creole. We have the Indigenous Storybooks project; we have the site for Kenya, we have Jamaica with Jamaican Creole; Liberia. In fact, I think we've just set up one for Namibia, which is very exciting. And Nigeria, Pakistan. And we've got a site for South Africa as well, and Tanzania, Zambia, and a site for Storybooks African Languages. All free and open access; you just go to globalstorybooks.net.

On the dropdown menu, we have all the languages that are available in both print and audio. That's very exciting, because when you learn a language, it's certainly very helpful to able to listen to the language, and also to read it as well. So, I'm going to take you to the Swahili site; let's go to *Andiswa Soccer Star*, because we did utilize that story in one study. Because the stories have a Creative Commons license, we know here who actually wrote the story, who illustrated the story, who translated the story. And here we see – here we have our story that's available in Swahili and

I'm going to just play this for you; it's just so wonderful to actually hear a language [*plays an audio clip*] – I hope this comes through.

> Andiswa alikuwa anawaangalia wavulana wakicheza mpira wamiguu. Alitamani kujiunga nao. Akamwomba kocha kufanya nao mazoezi.

For those who don't understand Kiswahili, this is the English:

> Andiswa watched the boys play soccer. She wished she could join them. She asked the coach if she can practise with them.

You can also toggle to French as well, on this particular site. You can go down and read the story and listen to that story in Swahili. And, also, we've got it in Zulu, Arabic and other languages. But if you go to the home site here, you'll also see that we've got many African languages under 'languages'. The reason why they're in this particular link is because we haven't yet translated all 40 stories into these languages, *or* we haven't yet done the audio for these languages. But there are still a wonderful number of languages that are available.

Should we look at Yoruba? Let's see what we have in Yoruba. We have eight stories available in Yoruba. If we pick up a story here (*I Like to Read/Mo fẹ́ràn kàwé*) we've got Letta Machoga who wrote the story; it was illustrated by Wiehan de Jager and Vusi Malindi; we see that it was translated by Blessing Williamson and Victor Williamson; and we don't yet have the audio. So, you can see that this is a work in progress, but I think it already has much potential for sharing languages and resources worldwide.

I'm going to stop sharing and open this up for further conversation. And perhaps I can start with you, Sinfree. I think the protocol is to have a little conversation with you, before we open it up?

Sinfree Makoni

Yes.

Bonny Norton

So, okay, my challenge – Sinfree, is the African Storybook a decolonial project?

Sinfree Makoni

That's a good question. Let me answer this by reading to you a text that I am currently preparing for a fellowship I got from CODESRIA, and it's called the Advanced Fellowship in the Humanities. And this is the conclusion I've provisionally arrived at, at the moment. 'A straightforward definition of a decolonial project is impossible.' Then the question then becomes, why? This is my best reading of the scholarship, as it stands at the moment. Decolonial scholarship means different things, depending on where you are situated in the globe. What decoloniality might mean in South America, for example, may be very, very different from what it might mean in the African context.

In an African context, it's not clear whether in actual fact the emphasis on decoloniality is having the negative effects of emphasizing Eurocentric thinking, for the reason that the emphasis on decoloniality is having the contradictory outcome; in other words, by emphasizing decoloniality you're saying, yes, I'm trying to challenge Eurocentrism – but then you are giving the impression, which is false, that there are no other libraries of knowledge which existed prior to or parallel to Eurocentrism. So, decoloniality, in this bigger scheme of ideas in Africa, as the Malawian African historian Paul Cereza puts across, is historically inaccurate. That's one strand to it.

The other strand to it is the argument that is made by the Nigerian philosopher Táíwò, who says that it's possible that we have overstressed the decolonial aspect of it. Even if we have overstressed the decolonial aspect of it, the key thing, the key question is one that is raised by Lewis Gordon, when he says, decolonial thinkers must, from the point of view, go beyond decoloniality, for the sake of decoloniality. If the decolonization is to be effective, we need to be clear what decolonization is for. So, that is the sort of African problem, which I'll come back and discuss further. If you then move and come to the United States, decoloniality begins to be used more or less interchangeably with a quest for social justice. So, it begins to metamorphosize and mean different things. If you go into Denmark, etc., the difference between the notions of decoloniality in Denmark and in Africa is that in Denmark, the concern is not so much with decoloniality, but who are you decolonizing.

According to Julia Krabbe-Suarez, for example, in the Denmark case, the emphasis is on the people you are targeting. Who you want to learn to decolonize are the white, Danish-dominant individuals. We learned in the African case, following the thinking by Ngugi, it's more or less Africans wanting to decolonize themselves from coloniality – but if you move and then go to Eastern Europe, the story is a different story. The story is, then, the relationship between state socialism and decoloniality. The scholars in Eastern Europe see state socialism as an incomplete project of decoloniality, so that is why your question is very important, but very difficult to answer – because it depends where you are, and how you're going to respond to it. Am I responding to it from the United States, or am I talking from Cape Town, or am I talking from Europe, or am I talking from Eastern Europe, etc.?

The dynamics of what decoloniality means are such that it means different things in different intellectual trajectories. And, at the moment, all these things are moving in different directions. That's my long response to what you're saying. It's a useful question, but completely unanswerable – unless you say decoloniality in Nairobi. *Then* I can be able to sort of say, 'Oh, yes, yes, yes.' This is what it might mean – but if it's simply decoloniality as a project, then it's a bit unanswerable.

> **Comments from the chat box**
>
> **Brett Diaz:** I wish I could 'like' spoken discourse, because I love that 'what is decoloniality in THIS context'

Bonny Norton

So, Sinfree, interestingly enough, I think that makes a huge amount of sense. And, in fact, this is one of the reasons, as I started reading on decolonization, I realized that there were all these different traditions, one of which, of course, is also the Indigenous tradition. [*Holds up book cover of* Decolonizing Methodologies *by Linda Tuhiwai Smith, 1999*]

Sinfree Makoni

Oh, yes. Yes, yes.

Bonny Norton

I'm thinking here of *Decolonizing Methodologies* by Linda Tuhiwai Smith (1999), from New Zealand, and how she is grappling with decolonization; the Indigenous community has been absolutely central in placing decolonization on the research agenda. And as I grappled with what we mean by decoloniality, I'm thinking of Pinky Makoe; how does she see decoloniality? Interestingly, she draws on a Brazilian scholar to understand decoloniality in the African context. So, what you see is conversations that are also crossing borders. How are we learning from others across these different transnational borders, as well as epistemological borders? When we go and do our research, you're reminding us that we need to understand: What does decoloniality mean, in this particular context?

Sinfree Makoni

In this particular context, at this particular time. Then – once you have clarified that for yourself, you can then be able to move ahead. If you just frame it broadly, then it doesn't help you. In the forthcoming book that I've just completed with Anna Kaiper-Marquez and Loretta McQueen, in which Átila had a chapter, we argue that for decoloniality to take place, there needs to be fundamental shift, to use Lewis Gordon's terms, in the geography of reason; there needs to be shift in the way you epistemologically relate to your own tasks. And with that in mind, we identified six different dimensions or layers that are required in order for you to move forward. One, there has to be a shift from a closed to an open relational commitment; there has to be a shift that requires you to think anew and creatively; there has to be a shift which requires understanding power should not be reduced to a single element; there has to be a shift that requires an understanding of the mechanisms of the production of knowledge; there has to be a shift in how you can use meta language that comes from the environment in which you are in. Let me explain.

The applied linguists are clear about the multilinguality of the world, but the meta language that they use is still European meta language; they don't use meta language that comes from the environment that they're dealing with. So, if you're going to decolonize multilingualism, you need to talk about what multilingualism is understood as within the local folk lay-oriented discourses that you are making use of. So, you can't decolonize multilingualism using Euro American meta language, because Euro American meta language colonizes your own imagination of what constitutes language. So, you are required by the circumstances, by the logic, to look at the meta languages that are used within that environment to talk about language.

I buy the argument that, as Chris Hutton reminds me, that if we follow you on that one, it will be impossible to come up with a coherent international discourse of sociolinguistics because different communities will have their different sociolinguistics. My argument is, I'm willing to say, 'It's better to have a sociolinguistics that is valid to the local context than a sociolinguistics that is internationally acceptable but not valid to the local users.' That is the price I'm willing to pay, at least for the time being.

Bonny Norton

But interestingly, Sinfree, this does raise the question of who sits on review boards in journals, right? Because when you wish to publish your work, it goes to particular journals who have a particular advisory board, and they will come back and, depending on who's on those boards, ask 'Have you read this? Have you read that? Are you familiar?' So, one would have to decolonize editorial boards.

Sinfree Makoni

Yes, yes. The key thing, which is there, which John Joseph from Edinburgh reminded me, and which is a point which I want to make, is that the limitation of our arguments about decoloniality at the moment is that they don't talk about the need to decolonize the notion of a book. Right? The notion of a journal. We don't talk about – we have inherited the idea of a book since the printing press and all that; we are willing to decolonize everything without addressing the *fundamental* concept which we need to review and revise, which is the idea of a book as a carrier of scholarship. Because if we don't revise and rethink how the notion of a book is conceptualized, then all these other things are going to be difficult. Because they're still going to be carried out on the basis of this notion of a book that has *retained the same form* since the onset of the printing press.

Bonny Norton

Mmm. But then, of course, the paradoxes – my graduate students always remind me of the paradoxes. In our field, we are sitting with all these books. [*Holds up a book*] We are part of this paradox.

Sinfree Makoni

We are. We are.

Bonny Norton

We are part of this problem, right? Because this is how we are spreading ideas. So, I guess, in a sense, I guess you could argue that the Global Storybooks project, the African Storybook is, in fact, *not* a book; it is *not* a book, and there is the dissemination of ideas through free open technology.

Sinfree Makoni

Yes. It's true. It's true. When I was thinking about this, when I was preparing for my talk, for my conversation with you, I couldn't understand why you wanted to call it a book project, because the signals it sends are very different from what you are talking about – the form, the access, etc. It is a much more radical project, which loses its power when you use more acceptable terms like 'the book project.'

Comments from the chat box

Carolyn McKinney: In editing the 2nd edn of *Routledge Handbook of Multilingualism*, we have explicitly required authors to cite research in languages other than English and from Southern or periphery contexts and asked authors to co-author across North and South as well as constituted a South-dominated editorial board (we as myself, Pinky Makoe and Virginia Zavala) but I agree that the notion of knowledge construction and dissemination through peer-reviewed books is not decolonial.

Bonny Norton

Well, Sinfree [and Carolyn], I can tell you that, when we work with teachers, with parents, they will ask you, 'Where are the books? Where are the books?' We have to remember that as we grapple with decolonial ideas, we have to ask ourselves: Who do we speak to? Of course, in this [Penn State] site, we're talking to one another as scholars and as researchers, but in the back of my mind are parents and teachers who constantly remind me of resources that are needed in schools, of examinations that children need to sit, of tests that students need to prepare for. So, how do we work in this liminal space, in this complex space? Much like the translanguaging challenge – you know, we were struggling with the named languages on the one hand, but also the linguistic repertoires – how do we work in this complex space, where we want to see change, but we also need to understand the investments of different stakeholders, because we need to bring them with us. We need to work together.

If we don't work together, we're just going to have silos and people who are speaking to people who agree with them, right? So, the concept of the African Storybook – I love the idea you [pose and] I think the African Storybooks is a radical project; I do think it's radical with a small 'r' in many ways, but I think that the concept of a book is important *because* this is the language that people beyond academia understand. And while we can, of course, shift that, for sure, re-theorize the construct of a book, it's helpful to begin at least with a language that many people understand.

Sinfree Makoni

Yeah. I see what you mean, but my view is that people are much more radical and more open to change than we give them credit for – but you and me will continue on this. Chanel, you will take over and do the moderation. Me and Bonny will continue our discussions later on.

> **Comments from the chat box**
>
> **Cécile Vigouroux:** I agree with Sinfree, but to what extent speaking about decoloniality in Kenya, Uganda, or DRC is not a way to endorse recent colonial borders and ratify as unproblematic a nation-state framework of analysis?
> **Robin Sabino:** Rather than 'in this particular place', might we think of for 'these particular people{s}'?
> **Olusegun Soetan:** Robin, 'these particular people' could still connote a colonial view. What is the heritage idea of Yoruba as a group of people? Is it the Yoruba that came together in the 1800s or the Yoruba of centuries before European invasion of Africa or the Yoruba of 1914, when Nigeria was amalgamated?
> **Robin Sabino:** I was thinking of 'people(s)' as constituted groups of individuals in specific times and places and as such a bit more specific than 'place'.

Chanel Van der Merwe

Okay, no problem. Thank you so much, Professor Norton. There is a lot of comments based on the conversation you just had. One from Cécile Vigouroux, who says, 'I agree with Sinfree, but to what extent speaking about decoloniality in Kenya, Uganda or the DRC is not in a way to endorse recent colonial borders and ratify as unproblematic a nation-state framework of analysis?' And then – Robin Sabino then added to that, 'Rather than – should we not think of in this particular place, think of, for these particular people?' as an add on. So, you guys want to just comment on those two, for now?

Sinfree Makoni

Right. Let me respond to what Cécile is saying by paraphrasing from a book cited recently by Suleiman Yasir (who presented last week), which was co-authored by Jean-Loup Amselle and others, and which I think partially agrees with what Cécile is trying to talk about. And they talk about this, they're talking on Africa and pan-Africanism.

And let me paraphrase: What does it mean to say that Africa desires Africa, that Africans are engaged in the realization of a pan-African idea, with the full awareness of the history of this idea and the differences between pan-Africanism yesterday, with all its emancipatory force represented, and the pan-Africanism of today, keyed in toward the new advances in independent meaning? To desire Africa means to wish to create unity in pluralism. This, as I have said, is the meaning of remembering certain periods, hours, when ethno-nationalism abroad are working to control and limit the mobility of certain populations, including African populations, of course, and are scared of the notion which they consider the ultimate catastrophe – that natives will be replaced by migrants. They are likely to dislike the idea that it is a single country in which, as Pope Francis carelessly repeats, nobody should be in exile. To offer an African space without frontiers [this is where, for example, I think Cécile was going] – without frontiers to the initiative and the creativity of citizens who are no longer Moroccan, Malawian, Rwandan and so on, but African, is not to ignore that Morocco is not Rwanda, it is to desire an African future. The future of an African project is not given, but it would be what, together, we make of it (Diagne *et al.*, 2020).

This is my response to it. This is how I think Yasir Suleiman, the African philosopher who was talking to us last week, would respond. He would say, yes, you're right. What we need is to desire an African future without borders, though that does not mean that the identities of being Moroccan or Rwandan disappear.

Chanel Van der Merwe

Prof Vigouroux, would you like to respond to that? Are you happy with the response?

Cécile Vigouroux

Yes, I – thank you, Sinfree, for the quotation. Yeah – why don't we embrace other kinds of identities? Ethno-linguistic identities and stuff like that? You know, there are other kind of frameworks than the nation state, and as you know, we are increasingly going away or challenging in any kinds of societies, challenging the nation state framework, that proves to be extremely problematic in understanding language dynamics.

> **Comments from the chat box**
>
> **Cécile Vigouroux:** We have a consortium of journal editors who are working on new publishing and reviewing practices that embrace decolonialities.

Sinfree Makoni

Yeah. I agree with you, I think that's a conversation I want to have, I think, with Bonny and Christopher Stroud about this sort of linguistic citizenship thing that seems to be grounded in a charitable interpretation of the positive role of a nation state. And for me, also, the idea of citizenship, yes, I can see what you mean – but citizenship, by definition, discriminates against other people. So, I've always had mixed feelings. I can see what they're trying to get at, but my experience with citizenship doesn't convince me that linguistic citizenship will resolve the problem for most people, because you're always going to have people who are going to be discriminated against on that basis. Yeah, but it's not me who is supposed to be talking, it's everybody else. And Bonny Norton is the person that everybody has come to listen to – not me. Stop asking me.

[*Laughter*]

> **Comments from the chat box**
>
> **Anna Kaiper-Marquez:** Question for Bonny: Hi Bonny! I have found your definition of identity/identities really helpful throughout the years in my own work. I am curious how shifts in thought on decoloniality, globally South epistemologies, etc. have impacted your own definitions of 'identity' and poststructuralism and how these re/definitions have impacted your research?

Chanel Van der Merwe

So, Bonny Norton, from Anna and then we'll go to Sangeeta. Okay. Hi, Bonny, I found the definition of identity identities really helpful throughout the years in my own work. I'm curious how shifts in thoughts on decoloniality, globally South epistemologies have impacted your own definitions of identity, and poststructuralism, and how these redefinitions have impacted then your research?

Bonny Norton

Well, thank you very much for that question [Anna]. I guess, I always – when I read new research, I set it in conversation with my ideas, and see whether or not it works. For example, when I was thinking about the multiplicity of identity, I thought, 'Does this project, this African Storybook project, actually expand the range of identities available for vulnerable learners, for example, decolonial subjects, in Stroud's words?'. I put it out there as a question because I'd love to get feedback. It seems to me that this project, in fact, does expand the range of identities available – whether you're a poet or a digital innovator, or a community member, or a change agent. And because of the expanded range of identities, it seems to me, the decolonial project is in fact, one which expands the range of identities available to learners, teachers, translators.

But then, if you think of other research, like, on new materialism, I go back to Henrietta, who holds that camera in her hand. In the past, I just thought, well, she's got a camera, and of course, she's relating to people, as someone who has resources and someone who has some power. But I never ever thought of this as a material object, so to speak. Now I have heightened awareness about the material world that I wouldn't otherwise have had, if I had not started reading the research on new materialism and post-humanism. So, when I read new work, I bring a new lens to my work, and it helps me to sharpen my focus when I actually look at my data. And in the same way, when I look at Indigenous methodologies, I'm trying to take seriously, what does it mean, to have Indigenous ways of knowing?

When I look at my data, how can I bring those theories and understandings to bear on the analysis of data? It certainly has a very important influence on how I see my data. And I'm sure that for many of you, who are researchers, there are many ways of reading your data. And what I find exciting about being introduced to new ways of thinking, new ideas, is that I *revisit* data, and see new insights in the data. So, there is a conversation between new theories, and I do always have to ask – it's interesting, Sinfree made the point – is decoloniality just about social justice? Well, in the North American context, is it, or isn't it? Or are there particular qualities around decoloniality that make it different to the construct of social justice?

Therefore, what does this mean for how I go about doing my research, and how I analyze my data? I do think about what Sinfree says about 'decoloniality means different things in different places'; you don't need to think of it even in terms of nation-states. I think what Cécile is saying is, 'I'm not sure how helpful that [construct] is.' But, at the same time, I do feel that time and place are really important in terms of understanding of language and learning. So, it does remind me that I do need to look very closely when I'm doing research: What are the understandings of language and change and decoloniality in that particular context? So, thank you very much for that question.

> **Comments from the chat box**
>
> **Sangeeta Bagga-Gupta:** I perhaps missed something, but I think the metalanguage that Sinfree mentions is what I call 'naming practices' and the 'vocabularies' in the Language Sciences. For instance, concepts like 'L1, L2, codes, oral language, written language, Swedish, English, trans/plurilanguaging…' I wonder what trans/multi, etc., do for us analytically when we have made a shift from 'language' to 'communication and languaging.'

Chanel Van der Merwe

Thank you. Sangeeta?

Sangeeta Bagga-Gupta

It's a bit hard to come in with this very rich conversation that has taken place, both orally but also in the writing. And I think Lynn Mario makes a very important point there in terms of that as literacy scholars, we somehow get sucked into the hegemonies of the written word. And we are not attentive to in our transcription, in our writing, attentive to the richness of communicative repertoires that we pay homage to and are not theorizing. So, there is a very important point there, but I won't go down that lane, because I think that that is – there's much to be said there. I also want to engage with the point that Bonny you make regarding insights from new materialism and post humanism. But in my current writing, I wonder whether that itself also raises, call it alternative epistemologies or parallel epistemologies from the Global South, and there, I would say, the south, the north, and the north and the south. So, it's not a territorial way of looking at the Global South.

And I'll take up one example. About 10 years ago, my previous university where I worked at in Sweden got a major grant together with local, civil societal representatives for something that was called Spread the Sign. And there were 15 European nation states involved in that project, and a number of Deaf leaders. I wasn't involved, so I was kind of observing what was happening. And I noticed that after the first couple of years, the Deaf leaders and the Deaf community sort of withdrew. So, there was tokenism in that project; the project was related to translating from Swedish sign language to Portuguese sign language to British sign language, you name it, and so there were these 15.

One of the insights that, as a scholar, I learned together with other colleagues and students who use Swedish sign language was that this was a project for hearing people, for politicians and hearing people who don't know anything about Deaf culture, and visuality, and visual-oriented ways of being. So, the written script, for instance, is a very strong marker of visuality. And I was thinking of this as I was reading the text for today's seminar, and I was thinking of the comment that Sinfree made regarding meta language. And this is a concern I have generally for my own – I mean, I don't know any way of getting out of it. So, my question is embedded in this meta-language, or what I call naming practices within the language sciences.

How can we get away from these naming practices where we are – we have to say something to talk about people like me, and many of us here who language in a number of different named languages: are we multilingual or are we translanguaging, or...? And that is a question to this text. So, the naming practices – so what is translanguaging? For me, that is... I mean, I feel worried when I see this replacing multilingualism. And can we translate without creating bounded languages? So, could you reflect with me on that?

Bonny Norton

First of all, thank you very much for those comments, Sangeeta. We do, interestingly enough, on one of our sites on the Global Storybook site, have a Speech and Hearing site for sign languages. So, I'd invite you to check that out. What this brings to mind is my thoughts as a University Examiner on a thesis. At UBC, we have a process where we've got the academic Abstract that the student writes, and then we've got what we call a *'Lay Abstract for the Public'*. And I'm thinking, isn't that interesting? So, I read the academic Abstract that has huge amounts of meta language, ways of theorizing and conceptualizing. And then I read the Lay Abstract, which is for everybody else who uses regular language.

And I think, what do we gain and lose with these two genres, so to speak? We have one language with which we speak to the public, so everybody understands what we're actually saying. And then we have another whole kind of language, for scholars who understand what we're saying, and I guess – this troubles me to some extent – that we need these two genres. What are we gaining from the meta language? So, I just put that out there, because I was just reflecting on that very point. But the question is, how can we translate without named languages? Well, as you saw, this was our biggest challenge in this whole African/Global Storybooks project, where what we want to do is to promote language learning in multiple languages. And when it comes to actually making a translation, and in particular, doing an audio, you've got to have something that the majority of people are going to understand.

And, in fact, if you look at the literature on translanguaging, the earlier translanguaging work done in Wales – in fact, they were looking at named languages, they were looking at a kind of bilingualism, but now there's been a shift to looking at linguistic repertoires. What we found in our research is that you can work with both. Haitian Creole was one of the languages that we translated into, and there were very few materials available in Haitian Creole or in Jamaican Creole. So, in a sense, by making it a named language, teachers tell us that this, actually, was wonderful in their classrooms, because children see legitimacy in having their Jamaican Creole made available. Mauritian Creole is another one that we've done a lot of translation for.

In the process of navigating into and working with named languages, there's a great deal of translanguaging at that time as well. So, I do wonder – you know, people talk about multilingualism – in fact, even with Stroud's book, it's *The Multilingual Citizen*. So, even though one might be looking at many different ways of framing languages, the title of the book still, in a sense, draws on common understandings of multilingualism. So, I do grapple with this, the language that we use, how far we go with it, what we can learn from it. Maybe just going back to Cécile's point – what I find as a scholar, and as a teacher, and a researcher – I do work in different countries, different nation-states, so to speak, but more importantly, I work in different communities; I work not only with scholars, I work with teachers, I work with students, I work with the public.

And so, in a sense, I'm always having to grapple with these different communities. It's a bit like the Lay Abstract and the Academic Abstract: 'How can we speak to one another in meaningful ways?' is for me the challenge. I see, Salikoko, you've just come on. I see your image there, Salikoko. Did you have a comment?

> **Comments from the chat box**
>
> **Olusegun Soetan:** Your presentation was so enlightening and very engaging, thank you! As a translator for the African Book project, I have noticed that digital technology homogenizes cultural spaces, peoples and ideas; so, how can digital artists and content creators decolonize technology to improve cultural identities in the African Book project?

Chanel Van der Merwe

Before you go, Professor Mufwene – sorry. There are few other comments and questions in the chat box that I just made a list of. So, if we can quickly just go to Olusegun's question, and then we can go to you. Dr Norton, is it okay if we go a little bit over time – ?

Bonny Norton

I'm fine, I *love* this conversation. Thank you so much. Yes.

Chanel Van der Merwe

No problem. Okay. So, let's just read out this question. 'A lot of praise. Your presentation was so enlightening and very engaging. Thank you. As a translator for the African Book projects, I've noticed that digital technology homogenizes cultural spaces, people and ideas, so how can digital artists and content creators decolonize technology to improve cultural identities in this African Book project?'

Bonny Norton

Well, thank you [Olusegun]. You know, one of the things that I am always very excited about is how teachers, actually, are the ones who actually radicalize, so to speak, these homogenized spaces. That you can begin with a story that essentializes, perhaps, a cultural space, a community, and can completely reframe that. Much like looking at the data with *Counting Animals*. I mean, for me, it was just a simple vignette about African animals, and suddenly a young girl from Pakistan says, 'Let me tell you about animals in my country, or let me tell you about my world.' And the teacher encourages that, right? So, what I see, what excites me, is the ways in which teachers can do radical work – even when texts can be essentialized, the ideas can be essentialized – that doesn't mean they stay in boxes. It's an opportunity to learn, it's an opportunity for the teachers to say, 'I'm going to challenge this'. Much like I wrote in one of my earlier articles 'Demystifying the TOEFL Reading Test' (Norton Peirce, 1992) because I worked at the Educational Testing Service in the US.

And what for me is so fascinating is how teachers can take a test, and then basically do a complete discourse analysis of the strengths and limitations of that test, and by doing it, it's liberating, because students realize it's just human made! There's nothing magical about this particular test; somebody made it, we can deconstruct it, we can challenge it, we can discuss it, and then we can take the test. So, I see teachers doing amazing things with objects, with ideas, with stories. And I think that's why I like to work with policymakers, because we want to be sure that teachers have the space in which they can do that, because if there's somebody outside their door, right, looking in and saying, 'You can't use Swahili in this classroom, it's an English language classroom!' then, that's going to tie the teacher's hands.

But if policymakers, if we all – and this is where I do see the value of the research that we do – if we can speak to policymakers, bring them on board, so that they understand the logic of what we do, of the research, we may find a more productive relationship with work getting done in schools. That's why I think we have to all work together, because we can't just talk to one another, we have to talk to the policymakers because the policymakers control the teachers, right? We want to keep teachers safe, but we also want to feel that they have the authority to utilize their imaginations in creative ways. I have a lot of faith in what teachers do, but we also have to give them the space to do it.

Chanel Van der Merwe

Thank you so much. Prof Salikoko?

Salikoko Mufwene

Bonny, thank you very much for this brilliant exposé, I learned a great deal from that… and especially relative to the exchange between Sinfree and you. I want to underscore the fact that at the beginning of your presentation, you articulated clearly your interpretations of 'decoloniality', and I've written three of them. In my words, it's 'emancipation from dominance in the production of knowledge', who is producing the knowledge, then a second interpretation, viz., 'emancipation from the way in which knowledge has been produced', who has control and determine the standard, according to which knowledge must be produced and so forth. And a third one that is implicit in the books that you showed 'that in which language is the knowledge produced'.

So, Sinfree reacted in part in saying decoloniality takes a different meaning in different places at different times, coloniality itself as domination actually took different meanings in different places, and in different times, and so forth. But there is a common thread. It's that movement of emancipation, the need to change things, and whatever we do is going to be quite specific in different places, depending on what we are doing. I mean, the case of children's storybooks is going to be determined largely by the different cultures. However, these interpretations are not mutually exclusive, there is still decoloniality that we are trying to engage in and engage with. So, this thing about language having boundaries, don't they have boundaries? It depends on where you are.

I'm thinking of rural Africa, languages are associated with villages, and a lot of villages are monolingual. And if you have a particular part that is multilingual, it's like a cluster of villages next to each other. And the members of one cluster, usually the main village, and then you have a satellite village. With these languages, the village becomes the part, the setting that imposes boundaries on language. So, the notion of translanguaging is not coming from these villages, it's coming from situations where people from different ethnolinguistic backgrounds come to meet. The boundaries become difficult to draw, and then because there is a lot of osmosis across languages; then things go across the boundaries.

And I think I should note that the term translanguaging is conceptually contradictory, relative to how people want to use it, because it has language built in it. That's a recognition that languages do exist, and somebody is crossing boundaries. That does not make useless the notion of multilingualism and so forth. So, you can have boundaries, but boundaries don't have to be rigid. Boundaries can be porous, and that's the reality that we are living; and so we have to address it in a different way.

I'm going to conclude my remarks with an anecdote, two weeks ago, I received an email from a sociolinguist asking me how Cécile and I have used 'egalitarian multilingualism' in Africa: 'Are African societies egalitarian?' And I had to explain to the sociolinguist: 'Egalitarian multilingualism' does not necessarily presuppose an egalitarian society, egalitarian multilingualism is that the different villages speaking different languages consider their languages as equal; and they don't negotiate the interactions and relationships among the languages as being stratified, as opposed to the kind of multilingualism that the colonial administration instituted in Africa with a hierarchy of what languages are considered more prestigious or economically more powerful and things like that.' And this is another way of fighting coloniality. So, maybe we should also start thinking about coloniality itself, how we have conceived of it in order to fight it in decoloniality. Thank you.

Comments from the chat box

Desmond Odugu: If (a) the ubiquity of technologies that make digital storybooks possible are increasingly monopolized by the Googles/Amazons/Microsofts/Apples, and if (b) these techno-monopolies are manifestations of the state-run neoliberal capitalist project, should we expect such projects as the storybooks to meaningfully alter the exploitative traumas and crises of imperialism that persists both in the bodies of indigenous people/communities and their ecological environments? Note that access to that technology is never free, and the enticements of 'modernity' has always been big business for neoliberal monopolies.

Ron Darvin: Perhaps one challenge of decolonizing knowledge is that the metaphor of flow embedded in concepts of translanguaging, materiality, technology and globalization, is that within these flows are processes of regimentation, control and inequality that 'flow' can obscure.

Sangeeta Bagga-Gupta: Important remark @Salikoko! I will share a 2018 [article] where we reflect (through an empirical tracing of the concepts TL and newcomers) on the slipperiness of vocabularies in the Language Sciences.

Sangeeta Bagga-Gupta: Bagga-Gupta, S. and Messina Dahlberg, G. (2018) Meaning-making or heterogeneity in the areas of language and identity? The case of translanguaging and nyanlända (newly-arrived) across time and space. *International Journal of Multilingualism* 15 (4), 383–411. https://protect-za.mimecast.com/s/92-eCY6YG5tnDjL8TGDDDB

Chanel Van der Merwe

Thank you so much. Dr Norton, would you like to respond?

Bonny Norton

Yes, I think – thank you so much for that, Salikoko. Working in the Ugandan context, I was always amazed when we moved into the villages. What you say is, in fact, very consistent with our observations: there was often just one language that was spoken. Sometimes refugees would enter into the village – I'm thinking in Northwestern Uganda, in the rural area – there was only one language often spoken, too, but when refugees from Sudan came into a rural area, you had other languages – but in the urban areas, you saw many different, as you say, contact zones there. And so, this had an impact on language policy, because even when the government said you must use the local language up to grade three or four, *what* local language is that going to be? Because in the cities, there were at least five or six *more* languages spoken regularly in the schools, but this was not the case in the rural areas; there they could identify, very quickly, a local language.

So, it's a very complex situation, but I love the way you defined it much more elegantly than I did, with three aspects of decoloniality: who is producing knowledge, who controls it, and in what language? I think if we just keep asking ourselves those questions, and reminding ourselves to take those questions seriously, I think that will have an important impact on what work we do, who we work with, where we write, and what research we do – and maybe that is really the heart of decoloniality. Right? There is basically a common set of principles that we adopt, and then in our particular context in which we work, we ask ourselves those questions and seek to promote – I love that concept – emancipatory multilingualism? Was that the term?

Salikoko Mufwene

Emancipation movement, that is really the common thread, and you find it everywhere in whatever form of coloniality you are fighting against.

Bonny Norton

Mmm. Thank you very much for that. Yes.

Chanel Van der Merwe

Okay. Before I give over to Professor Makoni, just one more question from Desmond on the digital space. So, he asks if A, the ubiquity of technologies that make digital storybooks possible are increasingly monopolized by your Googles, your Amazons and Apples and so on. And if B, these techno monopolies are manifestations of the state-run neoliberal projects or neoliberal capitalist projects, should we expect such projects as the Storybooks to meaningfully alter the exploitative traumas and crises of imperialism that persists both in the bodies of Indigenous peoples, communities, and the ecological environments? Also, note that the *access* to that technology is never free, and the enticement of modernity has always been big business for neoliberal monopolies. So, how do you, then, unite the neoliberal projects of the Storybook with the emphasis in decolonization?

Bonny Norton

Okay, thank you, I think that's such an important question. And I have to reiterate that the way I see my world is that we live in multiple worlds and we utilize resources. Yes, many of these technological resources are generated in the West; in fact, I know Facebook is in the news lately; you will have seen attacks on the ways in which they reinforce inequity. But for me, it's always – and I think this is maybe my South African roots – that you've got to figure out how to utilize what's available and recreate it. And maybe it's my history as a teacher – that you see resources and then you've got to figure out if they're helpful. We know they have problematic origins – but maybe we can reuse them, reframe them, reinvent them in innovative ways.

Remember that little photo that Willy Ngaka took of the clay keyboard? I have to remember that people throughout the world want to enter the digital world. Look at the Ugandan student, who talks about, 'I want to know about the computer and I want to share it'; Henrietta, holding that camera in her hand; the teacher Betty saying, 'I now feel like a learned person.' I take very seriously investments in the digital. What we have to do is be innovative about how we use the digital. I think *that* is our challenge: that there are resources there, and we have to reclaim them and reinvent them. And so, I think that is the challenge; and I think the very way in which the Penn State forum is working is a classic example of taking technology, and in a very innovative way, bringing people together, globally, to have conversations that are meaningful to us. And utilizing technology in radically new ways. Because if you just think very simply about climate change: if we all had to fly across the world to meet together there, how many of us, like, 40 to 60 people, how much travel would we need to do, what costs would be involved, what climate issues? But the fact that we can actually all chat and talk to one another, across time and space is remarkable. I'm optimistic about the ways in which we can radically reuse technology for the emancipatory project that Salikoko is talking about.

Chanel Van der Merwe

Thank you so much, Dr Norton. I would urge everyone to go and look at the chat section, it's on fire, but I couldn't get to all the comments. Sorry about that, but I will now give over to Prof Makoni to make his final comments.

Sinfree Makoni

I'd like to thank everybody for what I think was a very interesting and exciting discussion.

I'd like to conclude by just making two observations which link up with previous conversations that we've had, particularly the work of Raewyn Connell. And I will paraphrase what she says. Then, I'll move on to expand on Yasir Suleiman's citation of Jean-Loup Amselle from our last session.

The issue is not one of trying to identify and enumerate what you think constitutes the core principles of decoloniality, because decoloniality is an epistemological project (Connell, 2019). And then, she continues: Because traditional societies were creolized, we therefore propose a more dynamically interactive epistemology, in which horizontal relations and interactions emerge, producing [what Connell aptly refers to as] solidarity-based epistemologies. Founded on mutual learning on a global scale, in which epistemologies enter into mutually respectful and beneficial dialogues, a solidarity-based epistemology is implicit in some of the work by Africanists who talk of 'braiding feminisms (Bulbeck, 1998; Connell, 2019).

Then, the other key argument made by French scholar Jean-Loup Amselle, which touches on the discussions that were being made about either named languages or translanguaging: All those approaches assume the preexistence of languages. I take the opposite position. I start off by quoting Sartre and stating that nonexistence precedes existence, that the non-existence of languages, like that of cultures and traditions, precedes their existence. It is not because languages exist that we speak them, but on the contrary, it is because they are spoken that they exist. People speak the languages that they speak (Diagne *et al.*, 2020). Thank you.

References

Afreen, A. (2022) Translator identity and the development of multilingual resources for language learning. *TESOL Quarterly* 57 (1), 90–114.

Andema, S. (2014) Promoting digital literacy in African education: ICT innovations in a Ugandan primary teachers' college (Doctoral dissertation). Retrieved from http://elk.library.ubc.ca/handle/2429/48513

Bulbeck, C. (1998) *Re-Orienting Western Feminisms: Women's Diversity in a Postcolonial World*. Cambridge: Cambridge University Press.

Connell, R. (2019) *The Good University: What Universities Actually Do and Why It's Time for Radical Change*. London: Zed Books.

Darvin, R. and Norton, B. (2015) Identity and a model of investment in applied linguistics. *Annual Review of Applied Linguistics* 35, 36–56. https://doi.org/10.1017/S0267190514000191

Darvin, R. and Norton, B. (2021/2) Investment and motivation in language learning: What's the difference? *Language Teaching* 56 (1), 29–40. https://doi.org/10.1017/S0261444821000057

Diagne, S.B., Amselle, J.L., Mangeon, A. and Brown, A. (2020) *In Search of Africa (s): Universalism and Decolonial Thought*. Cambridge: Polity.

Doherty, L., Norton, B. and Stranger-Johannessen, E. (2022) Translation, identity, and translanguaging. In W. Ayers-Bennett and L. Fisher (eds) *Multilingualism and Identity: Interdisciplinary Perspectives* (pp. 201–219). Cambridge: Cambridge University Press.

Makoe, P. (2022) Navigating hegemonic knowledge and ideologies at school: Children's oral storytelling as acts of agency and positioning. In C. McKinney and P. Christie (eds) *Decoloniality, Language and Literacy: Conversations with Teacher Educators* (pp. 46–62). Bristol: Multilingual Matters.

Makalela, L. and White, G. (2021) (eds) *Rethinking Language Use In Digital Africa: Technology and Communication in Sub-Saharan Africa*. Bristol: Multilingual Matters.

Maldonado-Torres, N. (2007) On the coloniality of being: Contributions to the development of a concept. *Cultural Studies* 21 (2–3), 240–270.

McKinney, C. and Christie, P. (eds) (2022) *Decoloniality, Language and Literacy: Conversations with Teacher Educators*. Bristol: Multilingual Matters.

Ndhlovu, F. and Makalela, L. (2021) *Decolonising Multilingualism in Africa: Recentering Silenced Voices from the Global South*. Bristol: Multilingual Matters.

Norton, B. (2013) *Identity and Language Learning: Extending the Conversation* (2nd edn). Bristol: Multilingual Matters.

Norton, B. (2021) Identity, language and literacy in an African digital landscape. In L. Makalela and G. White (eds) *Rethinking Language Use in Digital Africa: Technology and Communication in Sub-Saharan Africa* (pp. 118–136). Bristol: Multilingual Matters.

Norton, B. and Morgan, B. (2020) Poststructuralism. In C. Chapelle (ed.) *The Concise Encyclopedia of Applied Linguistics* (pp. 901–907). John Wiley & Sons Inc.

Norton, B., Stranger-Johannessen, E. and Doherty, L. (2020, January 19) Global storybooks: from Arabic to Zulu, freely available digital tales in 50+ language. *The Conversation*. See *https://theconversation.com/global-storybooks-from-arabic-to-zulu-freely-available-digital-tales-in-50-languages-127480*.

Norton, B. and Williams, C.J. (2012) Digital identities, student investments, and eGranary as a placed resource. *Language and Education* 26 (4), 315–329.

Norton Peirce, B. (1992) Demystifying the TOEFL reading test. *TESOL Quarterly* 26 (4), 665–691.

Pennycook, A. and Makoni, S. (2019) *Innovations and Challenges in Applied Linguistics from The Global South*. New York: Routledge.

Stranger-Johannessen, E. and Norton, B. (2017) The African Storybook and language teacher identity in digital times. *Modern Language Journal* 101 (S1), 45–60.

Stroud, C. (2001) African mother tongue programs and the politics of language: Linguistic citizenship versus linguistic human rights. *Journal of Multilingual and Multicultural Development* 22 (4), 339–355.

Stroud, C. (2018) Linguistic citizenship. In L. Lim, C. Stroud and L. Wee (eds) *The Multilingual Citizen: Towards a Politics of Language for Agency and Change* (pp. 17–39). Bristol: Multilingual Matters.

Tuhiwai Smith, L. (1999) *Decolonizing Methodologies: Research and Indigenous Peoples*. London: Zed Books.

Zaidi, R., Metcalfe, R. and Norton, B. (2022) Dual language books go digital: Storybooks Canada in French immersion schools and homes. *Canadian Journal of Applied Linguistics* 25 (1), 64–87.

8 Domination and Underlying Form in Linguistics

Nick Riemer

Nick Riemer

Thank you very much for asking me to be here today. Before I start properly, I'd like to acknowledge that I'm speaking to you from stolen Aboriginal land in Sydney in Australia. I'm on the land of the Gadigal people of the Eora nation – land that was never ceded to the European invaders, and that has been a site of bloody struggle and dispossession since 1788. I think it's important to begin by acknowledging that.

I suppose that the guiding question behind the chapter that was circulated for today's talk (Riemer, 2019) is: 'What kind of linguistics do we need in an era of accelerating climate catastrophe and mounting political authoritarianism?' In asking that, my point isn't to suggest that the investigation of language should be subordinated to explicit political agendas or that ideas about what language is like should be answered on political or other non-intellectual criteria. Scholarship shouldn't be politically instrumentalized. Academic research has to take its own course without any sort of external interference. But, of course, ideas about language are *already* political. The way that we approach language intellectually is a product of politics. It's inevitably shaped by the background social situation that we're in, and the interests at work in it. In turn, it contributes in all sorts of subtle but nonetheless real ways to that overall social situation. When we find ourselves in a situation as serious as the one that we're in today, it would be irresponsible, I think, not to ask about the political valencies and the social valencies of the ideas about language that we perpetuate in virtue of our membership of the discipline of linguistics. And I recognize in saying that that not everybody here, by any means, is a practicing linguist.

Something that has always struck me about linguistics is the extent to which concerns like the ones that I've just mentioned are absent on the whole from the mainstream of the discipline – the kind of linguistics that is taught in the so-called core of undergraduate linguistics programs. So I think we can profitably ask what it is about the discipline of linguistics that insulates it so thoroughly from wider political and social and ideological concerns. Why is linguistics generally so unable or unwilling to contemplate its own ideological and political properties? That's an important question. Certainly, if we compare linguistics to other disciplines in the humanities and social sciences, it seems to me that the prominence of those questions is much, much lower in linguistics than it is in disciplines like anthropology, to take one example that is otherwise in many ways close.

In pursuing these sorts of questions, it seems to me to be important to focus on a central feature of the discipline of linguistics as it's conceived in curriculum terms – that is, in terms of what undergraduate students simply *must* be taught in order to be able to be considered competent practitioners of the discipline. And this feature is the idea that language and languages ultimately have a single underlying form. I have a quite extended argument about this in the chapter. The question I'm interested in is, 'What are the political and ideological consequences of the idea that language in general or a given particular language has a single underlying form?' What I mean by 'a single underlying' form is the idea that the variety of surface manifestations of language can and should be seen as the product of a single latent structure. This is reflected in the way that linguistics is taught. When we teach students the canonical core subdisciplines of linguistics, when we teach them syntax or phonology, or historical linguistics, we typically ask them to solve problems in those fields. We give them data sets, and we ask them to get the right answer. The whole tendency of undergraduate linguistics instruction, at least in the Anglo-American tradition that I'm most familiar with, is geared towards that kind of problem solving, and aimed at uncovering the *single* underlying representation that is taken to constitute the real core of linguistic reality.

In the chapter circulated for today's meeting, I go through some of the most important reasons for doubting that language is the sort of thing which it makes sense to reduce to this single kind of underlying representation. I won't go through most of those arguments here. Maybe the most telling is simply the fact that linguists often or maybe mostly can't agree on what the underlying form might be in almost any subfield of the discipline. There's certainly no consensus in syntax or semantics, or for that matter, phonology or morphology, about exactly what those putative underlying forms are, or what the right way of uncovering them is. Even within generative phonology, for example, there's often dispute about what the appropriate underlying forms might be, and we can add to that a whole host of other considerations, all of which militate against the idea that language is the kind of thing which admits a discovery procedure that reveals a single underlying form.

Given all that, it's interesting to ask why the idea that language has a single form is so persistent in the disciplinary mainstream of linguistics. And what are the ideological effects of that persistence? Now, of course, linguistics – and especially formal linguistics as it's practiced in the modern west, which is the spiritual home of the single form idea – has often been accused of being a vehicle of undesirable political effects. These have mostly centered around the discipline's theoretical investment in an individualistic, rational, and also, of course, white subject. That is, essentially, the subject of classical liberalism translated into linguistic theory. There have been many attempts to identify the ideological values that this version of the subject conveys: people have talked about linguistics' investment in instrumental reason, rationalism, individualism, in what Jan Blommaert and others call 'homogeneism,' in ethnocentrism, or in colonialism (Blommaert & Verschueren, 1992). I don't have time to flesh out any of those critiques in detail here, I just mention them in order to bring out the idea that the mainstream practice of the discipline is a contested one, even though that contestation often has very little or almost no visibility in the mainstream of the discipline itself. But that's just one side of the story, because the overt intellectual climate of linguistics is also surely, I think, mostly 'progressive', to use a very general term. What I mean by that is that linguistics is 'officially' opposed to discrimination, and, above all, is anti-racist. If we go back to someone like Franz Boas, right at the start of the discipline's modern history, we can see that antiracist dimension clearly (Boas, 1945). Contemporary linguistics is also, of course, very explicitly opposed to prescriptivism. So there's what we might call a sort of contradictory ideological tenor to the discipline, if we contrast the latent reactionary ideological values that it's often claimed to be the vehicle of with the overt and avowed progressive ideologies that are explicitly transmitted in the course of students' formation in the discipline.

One of the points that I make in the chapter is that for the purposes of ideological critique of any discipline, it's really not enough to reason solely from that discipline's content. It's not enough to say, 'Okay, these linguistic ideas bear an analogy to colonialist or racist ideas,' or 'These linguistic ideas in their content are anti-racist or anti-discriminatory.' The analytical challenge for someone who wants to understand the ideological force or potential of a discipline is to account for the processes that are involved at the 'point of production' of ideological values in the discipline. The question should not just be 'What does the discipline say?' or 'What is the discipline's intellectual or propositional content' but 'What processes and what habits of mind, what dispositions does the discipline try to inculcate or produce in its subject?' I'm not sure whether that's clear yet, but perhaps it will become clearer as I go on. The hypothesis that I'm interested in exploring is the idea that *undergraduate education* is the most significant side of the ideological work that linguistics accomplishes. The reasons for that are fairly obvious, I think. It's plausible that linguistics' different effects on students might constitute the most significant concrete influence that the discipline has in the world. Linguistics programs internationally produce thousands of graduates annually, and if we want to talk about the effect that linguistics actually exerts in our world here and now, it seems to me that's a very good place to start. Probably a much better place, I would think, than looking at works of linguistic popularization, for example books by Steven Pinker or whoever it might be (Pinker, 1994). These certainly do enjoy a certain cultural currency, but I think they are a less important site of ideological interpellation than the undergraduate instruction which linguistics students are put through.

So, it seems to me to be important to start from the overall way in which linguistic theory is regularly presented to students, particularly in those parts of it that constitute the core of the discipline. Linguistic theory is essentially presented to students as scientific – as enjoying an epistemic authority which is qualitatively similar to that of the natural sciences. That's a very regular and deeply embedded feature of the way that linguistics undergraduate programs present themselves to students and the public. This offers us an opportunity to explore what Foucault in his essay 'What is critique?' called the ties between a naïve presumption of science on the one hand, and the forms of domination proper to contemporary society (Foucault, 1996). What is the link between the scientific framing of linguistics and the manifold forms of domination which are observable in contemporary society? Here is where the question of the unique form hypothesis comes in. The idea of approaching language scientifically, for undergraduate students, means discovering the unique form that underlies the diversity of speech. Intellectual effort in linguistics is almost always devoted to referring these complex and multifaceted ways we have of interacting with each other linguistically to a framework of general rules in such a way that the extraordinary diversity of human languages is reduced to the operations of a unique and singular underlying structure.

I'm only talking here about the way that the core domains of linguistics are presented to undergraduate students. I'm certainly not saying that this idea of a single underlying structure of language is never challenged: it certainly is. But the core of the discipline relies on the presupposition that language has a unique form, and what undergraduate education in linguistics consists of, to a large extent, is teaching students how to reduce linguistic diversity to linguistic uniformity. Students are encouraged to acquire reductive, universalizing and classificatory mental habits. That was certainly a feature of my own linguistics education, for example, and it's still a feature of the education that we give to undergraduates in the most important parts of the curriculum. This is, in fact, no less than *definitional* of the discipline as it's understood by most of its practitioners.

So, what are the effects of this inculcation of these kinds of mental habits? I think there are essentially two. The first is western ethnocentrism, as I discuss in the chapter. This is most obvious in semantics, where there's a very widespread presupposition that if a meaning can be paraphrased, or if an account can be given of the semantic representation that supposedly underlies a meaning, then that paraphrase and that account can be given in English. Ngũgĩ wa Thiong'o's talk here recently brought out some of the issues that this presupposition might raise, as does Sinfree's own work on linguistics (African Studies Global Virtual Forum, 2020; Makoni & Pennycook, 2007).

The ethnocentric prejudice conveyed by the fact that linguistics research is predominantly carried out in English is probably well-understood and not something that I need to go into in much more detail. I would, though, like to talk in the minutes that remain to me about the other ideological consequence of linguistics pedagogy which derives from the same reductive, intellectual dynamic. Fields of linguistics like phonology, morphology, syntax or historical linguistics revolve for the purposes of undergraduate instruction around problem sets. Students are mainly required to undertake concrete analysis of particular circumscribed data sets in a rule-governed way. They're meant to discover the rules and the representations that underlie the diversity of the surface data, and that allow that diversity to be reduced to a much more economical set of underlying norms. One thing that we can say about this, obviously speculatively, is that the kind of intellectual discipline that students are subjected to in this models the orderly, rule-governed, hierarchical and dispassionate decision-making norms that are essential to the ideology of contemporary bureaucratic administration and that we see everywhere in modern governmentality. In the chapter, for instance, I draw an analogy between the linguistics reasoning that undergraduates are expected to assimilate and the principles of bureaucracy that Max Weber articulated in the 1940s.

My suggestion – which, again, is a speculative one – is that the kinds of rule-based reasoning that students are encouraged to acquire naturalize and provide a kind of intellectual license for the kinds of coercive instrumental reason that are ubiquitous in contemporary society. Linguistics pedagogy arguably suggests that the rationalistic processes of contemporary administration and management replicate the very processes that are constitutive of rationality itself, as revealed by linguistics' exploration of language.

But this is only half of the story. The attempt that students are always asked to make to reduce everything to a single unique form creates a tension with the fact that multiple analyses of any theoretical problem can always be envisaged. So, even within a single paradigm, there are often several correct solutions to any given data set. That's just a consequence of the underdetermination of theory by evidence and it's a general feature of systematic inquiry in any kind of empirical venture. And quite aside from the variety of solutions that are often possible within a particular framework, there's the prior question of the choice of theoretical approach: the fact that there's an essentially discretionary choice that's open to linguists about what the governing parameters will be behind the theoretical framework they adopt. No one tells you that you have to be a generative linguist or a cognitive linguist or proponent of the natural semantic metalanguage or one of systemic functional linguistics or West Coast functionalism. You get to choose this, essentially, or you're forced into it through contingent institutional considerations – for instance the fact that, as a student, this is the framework you're introduced to.

So, from the perspective of the different theoretical paradigms that coexist in linguistics, there's a high degree of theoretical arbitrariness across the discipline, and a whole variety of competing accounts of what the best analysis of a particular empirical linguistic phenomenon is. There's really no discipline-wide agreement about what underlying forms look like, or the way that we should discover them, either within or between theoretical traditions. So how does that pan out in the classroom? This is where we begin to see the possible ideological effects of undergraduate linguistics education. In the classroom, the academic is essentially free to impose *their own* particular vision of the discipline on their students. The linguistics teacher isn't accountable for their choices of theoretical framework, for which they are likely to nevertheless make often quite unequivocal claims of scientificity. Pierre Bourdieu talks about philosophy as a site of a massive number of divergent theoretical trends, each one of which claims to hold the *unique* key to understanding how the world is (Bourdieu, 2000). I think we can say something rather similar about linguistics. It's a jockeying field of differing interpretations of language, all of which claim, at least implicitly but often explicitly as well, the status of scientificity for themselves.

How is that relevant? It seems to me that in the linguistics classroom, as in many other parts of the humanities, students quickly learn that linguistic experts can claim authoritative scientific or empirical uniqueness for their preferred theoretical framework, even in the absence of disciplinary consensus. As I'll describe in a moment, this becomes a model for the way that power is exercised in society more widely. The Chomskyan gets to say, 'This is what the underlying form of language is like,' the cognitive linguist gets to say, 'This is what the underlying form of language is like,' and so on throughout the divergent theoretical paradigms in the discipline. Those claims to reveal language's unique underlying form are usually not presented to linguistic students as contested. They're typically presented simply as *the way we're going to do things here*. There's a very interesting article by Aaron Lawson from some years ago now about linguistics textbooks, in which he shows the way that there's this discretionary authority operative, in which the textbook author is essentially dispensed from any accountability or any need to justify his or her choice of overarching theoretical paradigm (Lawson, 2001).

My suggestion is, and I will end on this point, that this exercise of arbitrary discretionary authority that is modeled for students in the linguistics classroom is the most important ideological consequence of linguistics. Its effect is to *habituate students to a certain exercise of arbitrary symbolic power*. The lecturer gets to claim to students that language has whatever underlying form their theoretical preference dictates, and they get to enforce that choice on students by examining them and giving them marks or grades in it. And students are required to submit to and assume this particular way of exercising arbitrary symbolic authority in the domain of theory, by gradually accepting the scientistic pretensions of a basically discretionary and subjective intellectual practice. As I note in the chapter, 'in submitting to their lecturer's theoretical authority over the thoroughly material stakes of their academic results, students reinforce dispositions that will be reengaged in the far more coercive world of labour-market exploitation which they will soon fully (try to) join.'

So, linguistics academics encourage students to develop generalizations and theories about linguistic aspects of our world in a highly reductive and abstract way, subject to fairly lax empirical controls. And what academics do, as they teach students to do this, is validate their own theoretical preferences and effectively shelter them from serious contestation. Academics thereby model for students the ways that claims of scientificity, reason and empirical responsibility can be deployed to legitimate individual interests. It seems to me that this serves as a model for students of the arbitrariness of the material and political order outside it. On the traditional model, students are taught linguistics at the point prior to which they're just about to enter the labor market as full-time workers. When they finish their linguistic degrees, they will go off and try and get jobs. The arbitrary authority of the linguistics academic in the classroom, I'm suggesting, is a model of and preparation for the arbitrary authority of the employer, the landlord, the political representative, etc. each of whom deploys a certain claim of naturalness or necessity to justify their own essentially discretionary and interest-based choices. So I'm suggesting that linguistics education, whatever its other effects, plays a role in normalizing the unjustifiable and unaccountable exercise of power. I don't think that's the *only* thing that it does, but I do think it's *one* thing that it does, which we don't talk about nearly as much in the discipline as we should, which is why I'm so grateful to you for having asked me to come here today.

Bassey Antia

Thank you very much, Nick. Sinfree?

Sinfree Makoni

Nick, thanks a lot for the interesting talk. I got to know your work through John Joseph, and it's good that John is around. Currently, at Penn State University in the Department of Applied Linguistics, we are increasingly interested in setting up a minor in applied linguistics. But listening to your talk, and reading some of your work, I'm led to ask the following question, which I think you ask as well: 'Is there a way in which linguistic theory fits in a kind of politics which most linguists would oppose? In other words, are you saying that teaching linguistics is, to some extent, a harmful project?'

Nick Riemer

Reflection on language and language practices is an essential part of education. But there are aspects of linguistics as it's currently taught which do seem to me to be harmful. Linguistics is a contradictory project. That's entirely characteristic of most disciplinary and ideological formations that we care to examine in any depth. Linguistics has an overt ideology, which students are often explicitly encouraged to embrace, which says there's no such thing as prescriptive grammar, and that there's nothing wrong or in need of grammatical correction in the way people naturally speak. For this way of thinking, our role as linguists is just to describe and understand the natural ways of speaking that people adopt. All of that is entirely unobjectionable and indeed progressive. But what I'm suggesting is that the intellectual tools that we bring to that task also cut in the opposite direction, for the kinds of reasons that I've explained in the talk and discussed in greater depth in the original chapter. So yes, I think there are harmful aspects to linguistics education. That's not surprising. Linguistics is a very complex disciplinary, social and intellectual formation. It would be astonishing if we could give it a completely clean bill of health. Linguistics is like everything else. It's contradictory, it's complicated. We shouldn't assume that it's just good. Everything in the structure of academic professionalism encourages us to think that we can do no wrong in our disciplines, but I think that assumption needs to be questioned.

Sinfree Makoni

What I want to explore is the following question: 'What is the image of society which an 18-, 19-year-old develops after attending courses in phonology, morphology, syntax, etc.? What is the image of society which is created in linguistics? What is the image of how individuals relate to each other conjured in a linguistics curriculum?'

Nick Riemer

Yes, that's an excellent question. Obviously, we don't know for sure, but we can speculate. We can draw inferences on the basis of things that students tell us or ways that they behave. But the answer to that question is always going to be interpretive. I'll just go on my experience, both as a student and now as someone who teaches linguistics. The thing that always struck me as a student was an intense awareness of the arbitrariness of many of the theoretical moves which are made in class, but which are nevertheless presented to students as in some way either necessary, or as validated by a greater sort of scientific reason or authority. How often when one listens to a talk in linguistics, or even an undergraduate lecture in linguistics, how often does one think, 'Yes, but –' – or one thinks, 'Well, you don't have to say that. You could say it in a different way.' Or you think that *this* might not be the explanation, but *that* might be. For any proposed explanation or analysis, there's always a field of alternatives of greater or lesser plausibility that pops up at the same time. Perhaps the most important thing that students learn about society when they're in the linguistics classroom, is that the lecturer can just *impose* one particular version of reality: the teacher has this demiurgic quality, which licenses them to say how the world is.

Bourdieu and Passeron, in one of their books, make this very clear. They're talking about high school education, but I think the point carries over to university education in the humanities as well. The teacher controls everything, the teacher gets to say how the world is, even when reason very clearly shows that it needn't just be like that. It could be another way as well. It might even be able to be the opposite way to the way that teacher presents it (Bourdieu & Passeron, 1985).

This seems to me a very basic example of the exercise of arbitrary power to which linguistics education habituates students, and I think it's striking the extent to which the particular theoretical options that linguistics lecturers have taken are never really foregrounded as *options* to their students. Linguistics teachers essentially say to undergraduates 'Look, we could approach this topic in all sorts of different ways, but I'm not interested in those ways. I'm interested in *this* way, and this is the way that I'm going to teach you and the way you have to do it in.' Once that conversation has happened, the rest of the course just proceeds down this track, where the student is taught that the teacher's particular theoretical preference is the way that you do it. They have to accept that, and that seems to me to be very influential on students. It was influential on me. One of the things that this suggests to students is that part of what power means is the ability to just do what you want and impose it on others, and you never have to be accountable for that. That is the same sort of authority that students confront with their landlords or with their employers. In both cases, we have unjustifiable forms of domination which are naturalized with reference to these much wider ideological values, like the way that theory choice is naturalized in linguistics education. Clearly, it's not *just* linguistics education that establishes this attitude to authority: I'm pinpointing something here that goes far wider and deeper. But linguistics education is an example of it.

Sinfree Makoni

Let me ask you my last question before I open up to the rest of the audience. I want to give you an anecdote of my own – my first encounter with Linguistics. I did my first degree in Linguistics at the University of Ghana, and we're introduced during that phase to transformational generative grammar, but there were a lot of mosquitoes buzzing around. We always used to wonder why the Linguistics that we were doing did not seem to have any relevance whatsoever to the mosquitoes that we were dealing with. And I've never been able to resolve all the nature of the conflict or tension between generative grammar and mosquitoes. Once in my next life, I'll start off my career with that. The point I want to raise, which I think is interesting to me, is this: 'If linguists don't generally agree on the object of analysis, this thing called language, what should applied linguists do?' When I was thinking about this question, I went back to some of the early work by Henry Widdowson in which he argues that, instead of applied linguists relying on what linguists say about language, they should form and create their own understanding about language.

Nick Riemer

That's a really interesting question. What strikes me is the fact that people were writing grammars and dictionaries of languages, and teaching languages and learning languages and of course using languages for practical purposes, long before theoretical linguistics came along, and purported to provide them with tools that facilitated those tasks. There's a sense in which applied linguistics is much older than theoretical linguistics, just to the extent that people have been coping with language since time immemorial. I don't think there's any doubt that theoretical linguistics has contributed some useful tools – the notion of the phoneme, for instance. But the kinds of theory that are advanced and taught in theoretical linguistics are usually not so relevant to issues that matter in applied linguistics, which is precisely why there's a disciplinary division between them. They also have very little to do with the kinds of processes that engineers use for tasks like automatic translation, or data retrieval from corpora. Theoretical linguistics of the kind taught to undergraduates is generally very remote from those concrete applications.

That's something of a problem for the theoretical wing of the discipline, and I think it's a good idea for applied linguistics to consider itself not as a subaltern sort of linguistics, or a poor cousin of the Chomskyans or whichever other linguistic theorists, but as independent. The translanguaging movement is one of the most exciting sites of theoretical renewal in the discipline. That's an example of how the flow of ideas can go from the applied side to the theoretical.

Sinfree Makoni

I think I agree with you that the applied dimension of applied linguistics preceded, historically, the emergence of theoretical linguistics. John, what's your view?

John E. Joseph

I don't have anything to add, but Salikoko Mufwene has his hand up. My view is that we should turn over to him.

Sinfree Makoni

Okay, that's fine.

Salikoko Mufwene

Nick, I think you put your finger on a deeply entrenched legacy from Ferdinand de Saussure. According to him, all members of a community share an identical linguistic system, and that's why we understand each other, but that is a disconnect with reality. There is a subset of cases where people in the same household speaking the same language and who have such a long experience with each other, sometimes fail to understand each other. And we understand each other, basically, because we cooperate. When we have a conflict in the same household, between partners living together, notice, everything you say becomes wrong, and you can say 'That's not what I intended' or 'That's not what I heard.' This is part of reality. And something else in linguistics, this notion of idiolect, we have really underused it. And we have different idiolects, first because we are not anatomically or physiologically identical. We are not mentally identical. We don't have identical life experiences from which we have developed our linguistic competences.

Therefore, we have to come up with a different explanation for why we understand each other, in most of the cases. That's not necessarily because we have identical systems. Now, with computers, we should think that what has been produced with one particular brand of computers, is not completely translatable into how another brand of computers works. And between us speakers and signers, it's more or less the same experience. That's something that any professor of linguistics should be attuned to. That's why when you give homework to students, you can expect all sorts of analyses, and the position shouldn't be, 'I'm the professor, therefore, my analysis is the one that prevails.' It should be, 'Why did this student come up with this different kind of interpretation?' Is everything wrong in it, or is there something that really makes sense to which we should pay attention? My conclusion has been, we understand each other not because we operate with identical systems, but because each of our systems is capable of making sense of what has been produced by another speaker or signer. What do you think?

Nick Riemer

I'm very sympathetic to much of that. Thank you. Maybe the aspect that I have the clearest thoughts on is the notion of idiolect. To me, the notion of idiolect is something that we might want to complexify, in the sense that I'm attracted to the idea that there is no unique description of *any* single set of linguistic data, whether that's the set of utterances produced by a whole linguistic community (a 'language' or 'dialect'), or the set of linguistic utterances that's just produced by a single person (an 'idiolect'). Something in me wants to hesitate to say that you and I, for example, Salikoko, have different idiolects, because to say that introduces a determinacy into the characterization of each of our individual ways of languaging. I prefer to say that the way that I speak, and the way that you speak, are each susceptible of a very large number of different interpretations and descriptions, which will make them seem more similar or more different to each other, and more internally unified or various, depending on the particular description that we choose.

If that's our starting point, then it becomes less useful to talk about us each having different idiolects, because what that presupposes is that we each have a *single* grammar underlying our utterances, and that each grammar underlying each idiolect is different. I want to block the move that says there is a single unique description of a particular style of speaking, because I think that linguistics is essentially a hermeneutic discipline: it's one which is about interpretation, which is essentially pluralistic. There is always more than one way of describing how any one person speaks or how any one set of linguistic facts can be described. And the idea of an idiolect strikes me as going in the opposite direction to that.

Salikoko Mufwene

I agree with your answer, and I must admit my soft underbelly of sociolinguistics that I haven't completely purged away from me. Did I hear you use the term 'languaging'?

Nick Riemer

Yes, I did say that.

Salikoko Mufwene

Okay. I like that, because that's something that is consistent with what is going on in the sense of complexity in emergence. In other words, we are always in the process of producing what we call language, and that is not a uniform process. It is internally variable, but variable in a way that I believe even sociolinguists have not captured here because variation as conceived of in sociolinguistics is still predicated on Saussurean linguistics.

Nick Riemer

I can't really say very much about studies of variation because I don't know enough about them. I'm conscious that the people that I've referred to so far have often been dead, white European men – Foucault, for instance – but let me invoke another and say that I'm a Wittgensteinian in these questions. I think that the role of the linguist is to describe very closely the different language games that we play. That's what 'grammatical' description means for Wittgenstein (2001). We should block the move to try to step behind the surface of ordinary language in order to find a single more simple or more explanatory thing that lies behind it, because that's not something that I think we can do. At the same time, a genuinely scientific explanation for language behavior is no doubt available – just not from linguistics, but from brain science or some similar field. As long as we want to go on playing our humanistic game of linguistics, I think it's a mistake to try and find something simpler than ordinary language which lies behind it and explains it. Whether that's an idiolect or universal grammar or syntax or grammatical rules, whatever it is, isolating that is the sort of move that is uncongenial to me.

Bassey Antia

Okay. Thank you, Nick. Maybe I could just pose one question to you, Nick. Is the scientificity of linguistics, the association with rules, predictability, and all of that, only being pressed into the service of a contemporary political order? Couldn't one also explain it in terms of the history of fetishizing the sciences with classical Newtonian physics as the model? Rules, predictability, and all of that? I think in the early 1920s, Edward Sapir even wrote an article called 'The Status of Linguistics as a Science'. I find in the history of the discipline and, in fact, of several disciplines, that there has been this embrace of physics as the model science, and to gain respectability many disciplines have kind of embraced the principles, the approaches in the natural sciences. But paradoxically, physics itself, which was the model of science, has moved away from rule-based predictability to – if you look at work by Heisenberg, he even talks about the uncertainty principle, so physics itself has moved away from some of the 17th-, 18th-century principles, but somehow linguistics has maintained – at least formal linguistics – has maintained that tradition. The point I'm trying to make is that the rule-governed nature of linguistics which we see today is actually continuing a certain tradition, rather than being exclusively at the service of a political or social order today.

Nick Riemer

Thank you. It's an interesting question. Obviously, there is a physics envy in linguistics, which manifests as a general fetishization of science. I think that comes from a general lack of understanding of the epistemological status of statements in linguistic theory. It's a young discipline in its modern guise. I don't think we yet really understand very well what the source of the intellectual value of our practices is. It's interesting that the linguists I know hardly ever refer to physics, but when they contextualize themselves they're very likely to talk about the relationship between linguistics and population genetics, or biology, or ethology. These are the sciences that are most salient for linguists who do descriptive work on under-described minority languages, for example. There's a real taxonomic and quantifying drive that I think I see everywhere in field linguistics and descriptive linguistics – for the very good reason that if you're trying to understand something unknown, then quantifying it is a clear first step. If I had to identify the scientific ideology that was most present in contemporary linguistics of the kind that I have most to do with, I would say that there's a very persistent kind of positivism in linguistics research, which is an orientation to things that are taken to be definite facts.

That's how scientism manifests itself, most prominently, I would say, in the contemporary discipline. There's this assumption that what the linguist is doing is uncovering objective, positivistic facts in the same way that a physical scientist is doing. Not a physicist, but somebody who does basic quantitative research, and what that perspective marginalizes entirely is the idea that the descriptive linguist might be in a relationship to language of the same kind that a literary critic, for example, is in relation to a literary text. We tend to think that those two things are entirely different. The aim of literary studies is not to discover the truth about a Shakespeare play, for instance. The aim of literary studies is to multiply interesting interpretations of new and canonical texts. We don't think of linguistics like that. We think of linguistics as discovering facts about language, not as offering interesting new interpretations of them. That's a sort of anti-hermeneutic presupposition. It's saying that the linguist is not fundamentally offering interpretations, but ultimately trying to discover the truth of the matter in a positivistic fashion. That seems to me to be the way in which a scientific ideology is most manifest in the areas of the discipline that I know about, anyway. I'm not sure whether that's a satisfactory answer, Bassey.

Bassey Antia

Yeah, absolutely. Diane Larsen-Freeman has her hand up.

Diane Larsen-Freeman

Thank you so much, Nick, and everyone. I have so many thoughts that I could probably consume the remainder of our time sharing them, but let me just say that I came of age into linguistics, not as an undergraduate but as a young postgraduate student. It was at the time that generative grammar was supreme in many linguistic departments. I witnessed the stranglehold it had, not just on students, but professors, some of whom subscribed to other theories, even some of whom were quite eminent, like my own professor, Kenneth Pike. Experiencing first-hand the domination of a universalizing and positivistic theory was quite a lesson. Of course, there is some value to generative grammar, and even those theories that we do not agree with give us something to push back against and clarify our own views.

As for applied linguistics, one difference from theoretical linguistics is its problem orientation (Brumfit, 1995). We are advised to begin with 'What is the problem we're trying to solve?' rather than 'What is the theoretical commitment that we bring?' For instance, I coined the term *grammaring* because a long time ago, I saw that the problem for second language students was that they were unable to make use of what they learned in grammar class. They weren't able to adapt to a changing situation. They couldn't mold their language resources because the students had been drilled in decontextualized, invariant rules. Understanding this problem convinced me that we needed to teach grammar differently, which in turn led me to find support in complex dynamic systems theory (CDST).

Having defined a problem, then, you can look to different theories for tools to apply – tools, for example, informed by different ways of conceiving language. And so the materials that I've prepared for language teachers have been eclectic because I think different theories have different strengths and can help us when we're trying to deal with diverse problems and languages. However, I do not want to leave the impression that applied linguistics is atheoretical. It's certainly not, and we have arcane theories ourselves.

And then to your very last point, I'm also interested in second language development, and, researchers in this field are being encouraged to replicate studies in order to validate them. However, some of us have just written a paper and submitted it to a journal, arguing that replication doesn't make sense from a CDST viewpoint. That's because you're never going to obtain the same results a second time. The players are different, the time is different, the use of language is different, etc. So, certainly, adopting a non-reductionist stance, I think, is one that's going to help us when dealing with the problems that we've identified. Thank you very much for a rich talk and a rich morning experience.

Nick Riemer

Thank you very much. The problem of replication is fascinating. It's reasonably often commented on by linguists themselves that replication, as a matter of fact, is very rarely enforced in the discipline. When someone goes out into the field and comes back with a shiny new grammar of a little described language, no one else is going to go and check whether it's accurate or not. Once it's published, it's immediately accepted as an authoritative record of the language. This is an instance of the demiurgic or discretionary kind of impetus that I think is everywhere in the discipline. I think you're quite right to highlight the incongruity of appealing to replicability as a sort of epistemological criterion for linguistics, because it often just doesn't exist. Yet we persist in thinking of ourselves as researchers who are subject to that kind of constraint and who have the authority that derives from it as well. It's a paradoxical situation.

Comments from the chat box

Sibusisocliff Ndlangamandla: I heard you mention Interdisciplinary Studies, I'd like to hear your views on a subordinate linguistics in the service of other humanities fields like psychology or computer science and so on? Without over emphasizing the inter/over transdisciplinary problems that humanity may be trying to resolve over time and space.

Bassey Antia

Okay. Thanks, Nick. Cliff, would you want to pose your question to Nick?

Sibusiso Cliff Ndlanga

Nick, what is your thinking around the interdisciplinary work whereby the field of linguistics is usually utilized in other areas like psychology or computer studies? Or maybe even trying to answer colonial or historical problems that have been going on and resulted in inequalities? In other words, not to look at it as maybe the grand or classical discipline of linguistics, but rather as a field that is moving or is evolving but – just adapting to other disciplines. I would like to hear more of your thinking around the interdisciplinarity, or maybe transdisciplinarity, for that case.

Nick Riemer

Thank you. That's a very interesting question. I'm not sure that I have anything very well-developed to say about it. Maybe it's worth starting by noting that in many ways modern linguistics – and John can correct me if I'm saying something wrong here – started with Saussure asserting very strenuously the need for linguistics to be an autonomous and self-standing discipline. Saussure wanted to carve out a space for linguistics that was independent and *disciplinary* and independent of other affiliations. There's surely no area of human activity which language is not involved in, often centrally. I think it would be ludicrous for linguists not to think that they have something to contribute to the study of those areas, or that ideas that have emerged in linguistics should be marginalized in other fields of academic research which deal in some way with language. But for me, the real question is not how linguistics can contribute to other fields. It's the question of how much linguistics should learn from work that might touch on language but that is outside its own ambit.

To me it seems that the discipline is often quite inward-looking, and often quite reluctant to take on board ideas that might have a certain currency elsewhere in the humanities, in particular. There was a great wave of critique, for example, that swept over the whole of the humanities in the 1960s and 70s. And despite the fact that linguistic ideas – specifically, structuralist ones – played a dominant role in stimulating that critique, the wider discipline of linguistics just remained remarkably immune, so there is a certain kind of isolationism that characterizes the discipline. I'd be interested to know whether other people agree with that. For me, that's a more salient question than the question of what linguistics can contribute elsewhere. The real question is: 'How can we learn from what has been thought and discovered in other parts of the humanities?' Maybe John wants to react to that.

John E. Joseph

Well, I really wanted to ask you about something else, but I agree totally with what you say. As Diane coined the word *grammaring*, I coined the term *hermeneophobia*, as a condition that we, as linguists, have – a sort of fear of interpreting, or fear of being perceived as interpreting, rather than observing. I wanted to comment, Nick, on your very striking pessimism about the state of linguistics and I wanted to say something that will make it even worse. It's based on my own experiences. This last year, in particular, I occasionally react against things colleagues of mine say. This year, because we've changed our curriculum on account of COVID, I'm involved in courses I haven't been involved in before; and some of them are based almost entirely on puzzles. And the view of some of my colleagues is that the essence of linguistics – undergraduate linguistics education – is puzzles, and all the things that you were saying ring absolutely true.

I complain about the – what you were saying about the one-answer mentality behind that. Another thing we have are learning outcomes. We're very focused on 'learning', we have to define learning outcomes for each course, and I say, 'We can't define learning outcomes. We can have certain things that we'll *aim* for'. But the idea is that we're controlling what the students do. And then the answer that comes back to me, and I wonder if you've had this as well, is, 'Yeah. Well, the things you're saying are fine for the very top students, but for the students who are just getting by, they're the ones for whom we need those learning outcomes, and they're the ones for whom we need that very directed sort of education.' So, I'm being accused of elitism. It's not nice to be accused – and maybe there's something to the accusation. I don't know, but it seems to me that the people accusing me are sort of aiming for a vision in which there's an intelligentsia who should be free, and then a great mass of mediocrity who need to have them put in their place and kept there. I don't know. That's what I wanted to ask your advice on.

> **Comments from the chat box**
>
> **Ashraf Abdelhay:** Very interesting point Prof John Joseph. We have been constrained by and even controlled by these accreditation questions. It is always lovely and fun to listen to your views.

Nick Riemer

I don't think I have any advice to give you, John. What that question reveals is another dimension of this whole problem, because I don't think we can talk about the ideological properties of the discipline and just stay in the classroom, like I tried to do in my talk. We have to consider the whole institutional context of the university that the classroom is situated in. What you just said brings out extremely well some very deep-seated tendencies in, I was going to say, the neoliberal university, but maybe it's deeper and older than that. In a lot of education, it seems to me that there's a very deep contempt for students and a contempt for their mental capacities, their ability to learn, their ability to grow intellectually. A lot of humanities education, in particular, seems to me to be about forcing them to submit to arbitrary regimes of authority and control of a kind that they soon find replicated outside the university, and it's about instilling mental dispositions essentially of compliance. Of course, students are also encouraged to be imaginative and to push the envelope – but never too far. Never too far, just the right amount. I'm pessimistic, too, and I think we need to look at contemporary linguistics as a particular cultural expression of, essentially and for want of a better term, contemporary bourgeois liberalism that is entirely intricated in the systems of domination and exploitation that characterize our world.

I'm not stupid enough to think that changing linguistics is going to change any of that. Obviously, it won't. Obviously, it's utterly marginal with respect to anything that actually matters politically, but it does occur to me that if we could get rid of the kinds of deference that we encourage students to adopt to arbitrary regimes of domination, then we might be performing a bit of a service. If we could emancipate education and the life of the mind in linguistics, I think that would be a positive cultural contribution, though it would just be a cultural contribution. Really, I think what we actually need to be doing is bringing down the stock exchange. But that's obviously not something that we're going to do be doing here.

John E. Joseph

Right. Thank you.

Comments from the chat box

Átila Calvente: I was trained in mainstream economics. And after decades I have felt in my work with ethics of local and cultural contexts development, farmers, biodiversity, agroecology, much more as philosophical enigmas. Nowadays children education need a language in complexity to face global warming, climate change, huge models of capitalist modes of monoculture that are destroying cultures, indigenous populations, life itself. We do need alternative sources of interpretations, epistemologies, from ecopoetry and pluralistic approaches. How should, could we validate ways to interdisciplinarity? I mean bringing pluralistic connections in terms of possibilities in theory, practice, práxis.

Átila Calvente: I liked many of your ideas, and your approaches on glottophobia, dissociations, and Baudrillard 'the process of reducing and abstraction material into a form.'

Nick Riemer: Thank you!

Bassey Antia

Thank you. Talking about the stock exchange, perhaps I should invite the economist, Átila, to come in with his question. Átila?

Átila Calvente

Thank you. Thank you. Really, it's a great opportunity to learn from you. So beautiful ideas you brought me, because I've been struggling with mainstream economics, as they model the function. Everything that cannot be explained, you get out of the equation: so, you don't consider social inequalities, the historical process of people that were enslaved in Brazil for centuries – forget about those! Just get supply and demand and a point of equilibrium; that's the price; forget about everything. That's what I learned in my undergraduate education in Rio de Janeiro. And then, after decades of work in reality, I felt that we need from ecopoetry, we need to speak to humble soils, to water, to nature, and we can *learn* a lot from them as we work with children, so they can *think* of other possibilities. So, I would like to ask you, how can I validate to be in the academics, so that I do not leave the academics? How can I validate my work? Bringing these possibilities of integration to language, to communication, so that economics makes more *sense* to whatever ideas we want to develop for public policies and interventions. I don't know if I could bring you my problems. I mean, in terms of alternative epistemologies and ways to approach those things. Thank you so much. Very inspiring.

Nick Riemer

Thank you very much. That's a fascinating question. Of course, I can't say anything about economics. I'm barely numerate, I have to say, so I'm the last person who should be saying anything about economics. I think there's a very close relationship and analogy, though, between our disciplines, which goes way, way back in the history of linguistic thought. Thomas Hobbes is someone who immediately comes to mind as one of the people who asserted an analogy between linguistic thought and accountancy (Hobbes, 2008). There's a commonplace in ideas about language – the idea that there's a fundamental similarity between words as tokens of thought, and coins as tokens of value. It's relevant that there's a heterodox economics and heterodox economists. There's the whole discipline of political economy which tries to reconceive economics in an entirely different way, just as there are heterodox forms of linguistics. What I try to do in the undergraduate teaching I'm responsible for is simply not hide from students the fact that there are always other ways of doing things, and that any particular theoretical proposition is almost inevitably one that is placed within a whole field of alternative possibilities, and shaped by the particular presuppositions that lie behind it.

I certainly don't think we should say that the particular kinds of analyses that have developed in 'classical' linguistics are completely bereft of intellectual value. I don't want to say that generative phonology has nothing of interest. I don't want to say that Chomskyan syntax has nothing of interest. These are intellectual pursuits which people have devoted an enormous amount of energy and imagination and intelligence to, and they should be respected on that basis. It's just that we should not see them as things which tell us the singular truth about a singular structure of language. Perhaps there's the possibility of some kind of hermeneutic approach in economics as well. I don't know, Átila – I don't know your discipline at all. Interestingly, there is a Sapir in economics as well. I don't know whether anybody here has read Jacques Sapir's book *Les Trous noirs de la science économique*, *The Black Holes of Economic Science* (Sapir, 2003). That was published over 20 years ago now, it was one of the books that really opened up to me the possibility of a different kind of linguistics, for many of the reasons that you're saying. I think it would be very fruitful to explore the connections and crossovers between linguistics and economics, generally. That's an interesting task which there are no doubt people here who can say much more about than I can.

> **Comments from the chat box**
>
> **Salikoko Mufwene:** Thank you so much, Nick, for a stimulating lecture. Nice to see the audience participate so constructively in the discussion.

Bassey Antia

Thanks. Thanks a lot, Nick. It's been a lively set of engagements we have had with you. At this point, I'll hand over to Sinfree to round up this part of the discussion, and thereafter, we proceed to the after-hours party. We are at the lobby of the hotel, at the conference, and we're having coffee. Sinfree?

Sinfree Makoni

What I'm going to try and do now for the next two or three minutes is to foreground ideas that I found quite interesting, which I will keep thinking about as we move along. I want to spend a bit of time talking about the issue of idiolect, and the relevance of idiolect as a sociolinguistic way of analyzing language practices. It's possible that idiolects may enable us to provide valuable accounts of the nature of language practices, let's say in urban settings, which are extremely complex, heterogeneous, etc. Following what Salikoko Mufwene was saying, what you'll end up with are grammars of individuals, because my own grammar reflecting my own life history is going to be different. If that argument is valid, just for once, then the question that people like Diane Larsen-Freeman who work in *grammaring* have to explain is, whose grammars are they writing? Because if the only grammar is the grammar of individuals, then it's not possible for Diane Larsen-Freeman to be engaged in an exercise in grammaring, because that is conceptually not feasible.

What is interesting there are the sort of tensions that seem to emerge within this. The other dimension that is quite interesting, I think, is that linguistics as taught or experienced globally may be very different. It would be quite interesting to – moving forward with the interest in languages in the global south, southern epistemologies, etc. – to see to what extent some of these experiences that we've been talking about may resonate differently across the globe from the way it is taught in Euro-American Universities (or not.) The sort of colonial or neocolonial dimension of contemporary applied linguistics is something that I find quite interesting. If there's anything that I've learned quite a lot from listening to Nick is when he was drawing similarities between linguistic analyses and, let's say, literary historians, [he suggested] that literary critics are interested in finding new interpretations to existing objects, for example. If that argument is valid, what then the applied linguists should be interested in are new ways of thinking. They should be interested in defamiliarizing usual common experiences, because it is through defamiliarization of the ordinary that I think we are able to make more hermeneutic progress in linguistics or applied linguistics. The last thing which is important to us, I think, is the responsibility, which I think Nick touches on, of the linguist in a post-truth world. Can a good linguist be racist at the same time? This issue is important, given the racialized nature of the world.

References

'African Studies Global Virtual Forum: Decoloniality and Southern Epistemologies–Ngugi wa Thiong'o,' YouTube video, December 22, 2020. https://www.youtube.com/watch?v=LcHsqXB2dxM.

Blommaert, J. and Verschueren, J. (1992) The role of language in European nationalist ideologies. In P. Kroskrity, B. Schieffelin and K. Woolard (eds) *Language Ideologies* (pp. 355–375). Special issue (1992) *Pragmatics* 2 (3) 235–453.

Boas, F. (1945) *Race and Democratic Society*. New York: J.J. Augustin.

Bourdieu, P. (2000) *Pascalian Meditations* (R. Nice, tr.) (p. 44). Stanford: Stanford University Press.

Bourdieu, P. and Passeron, J.-C. (1985) *Les héritiers. Les étudiants et la culture*. Paris: Minuit.

Brumfit, C.J. (1995) Teacher professionalism and research. In G. Cook and B. Seidlhofer (eds) *Principle and Practice in Applied Linguistics* (pp. 27–41). Oxford: Oxford University Press.

Foucault, M. (1996) What is critique. In J. Schmidt (ed.) *What Is Enlightenment? Eighteenth-Century Answers and Twentieth-Century Questions* (p. 388). Berkeley: University of California Press.

Hobbes, T. (2008) [1651] *Leviathan* (p. 19). New York: Routledge.

Lawson, A. (2001) Ideology and indoctrination: The framing of language in twentieth-century introductions to linguistics. *Language Sciences* 23, 1–14.

Makoni, S. and Pennycook, A. (2007) Disinventing and reconstituting languages. In S. Makoni and A. Pennycook (eds) *Disinventing and Reconstituting Languages* (pp. 1–41). Clevedon: Multilingual Matters.

Pinker, S. (1994) *The Language Instinct*. London: Penguin.

Riemer, N. (2019) Linguistic form: a political epistemology. In J. McElvenny (ed.) *Form and Formalism in Linguistics* (pp. 225–264). Berlin: Language Science Press.

Sapir, J. (2003) [2000] *Les Trous noirs de la science économique*. Paris: Le Seuil.

Wittgenstein, L. (2001) *Philosophical Investigations* (E. Anscombe, tr.), Oxford: Blackwell [1953].

9 Decolonizing Multilingualism: A Practice-Led Approach

Alison Phipps and Piki Diamond

Sinfree Makoni

Piki, say thank you to your aunt for looking after the kids while you spend time with us on this particular session. Again, thank you to both of you.

Alison Phipps

Fàilte. Greetings to you from the places where my mind, heart, spirit and times body has been over the last 18 months. Right now, I'm in the City of Glasgow, so *Oidhche Mhath* – Good Evening – would be the Gaelic for that. And a huge thank you to all of you for coming, for staying up late, for getting up early, or just having a normal day and coming to this on normal time. It's a real pleasure for me to be here. And I was just saying to Sinfree what a delight it is to not have to wait 18 months to two years before I see my colleague, Piki, again who lives about as far away from me in the world as it is possible to live from Glasgow to Auckland in Aotearoa, New Zealand.

I'm just going to give you a bit of an insight into the kinds of things I've been thinking about, both in the book, but also since then with my work on *Decolonising Multilingualism*. I'm also going to take it beyond some of the things that I may speak about in the book. First of all, I'd like you to know that where I am in the world – and I kind of hope where you are in the world – is *atua whakahaehae*. That is the full moon. For indigenous peoples, and those who practice biodynamic care of the earth, this expression has a great deal of resonance all around the world. It's a really important concept, and it's something that means different things in different ways in different parts of the world.

Gathered in a work of love and law that is as old as time itself.

In my forthcoming chapter, 'Recovering Lost Arts of Languaging from the Four Directions', in the volume edited by Heugh *et al*. (2021), I draw on the work of Alcock and Labuscagne (2014) and their documentation of linguistic terms used in the southern hemisphere.

The cardinal directions in South Africa in previous times were partly based on the Sun, as indicated below (all references cited in Phipps, 2021a):

- Northern Ndebele: *buhlabalanga* = east (Skhosana, 2009) and *busubelalanga* = west. The term for the Sun is *llanga* (Ziervogel, 1959);
- Southern Ndebele: *ipumalanga* = east (Skhosana, 2009) and *itjhingalanga* = west (Shabangu & Swanepoel, 1989). The term for sunrise is *ukuphuma kwelanga* and that for sunset is *ukutjhinga kwelanga*. The word for the Sun or day is *ilanga* (Shabangu & Swanepoel, 1989).

The references, Alcock tells, us have been gathered into one of the first ever works to look at how those who were not schooled in the naming conventions of ancient Greek mythology chose to speak of what they saw in the night sky, and how to locate them when looking up, up, up into those pinpricks of light, or dust or ancestors.

It is disorienting, for me, to hear these words, stripping away the cognitive dominant framings of northern science and stories of the stars, and reorienting the world through the beliefs, customs, observations and, most of all, naming conventions in myriad languages of Southern Africa. I am lost. I don't know where I am. I don't understand my location in the world. And that has long been my experience wherever I stand looking into the sky and hearing the ways that the moon, the sun, or the stars are called.

'We lost our breath among the hostile winds,' says the poet Kofi Anyidoho (2009).

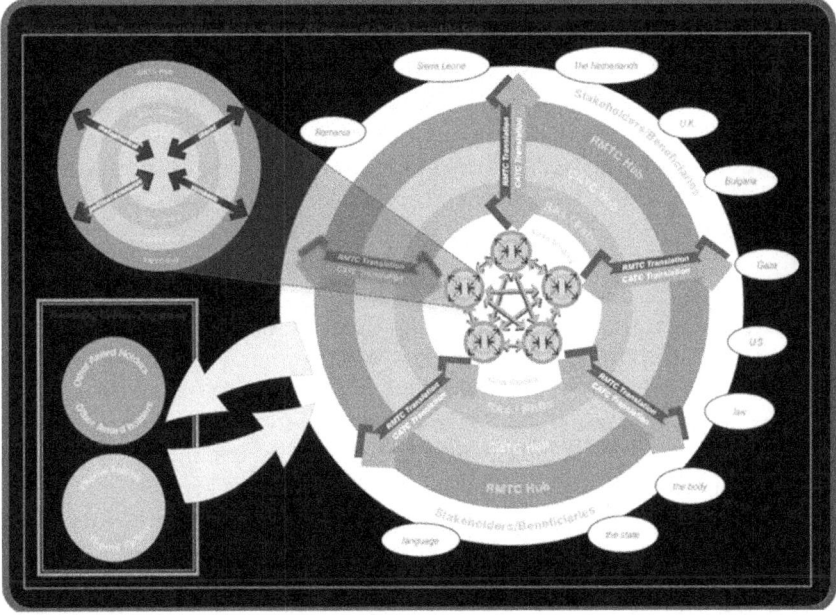

Figure 9.1 AHRC Grant Ref: AH/L006936/1

Let's move from the poetic, the indigenous, the southern skies, into a diagram (Figure 9.1) that perhaps gives you a different way of looking at multilingual work. This is from a project called 'Researching Multilingually'.

This was a £2.5 million project that ran over three years, 11 countries, 22 researchers, five case studies and two hubs. This is a tidied-up version of what I drew on the back of a napkin when I was trying to think about how we might persuade a really quite hostile UK government in terms of thinking about other languages, or languages other than English, to take a look at what we might find when we looked methodologically at law and medicine, at literature, at education, at anthropology and sociology and political science, and how they deployed languages in their research methods. The rest is history. The AHRC gave us the money (AHRC Grant Ref: AH/L006936/1). Working on the grant project was a little like a multilingual apocalypse at times, as we worked across the different countries of the world to follow this research. But it has continued to grow and has now led to a number of projects that have also been funded by the UK government.

In these projects, we're trying to undertake international work to consider indigenous languages and non-European languages more seriously and see why communicating in languages other than the dominant global languages might be so important. In that first project we were looking at what happens to languages under duress.

We were also concerned to look at language as a social construct and as a category. We looked at how we research interpreting, translation and multilingual practices in challenging contexts under pain and pressure. We worked from the Gaza Strip to Ghana, Zimbabwe, Aotearoa. We worked in Bulgaria as they signed up to the UN and EU Convention on Refugees and on Human Rights. And while we were doing so, we documented, described and evaluated appropriate research methods, both traditional and arts methods, together with practice-based methodologies. Then we up ended the 'normal' routines of academic representation, giving control and voice to those normally denied representational power as artists from the global sense. So, we employed two artists from Ghana, a textile artist, a musician and filmmaker; and a poet and playwright from Zimbabwe. Doing this in 2014 was groundbreaking. Now we are seeing initiatives like this following on from this project. But we are also seeing a turn back to decolonial thinking in the wake of social movements which have arisen during 2020 and 2021.

And yet, our research largely failed in that we failed at researching multilingually. We found it incredibly difficult within the dominant Anglophone, Anglonormative contexts of research in the academy to research multilingually. We kept trying and we kept not managing until we tried to do it as an intentional practice. I think this quote from Achille Mbembé really for me instantiates why we failed. 'We should first remind ourselves,' he says, 'that, as a general rule, the experience of the other, or the problem of the "I" of others and of human beings we perceive as foreign to us, has almost always posed virtually insurmountable difficulties to the western philosophical and political tradition' (Mbembé, 2001: 2). It's a little like me looking up at the northern stars and trying to see the southern skies and then trying to name them.

We also realized that the way that we, in applied linguistics, in sociolinguistics, in linguistic disciplines, in disciplines of modern languages, and even in literary studies, have looked at languaging, at the way we use and deploy language under the Anthropocene, has been largely extractivist. And my colleague, Michael Cronin, talks about it like this. He said, 'We have an extractivist attitude to language which we use as the fossil fuel of rhetoric, and we then burn it in the universities.' We mine data. We codify it. We analyze it. We extract it. These are very violent metaphors on *Papatūānuku*, on Mother Earth. So, we were trying to think about how we might shift from that, but also to shift from what Ngugi wa Thiong'o (1986) says of the dominant experience of the peoples of the Global South: 'Accept theft or die.' What we noticed a lot in our work was we talk – we talk a lot in the Global North and in English about my language, I speak […], I have […], my English […]. Or, why are you learning this? For purely functional reasons it will get you a good job through which to extract more capital. We were really critical of these paradigms within language studies.

Because we could see that within the academy, the academy is, as Pillay (2015) has said, 'a place of epistemicide, a place of the killing of knowledge because,' Pillay says, 'the university is a place of authoritative knowledge, certified knowledge, it is at the heart of epistemic violence. It is where authorized and legitimate knowledge is cultivated, preserved and protected but also changed.' And it's largely for this reason that it's so important for me to *mihi* to my friend and colleague, Piki Diamond, who is working with the Treaty of Waitangi, or *Te Tiriti Waitangi*, at the Auckland University of Technology. She is really responsible for trying, and largely succeeding, in taking forward a view of the university that will counter the epistemicide that has happened.

When we moved into a context of practice, with our research, we were asked by our funders to take our work and perform it in the centers of world power. They wanted us to go to New York, or the West End of London, or the Edinburgh International Festival, or maybe Paris, and instead, we chose to go to the center of the world. We looked at where the lines of longitude and latitude cross, the Greenwich Meridian and the equator. We went to the equator, and we started to work with equatorial epistemologists, as we called them, on a production called *Broken World, Broken Word* (Phipps *et al.*, 2016). We gave our understandings, our data, and our generative themes to the young people of the Dangbe rainforest in Ghana, and we asked them to improvise and make something with our work. But we didn't just ask them to do it as a dance piece; we asked them to do it by making English come last (Phipps *et al.*, 2020). When my white body turns up in a space anywhere in Africa, I am read in a particular way. People will initially speak to me in English. We decided we were not going to have that; we were going to put English last. So, our work, in the production that we did, worked in 18 languages. Most of the time, as the principal investigator, was responsible for all the documentation, the risk assessments, the funding, the account transfers and the breaking of a bank at Medina Market in Legon, was basically to not understand what was happening. And it was precisely from that insight, one which Piki had taught me, that I was properly humbled as a linguist and enabled to access worlds where the world was not transparent or coherent to me, and I might begin to have a taste of something different.

In producing and devising our production, *Broken World Broken Word*, we worked intentionally in 20 languages, English last, in devising, improvising (Tordzro, 2017). Never quite sure what was going to happen next, what we were going to eat next, what we were going to sing next, when we were going to go to bed next, when the rains would come. The women in the local township and the parents came and said that what they wanted to do was design their own costumes, so here they are, designing their own costumes [*shows picture*] PSU African Studies (2020, November 2) with what's now a small microenterprise run by the women themselves.

We discovered that when we worked intentionally in multiple languages and translanguaging, the rural power of languages will expose urban power. It will be opaque. It will need us to take more time for translation. It will need us to slow down. It will need us to accept that we are not coherent to one another all the time, but instead, that untranslatability is important. Uncomfortable as it may be, particularly to those who are supposed to audit and account, it will ultimately produce work that is more fully embodied by the people who are making it.

When we looked at this through an Applied Linguistics lens with the dancers, we noticed that the production ended up being more efficient and more economical because we'd worked more slowly and deliberatively, however counterintuitive this may be. We'd unearthed a whole range of different paradoxes in the work we were doing. And I think this might be because decolonizing multilingualism in these ways is fundamentally about changing the human relationships of power around speech and language. To decolonize languages is ultimately to de-create primal, ceremonial actions of cultural safety in the soft symbols of the speaking animal-body of the human. It's not merely an epistemological or cognitive task (Phipps, 2021b). We have to experience it viscerally (Santos, 2018).

It's also I think a part of what Conn-Liebler (1995) has talked about were the resonances of rituals like greeting and meeting and eating together, like clothing the body, like moving the body in dance, within modern cultures, these 'resonances are not vestigial, atavistic, but perennial expressions of enduring human concerns. They are not survivals of relics from bygone days, instead a bit like the full moon, they address the matter of survival itself, which has never disappeared from the arena of modern anxiety.' So, in this little book and in this short manifesto you've learned, there's the beginning of a few steps that we've taken together with those who are part of authoring the experiences in the book.

The book looks at the mind, the heart and the body. We look at what it means to not be able to speak for pain – embodied or emotional. And then with Piki, we very much looked at the life of the mind and how we might decolonize the mind – decolonizing the mind through learning the 'mihi' as part of the Treaty of Waitangi because we all 'lost our breath among the hostile winds'. The breath of the languages I spoke in the ancestry of my people who were cleared as part of the same colonial enterprises that rendered Aotearoa, New Zealand, a country that breached its treaty for so many years, that sent so many people to colonize the Americas and all South Africa and South Asia. My people in my family were actually from Ireland six generations ago to work in the cotton mills of Lancashire. They too lost their idioms, their dialects, their dances, their cloaks among the hostile wind. 'Atua whakahaehae'.

Piki Diamond

Tēnā koutou kātoa, tēnā koe Alison. I te taha o tōku pāpā, kō Ramaroa-Kupe te maunga, kō Hokianganui-ā-Kupe te moana, kō Matariki te awa, kō Ngāpuhi te iwi, kō Ngāti Whārārā te hapū. I te taha o tōku māmā, kō Tongariro te maunga, kō Tauponui-ā-Tia te moana, kō Whanganui te awa, kō Ngāti Tūwharetoa te iwi, kō Ngāti Te Maunga te hapu. Kō Piki Diamond āhau. Kia ora everyone from Aotearoa, New Zealand from the south; the furthest south you can get before you hit in icy Antarctica. What I just gave there was who I am or from whence I came, from which whenua (soils/land/placenta) I came from and from which waters I had come from. They are my mountains, my bodies of water that replenish us and the rivers in which move their waters in our people. And also, Tūwharetoa and Ngāpuhi are my greater extended family, my tribes, my clans. And then the word hapū is also the word we use for when women are pregnant. It actually means to swell. But we may regard it in terms of peoples, it's our extended family, so it's the idea of swelling. Thank you, Alison, for the kōrero (talk). It's so interesting listening to Alison when she presents because I find new things every time I hear her.

But I just want to talk about the mihi. What I gave you was a pepeha, and the mihi is to greet and acknowledge. And it's one of the three stages of engagement, rituals of engagement. And the mihi – she talks about the mihi in the book. And it was such an interesting journey for us. And I guess for me it was just the norm. Everything I did with Alison is normal for how I am. The word manaaki is so highly regarded and it means to host, to care, to be hospitable. And it's a way of being that I've been raised in, so it is very much my norm when I met Alison and took her for a bit of a journey and got lost. And then we found ourselves in the mist, knowing that once we're in the mist we're on the right way. How powerful these ways of knowing and engaging people are. They are so important and so needed, particularly at this time where things just seem to get more and more hostile.

And the mihi, as Alison mentions in her book, when we were traveling back from Chaz's place in Te Urewera, we had talked so much about her up-and-coming public lectures (Phipps, 2019: 73–79). And for me, I said to her, 'Perhaps you should write your mihi… our way' (Phipps, 2019: 79). Because too often we adopt the surface of a culture without understanding the why. So here in New Zealand and in Te Āo Māori (the Māori worldview) we had – it's almost – I call a formulaic way which is what you just heard of how to structure – it's a theoretical framework of how to structure our whakapapa, our genealogy.

But for Alison to do it that way would almost seem tokenistic. It would get to a stage of appropriation or misappropriation. So, I said to her, 'this is why we do it'. So, instead of giving her the formula, I gave her the why we do it. We do it to make connections, so that people know who is talking to them and who and where their ancestral lines that connect them back to the land so that they might connect to the land and experiences with, maybe past engagements with her peoples that people – her audience can connect to her. So that's why her mihi is very different to what I did. Now, for me, the expression is more authentic when you come from a place of the why. Why we do our culture, how we do it, instead of what we do, ask the question about that and I think, Alison, you see the philosophical and political reasons. You know I said philosophically we do it so that people know who's standing there talking to them. And then how can we make that connection?

So, for me, with Alison, it's like, oh okay, you're in Glasgow. My partner, and therefore my two girls, my twins, their father is Scottish from the Highlands. So, we have an immediate connection to the Highlands. From my father's side, you know, as part of the colonial rush to New Zealand, my ancestors were from Sussex. So, there is all of that intertwined into giving, or allowing, and opening up an experience for Alison, so she can learn from not only me, but also who I – being very, kind of, intentional about who she meets and who I give access to. Because there's people, too, that – people like Chaz, who have the biggest heart, but also – so giving – but what they have to give is so precious as well, and that we have to make sure that not just anyone is given access to them. This is probably why he's gone deep in the bush, he returned home away from urban life of convenience. He's less accessible, not a jump off the airplane and he's right there in the university.

I think that's more of where I'm coming from. I just want to talk a little bit about my background. I don't usually put a virtual background. I usually am at home, but I just wanted to acknowledge I've just come out of a – not a workshop, but similar to this, except it goes deep rather than wide into some real ethical issues around Te Tiriti and the epistemicide that is happening within our universities. And this is at AUT, Auckland University of Technology. This is a marae. So, for those who don't know what a marae is, it is like a spiritual home, a spiritual heart within our Māori communities that tell a story. So, the pous that you see – I'm going to see if I can do this. I feel like a weather person. [*pointing at virtual background; see Figure 9.2*] These pou (carved poles) are our ancestors. And then the tukutuku (lattice panels) here are talking about the environments. And then up here are kowhaiwhai (painted rafter beams) and that talks about the spiritual teachings and wisdom that come directly down through the people through our elders.

And what we have been doing is bringing everything back to our marae when we talk about treaty, Te Tiriti. This one is called Te Pūrengi and is very unique for the many female ancestors held here. The center pole, which we call the poutokomanawa – manawa means heart – so it's the central part it is the nexus, the stories of where our heart lies. And this is a wahine (female), some say Hine-te-iwaiwa as a personification of the divine female energy, and she is actually holding a baby and the umbilical connects to her into the ground. Above her are two male portraits which talk about the protection. Bringing it back to this place, the marae, the whare (spiritual house) is a microcosm of how we understand the world. And starting to use the whare as a teaching space to be able to talk and teach our non-Maori, our allied staff about how to engage with Māori people as tangata whenua (indigenous people) of Aotearoa.

But before I hand over to Sinfree, I would just like to finish with a little bit of poetry about this feeling of de-creation developed from this passage in 'How Can We Find Our Way South?' (Phipps, 2021a).

> 'East is not east nor, for the majority, is it buhlabalanga, or ipumalanga, and west is not west nor, for the majority, is it busubelalanga or itjhingalanga. It is a powerful stranger. Nor, dear reader, do I know whereabouts you are located, to the north,

south, east, or west of me as I write. On the spherical globe that is cartographized into these cardinal points, we are always dealing with fictions, even beyond the geopolitical locales, or metaphorical thinking, which underscores the many new users of 'south' to characterize thinking, intention, and stance.

My stars, are not your stars.'

Actually, right now, you can't see my stars because it's raining, as usual, in Glasgow. We're not actually in a turadh, which is the Gaelic word for that five-minute intervals you get between the rain in Scotland.

'My stars, are not your stars.
We are not under one Sky
We are under our sky.
We are not of one earth
We tend our earth.
My words are not my words.'
And they never were my words. They are the words of my mother who taught them to me and her grandmother who taught them to her.

'My words are not my words.
Your words are not your words.
Both were under the great stories of the sky.'

Thank you.

Sinfree Makoni

Thank you very much, Alison and Piki. Let me ask a couple of questions, I think more to clarify issues for myself, and it's a reflection of what I'm not sure about. Assuming, for example, one publisher says to you that can you come up with a book or a textbook entitled *Non-Extractivist Research Methodologies*. What would that look like? What would you write about, for example, in such a book? The argument, so far, has been somewhere, rightly, against extractivist research methodologies. But now you find yourself in a situation in which you are being asked to put together something that approaches a non-extractivist research methodological orientation. What would that look like?

Alison Phipps

Piki, do you want to go first, or do you want me to take it?

Piki Diamond

You go first.

Alison Phipps

Okay, all right. A lot of it for me is about starting with practice and with art and with improvising and devising, rather than starting with a plan, a linear chart, a project scheme, a book outline, a set of questions about which data I will get from where and when, which puts me at a more lost place. So, when I feel I am close to working with non-extractivist methodologies, it's when I don't have a plan. When I'm in a room often with young people who have a very particular way in which they wish to speak into the world or show the world what it is they understand. And at that point it's about working together on what it is we might want to do.

So, for me, it's much more about enabling a space where work can be made. And then after that, it involves a multiple exegesis. So, for example, the dance project I mentioned that we did in Ghana in 20 languages, I have no idea who extracted what from whom, other than that we all put on a lot of weight from eating too much fufu. But in that process, it was additive, not extractive. And in that process, we saw more knowledge made rather than me turning up with the recorder, sitting down, doing an interview, recording the self saying, 'if you want to hear this, you can,' knowing full well that the people will have real issues trying to get a hold of a recording, and having the wear-with-all to download it overseas. All those logistical material issues are involved in that kind of approach. And also, the research wouldn't be theirs.

Whereas, actually, what was made and filmed by the young people, who also learned how to film it, was a series of dance pieces and orchestral score that they made for the instruments they wanted to work with, and a series of songs that they danced to. All of that was additive to the community, so there are new songs that that community sing. There's new cloth in that community bringing back the traditions that they'd lost of tie-dyeing batik in the village, thanks to my colleague Naa Densua Tordzro (2020). What we had was a bit of a budget too for making costumes. Normally a costume budget would go to the National Theatre, they would bring their costumes, and it would stay within quite an elite circle. And this way, the moms of the kids in the production were able to then start their own microenterprise that they'd wanted to do for years but couldn't.

For me, it's a wider question. It's like the additive nature of it rather than the extractivist nature of it. So, looking at what it is we might want to make together and how that might happen. And to me, that's also where it becomes artistic, because the arts add to it. There's a making involved in that. There's a creative process. And that then the additive process, if you like for the scholars, but which increasingly I'm seeing is something that is also done collectively, is the exegesis of what has been made. Seeing that done in a team where you'll compare what the applied linguists thought they saw to what the anthropologists thought they say or to what the educationalists thought they saw, to what a dance choreographer thought they saw, to what I thought I didn't see, will look very different. Bringing those perspectives together means that you're not just seeing through that lens of 'this is the way this discipline has always done it'. But it's also not strictly interdisciplinary either. It's actually enabling a bit of a dance of multi-disciplinarity on trying to see what we might find as a result of that. But I don't know if, Piki, you want to comment on how you see that.

Piki Diamond

Yeah, I want to pick up on something you mentioned, Alison. You talked about improvisation, and I relate it to our word, which is more *way-finding*. I think the movie *Moana* has socialized that term. But it's a way of being within the Pacific that we are way-finders (Nicholson, 2020; Spiller *et al.*, 2015). So that is about not us determining where we're going, or us pre-charting and pinpointing with the map. We were talking about this yesterday in a wānanga, and how there's always a roadmap in our strategies. At the institutional level, we're actually in a space where others are telling us where to go, but their strategies and roadmaps do not recognise that we're indigenous people. As Dr Valance Smith and myself facilitated designing tikanga, an ethic of practice on how we might honor Te Tiriti with staff across the university, Valance described this state of unseen and unknown to that of our wayfinding ancestors. 'The mist is upon us, and it's so dark that we can't see, so we need to feel our way. And sometimes just being still is what we have to do, and we go around in circles until we see a tohu, a sign – the sun, the moon, the stars, where we can navigate from' (Personal communication, 30 October 2020).

I think, for us, we're currently really deep in that at the moment with our staff at AUT, in terms of how we respect and honor Te Tiriti o Waitangi. In the wānanga yesterday, we began to address that problem because at the moment, it is highlighting the systemic racism. The systemic racism is seen through the Te Tiriti lens. Te Tiriti establishes that we uphold the Māori worldview and the west worldview, the indigenous and the Global North, and that is what we are trying to do. Advocating not for an either/or, but rather asking, how can we work together? So, we are way-finding. Dr Valance Smith and I have found ourselves leading it, not intentionally, just because we are the people in the spaces and places that could make some movement. Because we are both within central units. We're not confined to a faculty. So we are in those spaces that go across the institution, rather than in pockets of the institution. So, we were able to see what was happening all around, but there was no coordination.

So, in some ways, we choreograph people, but our choreography is actually to hold the space. And the people determine where they want to go. We just activate where they want to go. We blow some wind, basically, if I can use that sailing term. This whare is called Te Pūrengi (see *Figure 9.2*). Now pūrengi are the ropes that are on the sails that tell us which way to go. And it's what I would find myself using, along with Valance. Valance and I work in partnership to hold the space of Mana wahine, feminine energy and mana tane, masculine energy. So we are always in balance. We work like that to hold each other accountable, and to make sure that the energy is balanced within the spaces that we work with.

So, I think there is this way-finding approach, where we don't have the answers. There is humility in the leadership. We know that we're only there as a service to the people. If we can't help the people grow what is so necessary, then we need to get out of their way and let someone else step up. I would love for someone else to step up, but at the moment, it's my cultural and ancestral responsibility, my duty. So, I think that's where we're at currently. We started the first gathering with all of our tangata whenua (Māori indigenous peoples) staff and students from the university, and asked them, what did they want? And it started with our values, the Māori values that we hold in the university: aroha, tika, pono; love, justice and truth. So, it's about holding people accountable. If the university wants to adopt those Māori values, they need to be held accountable in the practice of them. So, we delivered that yesterday to

Figure 9.2 Te Pūrengi, ancestral house of Auckland University of Technology, Aotearoa New Zealand. Credit: Office of Māori Advancement, AUT

what we call tangata Tiriti (people granted access to Aotearoa through government policies), those staff who are our allies to the cause – we had just over 50 staff members there.

We're still small, but at this time of year, we're coming to the end of our academic year. So, most of the staff should be marking assessments but noted that they wanted to come to this space instead because: one, they're sick of being on the screens, and two, they needed some healing themselves, and they knew they would find it in this space. And I think that's an important part to us, the healing in these creative spaces that we provide and the environment that we provide. The way I see it, our staff have been warriors and out on the battlefield. And so, my ambition is always to create a space of healing and sanctuary for them. So, when I get a chance to design wānanga or workshops, I look to design places of healing, downloading, purging, crying, screaming, getting all that out of them, which then allows them to create when they're not in that sort of anxiety survival mode. They can – they remember why they are here. They remember who they are. I think that's part of the way-finding that allows the environment – when you design the environment for them to do that, they begin to see the signs. Their vision starts to clear. They're not clouded by all the bureaucratic management tick-boxing debris that's floating around. I hope it answers that.

Sinfree Makoni

I will try and explain what I understand you are saying before I hand over to Magda. So, your argument is that non-extractivist research methodologies are fundamentally unplannable improvisation, in which research methodologies are analogous to spontaneous dancing. If I frame it like that, does that capture the idea?

Alison Phipps

Though I think – I would come in and say that they are rooted in a lot of discipline. I mean, I love paradox, Sinfree. But it's a really hard space. My colleague, Francis Nyamnjoh (2019) at University of Cape Town, speaks a lot of the need for a convivial scholarship and that we are in an unconvivial times. And therefore, for me, non-extractivist experiences might be a better way of talking about it, our methods of creating conviviality. Because when we're not afraid, when we're not afraid to learn a language and make a fool of ourselves, because you have to when you're learning a language, there is no way to learn to speak another language without making a fool of yourself.

I've got a two-year-old granddaughter. The things she says in English and in Tigrinya – she's a Tigrinya speaker as well – are hilarious. She's making lots of mistakes according to the codified way in which the authors of the Oxford English Dictionary have extracted the pure form of the English that we teach to enable elite people to gain more capital in the world through language as one of the things that that does. So that need for space of error, of failure, of repeatedly falling down, is what you do in two particular areas of the endeavors we learn within the academy. One of them is the learning of other languages. Yeah, I want to see mistakes, I say to my students. I want to see thousands of them. The more mistakes, the better, because that's how you learn. And then, equally, when I'm in the space of the performing arts, be it at the space of poetry or the space of drama – how many times do you have to forget your lines to be able to remember your lines? So I think, Sinfree, that something for both Piki and I, in the different ways, but actually in the similar ways that we're working, is about acknowledging the disciplines and the habits of the body, in order to be able to try to find a space within that paradox where we might do work. This, perhaps, does less harm than has been done in the past, or at least changes the kinds of harm we're doing, so we can recover from the ones who have harmed us in the first place.

Piki Diamond

I think just to pick up more on that spontaneity in the extraction and, Alison, what you are saying around what we are extracting. For me, my undergraduate degree is in visual arts, hence, why I always talk about arts. But it's also coming from an ancestral line of healers as well. When I create my learning experiences using curriculum design, what I'm wanting to extract from people is their way to their spirit. So, it's calling forth. Allowing spontaneity is allowing to release the spirit into these spaces so that it can have a voice, so that it can be. You know, we have these clichéd words like being authentic. But if we don't let the spirit flow, then it cannot be authentic, you know. It's appropriation. It's tokenistic. So that's why when I did the mihi with Alison, I said it comes from your spirit, comes from your lens.

The formula that we have in Te Ao Māori has a history that is bound to this land, so we have mountains, rivers, lakes and oceans. Now for some of our colleagues who are landlocked, or in deserts, they don't have lakes or bodies of water, or some don't have mountains. So, we need to be able to allow the spirit of their lands to come through, so they acknowledge the whenua, the lands, the path of our mother in which they have been rooted from to come forth and have a space within Aotearoa. So, yeah, the extraction is more about moving the barriers and calling forth this spirit.

> ### Comments from the chat box
>
> **Busi Makoni:** Whose mind has to be decolonized? The colonizer or the colonized?
>
> **Chanel Van Der Merwe:** Thank you for brilliant conversation! Can the speakers please explain the relationship between non-extractivist methodologies and authorship? How is authorship negotiated? How is authorship presented?
>
> **Finex Ndhlovu:** I may have missed this, but can Alison clarify what her understanding of the phenomenology of multilingualism that is to be decolonised? Multilingualism means so many different things to different people.

Alison Phipps

And can I maybe pick up on one of the questions in the chat, Magda? Would that be okay?

Magdalena Madany-Saá

Yes.

Alison Phipps

I can see Busi Makoni, you've asked the question, 'Whose mind has to be decolonized, the colonizer or the colonized?' And I love getting this question, because I don't think there is anybody in the world who has not been touched by processes of colonization. I do believe that everybody in the world has a different duty within that, a different road to find or to improvise out of that process. And I was asked to do a talk on the book, launching it just when it first came out by one of my Ethiopian colleagues. And his first – he's known me for a long time, and he was joking – but his first question to me was, 'So Alison, is this cultural appropriation?' I just finished his sentence, having done this a few times in the past, and just said, say it's the Ethiopian lawyer in the western suit and tie to the woman from Scotland who has just been asked to wear an Ethiopian dress.

And so that's a question of about why we draw lines all the time: whose mind, whose body, whose heart, mind and spirit has to be decolonized? It's very hard to draw boundaries around those things in any way that makes any sense when we subject it to severe pressure. And so, when I talk about decolonizing in my mind, I'm thinking about the way in which the cotton mills of Lancashire were part of the colonial enterprise and the part that my ancestors on my maternal side played within that. But I'm also thinking about the languages they lost. I'm thinking about the Cornish tin miners who spoke Cornish, a language which is now extinct, and therefore is one I can't speak, that wound of language that would have come through in a world that values multilingualism but no longer does. I question what it might mean to find my way back into families of those languages again.

I think, for me, what's been very interesting in the work I've done around the world with refugees is seeing that process that I went through of recognizing the places where my language genealogy had changed, where those that were in embryo – happening for the refugees who've just arrived in the UK or in other countries – where integration was all about them learning our English. And that was the sign of integration, rather than what we've been doing in Scottish society.

I can see a really good question that's just asking me to be a bit more practical about what this might look like. What does this look like in policy terms in Scotland? There's a project at the moment to see us sharing lives and sharing languages instead of placing all the burden on people who have come from highly traumatized contexts and then expecting people to arrive and instantly start to learn a language which is associated with colonial powers, with trauma, with interviews about how people have experienced trauma, maybe with deportation notices, with eviction notices, with detention notices, a highly codified language which is trying to extract life from people. A necrolinguistics, you might even say, of some of what we see.

And for me, in the role that I have with the Scottish government, which is to convene the group that is responsible for integration, we have said absolutely that this is a mutual task for the whole society, learning from the work that Piki has been doing with the treaty, the biculturalism in Aotearoa, New Zealand, and saying we need to – we need to remember our own languages. Absolutely. We do need to take care to 'manaaki', to give hospitality to the languages that are on the verge of extinction in Scotland of Scots and of Gaelic. We need to bring in sign language, and we passed the sign language bill in Scotland recently, because we need to make sure that we're trying to work for as much inclusion as we can. But we also need to enable people to walk alongside each other in different languages. There's a lovely little project run from the Scottish refugee council where people will go to a supermarket with people who have newly arrived, and they will share their language with one another. What's that? That's 'zaati' in my language. Oh, we call that cooking oil. What's that? That's 'chahi' in my language. Oh, we would call that tea. What's that? That's 'bun' in my language. Oh, we would call that coffee.

So, there's a little bit of a meeting and an understanding that our worlds are radically multilingual and multilingualized, and they actually are for the majority of the world's populations. Multilingualism is the mother tongue. And that, for me, the journey of decolonizing, the improvisation of decolonizing, is enabling us – again, going to the question in the chat – enabling us, in the work that we do of decolonizing, to create a practical scholarship that acknowledges that we must work multilingually and we do work multilingually, that we all are standing on the top of multiple translations when we only write in English or only write in French. And that we begin to do that – not that we are perfect speakers of other languages instantly, but that we begin to do it. And that translanguaging, I think, offers us an approach to that, a way of enabling that.

Doing scholarship in a way that is messing with the form of the academic monograph, messing with the idea that everything has to be purely in English, is part of that de-creative work. Just beginning to break it open is at the start of a journey. It is not complete. It's the very first step, and it's one that has to be a collective journey. And I think that will, then, lead to a different phenomenology of multilingualism to the one that, certainly, I have at the moment, which is really quite an activist stance, advocating and activating within Scottish society. But there are a lot of other places with governments that are predominantly monolingual in focus, so we have a long way to go.

> **Comments from the chat box**
>
> **Finex Ndhlovu:** Thanks Alison. I think you answered my question where you spoke about an 'activist stance'.

Piki Diamond

If I can just add to that, in terms of practical. For an example, and I spoke briefly about this around our values, and I gave some very literal translations. It's interesting, when people take our language, when the institution takes our language, even though it was actually gifted by a rangatira (Māori leader) at the time, it was not the translation I knew growing up on the marae. Instead of translating love, justice and truth, AUT has translated them to compassion, integrity, and respect. So, what has happened has been a redefining of what it is, and then a strategy put around it to implement it onto our staff, which is a misuse. That's what has come out of the two wānanga that we have had, especially one with tangata whenua, Māori staff and students, and the hurt it has caused. And it's a grievance on – and a transgression on – what we call mana, our integrity, our divine and invested power.

So, we had put forward some suggestions on how they can correct it. One of them is that the institution cannot use it until such time that they go through some series of cultural safety learnings and what they actually mean, so that it's not just this relocating into and changing into a western paradigm. And it's just finding this western – a façade, a Māori façade that is still locked in that very English paradigm. So, we're starting to pull back and say, actually, no, that's not good, that is not part of who we are. There's not a relationship, that's an abuse, so we're not going to have that. And so, we're starting to see how we can actually correct those unconscious acts that had been normalized within the institution.

Alison Phipps

I think, I mean, maybe also just add. Piki is really lucky. She might not think that at times, but she's really lucky and that there is a treaty, there's a document, Te Tiriti from 1848 I think.

Piki Diamond

1840.

Alison Phipps

There you go, 1840. And there's something wonderful about having a document that you can go to and say, 'uphold this.' And I think it's where, you know, for me, increasingly I can see the importance and value of legislation. So, a lot of the work that I do within UNESCO at the moment is looking at, for example, the ratification of the treaty of the convention on intangible cultural heritage where languages are an intangible mode and really important within oral cultures. It is important that we'll actually acknowledge that not all of our – not everything that we know is held in the pages of books. And that actually, that's really quite a recent human technology and certainly its wide availability is a very, very, very recent thing, and its digitalization even more so. I mean, I was beginning my PhD when the first emails were being sent. So, you know, these are technologies we have. Socially we're all like stumbling infants in the ways we're using it. And anyone who's on social media will know what a sewer that can be, and how we behave like little children in that space. We haven't yet learned to use these technologies of knowledge well. Whereas there are other technologies that have been around for a long time like oratory, like poetry, like arts, like song, which many anthropologists will tell you came before speech. And that speech is a kind of singing, as Merleau-Ponty (2002) says, that great phenomenologist of sound.

It is really important to make sure that we have protection on what we find important. I really have learned from my time with Piki and in Aotearoa, New Zealand. As a visiting scholar there, I come under the treaty; so, I have to sign a document to say that I will uphold it. And having to sign that document, for me, meant I must send a lot of messages to my Māori and my Pākehā (white-skinned) friends to say, 'what do you think this means for me? For me, honoring the treaty in the way that I might want to, what might not it mean to me for me?' Everyone got back and said the same thing, which was, 'you need to learn the language, you need Te Reo Māori, you need to humble yourself again, and you need to learn the language.'

And through the work that Piki did with me, I went into the world of greetings. The way that, you know, whenever you walk down a street anywhere on the continent of Africa, it will take you 10 minutes to get past the first person you meet because you have to ask about the aunts and the parents and broken leg of the chicken and whatever. You demonstrate in the greeting what is in the old forms of words, 'good day' or 'good morning.' These old greeting forms, when you dig into them, embody a whole philosophy. When you find that deep meeting, you realize that they are about wellbeing and peace keeping in the same way when you say A-salam alaykum, you know, peace be upon you and peace be to you. That that is a greeting that goes and comes back.

And that for me, and the greeting that is a pepeha, takes time to say, 'so, this is my mountain, this is my river, this is my canoe, these are my maternal grandparents, my paternal grandparents, and then this is a story that I would wrap around them.' What do you do when you do that is you cease to be born, you cease to be mono, you cease to be, for me, visiting speaker, you cease to be in the context of work that I've been studying and doing within the Gaza strip, you cease to be anime and anime, and you become someone who has a mountain, a river, a canoe. You become somebody who has paternal and maternal ancestry. That then makes it multiple. When you make something multiple, you give everybody the opportunity to begin to connect to you as a human being. And in that connection that we make through the greetings in language, we begin to do the work of peace.

For me, those rituals or ceremonies, those greetings in a language are really important. So, in earlier works that I did, I wrote a book called *Learning the Arts of Linguistic Survival* (Phipps, 2007) and I was prompted to write this because I was quite angry about what was happening in tourism where lots of people, particularly English people, were going overseas and speaking very loudly in Spain and demanding beer, or at least that was the story. And I wanted to learn tourist languages. So, I learned some Portuguese and I learned some Italian and I learned a bit of Spanish. And I kept hearing in the elite circles of the academy, oh, you know, when we teach languages, we're not teaching people just to order a beer or a cup of coffee, you know. And yet, what I found, as is usual in these journeys of scholarship and improvisation, as I spoke with people and as I learned new languages, was that we are precisely in the business, in a deep philosophical way, in languages of teaching people to order a cup of coffee, and to share a piece of bread, and to sit at the table together, and to greet, and to eat, and to sit with one another, because that is where we make human life together.

My colleagues who work with me within the UNESCO Chair, particularly those from Ghana and Zimbabwe, will repeatedly tell me whenever they're concerned about the fraught atmosphere around the tense culture wars we're fighting together at the moment. They will always remind me that the divisions that we have within our own society, be they racial or class or linguistic, also exist in their own contexts. And that, for them, decolonizing, decentering work is peace-building work, and it also needs to stop by an acknowledgment of the other, often through trying to try on the words of another in an intentional attitude of peace.

Magdalena Madany-Saá

Thank you so much, Alison and Piki. I've never seen anybody like you just answered all the questions without me having to moderate anything, so that's brilliant. Thank you. The only question that was not the answered is by Brett because he just wrote, 'I want to ask a question.' So, just in case if – the people that made the questions, if you require more clarification or have a follow up question, please let us know. And meanwhile, I will go back to Brett, please. You can ask your question.

Brett Anthony Diaz

Thank you. And so, I'm going to try to ask a question that I've been forming throughout the presentation, and so it might be unclear and make no sense and I hope that it doesn't offend anybody when I ask it. The thing that I kept wondering about is, do you think that we can ever be comfortable reaching a point in which we can't find a way to talk about or to understand each other, so that we don't have to extract or reframe, or exploit some sort of experience? If so, what would it be like? Can we become comfortable with, can we let something coexist and not be constructive, then let it be dynamic and let the meaning emerge from the meeting of the two rather than trying to 'explain' an authentic or true meaning?

Alison Phipps

I'm going to let Piki answer that one. It's such a good question.

Piki Diamond

That's a really good question. No offense received, very well asked as well. I guess what really struck me with the question was are we ever going to be comfortable? My question back to you would be, do we ever want to become too comfortable? Isn't there always something beautiful about the uncomfortableness? You know, so it's all about expectations, I guess. And this is one part of the way-finding; it's a journey and it's seeing you as a relational being. I think that's what Alison was talking about in answering whose mind is to be colonized and decolonized. The coexistence of people. I think, when you're asking the question for me, we do need to go back to those primal spaces as well, almost pre-language that Alison touched on in terms of song and imagery. Like I said, I'm an artist, so when I'm making sense of what is being said to me, I'm drawing constantly to find the form of what is being said to me. And I'm seeing pictures in my head. For me, I have to find that picture and the image that I can show the other person and ask, 'is this what you're talking about?' And then we create the meaning together from the picture. So, it's almost going back to that primitive form of language to co-create that meaning and that understanding together.

Comments from the chat box

Busi Makoni: Primitive?

Brett Anthony Diaz

I really appreciate your example there because I think, for me, I have a lot of trouble in the multilingual space because for me – and, you know, Makoni knows this – I see language quite diffusely. It's hard for me to actually conceive of language when I'm not speaking purely academically. So, the idea that we can have meaning without intersubjectivity struck me as very strange. This idea of drawing up a meaning and being respectful of where it comes from, for me requires the outside and the inside. And to remake what it means every time it's reproduced. And so, I'm just wondering how we can manage that and if it's possible, like you said to ever truly be comfortable, sort of, walking away and saying, 'I think I know what that meant, but I can't be sure and I'm okay with that. And I can't tell you what it meant; I can only tell you how I understood.'

> **Comments from the chat box**
>
> **Busi Makoni:** Children who come from different language backgrounds enjoy a 'conversation' even when they do not speak each other's languages, perhaps that is the comfort level we need.
>
> **Mari Haneda:** To the presenters: Do you consider your approach similar to arts creation from the new materialist perspective?

Alison Phipps

Yes, I think it's such a good question and it's such an important one. I think it comes from within the academy, we want coherence. We want to understand. I certainly spend all my time trying to understand. It's my go-to place. And yet most of the world is entirely incomprehensible to me. Every time I walk into the university library, I know I'm really going to spend my time on level 6 and there are 13 floors. And I'm not going to get past one stack in terms of what I can read in the library in a lifetime. You know, the last person to read anything, we are told in the West, was either Goethe or Coleridge, depending on whether you speak German or English. So, I think there's no pure place to stand in this and that to me is always really helpful. But I'm also finding increasingly that the work of my colleague, Angela Creese, has been really helpful because we've been having two different spaces. I've looked a lot at languages and categories. She's looked a lot at languages and constructs. And yet, when we've been in dialogue together, we've all often been set up to debate this deliberately because the funders wanted two women to have an argument. And actually, again and again we found we were just entering into dialogue and conversation saying, 'but it's both,' and we were bringing in what I would call a complete transformational paradigm, saying how can we have language as category and, also, as constructs. What would that look like? And where we've ended up, really, her in a quite – an abstract philosophical way, I think, coming out of applied linguistics – and me of a performing arts perspective, is to both start using the word *repertoire*. So, the question that there is there around, you know, is this similar to arts creation from the new materialist approach, that Mari has asked. Absolutely, I would say.

But that I see that the creation of language and speech in everyday life as a, sort of, sub-conscious creative artistic practice in the world. And how we go about that, how we care for words in a culture of lies, to use Marilyn Chandler McIntyre's (2009) book, that beautiful book that she wrote of philosophy, *Caring for Words in a Culture of Lies*. I just think it's really important. And the idea of the *repertoire*, rather than of languages, is increasingly helpful to me. So, going into a space that is multiple, with multiplicity in it, I'm thinking, what are the repertoires here that we might deploy to get enough sense, rather than to get perfect sense. Knowing that, actually, most of the world functions really well on enough sense, as you will know if you've ever tried to order a coffee as a tourist in a context where you don't speak the language. So, I think for me – there's a whole chapter in the book on gist, and getting the gist, and what it's like.

And for me, in a family where most of the time I don't understand the language that the family speaks, the language of my foster daughter who is an Eritrean refugee. When I'm with her family, I desperately want to be able to speak to her mother, but we can only speak to each other in gesture.

Piki Diamond

I just want to attend to a question in the chat, there's a question mark around what I meant by 'primitive.' So, I just want to define that that's more – and I probably used the wrong word, but as human beings, we have these forms of communication. And oratory was one of the last forms of communication, so there were these – so not primitive as in, you don't know anything or less intelligent, but actually a natural form of progression in terms of our ways of communication. And in terms of that relationship with academia, like some of this language is beyond me. I'm going to be straight out, I'm not a deep linguist. I'm actually monocultural, still trying to remember my own language. So, sometimes Alison brings me in on this and I feel like such an impostor. But it's about the experience – when I say primitive, I'm talking about those intuitive, tacit knowledge expressed, the pre-spoken language ways of communicating. The body language, those sorts of gestures, those drawings, music, different ways in which vibrations of communications were delivered or exchanged among people.

> **Comments from the chat box**
>
> **Busi Makoni:** Turning to academic authorship, how is this way-finding approach ever going to be acceptable as an example of good, rigorous research when those in decision making positions (editors/reviewers) do not view such an approach as epistemological?

Alison Phipps

I think one of the things we've done quite a lot for my team, and particularly in policy circles, is deliberately bring in these other artistic forms, or more primal ways of responding. And so, maybe just to give you an example, I was asked to author a report for the European Parliament on Cultural Work with refugees (Phipps, 2017).

So, I did what I normally do, which is to say, 'I'm not doing it on my own,' because we can't do this on our own. We need multiple voices, and we need to model that. But also, I said, 'I'd like to bring my colleague from Ghana who is a Ga speaker and a singer, and I would like her to be part of the presentation of the report in the Culture Committee of the European Parliament. And I would like to do it in a way that means that she will interrupt what I am doing and that the members or delegates, say MEPs, the members of the European Parliament, won't know that this is about to happen.'

And so, I was presenting my stuff, you know, with a tidy diagram that looked all very plausible with nice straight lines, and linear models. And then suddenly somebody stood up in the gallery of the European Parliament and started to sing. And sang in a language that wasn't one of the 28 languages of the European Union. And it was a moment utter consternation: 'Oh, wow, incredible! Oh, beautiful!' I mean, these gasps of surprise. In the 60 years of the Culture Committee at the European Parliament, no one had ever presented in song. In the Culture Committee, the *one* committee that you would imagine would be hospitable, we'd talked about, we'd not shown it in action. And then we moved together to do an exegesis of that, to say if we're going to do cultural work, we need to do cultural work. If we're going to decolonize multilingualism, as I say in the book, we need to *do* it, not to *talk* about doing it. There'll be plenty of opportunity to talk about doing it; in a forum like this, as we reflect back and think how could we have done that better? What do we do this time?

So, as we moved from doing our work in Ghana and we moved into doing some work on the invitation of our Zimbabwean colleagues, or with a refugee group, here in Glasgow, on their invitation to do multilingual performance and multisensory performance, using these new materialist methods, we reflected and thought, 'well, we did that well and that worked well, but that wouldn't work here. I wonder if this would work here.' And so, we're never actually going to arrive. We're always going to be, I think till the end of our days, actually, laying something down a little like the way-finders might, you know, mark a tree or leave a stone by the side of the path that tells you which way to go, and others might find their way a bit further on. But I think this is just for this moment, this is as far as we've got in that work.

And maybe just to come to one of the question in the chat, which is the question of academic authorship that has been asked, and how is this way finding approach ever going to be acceptable as an example of good rigorous research, when those in decision making positions, editors and reviewers, do not view such an approach as epistemological. I'm actually really seeing a lot of hope around this at the moment. The publishers that I've worked with 20-odd years now, Multilingual Matters, are open to this. They are really welcoming manuscripts that will work in different ways. They've recently published a manuscript by Adrian Blackledge, which presents his autoethnographic material on translanguaging in a market as a play script.

They have published my own book. They are publishing several more, which are collaborations between artists, practitioners and scholars. And they're actually asking people who, a little like me, maybe don't have that much to lose in the publishing game, because we're in tenured, secure positions, to be the ones who break the mold so that it is safe for others to say, 'look, these people did it, and these people did it, and therefore, we can have a go.' And so Piki and I, we're in a Aotearoa just a few weeks ago with 20 of those who are in my research group, my research team doing PhDs, all thinking about these aspects, these questions about how we might put together authorship that looks at questions of decolonizing authorship, the rights about attempts we've made to do it, that looks at how we challenge the people who bean count and ask how many people have cited our work, or what the rankings are in the journals. So, with a publisher that isn't necessarily one of the big global houses, that is, actually saying, 'let's work with the family firm, let's work with the smaller publisher, let's work with people who want to have a go and see what they can enable,' rather than what we all know academic publishing is these days, which is you basically do all the work of a good publisher, and you don't get paid for it, and you are expected to be really quite ruthless around what authorship looks like. And I think we're nowhere close to it, but in asking the question whether our publishers in the room – are publishers a part of that improvisation on way-finding and thinking that they're beginning to do together.

Piki Diamond

I've just – not so much probably on authorship, but also in terms of research outputs and stuff like that, as people who design conferences, how we accept abstracts. And we're actually going to share an abstract that I submitted and was accepted, and I ended up using it as a workshop piece. So, it actually was the framing of my workshop, and I submitted it just because, you know, sometimes people say that [they are open to receiving creative abstracts], but we are so used to just submitting an abstract in this academic form, that no one actually does submit something creative. So, that's sort of sometimes put out there to appear nice, and doing the right thing, but to receive it can be another question, for those who actually want to review – when it comes to reviewing an abstract that's in poetry.

But I'm going to just share that one right now.

Alison Phipps

Go for it.

Piki Diamond

>She stands tall at Rongo's threshold
>The kuia calls and silence falls
>'Haere mai haere mai haere mai'
>Manuhiri stand at Tū's threshold
>Women step first upon his earth
>The call is answered
>'karanga mai, karanga mai, karanga mai'
>Ka-ranga, activating the
>Weaving of time and spaces

Of known and foreign faces
This is the dignity of
mana wahine.

Tangata whenua dictate tikanga
in this space
Manuhiri still to prove
Their case
On Tu's open land
If they come as friend or foe
He hoa? he hoariri ranei?
Before stepping over Rongo's threshold
Breath must be shared.

Either way we are hoa
So, let's deal with our grievances
At this threshold of time
Rectifying where tikanga was displaced
Where manaaki did not take place
Instead, our home, our land
Invaded that saw her value
In property.
Her worth measured by the £
Disregarding her heart
Her true value as
our Māmā.

Whenua providing
For us to
Reciprocate her unconditional love
Her Aroha. Aro-hā
paying attention to her breath
To take care of her
To manaaki Papatūānuku
To mana-aki Papa-tū-ā-nuku
To encourage integrity
So that we-she can live with dignity
This is her and our...
Mana motuhake.

Dear conscience of the Crown.
You wanted to dictate tikanga here
With your man-made law
Vulnerable to corruption
But now our mother is dying and with that
the people die too
and guess what?
So, do you.
So, before our demise is upon us all.
Titiro, whakarongo
Let's kōrero.

Kōrero mai, kōrero atu
Pātai mai, pātai atu.

No longer shall we go head-to-head
Taking this time for hearts to be heard instead
It's time to action mana-ā-kī,
so that we can stand as one with dignity
where our words and actions are joined with integrity.
Let the hearts, ngā manawa take their rightful place
tuakana and vanguard of our grace,
Carving a pathway for its teina,
te hinengaro to unveil diverse truths
of tangata mauri.
So stand, e tū i te mana o te wa,
in this time of integrity
Let us take our place as people of the land
To host you, to welcome you
Into our world
With tikanga derived from te ao māori
Let us manaaki
Let us mana-aki
Let us
mana-ā-kī. (Diamond, 2022)

Alison Phipps

[*Singing*]

This newfound excitement about decoloniality is precious. It's easily critiqued. That's not exactly a hard thing to do as a scholar, not least of language, but the reinterpretations, the diversity of knowledges coming into view overhead is a little like blinking up into the Milky Way on a clear night. You are lost. Words fail. Then, you begin to find points of familiarity, and you give these names from where you stand. You are not lost. You are not found. Kia ora, everybody. Thank you very much.

Piki Diamond

Tēnā koutou kātoa

Comments from the chat box

Mario López-Gopar: Thanks for the wonderful presentation and conversation. Based on the conversation, I wonder if 'multilingualism' is the proper word to use, especially because it is still heavily connected to 'oral' and 'written' 'language', excluding 'other' modes of representation and 'other' interlocutors connected to 'othered' epistemologies and ontologies? Gracias, Mario.

Mari Haneda: A great question – I was thinking about that, too, Mario.

Magdalena Madany-Saá

Thank you so much. Dziękuję bardzo. This is the end of our formal presentation, so I will soon stop recording, just last words from Dr Makoni. And afterwards, we still have three beautiful questions, if you still can stay for a while, but I would like to finish the recording and the formal part of the session. Dr Makoni, over to you.

Sinfree Makoni

Thank you very much to Alison and to Piki for finding the time to come and share their experiences with us. And thank you to everybody else from across the world for finding time to join us once more on this journey that is taking us where, we are not very clear. What was very interesting about this presentation is that it reinforces some of the things that we have been doing. For example, there were a couple of sessions, previously, where we had poets or applied linguists coming in to read their poetry. And then there was another session where we had one of us who is a musician, who can sing and is also a scholar of language and literature. So, it was very interesting to listen to Alison and Piki talking about music, poetry and how all of them can be blended together.

So, what we were trying to do in a number of different sessions, previously, have been reinforced in their own session. There are a number of issues which came up, and which we may be able to focus on as we go on, including the issue of extractivist research and issues of authorship. Another aspect that we did in their terms talk about is the notion of work. What does it mean to say, 'this is my work?' And then there are a number of fascinating quotations from Alison and Piki, which I'm going to repeat, and which I think are very interesting. One of them, if I got it correctly, is that we have all, to varying degrees, been touched by colonialism. It is naïve to imagine that you are above colonialism and it never affected you. And then the statement 'multilingualism is a mother tongue' reminds me of the statement which was made about three decades ago by one British anthropologist writing about Africa, when he said multilingualism in Africa is a lingua franca. And so, another aspect which I thought was very interesting was the connection that Alison was making between the discussions about their work and issues about building peace.

Then, the last thing I want to talk about briefly is the issue of publishing. Magda, myself, and Rafael are experimenting with what we are calling conversational chapters where, for example, we have Alison and Piki's conversation today, and then we'll try and convert that into – we'll capture the conversation that has taken place, and we'll do minimal editing of the nature of the interaction, in order to blur the distinctions between a conversation and a conventional academic chapter. And we've approached Multilingual Matters – we'll know whether, for example, they are interested in what we are doing. I should say this to you, but I shouldn't say that we also cite the fact that Alison is one of the people who is taking part in this project, and that they published Alison's work on *Decolonising Multilingualism*, to try and enhance the probability that Multilingual Matters will be interested in our experimentation. So, Alison, there was some background idea why we wanted you to come. [*Laughs*] I'm not supposed to tell you this, but then I thought, no, I should. Let's be honest.

[*Laughter*]

Alison Phipps

I love the fact we're, (a) recording, and (b) the mischief under the full moon. I think it's the full moon. [*points at the sky*] Mission accomplished.

Sinfree Makoni

Yes, yes. Mission accomplished. [*Laughs*] Thank you very much to everybody.

Comments from the chat box

Ofelia García: Thank you for a conversation that has felt healing five days before our election. I was touched by the convivial scholarship and I'm glad you're holding that conviviality. May we all take up this way-finding as we face a difficult week.

Elka Todeva: Conviviality is what I am also taking away. Благодаря (seeing for the first time the deep meaning of the Bulgarian 'thank you' because of you).

Hala Almutawa: Thank you so much!
Judith Purkarthofer: Thank you so much for this inspiring talk!
Kim Hansen: Thank you so much!
Betty Dlamini: Thank you! Siyabonga! Asante sana! Medase! In ice. E se

---

References

Alcock, P.G. and Labuscagne, L. (2014) Venus rising: South African astronomical beliefs, customs and observations. *Monthly Notes of the Astronomical Society of South Africa* 73 (12), 280–286.

Anyidoho, K. (2009) Gathering the harvest dance. *Black Renaissance* 9 (1), 140.

Conn-Liebler, N. (1995) *Shakespeare's Festive Tragedy:The Ritual Foundation's of Genre*. London & New York: Routledge.

Diamond, P. (2022) Mauri ora: In pursuit of tohungatanga, wisdom and peace in higher education. DPhil Education (pp. 88–90). Auckland University of Technology.

Heugh, K., Stroud, C., Taylor-Leech, K. and De Costa, P.I. (2021) A sociolinguistics of the South. In K. Heugh, C. Stroud, K. Taylor-Leech and P.I. De Costa (eds) *A Sociolinguistics of the South* (pp. 1–19). New York: Routledge.

Mbembé, J.A. (2001) *On the Postcolony*. Berkeley: University of California Press.

McEntyre, M.C. (2009) *Caring for Words in a Culture of Lies*. Grand Rapids, MI: Eerdmans Publishing Company.

Merleau-Ponty, M. (2002) *Phenomenology of Perception*. London: Routledge.

Ngugi wa, T. o. (1986) *Decolonising the Mind: The Politics of Language in African Literature*. Kampala: East African Educational Publishers.

Nicholson, A. (2020) Te Hihiri: a process of coming to know. *MAI Journal* IX (2), 133–142.

Nyamnjoh, F.B. (2019) Decolonising the University in Africa. In *Oxford Research Encyclopedia*. Oxford: Oxford University Press.

Phipps, A. (2007) *Learning the Arts of Linguistic Survival*. Clevedon: Channel View Publications.

Phipps, A. (2017) *Why Cultural Work with Refugees?* Brussels: European Union. Retrieved from http://www.europarl.europa.eu/RegData/etudes/IDAN/2017/602004/IPOL_IDA(2017)602004_EN.pdf

Phipps, A. (2019) *Decolonising Multilingualism: Struggles to Decreate*. Bristol: Multilingual Matters.

Phipps, A. (2021a) Coda: Recovering lost arts of languaging from the four directions. In K. Heugh, C. Stroud, K. Taylor-Leech and P.I. De Costa (eds) *A Sociolinguistics of the South* (pp. 249–253). New York: Routledge.

Phipps, A. (2021b) Decolonising the languages curriculum: Linguistic justice for linguistic ecologies. In T.a.R.-A. Beaven, F. (ed.) *Innovative Language Pedagogy Report* (pp. 5–10). Research Publishing.

Phipps, A., Tawona, S., Tordzro, N.D. and Gameli, T. (2016) *Broken World, Broken Word: The Show*. University of Glasgow: RM Borders.

Phipps, A., Tawona, S., Tordzro, N.D., Gameli, T. and Densua, N. (2020) English last: Displaced publics and communicating multilingually as social act and art. In E. Scandrett (ed.) *Public Sociology As Educational Practice: Challenges, Dialogues and Counter-Publics*. Bristol: Bristol University Press.

Pillay, S. (2015) Decolonizing the university. See https://africasacountry.com/2015/06/decolonizing-the-university/

PSU African Studies. (2020, November 2) *African Studies Global Virtual Forum: Decoloniality and Southern Epistemologies–Phipps/Diamond* [Video]. YouTube. See https://www.youtube.com/watch?v=c7wXLoMfzK8&t=849s

Santos, B.d.S. (2018) *The End of the Cognitive Empire: The Coming Age of Epistemologies of the South*. Durham & London: Duke University Press.

Spiller, C., Barclay-Kerr, H. and Panoho, J. (2015) *Wayfinding Leadership: Ground-breaking Wisdom for Developing Leaders*. Huia Publishers.

Tordzro, G. (2017) *Broken World, Broken Word: The Documentary*. University of Glasgow: RM Borders.

Tordzro, N.D. (2020) Se anomaa entua obua da: 'The bird that does not fly does not eat'. Retrieved from https://www.mideq.org/en/blog/se-anomaa-entua-obua-da-bird-does-not-fly-does-not-eat/

Epilogue

Višnja Milojičić and Rafael Lomeu Gomes[1,2]

As we bring this volume to a close, we would like to reflect on how our chapter authors have collectively theorized on decolonial issues. One lesson which emerged for us relates to the need for more widespread theorization from Southern perspectives. According to de Souza and Nair (this volume), a crucial aspect of decolonization relates to framing global constructs using Southern lenses. As de Souza suggests in relation to Indian constructs, '[I]f we *infiltrate* the conceptual universe with Indian concepts, if we *elevate* Indian concepts to a certain respectable status in the Humanities and Social Science discourse, if scholars begin to use Indian phrases – instead of saying, for example, "It was a Herculean task," we could say, "It's a Hanumanian task,"' we then begin to 'flatten the asymmetry of power' between the academic spheres of South and North. Notably, linguistic anthropologist Arthur Spears similarly puts this practice into action when he speaks of 'segregation' in the United States as 'American apartheid' (Spears, 2022), rather than adopting the Global North construct for this phenomenon. Moving beyond theory and into praxis, Phipps and Diamond (this volume) suggest that decolonizing multilingualism as well as Global South/North relations involves, firstly, 'put[ting] English last,' and secondly, moving past tokenistic appropriation of Southern cultures by getting at the core of why such cultural practices exist in the first place. For the authors, such praxis serves to grapple with the fact that 'too often we adopt the surface of our culture without understanding the why.'

Another issue which the volume grapples with is Northern scholarship's unabashed appropriation of Global South theories into their academic spheres; that is, the incorporation of Southern theories into Northern theoretical frameworks without the granting of credit to Southern thinkers for them. Here, again, we see the authors of this volume challenging this practice, through both their narrative and citational practices. For instance, Robin Sabino (this volume) draws on theories developed by African linguists and historians, including Jamaican historian Neville Hall's (1992) notion of *hubristic eurocentrism*, as a starting point for her own theorization of the African linguistic context. On her part, Norton (this volume) cites largely Southern works, from Pennycook and Makoni's (2019) decolonial scholarship to Ndhlovu and Makalela's (2021) volume on multilingualism in Africa. Finally, Phipps and Diamond (this volume) illustrate the importance of drawing on Southern epistemes, including poetry, song and dance, in both academic research and activism. Such examples serve to illustrate the importance of theorizing not just *on* the South but *with* the South (Pennycook & Makoni, 2019).

Central to the issue above is the necessity of creating more equitable flows of knowledge between South and North. Comparing the politics of knowledge production and circulation between South and North to the process of the global production of material goods, Cusicanqui (2012) has alerted us to a potential danger in such flows of knowledge. That is, she has claimed that [Southern] 'ideas leave the country converted into raw material, which become regurgitated and jumbled in the final product' (Cusicanqui, 2012: 104). A pernicious consequence, she concludes, is that while certain themes and sources gain visibility, others remain unacknowledged. More worryingly, when the uptake of ideas that have emerged in the struggle led by Indigenous social movements in the South is devoid of its political impetus in Northern academic circles, the potential of effecting meaningful change is lost. Along similar lines, Tuck and Yang (2012) have argued for an understanding of decolonization *not* as a metaphor. Remaining wary of the ways in which decolonization discourse has been superficially taken up in educational research and advocacy, as reflected by increased calls for decolonizing schools, methods and student thinking, they argue for an ethics of incommensurability. According to such ethics, 'opportunities for solidarity lie in what is incommensurable rather than what is common across these efforts' (Tuck & Yang, 2012: 28).

In the introduction, we are presented with the following question: 'How is decolonial linguistics practiced?' The normative undertone of any univocal attempt to answer this question – as if it were possible to come up with a one-size-fits-all 'decolonial playbook' – would probably run the risk of contributing to the creation of a new canon, a new hegemonic system of knowledge production and circulation in linguistics. That is, lacking the capacity of being contextually relevant while retaining its political thrust, such an attempt would probably be incapable of constructing more equitable conditions in the circulation of knowledge. We believe, however, that one of the major strengths of this volume lies in its presentation of decolonial linguistics in its multiple shades. The reflections triggered by Cusicanqui (2012) and Tuck and Yang (2012) encourage us to remain vigilant, regardless of the shade a locally contextualized decolonial linguistics might engender (e.g. Deumert *et al.*, 2020; Idem & Udoh, 2022; Landulfo & Matos, 2022; Resende, 2021; Souza & Nascimento, 2022). Yet, communicating across differences is not only feasible but also desirable in order for solidarity to be established.

Another avenue for acknowledging decolonial linguistics in its multiple shades involves highlighting the relevance of affect within Southern contexts, including the importance of having an outlet for queer, Black, and Indigenous rage. As Milani (this volume) suggests and as Busi Makoni (in Milani, this volume) and Ofelia García (in Milani, this volume) have underscored, the rage of persons from the Global South is frequently trivialized within Global North academic contexts, at the same time as the humanity of such individuals is concurrently invisiblized. For instance, Black women are rarely cited in academic circles and often remain invisible within conversations surrounding feminism (B. Makoni in Milani, this volume; see also Makoni, 2022). Furthermore, Northern scholars such as Bickerton (1990) have constructed Blacks as less intelligent (e.g. in language learning) when it comes to the learning of European languages (Mufwene, this volume). Given the above realities, the importance of providing an outlet for Black rage, as well as the rage of individuals living within Southern contexts more generally, remains a meaningful yet heretofore oft-ignored issue within decolonial research – but one with which we hope future Southern scholarship will continue to engage.

Drawing inspiration from Sarah Nuttall (2022), who views narrative from the perspective of rain cycles, we might liken the role of this epilogue to the culmination of a particularly vigorous yet refreshing autumn shower. As this particular pluvial cycle comes to a close, we hope to have left the reader with more questions than answers, while at the same time feeling better equipped with a diversity of possible lenses through which to view the world, in all of its turbulent glory.

Thus, in the words of our late beloved forum member, economist and environmentalist Átila Calvente (Calvente in Madany-Saá, this volume), 'The rain teaches softness and lightness... The lakes cultivate serenity... The streams, the movement of life itself.'

Notes

(1) Rafael would like to acknowledge that work on this Epilogue was partly supported by the Research Council of Norway through its Centres of Excellence funding scheme, project number 223265.
(2) In April 2023, we learned that a number of women spoke out against Boaventura de Sousa Santos by voicing sexual and moral harrassment accusations against him. Now, and moving forward, we stand with these women. Decolonization is and has always been intersectional, and we support these women's voices and their right to be heard and acknowledged. Thus, rather than citing de Sousa Santos in our epilogue, we would like to encourage the reader to read and reflect on 'The walls spoke when no one else would: Autoethnographic notes on sexual-power gatekeeping within avant-garde academia' by Lieselotte Viaene, Catarina Laranjeiro and Miye Nadya Tom.

References

Bickerton, D. (1990) *Language and Species*. Chicago: University of Chicago Press.
Cusicanqui, S.R. (2012) *Ch'ixinakax utxiwa*: A reflection on the practices and discourses of decolonization. *The South Atlantic Quarterly* 111 (1), 95–109. https://doi.org/10.1215/00382876-1472612
Deumert, A., Storch, A. and Shepherd, N. (eds) (2020) *Colonial and Decolonial Linguistics: Knowledges and Epistemes*. Oxford: Oxford University Press https://doi.org/10.1093/oso/9780198793205.001.0001
Hall, N.A.T. (1992) In B.W. Higman (ed.) *Slave Society in the Danish West Indies: St. Thomas, St. John, St. Croix*. Baltimore: John's Hopkins University Press.
Idem, U. and Udoh, I. (2022) Baptism of indigenous languages into an ideology: A decolonial critique of missionary linguistics in South-Eastern Nigeria. In B.E. Antia and S. Makoni (eds) *Southernising Sociolinguistics: Colonialism, Racism, and Patriarchy in Language and the Global South* (pp. 90–111). https://doi.org/10.4324/9781003219590-7
Landulfo, C. and Matos, D. (eds) (2022) *Suleando conceitos em linguagens: Decolonialidades e epistemologias outras*. Campinas, SP: Pontes Editores.
Makoni, B. (2022) Black female scholarship matters: Erasure of black African women's scholarship. In B.E. Antia and S. Makoni (eds) *Southernising Sociolinguistics: Colonialism, Racism, and Patriarchy in Language and the Global South* (pp. 131–145). https://doi.org/10.4324/9781003219590-10
Ndhlovu, F. and Makalela, L. (2021) *Decolonising Multilingualism in Africa: Recentering Silenced Voices from the Global South*. Bristol: Multilingual Matters.
Nuttall, S. (2022) On pluviality: Rain as method. *African Studies Global Virtual Forum Series*. The Pennsylvania State University.

Pennycook, A. and Makoni, S. (2019) *Innovations and Challenges in Applied Linguistics from the Global South*. New York: Routledge.

Resende, V.M. (2021) Decolonizing critical discourse studies: for a Latin American perspective. *Critical Discourse Studies* 18 (1), 26–42. https://doi.org/10.1080/17405904.2018.1490654

Souza, L.M.T.M. and Nascimento, G. (2022) Questioning epistemic racism in issues of language studies in Brazil: The case of Pretuguês versus popular Brazilian Portuguese. In B.E. Antia and S. Makoni (eds) *Southernizing Sociolinguistics: Colonialism, Racism, and Patriarchy in Language and the Global South* (pp. 67–89). https://doi.org/ 10.4324/9781003219590-6

Spears, A. (2022) Contextualizing, assessing, and rethinking decoloniality. *African Studies Global Virtual Forum Series*. Philadelphia: The Pennsylvania State University.

Tuck, E. and Yang, K.W. (2012) Decolonization is not a metaphor. *Decolonization: Indigeneity, Education & Society* 1 (1), 1–40

Index

Note: References in *italics* are to figures.

Abdelhay, Ashraf 1–11, 34, 39, 40, 41, 114, 155, 204
Abiria, Doris 165
accent 94
Achebe, Chinua 120, 141n2
acronyms 124–125
Adam, Lucien 48, 85
adjectives 52
affect 142, 148–149, 161, 238
Afrern, Asma 168
Africa 9, 10
   Bantu languages 51, 52
   decolonial linguistics 172–173
   decolonization 1
   Kikongo 51
   languages 3–4, 18, 40, 44, 50–51
   pan-Africanism 177–178
   pragmatics 140
African Storybook 169–170, 176–177
   see also identity and the African Storybook initiative
Afro-Caribbean 86
Ahmed, Sara 149
AIDS 142
AILA (American Immigration Lawyers Association) 143–144
Al Qaws 156
Alcock, P.G. 210
Alkateb-Chami, Maya 103, 108–109
Alleyne, Mervyn 86
Allin Kghaway 5
Amselle, Jean-Loup 188
Amsler, M. 90
Andema, Sam 165, 167, 168
Anderson, Miranda 102, 103
anger *see* queer anger: alliances and affective politics
Antia, Bassey 195, 201, 202, 203, 206, 208
anti-racism 192

Anyidoho, Kofi 210
Aotearoa, New Zealand 214–215, 231
apes 24
applied linguistics 2, 7, 38, 66, 94–96, 164, 196, 198, 202–203
   identity and investment 167
   posthumanist applied linguistics 98–101
   second language development 110
   undisciplined applied linguistics 147
appropriation 6
Aristotle 99, 116
   On Interpretation 89–90
associationism 92–93
Atshan, Sa'ed 143
Auckland University of Technology (AUT) 213, 216
   Te Pūrengi 219, *220*
Augustine of Hippo, St 91
Austin, J.L. 126

Bade, David xviii–xix, 4, 8–9, 13–43, 43n8
Bagga-Gupta, Sangeeta 27–28, 29, 32, 36, 39–40, 50, 60, 64, 65–66, 102, 116, 158–160, 180–181, 185
Bain, Alexander 93, 98
Baissac, Charles 48, 85–86
Baker, G. 92, 119n7
Bantu languages 51, 52
Barad, K. 79
Baugh, John 44, 58, 59, 65
bees 38
Bhagavad Gita 16, 28
Bhattacharya, K.C. 120
Bickerton, Derek 58–59, 65, 70, 238
biosemiotics 98
black female scholarship 7, 150–151, 238
Black Lives Matter 158
Black rage 238–239
Blackledge, Adrian 98, 230

241

Blommaert, J, 191
Boas, Franz 57, 192
Borba, Rodrigo 145–146, 156
borrowings 131
Botswana 154
Bourdieu, Pierre 95–96, 97, 106, 107–109, 112–113, 170, 194, 197
brain 88, 91
Braine David 88
Brazil 133, 136, 138–139
    see also Calvente, Átila
Broken World, Broken Word 213–214
buen vivir 5
Bulwer, John: *Chirologia* 102
Bybee, J. 69

Cacaio Project: Education for Environmental, Esthetic and Moral Development xi
Caine, Anisa 37–39
Caldas-Coulthard, Carmen 153
Calvente, Átila 206–207, 239
    articles by xiv, 174
    dedication to vii–ix
    in memory of xi–xiv, 163
    poetry 169
Camus, Albert 108
"Cartesian" concept of mind 91, 119n7
Cashman, Holly 155
    Queer, Latinx and Bilingual 143
caste 127–128
cataloguing 19
CDST (complex dynamic systems theory) 203
Cereza, Paul 173
Cestaro, G.P. 91
Chandogya Upanishad 17
Chaudenson, Robert 58–59
Cheshire, J. 85
Chinese trade & language 47, 55–56
Chomsky, Noam 8, 14–16, 18, 21, 22, 23, 25, 35, 42n2, 43n8, 46, 57–59, 93, 96, 112, 194
Christie, P. 70, 165
cladograms 48
Clark, Andy 89
clefting 51, 52
Clough, Loretta 106
Cobain, Ian: *The History Thieves* 120
Coetzee-Van Rooy, Susan 102, 113
cognitive justice xviii
cognitive linguistics 195
Collingwood, R.G. 31
'colonial linguistics' 2, 48, 54, 58, 64

colonialism 2, 120, 165, 234
coloniality
    defined 2, 165, 184
    of language 164, 185
colonization 61–63
Comaroff, Jean 67
Communist Manifesto 17
complex dynamic systems theory (CDST) 203
Comte, Auguste 93
Confucius 17
connectionism 93, 94–95
Connell, Raewyn 188
Conn-Liebler, N. 214
Conrad, Joseph: *Heart of Darkness* 120, 141n1
conventionalization 69, 83
'conversational books' 5
Cottingham, J. *et al.* 92
    Passions de l'ame 91
Cousin, Victor 93
Cram, David 106
Creese, Angela 98, 228
Creole linguistics 72
creoles 48–49, 50, 51–52, 58, 59, 61, 65, 69, 86
Cronin, Michael 7, 213
cross-cultural communication 131
Cusicanqui, S.R. 238

Danish West Indies: linguistic contact xix, 68–86
    agency and identity 78–79
    Americans 71
    aptitude and phonological learning 74–75
    British occupation 71
    Dutch resources 71
    giving Jack his jacket 68–70
    history and demographics 71–72
    identity and linguistic resources 70
    in-group communication/identity 76
    Moravian missionaries 72, 73
    morphology 76–77
    phonology 76
    resistance and assimilation 76
    sound files 78
    St. Croix 71, 72
    St. John 71, 72, 73, 79
    St. Thomas 68, 70, 71, 72, 73, 79
    syntactic variation 77–78
    as U.S. Virgin Islands 71, *81, 82*
    Western hegemonic ideologies 70
    discussion 79–86
Dante Alighieri (1265–1321) 91, 119n6
Danziger, Kurt 161

Darvin, Ron 166–167, *167*, 185
Darwin, Charles 46
Davidson, Sara 168
Davies, Alan 94, 97, 100, 119n8
Dawkins, R. 130
de Jager, Wiehan 172
de Souza, Peter Ronald 6, 9–10, 120–141, 237
decolonial linguistics 3, 7, 64, 66, 172–173, 237, 238
   iconoclast's approach to decolonial linguistics xix, 9, 44–67
   see also shades of decolonial linguistics?
decolonial scholarship 172–173
Decolonial Voices, Language and Race 1
decoloniality 4, 10, 27, 57, 66, 123, 136, 172–175, 184
decolonization xviii, 1–2, 122, 124, 173, 237, 238
decolonizing multilingualism: a practice-led approach xix–xx, 10–11, 210–235
   mihi 215
   'Researching Multilingually' *211*, 211–212
de-creation 6–7
dedication vii–ix
DeGraff, Michel 44, 48
Democratic Republic of Congo: languages 53
den Besten, H. *et al.* 70, 73
Denmark 71, 73, 75, 173
Derrida, Jacques 64
Descartes, René 17, 89, 91, 92, 119n7
Deumert, Ana 45, 116
Diamond, Piki xix–xx, 5, 6, 8, 21–22, 210–235, 237
Diaz, Brett 147–148, 149–150, 153, 156, 160, 173, 226–228
Differences (journal) 146
digital technology 165–166
disobedient scholarship 161
distributed cognition 89, 95, 98
Doherty, Liam 168, 170
domination and underlying form in linguistics xix, 190–209
   anti-racism 192
   arbitrary discretionary authority 195, 197
   curriculum 191
   progressive climate 192
   theoretical paradigms 194
   undergraduate education 192
   unique form hypothesis 193
   western ethnocentrism 193
   see also mind over body in history of language analysis

Douglas, Frederick 17
Dumont, Louis 127

Early, Margaret 165
Eberhard the German: *Laborintus* 90–91
economic growth 53
Ehlich, Susan 146
El Kirat El Allame, Yamina 63
elevation 6
Elias, Norbert 95
embodied cognition 89
emotion 149
empire of critique 143
Encyclopedia Britannica 17
Encyclopedia of Language and Linguistics, The 15
enslavement of minds 120
Epicureans 93
Epicurus 89–90, 91
epilogue 237–239
ethnocentric prejudice 193
etymology 131, 134–135, 136–137
Euro-Caribbean 86
Eurocentrism xviii, 4
'European culture' 55
European Parliament 230
extended cognition 95, 98
'extended mind' 89

Fabrício, Branca Falabella 145–146
Fanon, F. 131
Fazendo Gênero 152
Fazl ibn Mubarak, Abdul: *Akbar Nama* 123–124, 141n4
Floyd, George 151
foreword xvii–xx
Foucault, M. 143, 192
Freud, Sigmund 95

Gaelic 210, 217, 223
García, A. 98
García, Ofelia 156, 157, 238
García León, Javier 153
Gassendi, Pierre 91
gaze 158, 159
Gee, J.P. 95
generative grammar 22, 35, 198, 202
Gibson, James J. 95
giving Jack his jacket *see* Danish West Indies
Global North 66, 121, 237, 238
Global South 66, 237, 238

Global Storybooks 163, 168–169, 170–171, 176
global trade 50
Global Virtual Forum 5
Goa 120
Goldsmith, John 44, 56–57
　Battle in the Mind Fields 44, 56
Gomes, Rafael Lomeu 27, 33–34, 36–37, 101–106, 109–111, 114, 147, 153, 237–239, 240n1
Goodman, M. 74
Goodman, Paul 30
Gordon, Lewis 173, 174
grammaring 202, 204, 208
Graves, A.V. 73
Greenberg, Joseph 58
Gullah 45–46, 52, 65
Gumperz, John 30, 32, 33, 37

habitus 95–96, 97, 107–108, 114
Hall, Neville A.T. 70, 83, 237
Han, Byung-Chul: *What is Power?* 21
Haneda, Mari 27, 29–30, 31–32, 33, 36, 158, 228, 233
Harris, Roy 2, 3, 8, 13, 15, 17, 22–23, 29, 30–31, 32, 37
　The Language Machine 19, 43n6
Hartley, David 92
Harvey, Sean: *Native Tongues: Colonialism and Race from Encounter to the Reservation* 35, 47
Hebb, Donald O. 95
Hegel, G.W.F. 56, 131
Heidegger, Martin 37
Heisenberg, Werner 201
Heller, Monica 33
Henry, Patrick 17
Herder, Johann Gottfried 92
hermeneophobia 204
Hesseling, D.C. 72
heterochrony 144
heterotopia 144
Heugh, K. *et al.* 210
historical erasure 120
HIV 142
Hobbes, Thomas, 17, 92, 207
homogeneism 191
Hoppers, Catherine 66
horses 13, 21, 23–24
Hull, Gloria *et al.* 151
Hume, D. 31
Husserl, Edmund 95

Hutton, Chris 6, 7, 175
Hymes, Dell 7, 9, 29, 30, 32

iconoclast's approach to decolonial linguistics xix, 9, 44–67
identity and the African Storybook initiative xix, 10, 163–188
　decoloniality 172–175
　Global Storybooks 163, 168–169, 170–171, 176
　identity and investment 166–167, *167*, 170–171
　language immersion 169
　languages 171–172
　linguistic citizenship 164, 165, 170–171
　literacy 167–169
　poststructuralist theories 164, 166
　translanguaging 170–172, *171*, 181–182, 185
'identity options' 2
idiolect 199–200, 208
IGALA (International Gender Language Association) 154
imagination 92
India: transcription company 8
　see also Keywords for India
indigeneity 5
indigenous knowledges and languages 5
Indigenous Storybooks 168
Indo-European languages 46, 47, 48–49
infiltration 6
information science 20
Integrational Linguistics 3
intellectual domination 120
internal decolonization 139
International Gender Language Association (IGALA) 154
International IPRA Conference 138
intersectionality 152
intracranialism 88, 96
invisibilization 120
Israel *see* queer anger: alliances and affective politics
Ituri Forest Pygmies 38

Janks, Hilary 154, 158, 161
Japanese 58
Jespersen, Otto 46
Jones, Shelley 165
Jones, Sir Lawrence 46
Jones, Sir William 34
Joseph, John E. 9, 84, 88–117, 175, 196, 198, 204–206

Kachru, Braj 22, 35
Kaiper-Marquez, Anna 1–11, 174, 179
Kendrick, Maureen 165
Keywords for India xix, 9–10, 120–141
   acronyms 124–125
   borrowings from English 125
   caste 127–128
   context 124
   diachronicity 126
   etymology 131, 134–135, 136–137
   fragments of language 125–126
   high-value words 125
   izzat 121–122
   jhanjhat 122
   jhoota 129
   jootha 121, 127, 128–129
   listening 126
   material culture words 124
   orality-literacy continuum 126
   strategies 121–122, 125
   swaraj 121
   synchrony 126
   tension 122
   'time pass' 121
   truth 126
Khubchandani, Lachman 136, 138
King James Bible 16
Kinginger, Celeste S. 105
knowledge 39
Krabbe-Suarez, Julia 173
Kramsch, C. 2
Krashen, S.D. 94
Kretzschmar, W.A. 81, 83

Labov, William 111
Labuscagne, L. 210
LaCharité, D. 75
Lakoff, G. 89
Laks, Bernard: *Battle in the Mind Fields* 44, 56
Language (journal) 53
language as myth 3
language change 70
language immersion 169
language learning 221, 226
language organ 18, 20
language professionals *vs.* planners 138
language rights 114
language variation 111–112
languaging 7, 8, 84, 200
Lantolf, Jim 105
Laranjeiro, Catarina 240n2

Larsen-Freeman, Diane E. 110–111, 202–203, 204, 208
Latin America 2
Latour, Bruno 98
Lawson, Aaron 195
learning outcomes 205
Lee, Eunjeong 156
Lees, Robert 22, 35, 143
legitimate discourse 170
Levon, Eric 144
lexifiers 48
Leymarie, Cassie 153
LGBT rights 142–143
libraries 18–19
Lingala 53
linguistic citizenship xix, 2, 10, 164, 165, 170–171, 178–179
linguistic form: a political epistemology *see* domination and underlying form in linguistics
linguistic incontinence 136, 138
linguistic memories 69
linguistics as a discipline 46, 66
literacy 167–169
living theory and theory that kills: language, communication and control xviii–xix, 8–9, 13–43
Locke, John 92
López-Gopar, Mario 233
Lorde, Audre 151
L'Organisation Internationale de la Francophonie 53
Love, Nigel 22
Lucido Santos, Joey Andrew 161
Lucretius 91
Luther, Martin 17

McCawley, Jim 35
McElhinny, Bonnie 33
McEntyre, M.C. 228–229
Machoga, Letta 172
McKinney, Carolyn 165, 176
McQueen, Loretta 174
Madany-Saá, Magda xi–xiv, 54, 56, 60, 64, 127, 131, 135, 140, 163, 222, 226, 234
Magens, J.M. 72, 73, 76
Maikey, Haneen 156
Makalela, Leketi 165, 237
Makoe, Pinky 165, 174, 176
Makoni, Busi 7, 104, 147, 150–151, 153, 157, 222, 228, 229, 237, 238

Makoni, Sinfree 1–11, 13, 18, 21–26, 32, 37, 39–40, 41–42, 45, 57, 67, 79–83, 99–101, 116–117, 131–135, 140, 145–147, 160–161, 164, 172–179, 187–188, 196–199, 208–209, 210, 217, 220, 234
Maldonado-Torres, N. 165
Malindi, Vusi 172
Mandarin 47
Māori 215, 216, 219–220, 224–225
Marie Antoinette 17
Mario de Souza, Lynn 133, 135, 136–137, 139, 140, 180–181
Marley, Bob 67
Marx, Karl 106
Maturana, H.R. 95
Mauss, Marcel 95
Mbembe, Achille 212
Mbiti, J.S. 33
Meillet, Antoine 48
Meinhoff, Karl 50
Meintjes, L. 212
Meireles, Cecília xii
meme 130
Merchant of Venice, The 93
Merleau-Ponty, Maurice 95, 119n9, 225
Mesthrie, Raj 44
metalanguage 6
Metcalfe, Robin 169
Mignolo, Walter 2, 147
Milani, Tommaso xix, 4, 10, 142–161, 238
Milojičić, Višnja 1–11, 40, 237–239
mind over body in history of language analysis 9, 88–99
  approaches to locating language 88, 118–119n2
  discussion 99–117
Moita-Lopes, Luiz Paulo da 147, 149
Montesquieu 92
Moorosi, Mantsoaki 147
Morris, K.J. 92, 119n7
Msibi, Thabo 145–146
Mufwene, Salikoko S. xix, 5, 9, 26, 33, 34–36, 40, 41–42, 44–67, 69, 85–86, 111, 112–113, 182, 184–185, 186, 199, 208
Multilingual Matters 230–231, 234
'multilingual turn' 6
multilingualism 100
  defining multilingualism 174–175
  egalitarian multilingualism 185
  in Europe 136
  in India 136

'is a mother tongue/lingua franca' 234
  meaning of 5
  queering 145
  research on 143
  see also decolonizing multilingualism: a practice-led approach
Munari, Bruno viii
Mutonyi, Harriet 165

Nair, Rukmini Bhaya xix, 6, 9–10, 120–141, 237
  Narrative Gravity 123
Namazzi, Elizabeth 165
native speaker 3, 94, 96–98, 99–101
'natural approach' in language teaching 94
Ndhlovu, Finex 165, 222, 237
Ndlanga, Sibusiso Cliff 203–204
nepantla 5
neural networks 95
New Zealand 214–215, 231
Ngaka, Willy 165
Ngudiankama, Adrien 33
Ngũgĩ wa Thiong'o 193, 213
Nguni languages 104
Niasse 2
Nietzsche, Friedrich 28, 123
Nigerian pidgin English 53
nite 5
non-extractivist methodologies 7, 217, 218, *220*
Norton, Bonny xix, 2, 10, 163–188, *167*, 237
Nuttall, Sarah 239
Nyamnjoh, Francis 221

Oates, Lauryn 165
Odugu, Desmond 109, 156, 185
Oldendorp, C.G.A. 74–75
Olson, David 29
Olwig, K.F. 70
Ono, Yoko 17
Ostler, Nicholas: *Empires of the Word* 53
Owomoyela, O. 73
Oxford Handbook to Bourdieu 104
Oyewumi, Oyeronke 60–61, 63, 67

Pable, A. *et al.* 3
Paikeday, Thomas M. 119n8
Palestinian rights 143, 156
Parallel Distributed Processing 94
Passeron, J.-C. 197
Peirce, B.N. 75
Penn State University 196

Virtual Group xii
Pennycook, Alastair 6, 45, 164, 237
Pennycook Makoni 20 6
Phipps, Alison *et al.* xix–xx, 5, 6, 7, 8, 210–235, 237
phonetics 94
phonology 94
pidgins 48–50
Pike, Kenneth 202
Pillay, S. 213
Pinker, Steven 192
Planer, Ron 33, 40
Pontopiddan (physician) 73
population 6
positivism 93, 202
'posthumanist' theory 98–101
poststructuralist theories 164, 166
Pratt, Mary Louise 2
Prinsloo, Mastin 79
publishing 234
puzzles 205

Quechua 51
queer anger: alliances and affective politics xix, 10, 142–161
  intersectionality 152
  legitimacy 152
  normativity 146
  queering multilingualism 142, 148, 154–155, 157
  undisciplined applied linguistics 147
  whiteness 145

race 96, 150–151
rage and activism 154
Reagan, Ronald 142
reflexive pronouns 58
Renan, Ernest 92
repertoire 228–229
replication 130, 194, 203
Rhodes Must Fall 32
Richardson, John 149
Riemer, Nick xix, 4, 5, 190–209
Roberts, Monty 13, 21, 23–24, 25, 26
Rosenstock-Huessy, Eugen 13, 17–18, 22, 31, 39, 42n1
Rothberg, Michael: *The Implicated Subject* 144

Sabino, Robin xix, 9, 68–86, 109, 177, 237
Said, Edward 20–21, 108, 120
Samarin, William 55

Sanskrit 46, 134–135
Santos, B. de Sousa xviii, 146, 240n2
Sapir, Edward 201
Sapir, Jacques 207–208
Sapir-Whorf hypothesis 61, 63, 64
Sartre, Jean-Paul 188
Saussure, Ferdinand de 46, 107, 199, 204
Savage-Rumbaugh, Sue 24
Schechter, Ingrid 168
Schlegel, Friedrich von 47, 92
Schuchardt, Hugo 49
science 18, 20, 25, 41, 83, 192–195, 197, 201–202
Scotland 223
Scott, Bell 151
second language acquisition 100–101, 110, 203
Sedgwick, Eve Kosofsky 149
self-reflexivity 160
Semitic languages 92–93
Senegal: Wolof 53
Sensbach, J. 72
serial verb constructions 52–53
Severo, Cristine 1–11, 26, 32, 109, 153
sexism 150–151
sexuality 4, 155, 156
shades of decolonial linguistics? xviii
  authorship and decolonizing multilingualism 6–7
  characteristic features of decolonized linguistics 4–6
  decolonisation in an unequal digital world 8
  decolonization and black female scholarship 7
  decolonization of linguistics? 2–4
  decolonizing linguistics and extractivist ideologies of research methodologies 7
  meaning of decolonization 1–2
  organization of the volume 8–11
Shank Lauwo, Monica 165, 168
Shepherd, Nick 45
Sherris, Ari 161
sign language 24, 102, 181, 223
situated cognition 95, 119n9
SLI (standard language ideology) 8
Smith, Barbara 151
Smith, Dr Valance 219
Smith, Linda Tuhiwai: *Decolonizing Methodologies* 174
social justice xviii, 173
Social Semiotics 149
sociolinguistics 66
Sociolinguistics of Protesting, The 155

Soetan, Olusegun 177, 182
South Africa
   African Storybook 167–168
   Saide 167–168
Southeast Asia 13
Southern multilingualisms 5, 237–238
Southern Theory 7
Spangler, Eve 143
Spears, Arthur 237
Spinoza: *Ethics* 39
Sprauve, G. 73
Stammbaums 48
standard language ideology (SLI) 8
Sterelny, Kim 33, 40
Stewart, S. 4
Storch, Anne 45
Storybooks African languages 168
Storybooks Canada 168
Stranger-Johannessen, Espen 165, 168, 169, 170
Stroud, Christopher 2, 164, 166, 182
Suleiman, Yusei 178
Suma Qamaña 5
sumak kawsay 5
Swahili 170, *171*
Sweden 142–143, 158–159

Táíwò 173
tat tvam asi 27–29
Taylor, Talbot J. 13, 15, 24, 38
Te Ao Māori 215, 221
Te Reo Māori 225
Tembe, Dr. Juliet 163, 165, 168
Terrell, T.D. 94
Thatcher, Margaret 142
theoretical linguistics 19, 58, 100, 198
theories of mind 90
Thich Nhat Hanh 27
Thomas Acquinas, St 33, 91, 119n4
Thompson, J.B. 95
Tom, Miye Madya 240n2
Toolan, Michael 17
Torrance, Thomas 33
trade 53–54
translanguaging 99–100, 170–172, *171*, 181–182, 185, 224
Treaty of Waitangi 213, 214, 219
Trump, Donald 25
trust 38
Truth, Sojourner 151
Tuck, E. 238
Turner, M. 89

ubuntu 5
Uganda 163, 165–169, 186
undergraduate education 192
UNESCO 226
unique form hypothesis 193
United States
   decoloniality 173
   decolonization 1
   Native Americans 35
Universal Grammar 15, 36, 96, 98
University of British Columbia 168
University of Chicago 19–20
University of Illinois 22
US Virgin Islands *see* Danish West Indies: linguistic contact

Valla, Lorenzo: *De voluptate* 91
Van Der Merwe, Chanel 13, 68, 79, 99, 177, 179, 183, 186–187, 222
van der Voort, H. 70
Varela, F.J. 95
vernacularization 69, 83, 86
Viaene, Lieselotte 240n2
Vigouroux, Cécile 55, 106–108, 112, 177, 178
Vinson, Julien 48, 85
Virgin Islands
   Dutch Creole 69
   linguistic resources *81*, 81–83, *82*
vocabulary 6
von Uexküll, Jakob von 98

Warner, Michael 142
way-finding 218–219
Weber, Max 95, 193
Weil, Simone 6–7, 17, 20
Welch, Tessa 163, 168
Western biases 64
western ethnocentrism 193
Wetherell, Margaret 149
White, Goodith 165
"white man's burden" 120
Widdowson, Henry 198
Wiegman, Robyn 146
Wiener, Norbert: *Cybernetics* 20
Wierzbicka, A. 89
Wilkerson, Isabel: *Caste* 127
Williams, Carrie-Jane 165, 166
Williams, Meredith 38
Williams, Raymond 121, 124, 130, 134–135, 139
Williamson, Blessing 172
Williamson, Victor 172

Wittgenstein, Ludwig 38, 200
Wolof 53
World War II 130
Woschitz, Johannes 111
Wright, Z. 2

Yang, K.W. 238

Zaidi, Rahat 169
Zavala, Virginia 176
zoosemiotics 98, 99

For Product Safety Concerns and Information please contact our EU Authorised Representative:

Easy Access System Europe

Mustamäe tee 50

10621 Tallinn

Estonia

gpsr.requests@easproject.com

www.ingramcontent.com/pod-product-compliance
Lightning Source LLC
Chambersburg PA
CBHW080409300426
44113CB00015B/2448